The Volvo Experience

Alternatives to

Lean Production in the

Swedish Auto Industry

Christian Berggren

Published in the United States under the title
Alternatives to Lean Production:
Work Organization in the Swedish Auto Industry
by ILR Press, Ithaca, New York

First published 1993 in Great Britain by
THE MACMILLAN PRESS LTD
Houndmills, Basingstoke, Hampshire RG21 2XS
and London
Companies and representatives
throughout the world

Reprinted (with a new introduction) 1994

ISBN 0-333-59338-3 hardcover
ISBN 0-333-61816-8 paperback

A catalogue record for this book is available
from the British Library.

Printed in Great Britain by
Antony Rowe Ltd
Chippenham, Wiltshire

To the Centre for Corporate Change at the Australian Graduate School of Management, which provided my family with such a happy year in Australia and me with the opportunity to finalize this book

T he assembly line is no place to work, I can tell you. There is nothing more discouraging than having a barrel beside you with 10,000 bolts in it and using them all up. Then you get a barrel with another 10,000 bolts and you know every one of those 10,000 has to be picked up and put in exactly the same place as the last 10,000 bolts.

Walker and Guest, *The Man on the Assembly Line*, 1952

T o have the human body work like a machine—consistently, continuously, hour in, hour out, to produce a product—is inhuman. . . . It's dehumanizing to work at such a pace that you can't even stop to have a cup of coffee or smoke a cigarette or go to the bathroom. You have no freedom from the production. It's like you are incarcerated from the minute you get there until it's time to leave. . . . We are prisoners of the assembly line. You're tied to a machine and you're just another cog. You have to do the same thing over and over again, all day long.

Feldman and Betzold, *End of the Line*, 1988

Contents

Introduction to the Paperback Edition/vii

Preface/xi

1. The Assembly-Line Regime and the Volvo Trajectory
3

2. The Evolution and Transplantation of Toyotism
22

3. The Swedish Automotive Industry: Small-Scale Car Makers,
Global Truck Producers
56

4. Pressures for Change: The Labor Market and Trade Unions
71

5. Organizational and Technical Design of Swedish Automotive Assembly
90

6. Competitive "Craft Work" in Two Bus Plants
101

7. Pioneers in Car and Truck Assembly: Volvo Kalmar and Volvo LB
119

Contents

8. Innovations in Uddevalla, Stalemate in Gothenburg
146

9. Methodological Problems in Comparing Working Conditions
184

10. The Degrading Monotony of the Assembly Line
194

11. Assembly Designs and Working Conditions: A Five-Plant Comparison
206

12. Shop-Floor Power and the Dynamics of Group Work
221

13. Toward Postlean Production
232

Notes/257

References/267

Index/277

Introduction to the Paperback Edition: The Lessons of Volvo's Uddevalla and Kalmar Plants

The central theme of this book is about the "Swedish trajectory" in the automotive industry, its innovative production design and work organization, and the competitive and labor market pressures that brought Swedish automakers, above all Volvo, to develop this model. Two small car plants constitute landmarks in this trajectory: the Kalmar plant from 1974 and the Uddevalla operation from 1989. In November 1992, in the midst of a severe economic crisis in Sweden, Volvo announced that it would close these two car plants: Uddevalla, in 1993, and Kalmar, in 1994. (The latter builds Volvo's top-of-the-line model, the 960, making its closure more complicated.) As a result, all of Volvo's Swedish assembly will be concentrated in the main, traditional line plant in Gothenburg, where Volvo's headquarters and design and engineering departments are located. This decision raises important questions. Were the critics of Volvo's alternatives to lean production right? Was Uddevalla just a "noble experiment in humanistic manufacturing," a short-term answer to the industrial labor crises of the 1980s, when Swedish manufacturers had so many difficulties in recruiting and keeping production workers, but an experiment doomed to fail in the hard times of the 1990s?

Volvo's official justification for the closings cited its heavy losses due to under-utilization of production capacity. Indeed, by 1993, the Swedish market had virtually collapsed. New automobile registrations plummeted from 340,000 in 1988 to 150,000 in 1992, the worst figure in more than thirty years, and are expected to decline even further during 1993, to 125,000 cars. In 1992, Volvo's total operating loss was approximately U.S. $300 million, of which Volvo Car accounted for more than half. The Uddevalla and Kalmar plants were at a distinct disadvantage in such a market because they were equipped only for final assembly.

But it must be recognized that Volvo's decision to consolidate its production, in the face of ailing volume and sales, in no way nullifies the importance of the question. What was the economic performance of the two plants and, in particular, of the radical non-line Uddevalla plant? As I have argued, contrary to the assertions of many American critics, Uddevalla was a remarkable success in terms of productivity and commercial potential.

This is borne out by a comparison of Uddevalla and Kalmar with the traditional Gothenburg plant.

1. During the three years Volvo Uddevalla was in operation, *productivity* (assembly hours per car) improved by more than 50 percent. From the last quarter of 1990 to the last quarter of 1992, the plant cut the assembly time at an average rate of one hour per month. By mid-1991 Uddevalla's performance equaled that of Gothenburg's assembly line. From then on both plants improved rapidly, but Uddevalla had an edge. Furthermore, its rate of improvement was particularly high in the second half of 1992, when a new management introduced a radical, process-oriented, flat organization, made up of only two hierarchical levels. None of its managers doubted that the plant could reach the target rate of 25 hours per car by mid-1993. (Interestingly, within Uddevalla there were no significant differences between the larger assembly teams working in long cycles of 1.5 hours and mini-teams working in very long cycles of 7 hours.)

Kalmar was the most productive of the three Swedish plants. Because it had been building cars since 1974, Kalmar had had many more years than Uddevalla to develop and fine-tune its operation. Production design and work organization were less radical than at Uddevalla, but the plant's participative management was very effective in fostering continuous improvement and a commitment to quality.

2. Uddevalla also had an edge in *customer satisfaction* when compared with Gothenburg. According to surveys carried out by J. D. Power for the 1992 model year, U.S. customers ranked cars built at Uddevalla consistently higher than those built at Gothenburg. U.S. customers reported 124 problems per 100 vehicles within 90 days of purchase for Uddevalla-built cars of the 900-series; cars from the Gothenburg plant had a corresponding figure of 144. (The 1992 average for European cars in the United States was 158.) Uddevalla achieved this score more or less spontaneously, as a consequence of the assembly teams' competence and dedication. Not until the fall of 1992 did the plant introduce and train workers in the rigorous routines and procedures that are needed for achieving world-class quality in the auto industry. The result was a further substantial improvement in the plant's quality performance.

Again, Kalmar's commitment to quality made it the best performing of Volvo's assembly units. When the plant started to build the Volvo 940 in late 1992, it immediately reduced the number of faults reported by J. D. Power to half of the Gothenburg score! In the statistics for model year 1993, reported in May, Kalmar-built 940 cars reached the same level as Lexus (57 complaints per 100 cars).

3. The single most salient advantage of Uddevalla's parallel team assembly and broad worker competence was its high *flexibility*. One indication of this flexibility was the minimal effort needed to introduce annual model changes at the plant. The three annual model changes introduced from 1990 through 1992 cost between 25 and 50 percent less per car than at the Gothenburg plant. Uddevalla needed to invest less in tools and training, and returned to normal productivity after the model change in half the time required by Gothenburg. In 1992, the best Uddevalla teams needed to build only two to three cars (approximately one day) before resuming 95 percent of normal production pace. The least efficient teams needed five to six cars, or two days.

After the plant had concluded the official breaking-in phase and reached the corresponding performance targets in mid-1993, it planned to take advantage of its flexibility by adding special vehicles, such as police cars, extended wagons, and other "quixotics," to its production of regular cars. Preliminary tests demonstrated that Uddevalla could assemble such cars in less than half the time needed at Gothenburg.

4. *Combining custom-order assembly and short delivery times* was another Uddevalla specialty. In Volvo, as in many other car companies, efforts to improve efficiency and productivity have focused on the industrial system, the components supply, and above all, the assembly hours. Much less attention has been devoted to the efficiency of the commercial and distributional systems. At Uddevalla, however, there was an early awareness of the importance of fostering close contacts with the market. Unfortunately, Volvo's system for evaluating plant performance focused only on production parameters such as assembly hours and quality indices. In the company's strongly departmentalized organization, design, distribution, and marketing were strictly separated from the production operations.

When productivity reached the Gothenburg standard in 1991, however, Uddevalla established direct deliveries from the factory to selected outlets as well as direct communication with all Swedish dealers. One year later, the plant started to build all cars for Europe based solely on customer orders. As a result, dealers could offer customers individually specified and equipped cars within four weeks, instead of persuading prospective buyers to accept prespecified "package cars." The total lead time was cut from two months in 1991 to one month in 1992, with further radical reductions planned for 1993. The resulting savings in finished product stock equaled the value of the entire assembly time!

For all those interested in the development of competitive humanistic manufacturing, this evaluation of Uddevalla carries an important message. The plant was not only a bold step in creating a humane workplace, but a success in a wide range of performance measures. Rapidly improving productivity and quality was combined with superior flexibility, low-cost tooling, unparalleled customer orientation, and a unique responsiveness to market demands. In May 1993 the plant was laid idle. But Kalmar was still fighting for survival, refusing to accept its death sentence. In terms of productivity, quality, engineering competence, and supplier cooperation, it is clearly superior to the Gothenburg line plant.

By closing Uddevalla, Volvo's management has abandoned much of its pioneering position. Within Volvo, the struggle between different production concepts and management strategies continues. In an article in *Sloan Management Review* (Spring 1993: 85–86), Paul Adler and Robert Cole stressed that "these plant closings should not close the debate over the significance of their innovations. . . . Whether the advocates of work reorganization within Volvo will be able to refocus their efforts on reforming Volvo's other facilities remains to be seen. Whatever the case, there is much to be learned from the Kalmar and Uddevalla experience." The intention of this book is to present this remarkable experience in depth, and in its social context, for anyone interested in making use of it.

Preface

Human beings are created for work. Seldom is work created for human beings. Can work be changed so that it meets human needs and fits human capacities? This fundamental question guided me during the ten years in which I conducted the research that formed the basis for this book.

My original interest in working conditions and the prospects for change in mass production was born in the mid-1970s when, as a blue-collar worker and rank-and-file union activist at a refrigerator factory, I participated in industrial work in its most Fordist form. After studying industrial sociology and engineering, I was granted the opportunity from 1981 to 1983, through the Swedish section of a project initiated by the Massachusetts Institute of Technology entitled "The Future of the Automobile," to become acquainted with many production installations in the Swedish motor vehicle industry. I visited and studied factories producing engines, buses, trucks, and cars. My main interest was to find technologically and economically feasible alternatives to the restrictive work organization of scientific management. Observations and interviews with experts were the chief methods of investigation.

From 1984 to 1987 I was involved in a joint labor-management study entitled "Evaluation of Work Organizational Development in the Volvo Group." My assignment was to audit developments in Volvo Trucks, especially at the LB plant in Gothenburg, Sweden, which at the time was a controversial pioneer of decentralized group work within the company. The LB workers' assessment of their work was very clear: it was much better than the assembly line but fell far short of their wishes to perform holistic, nonfragmented work. LB's economic performance was also ambiguous—better than the traditional plants' but far from the company's targets in several respects. According to the study, a much greater departure from the assembly-line regime was needed.

I wondered how representative this research was, given that it was based on a single production unit. To answer this question, I began a three-year follow-up study in 1987, with the goal of examining all the factories I had studied in the mid-1980s, as well as Saab's and Volvo's new projects in Malmö and Uddevalla. This amounted in all to twenty studies of changes in technology, shop-floor organization, and working conditions. Six of these studies are presented here.

The central object of this book is to discuss the development of work organization and production design in Sweden. The Swedish "trajectory" is contrasted with the expanding Toyota system. My analysis of Japanese lean production is based in part on studies I conducted in 1984 of supplier relations and working conditions in the Japanese automotive industry and in 1990 of Japanese transplants in North America. Principally, however, I have made use of the extensive literature on the Japanese production philosophy that has emerged in the United States and Germany.

Much of the material in this book was included in the thesis for my doctorate in industrial management, which I received from the Royal Institute of Technology in Stockholm in 1990. Financial support for the protracted research as well as for most of the rewriting and translation was generously granted by the Swedish Work Environment Fund.

A great number of people in and around the Swedish auto industry—engineers, production managers, trade union representatives, and assembly workers—have contributed to this work by cooperating in surveys and interviews, participating in seminars, and commenting on a long series of work reports. Tomas Engström at Chalmers Institute of Technology made it possible for me to participate in the MIT project "The Future of the Automobile" in the early 1980s. Together with Lennart Nilsson at the College of Education in Gothenburg, Tomas has since played a unique role in the planning of Volvo's Uddevalla plant. In the evaluation of work organization within Volvo, I enjoyed the benefit of collaborating with Anna Holingren, also at the Royal Institute of Technology. This was an exciting period of "high-speed" research. Since the start of the 1980s, Kajsa Ellegård of Gothenburg University has also undertaken a series of studies within Volvo. Our continuous exchange of ideas has been of great value.

In Japan, I carried out a study of production pyramids and suppliers, from advanced components manufacturers to underpaid home workers, together with Toshiko Tsukaguchi. Her deep understanding of Japanese society and culture was of crucial inportance for the results.

Six years later, I got the opportunity to make an extensive field trip to Japanese transplants in the United States and Canada together with Torsten Björkman and Ernst Hollander of the Royal Institute of Technology. I thank them for their intensive cooperation on this project.

Peter Unterweger from the United Auto Workers (UAW) in Detroit has for several years been of great help in my efforts to follow the American debate on the Japanese transplants. Nomura Masami at Okayama University has contributed to my further understanding of the intricacies of Japanese labor deployment and personnel management, thereby elucidating the limitations of the current transplantation process.

From the start, Jonas Pontusson at Cornell University has offered indispensable support and constructive criticism on successive versions of the manuscript. Peter Mayers has put enormous effort into the work of translating this book. Professor Robert Rehder, from the Robert O. Anderson Management School at the University of New Mexico in Albuquerque, very kindly examined the manuscript after translation and gave me invaluable encouragement as I continued my work.

While writing the final version of the manuscript, I had the benefit of being a visiting fellow at the newly established Centre for Corporate Change at the Australian Graduate School of Management in the University of New South Wales. I enjoyed both generous support from the director, Dexter Dunphy, and Stephen Frenkel's thoughtful criticism and suggestions. Furthermore, the experience gave me the opportunity to finalize this study from the useful perspective of a distant continent. This also made it much more easy to take full advantage of Erica Fox's meticulous copyediting of virtually every page, for which I am deeply indebted.

The Volvo Experience

1.

The Assembly-Line Regime and The Volvo Trajectory

Seldom have changes in the labor market and industrial work been described from such different perspectives as during the past decade. Authors such as Barry Bluestone and Bennett Harrison (1988) have shown how insecurity and low-wage work have spread to many parts of U.S. industry, how union-negotiated employment conditions have worsened on such matters as vacations and sickness pay, and how the internal labor markets of large U.S. companies have deteriorated or disappeared—in short, how the prospects of high school graduates have declined sharply since the 1960s. At the same time, Michael L. Dertouzos, Richard K. Lester, and Robert M. Solow write in the well-known MIT report on industrial productivity *Made in America* (1989:134–35): "We see an unprecedented opportunity in the new technologies for enabling workers at all levels of the firm to master their own work environment. This marks a major change from even the recent past. . . . If American industry can seize this opportunity, individuals may experience a new measure of mastery and independence in the job that could go well beyond maximizing productivity and extend to personal and professional satisfaction and well-being."

One of the most significant contributions to the optimistic "flexibility debate" focuses solely on the auto industry. *The Machine That Changed the World* (1990) is based, unlike many other works in this genre, on comprehensive empirical material and impressive comparative studies. As do many others, James P. Womack, Daniel T. Jones, and Daniel Roos claim that mass production is approaching its demise and that Japan leads the way. They maintain that Japanese auto companies have blessed the world with a completely new approach, lean production, which "combines the best features of both craft production and mass production—the ability to reduce costs per unit and dramatically improve quality while at the same time providing an ever wider range of products and ever more challenging work" (277). According to the authors, lean production will mean a global revolution: "Lean production will supplant both mass production and the remaining outposts of craft production in all areas of industrial endeavor to become the standard global production system of the twenty-first century. That world will be a very different and a much better place" (278). They believe the Japanese management system entails dramatic improvements in both productivity and working conditions. Unfortunately, however, they submit no evidence whatsoever for their optimistic judgments. They carefully review productivity levels, yet, when it comes to conditions of work, they content themselves with cocksure assertions.

The Persistence of the Line Regime in the "Post-Fordist Age"

In 1990, there were ten Japanese-owned auto plants in North America. The Ford Company, moreover, had made major progress in adopting lean procedures. Have these plants achieved the revolution in assembly work alleged by the MIT researchers?

It is useful to compare the auto industry of the 1980s and 1990s with that of the 1950s—the heyday of classical Fordism—when some of the most incisive and penetrating studies of the nature of auto work were done, including those by Robert Blauner (1964), E. Chinoy (1955), and Charles Walker and Robert Guest (1952). In a summary of these studies, Blauner noted a widespread discontent among auto workers in an age of rising affluence and expectations. The reasons were many:

Workers on the line had no possibility of varying the pace of their work at their own discretion but were subjected to rigid, mechanical pacing.

The work was extremely repetitive—a most objectionable feature for a majority of the workers. According to Blauner, auto workers were more likely than workers in any other industry to consider their jobs constantly dull and monotonous.

It was difficult for the workers to gain a sense of purpose by orienting their efforts to the completion of a task. This problem, Blauner emphasized, did not arise from any lack of understanding of the process as a whole: "Automobile workers have a large amount of such understanding" (99–100). The root cause of the problem was the minute division of labor and the cyclical nature of the work, as embodied in the fact that the vehicle to which the worker had added a part immediately moved onward.

The workers were subjected to intense time pressure: "The fact that there is no other industry in which such a high proportion of the unskilled complained of job pressure suggests that it is the assembly-line technology and work organization and not just the lack of skill which is crucial."

The physical demands of the assembly work were severe, in contrast to other industries in which the majority of the low-skilled and highly repetitive jobs involving little freedom and control were not physically demanding. As a consequence of the intense job pressure and physical work loads, a high proportion of the workers reported that their jobs left them feeling very tired at the end of the day.

In conclusion, Blauner emphasized the importance of the technological structure: "The assembly line's inexorable control over the pace and rhythm of work is most critical; it is largely responsible for the high degree of pressure, the inability to control the quantity of work, and the lack of free movement."

If this was the character of work in assembly plants during the 1950s, what about the 1980s and 1990s? According to the MIT authors, the advent and expansion of lean production has meant a fundamental transformation of classical mass-production work. A reading of reports from the shop floor, however, such as *End of the Line* (Feldman and Betzold 1988), which consists of a series of accounts from workers at an American lean producer (Ford Michigan Truck Plant) or *Working for the Japanese* (Fucini and Fucini 1990), with its detailed description of a Japanese transplant (Mazda at Flat Rock, Michigan), yields a radically different picture. Factory layout, production control, and quality standards have all changed, but the basic nature of the work seems to be much as it was in the 1950s.

This impression was confirmed when I and two other Swedish researchers did a study of working conditions in six North American transplants in 1990: Nissan in Tennessee, Honda in Ohio, Toyota in Kentucky, Mazda in Michigan, CAMI (GM-Suzuki) in Ontario, Canada, and Diamond Star (Mitsubishi-Chrysler) in Illinois (see Berggren, Björkman, and Hollander 1991). True, the personnel policies had changed from the "massified anonymity" and depersonalization of the 1950s toward a strong emphasis on selection and individualization. Programs such as employee involvement, pay for knowledge, and quality circles, as well as well-publicized suggestion schemes served to enhance the personal commitment of all "associates." The "atrophied group structure" of the line in the 1950s had been replaced by an elaborate "team organization," which was intended to improve on the low normative integration of classical Fordist work. And job security, always very fragile in the American auto industry, was a paramount objective.

Yet the character of the work itself has not changed. If anything, the rhythm and pace of the work on the assembly line is more inexorable under the Japanese management system than it ever was before. Off-line jobs, such as those in subassembly (the senior workers' favorite positions, in which a personal work pace and "banking" were possible) have been outsourced or are geared strictly to the main line by means of just-in-time (JIT) control. Idle time is squeezed out of each work station through the application of *kaizen* techniques, while work pressure has been intensified and staffing drastically reduced in the name of eliminating all "waste" (*muda*). According to Blauner, auto workers resented the fact that the speed of the belt made it difficult for workers to detach themselves from the repetitive work. These difficulties have been aggravated by the combined JIT and quality pressure (zero defect) of the modern Japanized lines, which demand a high degree of mental concentration on work that is still very standardized.

Traditionally, management in American plants was strongly authoritarian ("drill sergeant style"), and labor relations were adversarial. The team organization characteristic of the lean producers emphasizes a different language and manner of communication: all employees are supposed to treat one another with respect and to work for the same goal, as good members of the "Toyota Team," the "Mazda Team," and so on. But the team concept is a far cry from democratic work organization and autonomous worker decision making. The emphasis on visibility and strict adherence to minutely prescribed standards in all tasks (exemplified by programmed worksheets and the like) restricts, even more than before, workers' discretion in the choice of work methods. Lean production may be fragile from a production control point of view, but its factory regime is rigorous with demands for perfect attendance, mandatory company uniforms, the prohibition of all personal articles, strict rules of conduct, and an elaborate system of sanctions. The MIT study argues that lean production, since it has no slack and no safety net, is based on trust and cannot operate if "the work force feels that no reciprocal obligations are in force" (Womack, Jones, and Roos 1990:103). Workers and unionists whom we interviewed during our tour of transplants in 1990 criticized precisely this absence of reciprocity. To quote the president of Local 2488 at Diamond Star: "They talk a lot about flexibility, but it's a one-way street. It's always the employees who are supposed to be flexible, never the company."

Lean production undoubtedly represents a major advance in productivity. But if one considers working conditions as well, it is a double-edged sword to at least the degree that the classical Ford system was.

The Swedish Contribution: A Different Kind of Teamwork

A very distinct assembly design and work organization developed in the Swedish auto industry during the 1970s and 1980s. The search for an approach that differed from the international mainstream was a contested process, stamped by sharp intramanagement divisions. Nevertheless, by the late 1980s, new solutions had materialized in a number of new facilities.

In the international context, the Swedish development had two distinct features. For one, the use of the assembly line—the standard production system for nearly all auto producers—was repeatedly questioned. To obtain more flexible work structures and more attractive jobs, many alternatives were tested—from buffered flow systems with automatically guided vehicles to the complete dissolution of the assembly line by means of parallel dock assembly, in which small teams of skilled workers built complete cars or trucks. The most advanced cases represented a major change in the technical organization of production, amounting to a drastic reduction of the horizontal division of labor. Fragmented and repetitive tasks were converted to functionally coherent jobs performed on stationary objects instead of a moving line; these jobs, moreover, were characterized by long work cycles (several hours or more).

For another, the traditional shop-floor hierarchy was replaced by group work, in many cases involving considerable autonomous decision making and thus a substantial reduction in the vertical division of labor. Teamwork certainly played a central role in the Japanese management system. The Swedish model differed, however, in four important respects. First, the organizational changes were strongly linked to changes in the production arrangement, which aimed at creating conditions whereby functional groups would have some technical autonomy. The work teams at the transplants, by contrast, were organized directly on the line.

Second, the Swedish version of teamwork was marked by a desire to increase the workers' organizational autonomy and scope for independent decision making. The teams often selected their own leaders or group representatives and performed tasks that earlier had been done by foremen and industrial engineers.

Third, the role of first-line management was changed from that of having direct control to coordinating, planning, and supporting. At the transplants, by contrast, teamwork usually went hand in hand with a strengthening of the managerial structure. In many cases—Nissan in the United Kingdom or Toyota in Kentucky, for instance—the team was organized directly around the foreman. These forms of teamwork entailed a reduction of worker autonomy and an increase in managerial control.

Fourth, in Sweden, the Metal Workers' Union strongly committed itself, both centrally and locally, to the development of this new organizational form. It was especially interested in strengthening the teams' decision-making prerogatives, as well as their prospects for developing collective competence.

Table 1-1 provides an overview of the differences between the Swedish and Japanese forms of teamwork. The Japanese model of the 1980s was a coherent and systematically realized concept in which teamwork was firmly rooted in an organizational structure shaped by management. The practices and policies developed in Japan were not uniformly implemented, however, in the overseas operations of Japanese companies. The unionized transplants in North America, for example, did not employ the elaborate personnel evaluation and wage-setting practice (*satei*) that plays such an important role in Japan. Consequently, first-line managers were considerably less powerful in the American plants.

The Swedish model was even less uniform and fixed. It represented a *social compromise* between different interests: between management's interest in delegating tasks and responsibility without yielding control and the trade union's aspirations to achieve a genuine shift in the balance of power. This meant, among other things, that the boundaries of the work teams' autonomy and decision-making power could not be deduced from some guiding concept. Rather, the boundaries were more like temporary outposts in a still-contested terrain.

Labor-intensive processes such as assembly entail a special control problem for management. A comprehensive decentralization of decision-making prerogatives from management to the work teams has considerable productive potential, but it also involves the risk that workers will make use of their increased resources to defend themselves from the demands of the economic system by restricting both their own work efforts and management's insight into the production process. This is one of the reasons work developments in the Swedish auto companies have often been hesitant and inconsistent. The Japanese model of teamwork escapes this ambiguity. Delegation of responsibility, for quality, for example, takes place within the framework of a tight regime, complete with precise visual control systems, intensive personnel selection, and a wide array of disciplinary measures. The possibility of collective worker action and of various forms of opposition and restrictions on output is thereby eliminated.

As early as 1979, Robert Cole observed important differences between developments in Swedish and Japanese companies. In Sweden, he noted, the aim was "to achieve a fundamental change in the basic structure of the organization, with rather open-ended possibilities for worker influence" (203). In Japan, "job redesign occurs in a context of unquestioned management authority" (201), with the emphasis "not on participation per se, but rather on achieving the consent of workers for policies which management wants to pursue. . . . Decentralization at Toyota Auto Body has been accompanied, if anything, by an increase in the authority and role of the foreman" (209).

Importance of the Assembly Design for Working Conditions

In Blauner's analysis, the technological structure plays a central role in determining the character of the work. The auto researchers at MIT take the opposite position: management is everything; with lean production, the same technology produces fundamentally different work. They flatly deny, without any empirical substantiation, that a different production design that expands cycle times from

TABLE 1-1. The Japanese and Swedish Models of Teamwork

Characteristic	Japanese	Swedish
Production arrangement	Trimmed lines with just-in-time control.	Sociotechnical adaptation and increased work content, most radically in complete assembly.
Relations between groups	Elimination of all buffers and variation in individual work pace.	Reduction of group interdependencies by increasing worker autonomy and allowing variations in individual work pace.
Supervision and coordination	Dense structure and strengthened role vis-à-vis both staff and subordinates. Foremen decide matters concerning training, promotion, and wages.	Reduced control (how much is a contested issue). Tasks shifted toward planning, and daily responsibility is delegated to the teams.
Administrative control	Team leader is selected by first-line management. Suggestions by the workers encouraged but decisions are taken hierarchically to ensure standardization.	Group leader/representative chosen by the team. The post is often rotated, but this is a controversial question.
Work intensity and performance demands	Intense managerial and peer pressure for maximum performance. No upper performance limits.	Performance limits are specified in contract between company and union. Actual work intensity varies, depending on the wage system and peer pressure.
Union role	Work organization, production pace, and job design defined exclusively by company.	Job content, wage system, and prerogatives regulated by contract. Union engaged in questions of plant management's structure and staffing.
	Clear structure of interests. Team closely tied to plant management.	*Autonomy—a social compromise.* Work organization expresses partly opposed interests.

minutes to hours and that makes it possible for workers to set their own pace could improve working conditions.

During the 1970s and 1980s, Sweden, unintentionally, was a laboratory of sorts for experimenting with different assembly systems. This made it possible to study empirically the significance of the production design on working conditions. In chapters 10 and 11, the line plant TC is compared with four other assembly plants, each representing a distinct production design along the scale from modified to long-cycle complete assembly. The comparison provides very clear results. The further one gets from short-cycle line assembly, the better the results in the areas of job variety, skill development, the taking of responsibility, and room for use of knowledge and skill at work. The further from line assembly, the less common are psychosomatic symptoms caused by work stress, such as stomach pains, headaches, and sleeping difficulties. The results show that the highly significant differences in the working conditions at these plants are directly related to their production design and, overall, the great potential in abandoning line assembly in favor of complete assembly and long work cycles.

There is a widespread management myth that the majority of workers prefer monotonous and mechanical jobs. This view was propagated by Henry Ford in the 1920s and has recurred ever since. My study of TC and other assembly plants yields a very different picture. In all factories and among workers of all age groups and educational levels, those with monotonous jobs expressed a strong desire for more variety and better development prospects. Moreover, the overwhelming feelings of boredom and tediousness on the line were not ameliorated by job rotation between different stations, an important and often heralded feature of the Japanese approach. This was sharply borne out at the TC plant, where 90 percent of the workers participated in extensive job rotation yet 80 percent considered the work to be so monotonous as to be degrading. Feelings of distaste at the prospect of work were widespread, and the frequency of physical ailments was high.

Based on the Swedish experience, there is a strong interdependence between changes in organization and technical design. The freedom of "organizational choice" is restricted in manufacturing. In processes where jobs are fragmented and standardized and autonomy is low, Taylorized forms of organization tend to reappear again and again. Thus, it has proved to be very difficult to implement group work at the assembly lines in Sweden, in the sense of self-regulating units assuming delegated responsibility. And it is not by chance that the Japanese version of teamwork, which takes place without changing the basic technology and work structure, is accompanied by a reinforced management structure, intensive personnel selection, and a rigorous factory regime. Much of the Swedish development in the 1970–90 period, which is analyzed in this book, can be seen as a search for a new model in which novel technical designs enable workers to perform holistic work tasks as the basis for robust and qualified group work and organizational decentralization.

The Volvo Trajectory

In the early 1970s, at the end of a long period of very high employment levels, workers throughout the industrialized world began to revolt against Taylorism. Turnover, absenteeism, and recruiting problems all worsened and wildcat strikes were a frequent occurrence. The "blue-collar blues" became a recurrent theme in the mass media, and there was great interest in alternative organizational forms and in humanizing industrial work. In most cases, however, the interest was short-lived. The long period of expansion was succeeded in the mid-1970s by energy crises and recession, and the interest in alternatives declined dramatically, particularly in Japan and the United States.

As David Jenkins (1981:17) has emphasized:

> A fundamental de-radicalization occurred. Lordstown proved to be not the first in a series of spontaneous revolts against the assembly line, as some observers expected, but rather both the first and last in the series. Monotony and fatigue at work, energetically discussed during a short period, faded from the public debate. The quality of work life appeared a low-priority question, and many companies which had been active in this area turned on the brakes.

Unlike much of the rest of the world, in Sweden the pressure from the labor market, despite some variations in the business cycle, never really ceased. Except for a few years at the start of the 1980s, unemployment remained at less than 2.5 percent. The labor force participation rate was high and rising; at the close of the 1980s, more than 85 percent of the population between sixteen and sixty-four years of age were in the labor force. At the same time, the wage differentials between different sectors and companies were small. This made it very hard for companies to compensate for a bad working environment and arduous work with high wages and good benefits. It also increased the engagement and interest of the trade unions in the work environment and organization.

The greatly increased product variation in the auto industry during the 1980s was yet another motive for developing more flexible and integrated production systems. This was especially true in the manufacture of heavy-duty commercial vehicles, trucks, and buses—products of great significance for Swedish industry. (Within the Saab-Scania group, the truck and bus division Scania has always been responsible for the majority of the corporate profit, whereas Saab, the car division, has experienced recurrent economic problems.)

Increased demand for flexibility was occurring internationally. What created the special climate for change in Sweden was the simultaneous pressure from product and labor markets. The heightened demand for flexibility and quality increased companies' dependence on a stable and committed work force. Concurrently, the high employment level made it difficult to recruit and keep workers in Taylorized industrial jobs. Creating new production systems adapted to human demands—what in Europe has been referred to as "anthropocentric production systems"—came to be seen as a strategic necessity for coping with personnel problems. Under these conditions, the influence of the unions in the companies' planning and investment decisions also increased.

The Volvo Group played a major role in the search for alternative production systems. The laborious development of a new auto assembly system is well illus-trated in the histories of the three Volvo factories Kalmar, LB, and Uddevalla. (A detailed analysis of each is in chapters 7 and 8.)

Planning for Kalmar was begun around 1970, during an intensive period marked by powerful demands for reform and rapid growth in volume. The plant was inaugurated in 1974. It was a small operation, with a capacity of thirty thousand cars per year per shift, but Volvo planned to build another factory of the same type in the United States with the capacity to make one hundred thousand cars a year. Three years after Kalmar was begun, however, Volvo's profits fell drastically, plans for the U.S. plant were shelved, and the organizational climate in the car division became much more conservative.

The truck factory LB was planned at the close of the 1970s and began operations in 1982. It had the capacity to produce six thousand heavy trucks per year per shift. At the time the factory opened, the reform climate in Sweden was rather weak, but the boom in trucks was without equal. Furthermore, Volvo Trucks in Gothenburg was encountering significant problems in the labor market, which was propelling the search for new solutions. An important point of departure was the conviction of management that "people won't want to work on a line in the future." The trade unions played very little role in the development of the Kalmar plant. In the planning of the LB plant, however, which began a short time after new labor legislation that strengthened the role of organized labor, the unions participated from early on and remained intensively engaged in shaping the decentralized group organization.

Finally, the Uddevalla project was begun in 1985, the year in which Volvo was the world's most profitable car manufacturer. Sweden was again in a period of intensive economic expansion, during which the labor shortage was acute. At the same time, an extensive debate was taking place about cumulative trauma injuries in repetitive industrial jobs. More broadly, there was renewed general interest in the reform of working life. Attempts to solve these problems and at the same time raise productivity through the comprehensive automation of assembly had failed both in Sweden and abroad. The trade unions participated with full-time officers from the start of planning for the plant, and the local of the Swedish Metal Workers' Union was actively supported by the national staff. Other sections of the auto industry also began projects for change, but none of them had as comprehensive and consistent ambitions as Uddevalla, where small, autonomous teams build complete cars (in ergonomically correct positions) in work cycles lasting several hours. The plant attracted wide public interest as an example of the most fundamental attempt so far to solve the problems of auto work identified by American researchers in the 1950s: the inexorable rhythm of the line (with no chance of varying the pace), the overwhelming monotony and repetitiveness of the work, the heavy physical strain, the lack of free movement, and the difficulty of gaining a sense of purpose and meaning in the fragmented work process.

The authors of *The Machine That Changed the World,* who never visited the plant but who were very eager to establish the virtues of Japanese lean production beyond any doubt, felt compelled to condemn the concept as neocraftsmanship nostalgia and "a return full circle to Henry Ford's assembly hall of 1903" (Womack, Jones, and Roos 1990:101). This superficial assessment missed the novelty of the concept: the combination of small-scale assembly with a largely automated materials-handling process, a computer-integrated information system, a comprehensive development of new assembly tools, and significant new forms of vocational training. At Uddevalla, the anthropocentric strategy within the Volvo Group culminated in what could be called a transcendent production system. Assembly work had the potential of transcending the confinements of Taylorized fragmentation and thereby attaining a new intellectual quality. Workers could thus achieve an intimate understanding of the production process and its individual functions, as well as a sense of meaningful participation in a large productive organization.

According to Womack, Jones, and Roos, Uddevalla would never achieve the levels of productivity of a conventional mass-production plant, to say nothing of lean production. In fact, the plant reached the productivity levels of Volvo's "mass-production" plant in Gothenburg in 1991, two years into operation.

In addition to the above factories at the end of the 1980s, an operation was begun at Volvo Trucks in Gothenburg in which integrated teams built complete chassis in docks. The purpose was both to develop a flexible form of production for the assembly of the most complex products and to upgrade assembly work in order to meet rising demands from the labor market, and especially from young workers.

The technical and organizational changes at Volvo must be understood against the background of the changes in Sweden's product and labor markets. They are not, however, a simple reflection of these changes. Both Volvo and Saab-Scania encountered the same overall driving forces for change in Sweden. In Scania's least standardized manufacturing section, the bus operation, new work forms were developed that were very similar to those in Volvo (see chap. 6). Saab was much less successful. Its attempt at the close of the 1980s to design an innovative assembly plant in Malmö was marked by incompatible approaches, and when the plant opened, Saab was in a sharp slump in sales. In 1990, the company had the capacity to produce 180,000 cars but it could sell only 90,000. So, although the Malmö plant managed to produce the best-quality cars in the history of the Saab, the new CEO from General Motors, which had taken control in 1989, found the situation untenable and closed down the factory.

Generally, Volvo—both the truck and the car lines—went much further in its innovations. Neither its Kalmar nor its Uddevalla factory had any counterpart at Saab. Volvo's "culture" and high profile were heavily conditioned by the interests and policies of its management and, in particular, those of the CEO,

Pehr G. Gyllenhammar. His orientation had great import, partly because of the absence of dominant owners at Volvo, which gave the CEO tremendous power. Other significant factors in the Volvo culture were the unions' strong position in the company and the unusually open perspective among its engineers, which allowed a great deal of space for trying new approaches.

The social conditions in Sweden were also very important. During the 1970s and 1980s, tellingly, the assembly-line regime was never questioned at Volvo's auto and truck factories in Ghent, Belgium. The Belgian car factory produced the same product as in Sweden, but conditions in the Belgian labor market were altogether different. Specifically, unemployment was higher than 10 percent, job security was much more limited than in Sweden, and unemployment as well as sickness benefits were considerably less generous.

A number of events in 1990 signaled that Volvo had entered a new phase. A decade's expansion was followed by sharp contraction, in the wake of a swiftly deepening recession in Sweden; severe downturns also occurred in Volvo's other two main markets (the United States and Great Britain). Gyllenhammar, who for twenty years had been at the helm of the company, withdrew as CEO and became chairman of the board. In the same year, a comprehensive and complex alliance was forged with the French state-owned Renault Corporation, a firm with technical, social, and cultural values very different from Volvo's.

Need for a Plurality of Production Concepts

Eighty years ago, the Ford Motor Company developed a single standard way of manufacturing automobiles. Toyota and the Japanese auto firms have taken this standardization even further, to the point where their plants in North America are considered clones of their operations in Japan. The opposite is true for Volvo. In a unique manner, the company's assembly plants embody a great variety of technical and organizational concepts, reflecting the place of each plant in the Volvo trajectory, the different market conditions for its three main product lines, and the different social conditions in Sweden, Belgium, and North America, the principal regions where Volvo operates. As a result it is difficult to speak of "Volvism" in the same way as one may speak of Fordism or Toyotism.

As the world's second largest producer of heavy trucks and the third largest producer of heavy buses, Volvo's international position in heavy commercial vehicles is very strong. Unlike cars, these vehicles are produced in rather small-scale operations. The demands for flexibility and responsiveness to special customer requests are exacting. In the late 1970s, the bus divisions at both Volvo and Scania pioneered modern forms of long-cycle stationary assembly in small teams (so-called dock assembly). After a difficult breaking-in phase, dock assembly became very successful.

In 1989, Volvo Buses decided to introduce the same concept in the newly acquired British Leyland Company. This was done at the same time that the Leyland plant in Workington was being refitted to make Volvo chassis. The object was gradually to spread the organizational model of work teams and stationary assembly to the production of British buses. In the United Kingdom, Volvo had no need to make its jobs more attractive; however, it expected to attain quality advantages by applying the Swedish concept. Another objective was to achieve symmetry with the manufacturing system in Borås.[1]

Volvo Trucks followed two production strategies. In 1990, a substantial expansion of the Ghent facility, which functioned more or less according to traditional principles, was planned. The objective in Gothenburg, however, was to expand the new dock assembly and increase capacity at the group-organized LB plant. Production in Volvo's truck division was thus less centralized and technology-intensive than in the car division. According to senior production managers, having two different production strategies was not a burden but an advantage—it corresponded to the differentiated product structure and labor market requirements of the 1990s. The large pool of disciplined Belgian labor was used for the rationalized line assembly of a simpler product mix. At the same time, alternative forms of production were developed in Sweden to supply the flexibility required for the most complex and customized types of assembly, as well as to answer the strong demands by workers for variation and expanded job content. This does not mean, however, that Volvo's capacity or interest in workplace innovation was confined to Sweden. Thus, in its greenfield site in Curitiba, Brazil, which produced trucks and buses, Volvo management did not "go native" in the sense of simply adopting local practices. Instead, it made considerable efforts to reorganize work, upgrade workers' skills, and develop a participative culture.[2]

By contrast, in the passenger car market, Volvo's standing was much weaker, the pressure for lean production was stronger, and the scale and standardization of production was far greater. A plurality of work concepts could be an asset in the truck business because of its mix of both standardized and widely customized products. In car production it was mainly a disadvantage, however, since it implied that the same models were produced using different methods in different plants also within Sweden.

In 1990, which was a year of plummeting sales, Volvo's total Swedish output was 160,000 cars. Of these, 75 percent were assembled at the Gothenburg plant TC, which in spite of a number of attempts at reform still operated largely on the basis of line production. The innovative Kalmar and Uddevalla plants accounted together for the remaining 25 percent. Kalmar, the pioneer of the 1970s, consistently outperformed the main plant, TC, during the 1980s but never reached the high productivity levels at Ghent. Uddevalla, which was opened in 1989, was still in the start-up stage. The plant had demonstrated its flexible capacity by coping with the introduction of Volvo's new 900 series much more smoothly than other production installations had done. In 1991, Uddevalla matched the performance of TC, but at both plants it was considerably below that of Ghent, which was one of Europe's most productive assembly plants in its segment. With a rapid stabilization of the work force, the potential for improvement within Uddevalla's "transcendent production" was great, and the plant was working intensively to make further progress (without much support from corporate management). So were the other plants, however, all of which were struggling to survive this period of excessive overcapacity at Volvo.

Dogmatic Emulation or Dynamic Synthesis?

Since 1980, Japan has been the world's number one car producer. Since 1985 it has also been the global leader of new technologies and product offerings. These accomplishments have been possible because of innovations and new approaches in a vast array of areas: relationships with suppliers are at the same time long term, collaborative, and intensely competitive; the product design process has a fierce tempo, and there are close relations between the departments of development and manufacturing; and the emphasis in production control is on continuous improvement. Japan's manufacturing excellence has been a result of its focus on the shop floor, a characteristic of late industrializers. The quality control (QC) techniques, JIT delivery system, and the total productive maintenance (TPM) philosophy emerged from this shop-floor focus. The personnel policy of the Japanese transplants, with its egalitarian thrust, commitment to job security, emphasis on working with pride, and involvement of blue-collar workers in process development, also entails important contributions. Intense domestic rivalry and a demanding and sophisticated product market have fueled the development of the Japanese auto production system. The auto companies have also been privileged to have acquiescent unions and highly dependent workers who submit to the relentless demands. Thus, Japanese firms—with the exception of a short period before the first oil crisis, when "humanization of work" was an issue in Japan— never had to confront and change the character of the work itself, such as its fragmentation, intensity, and inexorable mechanical control. Japanese workers have resented the work but complied.[3]

The range of Swedish innovations has been much more narrow, as is proper for a small nation. The Swedish auto firms of the 1980s were minor players in the industrial world, and their contributions of new ideas and organizational forms have been restricted to manufacturing and the handling of customers (Volvo in Europe pioneered lifetime service contracts and other forms of sophisticated services). As in Japan, there has been a strong shop-floor focus but for a very different reason: in Sweden, the labor market and its increasingly exacting demands triggered much of the innovation and change. Technical redesign of the production process to relieve workers of mechanical pacing, to make reintegration of fragmented tasks possible, and to create a basis for true team production (as opposed to administratively engineered teams) has been one important feature. Another has been the strong interest in improving the physical work environment and ergonomics through technical as well as organizational means. Yet another has been the endeavor to "democratize the workplace" and develop sustainable forms of shop-floor self-governance. Finally, there has been extensive labor-management collaboration; unions are independent and important partners in company activities, including the early phases of plant planning. This feature has become characteristic of the "Swedish management style," which generally is less authoritarian, more informal and egalitarian, and less inclined to rely on the formal powers of organizational position than the Anglo-Saxon type. (The development of the Swedish style has been closely related to the high degree of job security in Sweden, which has made employees less inclined to "blind obedience".)[4]

Since the close of the 1980s, the labor market in Japan has become increasingly tight. Criticism of the industrial conditions, the long working hours, and the trying physical environment are widespread. Manufacturing firms are encountering mounting recruitment difficulties, and there is soaring turnover among new hirees. Japan's Auto Workers' Union has become active in this field and has demanded a "new industrial policy." The prescription of Womack, Jones, and Roos (1990) that the West must adopt the Japanese production system lock, stock, and barrel (they explicitly warn against any attempts at modification) is out of sync with the current debate in Japan and, compared to Western "best practice," represents a regression in terms of working conditions as well as individual freedom.

After World War II, the Japanese approached Western countries, especially the United States, because they wanted to learn, transplant, and transform. The real challenge for the 1990s and the next century is to amalgamate the contributions of lean production and of European human-centered manufacturing to create new syntheses.

Theoretical References and Empirical Sources

From **The Degradation of Work** *to* **The End of Mass Production**

Research in industrial sociology during the 1970s was heavily influenced by the notion of the degradation of labor, as a result of the continuing spread of the organizational principles of scientific management. Harry Braverman's powerful study on this theme, *Labor and Monopoly Capital* (1974), had many successors in the so-called labor process school. In Germany, research largely followed the lines laid down by Horst Kern and Michael Schumann's exemplary study *Industriearbeit und Arbeiterbewusstsein* (1977). The debate in Germany was more sophisticated than in the United States or Britain, but it had the same general message.

The investigations I started in the Swedish auto industry in the early 1980s were inspired by these theories, but not in the sense that I sought their confirmation (that was all too easily found). On the contrary, what interested me was alternative forms of rationalization, leading to reskilling and enhanced autonomy. At the time this was a rather original point of departure. By the mid-1980s however, it was far from being so. A dramatic shift had taken place in industrial sociology. Braverman's theses, which earlier had met with such approval, were succeeded by notions, quite opposite in character, on the themes of flexible specialization and requalification. In the United States, Michael Piore and Charles Sabel played a critical role in this reorientation. In Germany, this role was played by Kern and Schumann, who, in a book with the title (typical for the time) of *Das Ende der Arbeitsteilung?* (1984), claimed that industrial rationalization had taken a new turn and tended now to dissolve the division of labor in precisely those sectors where earlier it had been most strongly rooted.

In my own work, this post-Fordist debate, with its stress on the demands and changeability of the market and the economic limits of the division of labor (themes wholly absent in the studies of the labor process school), has been an important inspiration. At the same time, there is cause to be critical of many of the ideas at the root of the thesis that there has been a shift in the industrial paradigm. The notion of "the end of mass production" is central to the flexibility theorists, starting with Piore and Sabel (1984), and has been picked up by Womack, Jones, and Roos. Piore and Sabel played an important role in "discovering" the Italian industrial districts as a mode of production and organization very different from the American Fordist model. Michael Porter (1990) elaborated on the competitiveness of these districts not only in textile, fashion, and design but also in a wide range of customized machinery. But paralleling the rise of flexible specialization, there has been an ever-increasing range of mass-produced goods, from video cameras and VCRs to microwave ovens and fax machines (see Cutler et al. 1987). True, many companies such as the auto manufacturers offer a great many more options and models than in earlier decades, yet they remain mass producers that are highly dependent on economies of scale (see Luria 1990).

In this new kind of flexible volume production, the Japanese car producers are the modern masters, representing a production system and industrial structure squarely different from the Italian districts, a point Piore and Sabel unfortunately gloss over. The Japanese preference for high volume and standardization as a basis for offering a variety of features and options is also stressed by Porter, whose massive study *The Competitive Advantage of Nations* (1990) contains a much more compelling analysis of the Japanese dynamism than is found in the MIT texts. Japanese firms are very competitive in such industries as cars, consumer electronics, semiconductors, and standardized machine tools. They have not invented any universal production or management system, however, and Porter finds them to be much less successful in industries demanding customization and individualized customer relations: "Japanese firms do not do well, by and large, in industries or segments involving a high degree of customization to individual buyers, narrow applications, heavy after-sale support, and small lot sizes" (411).

Another drawback of much of the flexibility debate is that the strong interest in changed product markets and new technology as driving forces for new production strategies tends to obscure the significance of labor market conditions and the role of trade unions, government policies, and national institutions in general.[5] It is precisely the importance of the latter set of conditions that the Swedish case powerfully underscores: high employment levels and strong trade unions were of decisive significance in the development of work patterns involving a qualitative enhancement of autonomy and self-management. This weakness in the flexibility discourse is closely tied to a reductionist perspective in which increased market variation and product flexibility are followed directly by new work forms and more qualified jobs. But which strategies companies use to cope with demands for flexibility and what the consequences for work are cannot be deduced from developments in product markets; rather, these consequences must be traced through empirical study. In the case of the careful empirical investigation of changes in industrial work, both the American industrial sociology of the 1950s and the labor process school of the 1970s are superior to the flexibility discourse. The workplace studies in Kern and Schumann's *Das Ende der Arbeitsteilung?* lack the methodological rigor, systematic approach, and massive empirical basis of the earlier *Industriearbeit und Arbeiterbewusstsein* (1977).

Piore and Sabel favor modern craft work that is able to take advantage of advanced technology yet flexible in meeting market demands, but they provide few empirical examples of firms that have such jobs. Their argument is further weakened by their attempt to portray the Japanese production system as a new form of "craft control." Womack, Jones, and Roos correctly reject this ill-informed notion in *The Machine That Changed the World* (1990). But their own treatment of the working conditions under lean production are sloppy and speculative, and the generalizations from the car industry to all forms of industrial production lack any qualifications. In some ways the book is more a piece of propaganda than of science. Nevertheless, their study is an important source for reference (and criticism) throughout my book. The comparative studies of plant productivity (and to a lesser extent productivity in research and development) are impressive, and the style of writing, in which all the parts seem to move in the same direction, is forceful and an obvious reason for its great impact.

In contrast to much of the flexibility debate, comprehensive field studies and surveys of working conditions play a central role in this book. Extensive interviews with managers, from the shop floor to the executive level, are also important. At the core is a series of case studies of the Swedish auto industry, carried out from the late 1970s through 1990. For the analysis of the often ambiguous working conditions in new work settings, German industrial sociology, especially Norbert Altmann's Institute for Social Research in Munich, has provided a major inspiration. The Scandinavian sociotechnical tradition and European studies of industrial democracy have been other points of reference, especially for the investigation of group work and participation. The development in Sweden is contrasted with the characteristics of Toyota's production system, in Japan and in the Japanese transplants. These comparisons depend on cumulative analysis of materials derived from many sources and lack the systematic character and empirical rigor of the Swedish case studies and surveys. In important respects, my discussion of the Japanese management system has been influenced by the Berlin project *The Future of Work in the Automobile Industry* (Jürgens, Dohse, and Malsch 1989).[6] As a whole, this book may be seen as an offspring of the broad debate of the 1980s among European researchers and industrial practitioners concerning anthropocentric or human-centered production concepts.

Plan of the Book

The focus of this book is automotive production and assembly work. It was in this process that the Fordist revolution had its most dramatic impact with the birth of the mechanical assembly line in 1913. It has been a classical terrain of industrial sociology ever since. The developments in the 1970s and 1980s have made a revisit imperative. Moreover, it was in the assembly plants that the Swedish auto firms experienced their greatest personnel and productivity problems and, consequently, where they were most innovative. A final reason for the focus is that the proportion of human assembly work in auto manufacturing has been increasing steadily for a long time because of the relative failure of mechanization in this area compared to machining or body welding.

Chapter 2 analyzes the dominant industrial paradigm of the 1980s, the Japanese production system, from the Toyota revolution to the experience of the transplants. I move from there to the Swedish experience. Chapter 3 presents the development of the Swedish automotive industry from 1970 to 1990, emphasizing the differences between the car, the truck, and the bus business. Chapter 4 highlights important features of the labor market and union structure and then summarizes the specific reasons for change in Sweden.

Chapter 5, a preamble to the case studies in chapters 6, 7, and 8, outlines the basic concepts and models that guide the subsequent case analyses. This conceptual framework differs in some respects from the frame of reference used in chapter 2; I have chosen to present each paradigm by focusing on its specific distinguishing features rather than applying the same structure everywhere, and these features are not necessarily in the same areas. Three broad themes recur in both the Swedish and Japanese cases—the forms and contents of skill development, the preconditions for autonomy, and the nature of teamwork and how these three issues are linked to technical and organizational design.

Chapter 6 addresses the Swedish pattern of assembly design from the periphery by analyzing the radical and unknown experiences of the bus manufacturers. Long ago they proved the viability of autonomous assembly of complex products in extended work cycles. Chapter 7 examines the first and second stages of the Volvo trajectory proper: the Kalmar car plant and the LB truck plant. Chapter 8 proceeds to the third (and last?) stage, the Uddevalla plant, elucidating how its original design came about as a rational solution to a number of pressing problems. This chapter also contains a discussion of the arduous and largely aborted process of change at Volvo's main brownfield plant, TC, which started operation in 1964.

Chapter 9 is a methodological prelude to the survey studies. This chapter discusses the problems and pitfalls of comparative studies of working conditions and possible solutions. Chapter 10 presents the survey results from the assembly line at TC as a benchmark for the subsequent comparisons. Chapter 11 analyzes working conditions in five assembly plants with different technical designs. Chapter 12 continues with an investigation of group organization and worker influence in everyday decisions. Finally, chapter 13 summarizes the empirical chapters and pulls together the different elements. Thereby I return to and elaborate on the main argument presented in this introduction—the need for a new synthesis in manufacturing as a strategy for postlean production.

2.

The Evolution and Transplantation of Toyotism

The development of the Japanese auto industry in the postwar period is exceptional in industrial history. At the end of the Korean War, in 1953, the Japanese companies manufactured a mere 50,000 cars. By 1960, the figure had increased tenfold, to nearly half a million. By 1970, it had gone up another order of magnitude, to 5 million. The 11 million mark was passed in 1980, making Japan the world's number one auto manufacturer. The level of productivity of the Japanese companies reached that of the American firms as early as the mid-1960s, and shortly after the Japanese passed them by. By the 1970s, the Japanese automakers were setting new world standards of quality as well.

The leading Japanese companies long pursued a "VW line," meaning that they concentrated on a few basic models that they manufactured year after year with incremental improvements. The companies concentrated their resources, as Ford had in the teens, on the development and fine-tuning of the production process (see Cusumano 1985). In the 1980s, however, the Japanese also took the lead in product development in the auto industry. Investment in research and development rose much more sharply than in Western Europe and the United States. Measured by the number of company patents approved in the United States in 1985, Toyota, Nissan, and Honda, in that order, led both their American and European competitors.[1] The rule of the strong yen, which was institutionalized by the Plaza agreement in 1985, reinforced the Japanese automakers' commitment to product upgrading and unleashed intense domestic competition to introduce new models and features. In the five years from 1982 to 1987, Japanese automakers introduced more than seventy new models while U.S. manufacturers released only about twenty and the European firms about forty. The Japanese firms succeeded in combining high manufacturing productivity with efficient design processes, which, compared with their American and European counterparts, dramatically reduced resource consumption, as measured by the number of engineering hours spent on the development of each new product.[2]

Some years after Japan had become the world's largest car producer and exporter, internationalization of production was begun. After a cautious start, the pace accelerated in the mid-1980s with the establishment of a growing number of transplants, principally in North America.

In this chapter, I shall first summarize some of the main features and conditions of the paradigmatic production philosophy of Japanese auto manufacture — the Toyota system — as it was developed in Japan during the 1950s and 1960s. I shall also relate Toyotism to Taylorism in three respects: work process and labor deployment, the managerial structure, and the employment relation. In the next section, the focus shifts westward, to the Japanese transplants in North America and the United Kingdom. My purpose is to analyze the preconditions for the impressive success of these factories, which are the principal exponents of lean production in the Western world, and to examine the nature of work in these plants. I devote special attention to four issues: skill development and qualification requirements (multitasking or reskilling), JIT control and worker autonomy, the nebulous meaning of teamwork, and the problem of physical strains and work hazards.

Rise and Defeat of the Independent Unions

When the Japanese auto industry began to expand under heavy state protection after the war, the production system of the American car industry was the reference point. Both the product and labor market conditions in Japan were very different, however, from those in the American car industry. For one, there was much less room for mass production than in the United States. Volumes were radically lower; in 1950, for instance, thirty thousand vehicles were produced in all. This was the equivalent of one and a half day's production in the United States. For another, the Japanese companies had a wide product spread; indeed, the auto firms had begun as manufacturers of light trucks. Moreover, the economic resources of the companies and the purchasing power of the home market were very limited. It was therefore necessary for the car manufacturers to adapt American methods to fit the efficient manufacture of lower volumes and, despite limited resources, to be able to expand. The crushing defeat of independent Japanese labor unions after a number of dramatic conflicts in the early 1950s gave the auto companies the opportunity to develop just such forms of low-cost rationalization.

After the war had ended and the Americans had forced democracy on Japan, the labor movement enjoyed an enormous upswing. Trade unions mushroomed in virtually all sectors of society, so that union density rose from almost zero in the autumn of 1945 to more than 40 percent one year later. Most of the new unions were organized as enterprise unions and comprised both blue- and white-collar employees. Japanese workers were eager to unionize in this feverish period and, as Haruo Shimada has noted (1988), enterprise unionism seemed to be the easiest and most practical way for them to achieve this goal. In the prewar period, before the authoritarian rule of the 1930s, Japanese workers had put forward three broad demands. The first demand concerned job security. The second concerned predictable and secure wages instead of the more prevalent output pay, which was considered capricious and unreliable. The third demand focused on the discrimination and segregation in Japanese firms, where workers were not treated as "full members" but often experienced scorn and a painful lack of respect from management.[3]

This "program" was aggressively revived by the postwar unions. After a series of major strikes in 1946 to stop management plans to fire workers, firms across the country were forced to announce "no-dismissal" pledges. During the war the government had prodded companies to introduce predictable and stable wages in the form of seniority (*nenko*) systems. The unions perceived this as a fair and objective basis for remuneration, and after the war the *nenko* principle was diffused further, despite management desire to eliminate it. At the same time, formerly pervasive divisions between blue-collar workers and white-collar staff were largely eliminated and workers gained "full citizenship" in the enterprise community. Moreover, in many companies unions also gained a strong influence on shop-floor practices and labor deployment.

For management, the strength of radical labor unions on the shop floor represented an intolerable loss of control. A determined counteroffensive was launched with the support of the American occupation authorities, which in the wake of the Cold War increasingly stressed the importance of Japan as a strong and stable ally. The pattern was set during a five-month conflict at Toshiba in 1949, which Andrew Gordon (1990:248) summarized as follows: "In a tactic that has since been replicated hundreds of times, the company refused to bargain with the existing 'first union' or to renew its contract, while it simultaneously identified a core of cooperative workers willing to lead a 'second union'. The latter repudiated the oppositional stance of the first union, accepted some dismissals, restrained its wage demands and supported management efforts at 'rationalization.' "

Workers in the auto industry had first been slow to participate in the general labor advance, but eventually a strong union developed at Nissan that took the initiative to form a national union of auto workers. Japanese business leaders considered this development very dangerous. In 1953 Nissan management, with determined backing from commerce and industry, found the time ripe for a showdown. The struggle concerned power on the shop floor, where Nissan's union had, through its shop committees, called into question the right of the company unilaterally to order overtime and reassign labor.[4] But the struggle was also about a basic principle of unionism, Was there to be a cohesive national industrial union or a system of company unions closely connected to company interests?

In a series of strikes and lockouts in 1953, the union at Nissan was crushed and its leaders were fired and a new "second union," loyal to the company, was formed. These events were a death blow to the national auto workers' union, which was dissolved in 1954. In sharp contrast, in the 1950s and 1960s, auto unions in Western Europe and the United States became increasingly powerful national organizations.[5]

The defeat of the independent trade union movement in the Japanese private sector had three important consequences: First, the companies got a free hand in matters of shop-floor organization and the supervision and utilization of the work force. Second, the defeat contributed to the critical lack of a social force capable of carrying out a general social welfare policy, as in Western Europe, or national contracts, as in the unionized sectors of American industry. Thus, employees' security, income development, and social benefits came to be wholly dependent on the company for which they worked. Third, small companies (up to one hundred employees) came to lack a union organization almost entirely. This helped strengthen the industrial dualism — the extremely large differences in wages and employment conditions between big and small companies — that had already existed before the war. This dualism became a very important aspect of the total structure of Japanese auto production.

In large companies, several early postwar gains were retained, albeit in a more restricted and controlled framework. These included job security for the core (male) work force, the seniority-based wage system, and the policy of treating blue- and white-collar workers equally and with respect. Thus, management's espousal of common goals and joint efforts to increase productivity was endowed with enough legitimacy in the eyes of most workers to become the long-term basis for cooperative labor relations.

The Toyota Revolution

The restrictions of the product market and the possibilities for management posed by the defeat of industrial unionism were the basis for the Toyota Revolution of the 1950s and 1960s. This new way of organizing production, materials, and suppliers came to set the norm for all Japanese auto firms. As at Ford, the Toyota system developed in a process of trial and error. The individual features were often not unique in themselves, but in their entirety they became a new production matrix. Demands for far-reaching economizing in the use of materials and workers formed the departure point for this revolution. Taichi Ohno, a key figure in Toyota's production development during the 1950s and 1960s, met these demands with new methods.[6]

Manufacturing in the smallest possible batches replaced the American philosophy of "optimal batch sizes." New materials-control methods, the *kanban* system, and JIT deliveries were developed to manage this small-batch production. "Inventoryless" manufacturing gradually became an overall method for streamlining processes and the flow of materials. Several important consequences followed.

One consequence was that setup times had to be reduced, which led to dramatic reductions in changeover times. At the start of the 1970s, after fifteen years of systematic work, Toyota could reset its press lines in three minutes, compared with three hours before 1955 (Cusumano 1985:284–85).[7] (The Western car industry still needed several hours in the early 1980s.)

As a consequence of the ever smaller buffers between different manufacturing steps, the production process became ever more sensitive to disturbance. Manufacturing quality, expressed as the goal of zero defects in every stage, therefore played a central role beginning in the 1960s. The export offensive following the oil crisis of 1974 further underlined the role of quality. As in many other areas, Toyota seized on methods developed in the United States but applied them far more rigorously.

Furthermore, small-batch manufacture led to the need for a highly flexible work force, with rapid and frequent relocation of personnel according to the production needs of the moment. To ensure such flexibility, Toyota invested heavily in work simplification, as Ford had done in the teens: As Shigeo Shingo noted in *The Toyota Production System* (1981:132), "This [flexible capacity] requires that the machines be developed and simplified, so that a new operator can perform the job independently after three days' training."

The principle of the minimum use of materials in work had its equivalent in least possible staffing. In the late 1940s, Taichi Ohno introduced the rationalization of cycle times on the assembly lines and multimachine tending in the machine shops. During the 1950s, each operator had an average of five to ten machines to tend; this principle was further extended during the 1960s and 1970s.

The principle of least possible staffing also had as a consequence that routine inspection work was integrated into the production line as the responsibility of the operators and foremen. As with the reduction of setup times, this no-fault policy led to new means and methods for avoiding unintentional mistakes, for example the *poka-yoke* principle, incorrectly translated as "fool-proof devices" [Shingo 1981:132]. But cycle-time rationalization, multimachine tending, and the integration of inspection work also contributed to greatly heightened work intensity. The absence of union-imposed limitations, in the form of ceilings on line speeds and staffing, played a central role in this connection. In an interview with Cusumano, Ohno conceded that "workers hated this and the technique of operating several machines at once. . . . Had I faced the Japan National Railways union or an American union I might have been murdered" (Cusumano 1985:306).[8]

Ohno succeeded in controlling the Toyota union, however, by using a mixture of methods: on the one hand, management threatened to dismiss recalcitrant workers; on the other, workers were promised long-term job security. Like many other large firms, Toyota was also able, as Gordon has emphasized (1990:250), to show "real creativity in building on the notion, rooted in the practice of the early post-war era, that blue-collar workers were full members of the enterprise, and they involved these men in self-directed (though circumscribed) endeavors to improve morale and raise output."

Another central feature of Toyota's production system, which originally arose for purely economic reasons, was the strategic decision, made in the 1940s, to refrain from vertical integration. As great a share as possible of components manufacture was assigned to suppliers (*sh'tauke*), which were closely associated with Toyota but economically independent. This required great efforts in the 1950s and 1960s to streamline the quality and delivery systems of these suppliers. In return, Toyota was able to expand during these decades, using much smaller investments than would have been required otherwise. Moreover, the much lower wage level of the small *sh'tauke* could be exploited in carrying out severe cost cutting.[9]

Toyota's suppliers were organized hierarchically in a veritable production pyramid. A few, relatively large firms were responsible for a complete function and delivered directly to Toyota. These in turn had a considerable number of parts suppliers connected to them, which often engaged even smaller firms for various subjobs.[10] During the 1970s and 1980s, many of the suppliers on the first and second levels could — in step with Toyota's expansion and ever more developed products — become advanced components firms with extensive research and development.[11] By contrast, at *sh'tauke* on lower levels, low wage costs and high flexibility (with no lifetime guarantees for employees) remained essential competitive advantages.[12]

At Nissan, management did not enjoy the same position of power as at Toyota — even after its victory over the union in 1953. Thus, work could not be made as intensive. One expression of the differences between Toyota and Nissan, and between the Japanese and American manufacturers as well, was labor's share of the value added. In 1980, after thirty years of nearly unbroken expansion, this share was but 46 percent at Toyota, whereas it was 85 percent at Nissan and 87 percent at Ford.

Toyota's capacity to achieve major increases in productivity in a "mature" industry without any technological innovations in either products or processes is indeed striking. This feat was achieved through extraordinary and incessant attention to shop-floor practices — work simplification, machine setup procedures, quality-control methods, and materials ordering. But why this attention, and why did it happen in Japan?

In a provoking analysis, Alice Amsden (1990) has pointed to the importance of Japan's character as a late industrializer to explain this phenomenon. In Britain, industrialization was based on *inventions* realized by entrepreneurs in processes of trial and error, whereas in Germany and the United States *innovations* emanating from systematic problem solving and the application of science were the driving force. In contrast, Japan, like other late industrializers such as Korea, based all of its industrialization on *borrowing* technology, which meant that even leading firms had to wage competition without the aid of any technological advantage. Borrowing, or *learning,* is also a creative process but of quite another type and demanding other skills than the Western process of industrialization did. As Amsden emphasizes, in firms competing on the basis of making borrowed technology work, the shop floor tends to achieve a strategic focus. Thus, production engineers acquire a very important role, as well as strong social recognition. In Japan, as in Korea two decades later, this resulted in a particularly effective shop-floor management and in general in a markedly technical orientation within management.[13] The shop-floor focus also resulted in a "Spartan regard" for staff functions as efforts were made to keep overhead costs to a minimum. This policy at Toyota — and at the Japanese manufacturing firms in general — was later followed by firms in Korea.

Small-Batch Manufacturing as the Basis for Flexible Mass Production

Does Toyotism represent an abandonment of the basic principles of mass production? A good deal of confusion exists around this question, often because *production in small batches* is confused with *short total production runs.* Shingo, an expert on Toyota's production methods, rejects the idea that the Toyota system is "the antithesis of the philosophy of mass production upon which American industry had been founded." He points out that Toyota, "with its Corolla, broke the world record for the number of vehicles produced of one and the same type." Moreover, he emphasizes, "the question in this area is not whether or not to mass produce, but whether to produce *large or small batches*" (my emphasis) (1981:110ff).

The Toyota executive made having small inventories a priority and chose therefore to concentrate on small-batch manufacturing. The object, however, was to produce the highest possible cumulative volume of each product. Long total runs were (and are) decisive for carefully preparing the manufacture of each part; standardizing tools, methods, and operations; streamlining suppliers; and developing the JIT flow. As Shingo points out, "It cannot be said the Toyota system is the antithesis of mass production; it is, on the other hand, the antithesis of large-batch manufacturing" (1981:112). In short product runs, tools and methods contain unique features for each manufacturing order and the prospects for standardization and bureaucratized control are extremely limited. By contrast, in the small-batch manufacture of long-run products, the same tools and methods are used a great many times. Flexibility is a matter of switching quickly between a number of standardized models — of retooling from model A to model B, for instance. The high frequency of such switching in the Toyota system has also meant that "resetting work" could itself be standardized and intensified. It has become part of the highly rationalized system of mass production. In Western long-run manufacture, switching has been a low-frequency, craft-type work, very different from the repetitive operations in production. The Toyota system's flexibility of mass production can thus be said to represent an extension of the sphere of influence of scientific management.

During the 1980s, these methods, which were originally developed to cope with quick switching between batches within the framework of long production runs, increasingly came to be used to enhance the capacity to break in new models. In the event of automation, moreover, the Japanese companies have, to a considerably higher degree than their Western counterparts, installed convertible rather than dedicated equipment. Combined with a highly efficient process of product design and an increasingly dynamic network of suppliers and assisting firms, this has enabled Japanese automakers to reduce their break-even levels for each single product. During the 1980s, the Japanese companies on average produced 120,000 units per year and model, compared with more than 200,000 for the European and American firms. The total runs (or accumulated volume) per model was also much lower: 500,000 for the Japanese models, 1.8 million for the European, and 2.1 million for the American (see Jones 1989).

Toyotism as a Complex Extension of Taylorism

Many analysts have claimed, in common with the authors of *The Machine That Changed the World* (Womack, Jones, and Roos 1990), that Toyota's personnel policy and production management amount to a fundamental break with Taylorism. This is misleading in several ways. I shall use Craig Littler's breakdown of the Taylorist approach (1978) to analyze this question: organization of the work process: minute division of labor, high degree of predetermination, standardization ("one best way"), and control; managerial process: a high degree of division of tasks and functional specialization; personnel policy and company-employee relations: a "minimum interaction model" marked by an individualistic and economistic approach. In regard to these three features, Toyotism entails a complex combination of continuity and change.

Highly Standardized Work

The work process in Toyota's production system has a short-cycle, highly repetitive structure throughout. Assembly takes place on machine-paced lines in which there are short instruction times, and training takes place directly on the job. It takes a couple of days to a week to learn what is necessary. Standard operations sheets prescribing movements and times are used at each work station. New operators are trained and performance is judged on the basis of these time-tables. As Shingo notes (1981:151–52), "The standard operation sheet is accordingly an important instrument for reaching Toyota's goal of being able to train new operators to perform the job independently after three days. . . . At Toyota it is insisted that the standard time be held to. . . . If deviations occur, the first question is if the operator's movements depart from the standard."

Work standardization is important in increasing work intensity, as Shimuzu emphasizes: "In order to eliminate parasitism and superfluous work motions, a thorough standardization that can be immediately understood and observed by everyone is necessary. In order to promote standardization complicated work tasks must be avoided as much as possible and work simplified. . . . When work itself is simple and repetitious, it is easy to identify parasitical and superfluous persons (oneself included)" (quoted in Dohse, Jürgens, and Malsch 1984:17).

The labor process in the Toyota system is thus designed according to classic Taylorist principles. At the same time, inventoryless small-batch production requires a work force that is not highly specialized but rather is capable of performing a number of different tasks. These different tasks, however, are mainly variations of similar simple jobs (three days' instruction time for production work is, as mentioned above, a general goal at Toyota). According to Eishi Fujita (1988:6), the reassignments often entail heavy burdens: "Transfers to an unrelated working position, mostly to a simple one everyone can do, does not make workers able to utilize their abilities and it is a heavy burden to them."

Representatives of the Swedish Metal Workers' Union were especially interested, during a visit to Japan in 1989, in the prospects for training in the auto industry. Their report revealed a great gap between the image of continuous learning for everyone in Japanese work life and the reality on the shop floor. Investments in advanced training could only be found in highly automated sections. In the case of such manual jobs as those on Nissan's assembly lines, the training consisted of a short introduction to the company plus workplace training lasting a total of two weeks. In the case of partly mechanized processes, such as the manufacture of electrical fans, a select few (about 2 percent) were trained each year in maintenance work. Because absenteeism was so low, the company saw no need to train more of its employees. In general, the workers' prospects for training were closely linked to advancement in the shop-floor hierarchy. Advanced training was reserved for workers who were promoted, as in traditional Western organizations (Grehn and Pettersson 1989:14). As I will explain, the difference is that the promotion system is much more comprehensive in Japan.

The feature of the Japanese production system perhaps most often associated with a different and broader way of utilizing personnel is that workers and foremen continuously offer suggestions for improvements. Rationalization activities (so-called *kaizen*) are not reserved for engineers but are the responsibility of everyone. The vertical hierarchy and managerial prerogatives have not been changed, however. Workers are encouraged to offer proposals for rationalizing standard operations by improving quality and productivity, but management exclusively makes the decision to change methods — precisely to ensure that operations remain standardized. At the close of the 1960s, it became mandatory at Toyota to attend quality circles and suggestion meetings; management set quotas, and the workers' success in fulfilling them was an important factor in the determination of the yearly bonus (Cusumano 1985:357).

It is certainly true that scientific management has not traditionally included making large-scale use of employees' suggestions for improvements to enhance performance, but this is not because the use of such methods would have contradicted the goals of scientific management. On the contrary; Frederick Taylor's follower Frank Gilbreth, for example, considered it crucial that the operators cooperate in developing the standard methods. No means were available for eliciting such cooperation, however. Instead, Taylor saw that workers used their skills to resist increasing performance demands. *Kaizen* is not based on there being a differently designed work process but rather a distinct employment relationship that includes novel forms of labor deployment and career systems.

In an analysis of the Toyota-GM joint venture NUMMI in California, Paul Adler (1991:59, 80), in contrast to other proponents of the Toyota system, stresses the intense bureaucratization and Taylorization but only to perform a reanalysis (or "revisionist reading") of both phenomena. There are different forms of bureaucracy, he argues. The traditional form, associated with Max Weber's famous "iron cage," is the "compliance bureaucracy." In contrast, NUMMI and the Toyota system represent a "learning bureaucracy," where the most intensely bureaucratic procedures "appear to serve the purpose of organizational learning." As for Taylorism, Adler distinguishes between the technical dimension — division of labor, standardization, and so on — and the social dimension of authority and control. In NUMMI, he asserts, "technical Taylorism" plays the central role, while the social dimension is democratized: "Taylorism can be oriented towards learning rather than social control if workers participate in the definition of the rules that govern their work, or the organization has some other way of assuring that the rules will reflect a shared understanding of the technical requirements of the job" (Adler 1991:63–64).

The designation of the Toyota model as a learning bureaucracy is pertinent and important in that it captures how the dynamics of the Japanese production system challenge and transcend our traditional understanding of some fundamental organizational concepts. Unfortunately, this quality of the overall system does not alter the utterly repetitive and fragmented character of the jobs or explain why the alleged democratic version of Taylorism is everywhere combined with such intensification of work and line speed.

Dense Management and Flexible Labor Deployment

Compared with the management structure of Fordism, the Toyota system's managerial organization is marked by a complex combination of continuity and innovation. When the Ford system was developed at Highland Park in the teens, it created the conditions for (and required as well, because of its high sensitivity to disruption) a considerably more extended system of managerial control than had characterized earlier forms of industrial organization. The Toyota system is even more dependent on comprehensive control and to a corresponding degree has a broader management structure. The position of foremen (*kumichō*) on the shop floor is extremely important. Foremen distribute tasks, choose work methods, determine operation times, assess employees' attitudes and efforts, and determine wages and advancement possibilities on the basis of the carefully worked-out system for individual evaluation. The union has no influence over either performance standards or individual wages. Further, in Japan, the foreman is also usually the union representative. Finally, the workers are organized in groups led by subforemen (*hancho*), which further strengthens the role of first-line management.

On the one hand, Toyota has not followed Taylor's ideal of having a highly specialized managerial apparatus with "functional foremen." On the other hand, production and shop floor management is even more densely staffed. In the early 1980s, for example, there was one subforeman for every five workers, one foreman for every fourteen workers, and one senior foreman (*kōchō*) for every forty-three workers. Thus, for every forty or so workers, there were eight subforemen, three foremen, and one senior foreman (Fujita 1988:20). This dense managerial structure plays a critical role both in avoiding disturbances and in mobilizing workers in rationalization activities.

Personnel Evaluation

The capacity to mobilize workers in the never-ending effort to increase productivity is closely linked to the career system and individualized personnel evaluation. In large firms, all regular employees, blue collar as well as staff, are normally classified in a grade or status system (*shokunoshikaku*). If, for example, a firm has ten different grades, workers entering the firm after junior high school start at grade 10, workers with a senior high school education at grade 9, and university graduates at grade 8.[14] During their first years of employment, new hirees in a certain job category all stay at the same grade level.

Advancement is linked to length of service, but depending on ability and attitude, employees enjoy different promotion speeds and reach different end positions. The promotion system is not directly linked to the organizational hierarchy, however. For example, Koshi Endo (1991) found that at one firm there were seven different status levels for production workers, from SS1 to SS7. Subforemen were selected from workers in the SS5 or SS6 category, while first foremen were appointed from workers in the SS6 or SS7 status. Consequently, there were workers with SS5, SS6, and SS7 status who were neither foremen nor subforemen. The same was true of white-collar employees.

Status is linked to one's wage, but within each grade there may be substantial individual differences. Decisive for an individual's promotion speed as well as for his wage within the grade is the personnel evaluation system (*satei*). Normally, every employee is evaluated once a year by his immediate superordinate, and the results are then checked by managers at one or two more levels.[15] The items evaluated have nothing to do with the work assignment. Thus, the system focuses on the capacity of individuals, not actual work requirements. The assessment includes objective factors such as performance but above all a range of subjective factors, such as an employee's eagerness to perform his job, his attitudes as a team member, and his potential ability to perform jobs more effectively. As a result of this practice, employees are highly dependent on the evaluations of their superiors. This was not the case in the original *nenko* (seniority) system, which the unions pushed for after the war as an unbiased and equitable system of wage setting. During the labor shortage of the 1960s, however, young and diligent workers grew increasingly impatient with their low starting wages and the slowness with which they were promoted. At the same time, management, which never was very happy with the strict seniority order, wanted to introduce more individualized methods of evaluation to increase its control. The result was the development of the *satei* system, which was superimposed on *nenko* principles and rapidly spread through the entire industry.

The focus of the wage and promotion system on individuals instead of jobs and positions makes the organization very flexible both at the shop floor and in the vertical management structure. While the work process is minutely standardized and rigid in terms of rules, procedures, and cycle (*takt*) times, labor deployment is elastic and worker treatment personalized. The system also fosters intense competition among rank-and-file workers (as well as among white-collar staff) over *satei* scores, with the result that there is a tendency for workers to comply and obey unquestioningly. According to Endo, this is especially true at Toyota: "The case of workers at Toyota is famous as one of the most extreme and Toyota workers are often disparaged in Japan for their lack of individual personality" (1991:13).

Furthermore, the *satei* system makes it difficult for employees to refuse overtime work or take off paid holidays, since such actions are assessed as evidence of a poor attitude. In the same way, the evaluation practice renders it hard for workers to decline to participate in nominally voluntary activities outside of working hours.

From Minimal to Maximal Interaction

The Fordist company-employee relationship was characterized by carefully defined tasks, relatively short and demarcated work times, and strictly economic compensation of employees. This was a highly productive combination at the time of the onset of mass production. The results, however, were instrumental work attitudes and little motivation to work. The Japanese model, by contrast, elicits "maximal commitment" from the regular, permanently employed work force.[16] The differences between these two relationships manifest in several ways.

First, work effort in Japan is regulated not by the job descriptions of individual employees but by the norm of "unreserved commitment to the company." This manifests as a constant readiness to be reassigned within and between sections and shops (Deutschmann and Weber 1987:32).

Second, the company's core employees have job security and "lifetime employment," in glaring contrast to American firms' hire-and-fire practices.[17] A by-product of the Japanese companies' obligation, which became especially palpable after the oil crises of the 1970s, is extremely narrow regular staffing. In the mid-1980s, Japanese car companies planned their staffing based on a rate of absenteeism of 5 percent, including vacations.[18] The severe demands for attendance arose not just from economic motives. They were also very important for maintaining "total commitment" and reinforcing work as the central life activity of the employees.

Third, the total work time in Japan is very high. In contrast to developments in the West after the war, it has stayed high despite very impressive rates of productivity. In 1986, a regular year's work time at Toyota was 1,990 hours and the average overtime was 370 hours, for a total paid work time of 2,365 hours (Fujita 1988). To this should be added various "voluntary activities." By comparison, in 1988, the average work time in the engineering industry was 1,580 hours in Germany and 1,500 hours in Sweden.

The number of used vacation days was about six days for the leading Japanese auto companies in 1985. Absenteeism on other grounds was one day per employee on average. At Toyota, the employees made use of only 26 percent of their vacation days, at Mazda 24 percent, and at Nissan 34 percent. One reason for these low rates was the narrow staffing policy (Jürgens 1986).

Fourth, work times in Japan lack clear boundaries, just as work tasks do. Employees are expected to prepare the work and put their machines in order before the work day formally begins. Likewise, they are expected to stay after the work day has ended to participate in quality circles, for example. The remaining leisure time for male employees is often taken up with activities such as training, company outings, corporate exercise, and gatherings with colleagues and superiors.

One consequence of this "unlimited" employment relationship is that it does not suffice for the individual to do "his job" well. In the intense competition over individual wages, bonuses, and chances at promotions, the worker's overall time and work commitment — work attendance, readiness to work overtime, participation in group and leisure activities, proposals submitted — play an extremely important role.[19]

Traditionally, the reaction of the working class to rationalizations has been characterized by spontaneous self-defense against what the Norwegian sociologist Sverre Lysgaard has called "the technical/economic system's insatiable, inexorable, unilateral demands" (1976:73). The extensive literature on "output restrictions" in American industrial sociology and economics indicates the significance of this behavioral pattern.[20] It was on account of this pattern that Taylor insisted on a sharp distinction between conception and execution. This was also why he argued in favor of an individualistic approach; in his view, workers in a group would inevitably reduce their efforts to the lowest common denominator. In other words, Taylor saw no possibility of controlling and molding "the gang" in accordance with the company's values and wishes.

The maximal employment relationship of Toyotism entails turning this pattern upside down. By means of a far-reaching integration of employees in the technical and economic system, based on the employees' dependence on the company as well as the promotion and personnel evaluation system, tendencies toward collective worker action—in Lysgaard's sense—are eliminated. "Spontaneous" cooperation between workers and management is thereby ensured. This cooperation is a necessity in Toyota's synchronized and integrated production process, where even trivial mistakes can have far-reaching consequences. The inventoryless and minimally staffed manufacturing system means the consequences of disruptions in production fall directly on the workers. Production quotas are usually constant, regardless of disturbances or absenteeism. This leads, as Richard Schonberger has noted (1982:61), to a situation in which "workmates put each other under a massive moral pressure" to turn in a good performance.[21] Peer pressure in the work group is thus a functional part of the production-control system. To use Lysgaard's words, the group organization of the Japanese production system, instead of constituting a defense against the "technical/economic system's insatiable demands," plays a role in enforcing these demands.

Japanese Transplantation

In the United States, the second oil shock of 1979 was followed by a deep crisis in the auto industry and rising unemployment. From 1978 to 1982, U.S. production of automobiles dropped from 13 to 7 million. Several studies showed a productivity ratio between the United States and Japan of 1:2 (see Altshuler et al. 1984). GM invested in a technological strategy, in the hope of catching up with the Japanese by means of a great leap in automation. This failed, however, as demonstrated by the inefficiency and low quality of the new high-technology plants, such as Hamtramck-Poletown in Detroit.

Coincidently, while the American car industry was in crisis, the Japanese companies began their efforts at internationalization in earnest. Nissan and Honda led the way in establishing U.S. manufacturing facilities, initially with a low profile and small impact. The turnaround came in 1986, when Toyota demonstrated, with its NUMMI factory in California (co-owned with GM), that it was possible to reach Japanese productivity levels in an area where GM's factories had failed dismally.

NUMMI became the success story of the year and aroused an enormous interest in the American auto world. The Japanese companies expanded rapidly after this; in 1990, they had ten assembly plants in the United States and Canada, with a total production of 1.7 million cars and light trucks. According to calculations carried out in 1987–88 in MIT's International Motor Vehicle Program, productivity in these factories — defined as the time required to perform a number of standard operations in body manufacturing and assembly — was nearly the same as in the plants in Japan; namely, 40 percent higher than in American-owned factories in the United States, and nearly twice as high as in European-owned plants (Krafcik 1988).[22]

The Japanese transplants also had much higher levels of quality than the American and European plants. This success was particularly noteworthy in that no other country's car companies had succeeded in preserving their American plants. The Europeans, who on the surface had better prospects, had failed to establish themselves in the United States. Volkswagen, the last remaining European transplant in the United States, had a worse and worse time making it in the 1980s. It drew the necessary conclusion in 1988 and discontinued its U.S. manufacturing operations. (An overview of the Japanese expansion in North America is presented in table 2-1.)

The establishment of Japanese auto companies in North America was followed by that of hundreds of Japanese suppliers. According to a 1990 study by the Office for the Study of Automotive Transportation at the University of Michigan, there were more than three hundred large or medium-sized Japanese-owned supplier transplants in the United States alone.

The Japanese auto companies have chosen Great Britain as their base for expansion in Europe. Nissan has been one of the pioneers, as it has in the United States. Production on a small scale began in 1986 in Sunderland, in England's crisis-stricken Northeast. Three years later, the output was 50,000 vehicles per year; the objective was to reach 200,000 in 1992. At the close of the 1980s, both Toyota and Honda revealed plans to follow Nissan and to make 200,000 and 100,000 cars per year, respectively, in Britain during the 1990s.

Japanese suppliers have also moved to Britain. According to Stuart Crowther and Philip Garrahan (1988), Nissan in Sunderland has sought to reproduce exactly the social and material conditions that have given the company total control over the production process in Japan. For example, by concentrating suppliers near the plant and on land owned by Nissan, the company gained decisive influence over these firms, especially regarding their product development, pricing policies, and industrial relations.

The establishment of Japanese production in the West has in some sense demystified the Japanese management system. Earlier, these companies' successes were ascribed to unique features of the Japanese culture. The growing number of Japanese auto plants in the United States and Britain has shown, however, that key elements in Japanese management and production philosophy can indeed be transplanted. At the same time, new opportunities have been created to investigate working conditions under the Japanese system. Much has been written about Mazda, Honda, and Nissan, in both the United States and Britain. The larger part of this material has a journalistic character, however; scientific studies are still in their infancy.

Rigorous Personnel Selection

The various transplants are similar in several ways. All of them manufacture Japanese products: many critical components are produced in Japan. This is true even of the joint ventures between Japanese and American companies, such as NUMMI. Insofar as local suppliers are used, they are required to satisfy much

TABLE 2-1. *Auto Transplants in North America, 1990*

Company	Location	Year started	Production (1,000s)	Production planned (1,000s)	Planned employment level
United States					
Honda	Marysville, Ohio	1982	430	510	8,000
Nissan	Smyrna, Tennessee	1983	240	440	5,100
NUMMI (Toyota and GM)	Fremont, California	1984	200	300	3,400
Mazda	Flat Rock, Michigan	1987	180	240	3,400
Diamond Star					
(Chrysler and Mitsubishi)	Normal, Illinois	1988	150	240	2,900
Toyota	Georgetown, Kentucky	1988	220	440	3,500
Subaru and Isuzu	Lafayette, Indiana	1989	70	120	1,700
Canada					
Honda	Alliston	1988	100	—	—
Toyota	Cambridge		60	—	—
CAMI Automotive					
(Suzuki and GM)	Ingersoll	1990	50	200	2,000

Source: *Business Week*, Aug. 14, 1989, and *Automotive News*, Jan. 7, 1991.

stricter demands for quality, frequency of delivery, and overall commitment than they have before.

With the exception of Nissan's plant in Tennessee, the design of the factories is very compact so as to achieve maximum utilization of space. The technical level is generally high. In the newer factories, for instance, transfer presses with extremely short setup times are standard. All the plants use mechanically controlled, high-paced assembly-line systems. The level of automation on the assembly lines varies. Mitsubishi and Chrysler's Diamond Star facility had more than one hundred assembly robots in 1990, but at other plants assembly is still almost completely manual.

The Toyota system is used at all the transplants, not surprisingly, most successfully at Toyota, in Kentucky. Nissan in Tennessee is somewhat of an exception; it is the most Americanized transplant in the areas of organization and management. Nissan, the oldest and for a long time the largest Japanese car company, has not wished to be Toyota's pupil and has only halfheartedly applied the techniques of its aggressive competitor.

An important cause of the transplants' high productivity is their extremely lean staffing, which assumes a very high attendance rate ("no-fault attendance policy"). To maintain this high rate, despite, for example, family problems (a large share of the workers at plants such as Mazda Flat Rock are women), social pressure and bonus systems are used. Regular disciplinary punishment is also employed and, as a last resort, dismissal.[23]

Another feature, attested to by all visitors, is the high work intensity. The *kaizen* method and the *andon* system (the right to stop the line) mean there are no upper limits on performance. As in Japan, management demands total commitment from the employees. Accordingly, workers are often required to work overtime, on short notice, because of disruptions in the inventoryless production.

A basic precondition for this system is an intense personnel selection system. All the transplants received a large number of applicants when they were established, and they screened out a great many of them in an extensive selection process. It has been usual to receive thirty to one hundred applicants for each place. Those who are chosen are in many respects elite workers, both physically and mentally: young, strong, intelligent, well behaved, highly motivated, and inclined to cooperate.

Applicants who have worked in the American auto industry are not given special consideration; quite the contrary, they are judged to have a handicap. Further, applicants' formal educational background is not considered important. This, of course, represents a chance for individuals who did badly in school but who are nonetheless ambitious and have a will to succeed in life.

The screening process, as it was presented by Toyota's personnel director in 1990, is exceedingly rigorous (see Berggren, Björkman, and Hollander 1991). Applicants first undergo intelligence tests. The lower half are then eliminated. Next comes a dexterity test, and again the less gifted are taken out of the running. Then come tests designed to reveal the applicants' ambitions, initiative, and creativity. Group orientation and social skills furnish further grounds for selection. According to Toyota's personnel department, the result of this process is a worker who is aggressively oriented to performance, who is bent on being the best, and who wants to succeed in a career.

It would be a mistake, however, to identify the personnel practices at the transplants with the policies pursued by Japanese companies in Japan. For example, Japanese researchers visiting transplants tend to be surprised when encountering their egalitarian wage policy, since this is very different from the practice in Japan. An element that is still conspicuously missing is the personnel evaluation practice, the *satei* system, although nonunion plants, such as Toyota in Kentucky, are reportedly in the process of introducing some form of individualized assessment system.

Significance of Social Conditions

The transplants have been established in high-unemployment, somewhat rural regions where the workers enjoy few job opportunities. The wages are relatively high, often twice as high as in industrial jobs outside the auto industry. These fac tors together have established the essential conditions for the new factory regime, including the possibilities for strict personnel selection and severe pressure for performance and discipline. The strategy of offering high wages combined with demands for maximum performance was recommended by Taylor as well, and Ford applied it with great success when he initiated his five-dollar day in 1914.

Mazda in Flat Rock, Michigan, and Toyota (NUMMI) in Fremont, California, established their operations in areas where Ford and GM, respectively, had had plants that failed. After twenty years of production in Fremont, GM closed down its factory there in 1982, putting six thousand people out of work in the process. According to Lowell Turner (1988:15), this plant closing and the ensuing loss of jobs "inaugurated a roller-coaster of dislocation and trauma" among the employees, who could not find jobs of comparable value in the region. With NUMMI, the well-paid industrial work returned. In a summary of the debate around the controversial factory, the *New York Times* concluded on January 29, 1989, that NUMMI was a place "where workers are thankful for their $15-an-hour jobs—but live in constant fear of losing them. For many, the memories are still vivid of the low-paying jobs or unemployment they endured after G.M. shut the plant in 1982. That fear is what seems to motivate workers. . . . 'We got a second chance here, and we are trying to take advantage of it. Many people don't get a second chance.'"

When Womack, Jones, and Roos (1990) attempt to explain the success of the Japanese companies, they never mention a word about the social preconditions. The adaptation of the labor force, the discipline, and the low absenteeism are all exclusively the result, in their view, of the splendid qualities of the production system and of the confidence of the work force in the new management. The same policy is assumed to enjoy the same success everywhere, regardless of social and labor market conditions. It is interesting, therefore, to compare conditions within the same corporate group at different factories in different social environments.

The Swedish-owned household appliance company Electrolux is an international group with a traditional Fordist personnel and organizational policy that has shown scant interest in employee involvement. Why, then, do some of its plants have nearly Japanese-style personal data on their personnel? This question cannot be answered without taking into account social conditions. This is illustrated by table 2-2, which compares Electrolux plants in Sweden (Mariestad) and Great Britain (Spennymoor). (The latter plant is in the same region as Nissan's facility in Sunderland).

Spennymoor differs from Mariestad with respect to the segmentation of the work force into those with permanent and those with temporary employment. The latter category can be as high as 20 percent of the work force at Spennymoor when orders are heavy. The insecure conditions of these workers strongly motivate the permanently employed workers to stand guard over their jobs in every way possible.[24] The technical level, moreover, is considerably lower at Spennymoor

Table 2-2. Personnel Data for Electrolux, 1989

Data	Mariestad, Sweden	Spennymoor, Great Britain
Company		
Short-term absence for illness	15%	5%
Other absences	13%	0%
Personnel turnover	25%	2.5%
Labor market		
Unemployment	0.9%	10%
Waiting days for sickness pay	0	5

Source: *Dagens Nyheter*, July 29–30, 1989.

(in inventory handling, for example). This can be explained by the much lower wage-related costs in Britain. The design of the work process differs as well; this too is connected to social conditions. Management in the British factory harbors classically Taylorist aspirations. In the words of the head of production: "We try to simplify the job and divide it up in shorter operations as much as possible, in order to minimize sources of error. . . . This is our way of reducing defects in manufacturing and increasing production at the same time."

At the Swedish factory, by contrast, another orientation prevails, as the plant manager stressed: "We are building an experimental shop for testing different forms of work organization. The idea is to eliminate the most repetitive jobs and replace them with robots. All this to attain more stimulating jobs."

Concessions as Union Strategy

American unions have been in a state of decline for a long time, as a result of falling rates of organization and incessant demands to accept concessions. The advent of the Japanese transplants has exacerbated these problems. Of ten assembly transplants in North America in 1990, only the four with some connection to the Big Three automakers had unions, and none of the more than 350 parts suppliers to the transplants were unionized (*Automotive News*, Jan. 28, 1991). To organize any of the new plants at all, the UAW had to make major concessions and sign contracts with very weak language (compared with traditional UAW contracts).

For the UAW locals at Mazda or Diamond Star, the experience of lean production was very different from that promised at the outset. Yet these union locals, which were truly pioneers, got little support from the national organization in their efforts to translate their experiences into a counterstrategy that could strengthen their members' rights concerning overtime rules, absence for sickness, freedom in the workplace, organization of work, and so on. Instead, the UAW hailed NUMMI as a model for the future and threw its support behind the entire Japanese factory regime.[25]

This approach, of confronting the Japanese companies with concessions, created two fundamental problems for the UAW. First, it undermined the overall basis for union organization. Nissan made clever use of this weakness in 1989 to prevent unionization of the plant in Tennessee, as David Gelsanliter (1990) has documented. Time and again, Nissan put the question to its employees: why pay membership dues to the union when it made so little difference? Second, this strategy deepened the division and discord that had arisen in the UAW during the first wave of give-backs in the early 1980s. The union mobilizing begun at Mazda in 1988 was directed not only at the company but also (and with great bitterness) at the UAW and its official line. This has been vividly described by Joseph and Suzy Fucini (1990).

In Canada, the trade union movement generally enjoyed more favorable conditions than in the United States at the end of the 1980s. The unionization rate was more than twice as high (40 percent versus 18 percent); there was a rather strong social democratic party, which in 1990 won the election in Ontario, the most populous province; and social welfare policy was considerably more developed than in the United States. The Canadian Auto Workers' union (CAW) was formed in 1985 as a break-away from the UAW. At that point, the Canadian section of the UAW had for several years strenuously opposed the concession bargaining pursued by Detroit since the great car crisis of 1979–80. On the national level, the CAW sharply criticized the Japanese management system in a declaration adopted in 1989: "We reject the use of Japanese Production Methods which rigidly establish work standards and standard operations thereby limiting worker autonomy and discretion on the job. We reject the use of techniques such as Kaizen (pressure for continuous 'improvement') where the result is speed-up, work intensification and more stressful jobs" (CAW Research Department 1989:12).

Yet at CAMI, in Ingersoll, Ontario, the management system and personnel policy were largely the same as at the American transplants. Sam Gindin, the head of research for the CAW, in an interview in November 1990, stressed, however, that the context was fundamentally different:

> While the UAW regards Nummi as exemplary and combats its critics, we regard CAMI as a compromise, which we must improve. At Nummi, Toyota's rigid attendance policy is regulated in the contract. The UAW cannot defend its members, but instead has to run around explaining how important a perfect attendance record is. At CAMI, on the other hand, attendance policy is a company rule, and the CAW can demand negotiations and file a grievance when management takes disciplinary measures. The Local is part of a lively union structure, it gets criticized and learns from others, along the way of building up its position for contract bargaining in 1992. The

UAW local at Nummi is completely isolated, and the critics which do exist in the plant, especially in the assembly department, don't get any support. It's a defeated union that only jerks now and then, but has no independence in relation to management (quoted in Berggren, Björkman, and Hollander 1991:53).

While the UAW pursues its low-key cooperationist policy toward the transplants, politics at the local level tends to be more adversarial. In 1991, the oppositional People's Caucus won the majority in the elections of the NUMMI local—a significant event that also demonstrated that the CAW's perception of the union as more or less dead was premature. In the same year, the radical leadership of the Mazda local decided to play hardball. In preparing the negotiations for the new contract, 90 percent of the workers voted to give the leadership the right to call a strike if needed. From this position the union was able to achieve significant gains, such as relaxation of the tight attendance policy; elimination of the "support member pool" (temporary employees); more union influence in company decisions about the outsourcing of work and the use of outside contractors; and a more stringent policy of worker protection, including the establishment of a written health and safety grievance procedure, a joint ergonomics training program, and union access to information such as symptoms surveys.

Working Conditions under the Lean Regime

On the surface, there are striking similarities between the Japanese practices and the European discussion of new production concepts involving reskilling and an "end to the division of labor." For instance, both German industrial sociology and the Japanese production philosophy emphasize teamwork, participation, and competence development. Yet the real content of these two approaches is very different. I shall try to demonstrate this by analyzing three aspects of auto work in the transplants: the character of skill formation, the JIT control system and increased work strictures, and the peculiar and elusive team concept.

Multitasking versus Reskilling

Japanese production organization is contradictory. On the one hand, it consistently applies the highly repetitive line system of Fordism in which there are strict requirements for standardized work operations. On the other hand, it stresses selection, flexibility, participation through submitting suggestions, and continuous learning ("multiskilling"). Toyotism's forms of labor utilization are considerably broader than Fordism's, but this is far from being equivalent to a general reskilling of production work.

First, the selection process does not favor applicants with occupational skills but rather those with no previous experience in the auto industry. This was precisely Ford's approach in the teens. According to Peter Wickens (1987:181), the personnel director at Nissan UK, the purpose of the careful selection process is indeed to procure first-class workers but above all to show the world that manufacturing is not a last resort where one looks for work because no alternatives exist. The selection process aims at raising status or revaluate, not reskill, production work. Nissan's purpose in sending this message is also to raise the quality of applicants to production management and industrial engineering, since it is supposed that highly qualified managers would be attracted by the prospect of managing a competent work force.

Second, a significant portion of the training of production workers is to socialize them into the company culture. In many transplants, the transfer of skills is not impressive.[26] The production head at Nissan in Sunderland, in an interview in 1989, rejected the notion of work cycles that were longer than 2.4 minutes: "In that case we wouldn't do anything but train people, and it would be hard to find substitutes and balance the line when absenteeism occurs" (*Ny Teknik,* no. 34). In comparison, cycle times at Volvo's Uddevalla factory were more than two hours, despite a much higher rate of absenteeism because of the large proportion of the work force who was female and generous social legislation.

Third, for most workers, the demands for flexibility mean they are alternating between similar repetitive tasks. This is multitasking, rather than multiskilling. To a varying degree, training in group-based problem solving, basic industrial engineering, and quality-control techniques is also provided,[27] but the bulk of the work still consists of very standardized and factory-specific operations. In contrast, genuinely skilled work is characterized by the possession of competencies of a general value to the labor market; individuals are endowed with independence and opportunities for choice.

Workers in skilled trades normally comprise a much smaller group at the transplants than has historically been the case in American auto plants.[28] Thus, the transplants compress the skill range in two ways. They elevate the traditionally unskilled production workers to some degree while significantly reducing the proportion of workers in skilled trades and the discretion and independence in their work. At NUMMI, for example, Toyota is determined to standardize maintenance procedures. In the words of the manager of the stamping department: "Fixing things isn't maintenance—that's repair. The general idea is to replace repairs with routine maintenance" (Adler 1990:68).

Increasing Work Strictures

A common conception is that the Japanese production system decentralizes decision making and increases the prerogatives of the workers. Few researchers have investigated how much room actually exists for such developments, however, or have framed the analysis in comparative terms: decentralization compared with what? Of great relevance in this context is Janice Klein's analysis (1989) of the introduction of Japanese production methods in an American engine plant that earlier used self-managing work teams in accordance with the Scandinavian model.

In the United States and Western Europe, Klein points out by way of introduction, most initiators of organizational reform see group organization as a way to empower the work force. This was the original approach in the American engine plant Klein studied, which began in the 1970s with self-managing work teams and broad competence development. Process buffers gave workers autonomy and sufficient time to take part in production decisions. Top quality was the goal. The plant's good yields made it a model in the company. Greatly increased competition created a heavy pressure to cut costs, however, and the company decided to introduce just-in-time control and statistical process control (SPC). The workers took an active part in introducing this system, but they soon complained that the new methods undermined the whole idea of employee participation in decision making. The workers thought management had reverted to a traditional control mentality and that they had lost their individual freedom and team identity.

After the introduction of the JIT philosophy, the buffers, which earlier had created autonomy for both individuals and teams, were discontinued. As a result, the workers became completely subject to the unalterable pace of the line and the rigid cycle times. The stress level rose, as did the incidence of health problems. Moreover, the greatly increased dependencies in the production system reduced collective autonomy. Work teams found it more difficult to hold meetings, and the room for independent decision making diminished. Performance measures were radically changed, as Klein's interviews with production managers revealed: "It is not a 30-day time span, it is a 3-minute time span. . . . It used to be that you had a monthly goal and you really shot for it. Now they have targets every day. It used to be that you could loaf a little bit, and other days you knew you were under the gun. Now you're under the gun all the time" (1989:64).

In Klein's view, the JIT and SPC methods allow for greater participation by employees, as compared to a traditional "command-and-control" factory. But compared with the earlier arrangement in the same plant, the losses in autonomy were striking. As Klein notes (60): "The attack on waste, it must be understood, inevitably means more and more strictures on a worker's time and action. Our conventional Western notions of worker self-management on the factory floor are often sadly incompatible with them."

Adler (1991) has contested that the loss of autonomy in JIT systems is regrettable. His study of NUMMI verifies that the very tight coupling of all work stations and teams in the low-inventory system results in a significantly reduced autonomy.

He argues, however, that autonomy is not a critical motivating characteristic of jobs and stresses that "the fact that this coupling was seen by workers as the most effective way of managing operations seemed to ensure its endorsement." Carrying the argument further, Adler maintains that autonomy is a kind of negative goal, the absence of external constraint. "The more important factor behind motivation and satisfaction might be the obverse—self-efficacy, or the power to accomplish significant objectives. When a job design . . . fits well the nature of the task, workers will feel empowered in a productive—as distinct from a political—sense, and this productive empowerment is a real source of satisfaction and motivation" (1991:72).

This line of reasoning has some strengths. But Adler fails to address the possibility that the alleged motivation and satisfaction may be in place *despite* the absence of autonomy and leeway in the job and because other and very different factors are more important, such as high pay and job security, competent and supportive management, and pride in the quality of the product. The strength of the oppositional unionists in this selected work force also suggests that there are important limits to the heralded motivation and satisfaction.

Visibility as a Means of Intensified Control

Production control of the Toyota type means that waste in the production system is reduced to a minimum by cutting down on reserves (both human and material). The system is stressed, and problems with workers, materials, or machines can be identified and removed, after which reserves are further reduced and the system is stressed again. Extra resources are considered as wasteful as producing scrap. It is just as important to identify sections that never have problems (and that therefore have "too many resources") as those that have problems often. Mike Parker, a prominent American critic of Japanese production methods, has termed this system "management by stress" (1988:11): "Stress rather than management directives becomes the mechanism for coordinating different sections of the system. The stress throughout tightly links the different parts to make the system 'self-regulating' for management's purposes."

One result is personal stress, since all employees are required to do their utmost. This is an important reason for the strong emphasis on visualization—making all processes immediately visible, as far as this is possible. In this way, everyone can see who is responsible for a problem. A powerful instrument for visualizing problems, whether caused by materials, machines, or workers, is the famous *andon* device. Under the Toyota system, each work station has an easily seen panel with three lights. Green means everything is okay, yellow means the operator needs help, and red means he or she has stopped the line.

The *andon* system was introduced by Toyota at the end of the 1950s and is applied consistently at the transplants. It has often been held out as an example of the transfer of prerogatives to the operators. It is important to understand the context, however. The right to stop the line functions as a replacement for the earlier negotiating system and the right to strike. Once a new product or assembly line has been broken in, the pressure is strong not to pull the cord, even when the tempo of production is very fast. Production stoppages are easily interpreted as the fault of the worker. The *andon* system is an effective instrument of control, but it is also a way of continuously intensifying work and selecting personnel. This function was described in Schonberger's study of a Japanese motorcycle engine factor in the United States (1982:87):

> The red light brings frowns, but plant management is pleased when many of the yellow lights are on. Yes, *on*. As one Kawasaki manager put it, "When the yellow lights are on, that means we are really busting ass." To follow this reasoning, we must understand that the main reason for the yellow is too few assemblers on the line to handle the rate of output. If no yellow lights are on, management knows that the line is moving too slowly or there are too many workers. Usually, the response is to pull workers off the line and assign them elsewhere so that it becomes hard for the remaining workers to keep up; so yellow lights begin to come on. . . . Pulling assemblers off the line exposes remaining assemblers and their supervisors to trouble, e.g., inability to keep up without sacrificing quality, which leads to an attack on the cause of the trouble—whether human or mechanical—so that it won't happen again. . . . Pulling assemblers off the assembly line is quite like removing buffer inventories between fabrication work stations.[29]

The Ambiguous Concept of Teamwork

The Japanese transplants in the United States have been strongly associated with the team concept. Yet Japanese experts on Toyota's production system and philosophy scarcely mention a word about teamwork. It was only after the Japanese companies had begun large-scale operations in the United States that they started to refer to their work organization as based on teams. In the United States the team concept was earlier associated with autonomous, self-managing work units. As used by the Japanese, the term has had a different—and shifting—meaning.

First, it refers to a company culture that lacks labor-management antagonisms, in which there is strong cooperation between the company and the union (in cases where the latter exists) and a climate marked by a strong sense of "we." All employees are supposed to be active and contributing members of the "company team." The team concept also extends to relations with suppliers. Customers and suppliers are supposed to work closely together "as a team."

Second, the team concept usually implies that the smallest units in the organization consist of groups led by team leaders. These teams play an important role in the company's control system for, among other things, maintaining a high attendance rate. One innovative feature of the transplants is that the title of foreman (supervisor) has been abolished, although the function remains. This has never been the case in Japan. New terms are used, which vary from plant to plant. "Group leader" and "coordinator" are common; the analogy with sports is thought to express the appropriate associations. In fact, the discretionary powers attached to these positions are great in most transplants. At Toyota in Kentucky (but not at NUMMI), the team leader is the foreman, so workers are not given any double messages.

"Team" is probably not the best translation for the Japanese concept of work group; perhaps "platoon" might be better, at least for those transplants that are not unionized. For example, a November 1990 visit to Honda's engine plant in Anna, Ohio, revealed the following picture: when the workers go on their shift, they receive (while standing) instructions concerning the day's tasks from the foreman. He talks for five to ten minutes in a microphone. After the shift is over, the workers may not leave individually. They are again gathered in the information area, where they are told about the next day's plans. The workers then march off to the dressing room as a single unit. The impression that one is watching soldiers in the military is strengthened by the dress code, which requires uniforms and prohibits personal adornments.

Robert Cole (1979:201) has emphasized that worker participation in the Japanese sense differs in content from participation in the Western sense:

> A second characteristic of job redesign at Toyota Auto Body is that the emphasis is not on participation *per se,* but rather on achieving the consent of the workers for policies which management wants to pursue, as well as on guiding workers in the direction in which management would like to see them move. This is apparent in the rhetoric the company uses; the term sanka (participation) is not used, rather the focus is on nattokusei (consent) and kobetsu shido (individual guidance).[30]

In many cases, the team concept is used without a clear connection to any particular way of organizing work. In Peter Wicken's view (1987:92), "teamwork and commitment" have nothing to do with group work. In criticizing Volvo's Kalmar concept, he asserts that "while group working, as it is sometimes called, may require people to work together, there is no reason why this should lead to teamworking and commitment.... Indeed it is possible to envisage the opposite occurring. The nature of teamworking in our sense can be developed among people working individually just as, if not more, easily among those working together. It depends on what you call the team."

"Teamworking" at Nissan UK includes a significantly stronger standing for first-line supervisors than in traditional British industry. The foreman recruits his workers himself. The company stresses that the foremen meet their workers daily in the teams' meeting place and that the usual distance between foremen and workers, in which there are no-go areas where foremen fear to tread, is absent. The official objective is to create a committed work force, without antagonisms between "us and them." Yet the Nissan team appears to have few safeguards against autocratic foremen, as Philip Garrahan and Paul Stewart have documented. The following comment by a worker was not atypical: "Everybody just kept quiet because the supervisors were never wrong.... I think the supervisors— the management—had all the power. If anybody said anything they would be kept back to clean the floors, daft things like that, they would find a way to get back at you" (1989:13).

The power relations and forms of control seem to vary considerably between plants. In unionized "team plants," the picture is more contradictory, and teams constitute more of a contested terrain. This is borne out by a study of the CAMI plant. Here, a group of researchers and unionists, "The Canadian Auto Workers Research Group on CAMI," launched a pioneering longitudinal research program in 1990 in which it planned to conduct field studies twice each year during a two-year period (see Huxley et al. 1991). The first intervention took place in March 1990, the second in November of that year, by which time the plant had reached full production for one of its product lines.

On both occasions, the researchers found a high level of participation in suggestion activities (71 percent of the respondents in the second study), and a majority of the workers supported QC activities. The assessment of the team concept was ambiguous, however. The social qualities were generally appreciated, but in the second round 41 percent of the interviewees thought teams were a way to get people to pressure one another to work harder, up from only 19 percent in the first field study. Also in the second round of observation, the research team discerned a growing overall disillusionment with CAMI's philosophy: 78 percent of the interviewed workers said that the management at CAMI still had all the power.

The "Double-Edged Sword"

"Henry Ford's sword was double-edged," Womack, Jones, and Roos claim in a critical part of their book *The Machine That Changed the World:* "Mass production made mass consumption possible, while it made factory work barren. Does lean production restore the satisfaction of work while raising living standards, or is it a sword even more double-edged than Ford's?" (1990:100).

Opinions are divided, they admit. There are those who call lean production "management by stress" and consider it worse from the workers' point of view than traditional mass production. But such a conclusion is altogether wrong, according to the MIT authors: "While the mass-production plant is often filled with mind-numbing stress, as workers struggle to assemble unmanufacturable products and have no way to improve their working environment, lean production offers a creative tension in which workers have many ways to address challenges. This creative tension involved in solving complex problems is precisely what has separated manual factory work from professional 'think work' in the age of mass production" (Womack, Jones, and Roos 1990:101–2).

Work experience from the transplants presents a different picture. It shows that lean production, even more than the Ford system, is a double-edged sword. On the positive side, a number of features have proven to be highly attractive to American workers.

Positive Features of Lean Production

Job security. Historically, Japanese plants have offered much better job security than American-owned factories. The significance of this difference grew steadily during the 1980s, in line with the increasing scarcity of stable, good-paying jobs for nonprofessionals in the American labor market.[31] A telling example occurred in 1988, when Nissan had considerable sales difficulties and completed cars were being stockpiled. In contrast to what American companies usually do in such situations, Nissan did not resort to layoffs or dismissals but rather retained all employees until the market improved.

Egalitarian character. The transplants have a consistently egalitarian appearance, while traditional American factories are marked by a glaringly obvious, razor-sharp distinction between blue- and white-collar employees. I was reminded of this when I visited a Mazda plant in 1990. An American engineer pithily described the hostility she felt toward the white-collar employees at the Ford factory where she had previously been employed as a blue-collar worker: "I hated those ties!"

Workers are required to work hard in Japanese plants. But the same demands are made on everyone, including managers.

Shop-floor focus. Production has high status and high priority at the company, and management values workers' proposals for improvement, if they suggest ways to increase productivity. Management of production seems in most cases to be of high quality, in line with the Japanese shop-floor focus.

Pride in work. All transplants see the quality of their products as central to their operation. The products are well designed, and suppliers maintain high quality and reliability. Many workers therefore also feel pride in the accomplishment of the enterprise.

A carefully selected work force. Transplants select their personnel extremely carefully. The process is stressful, but for those who are accepted there is a feeling of being one of the chosen. The book *Working for the Japanese* reports that it was precisely the high quality of the personnel at Mazda that the workers most appreciated about working there. The heavy emphasis on team-based problem solving in the selection of workers also has advantages at the workplace. Furthermore, "teamwork" appears to have a strong appeal for many workers, even if there is frequently disappointment about its practical meaning and the desire for a more democratic team organization is widespread.

As Womack, Jones, and Roos (1990) stress, the Japanese production philosophy also entails great improvements in cooperating with and developing supplier firms. Here, as in their methods for achieving efficient product development, the Japanese companies have set new world-class standards. The manufacturer-supplier relationship is much more difficult to transfer to the West than the production system, however, since the implicit and intangible aspects of the relationship are so decisive.[32]

The Down Side of Lean Production

Against the advantages listed above, the insatiable demands of lean production must be examined.[33]

Unlimited demands for performance. Regulation of the utilization of labor and the speed of work so as to reduce the risks of injury and exhaustion has been a central trade union demand in Western industrial production. The transplants do not accept any union regulation of performance demands or other limits on the utilization of labor. Richard Hill, Michael Indergaard Child, and Kuniko Fujita, in their report on Mazda (1988), quote a union representative who expressed grave worry about this: "The Japanese, through kaizen, etc. are exploring the limits of human capacity. That may be all right in cycles but it's not good to be pushed that way continuously and that's a danger with all of the transplants" (1988:28).

For Japanese management, it is not just a question of making more efficient use of labor power. The high intensity of work is also an instrument for pushing rationalization constantly onward. If, according to this perspective, workers perform their tasks at so calm a pace that they can occasionally read a newspaper, then there is no force driving forth suggestions for improvement. In comparing Japanese transplants with GM's plants, a striking feature was the relatively relaxed pace of work in the American plants, even in those that had high levels of productivity and quality, such as Buick City, in Flint, Michigan. Workers had time to talk with visitors and to read during short breaks at their work stations. This is unthinkable in Japanese factories.

Unbounded work time. Another classical reform tradition in Western industrial countries, especially in Europe, is the regulation and reduction of work time. This, too, is hard to combine with lean production. The extraction of overtime in the transplants tends to be very high (except during periods of serious market problems, as NUMMI has experienced for most of its existence). Because of the minimal reserves of materials and persons, orders are often given on very short notice. Strictly speaking, lean production is not buffer-free. The long and flexible work times comprise the hidden reserve that is squeezed out in the production process. These flexible work times are an important precondition of the system's productivity and reliability.

The companies' far-reaching power over work times, which means production quotas in principle must be reached regardless of what has happened that day or shift, is also a way to promote improvement. If disturbances have the consequence that workers must stay after the end of their "normal" workday, their interest in ensuring that these disturbances are not repeated is naturally increased. In Europe, the eight-hour workday has been a goal for more than a hundred years. In lean production, it no longer applies. This feature is not confined to Japanese producers. Ford, the "leanest" American automaker according to MIT, has since its recovery after the deep crises in the early 1980s relied on large amounts of overtime to avoid plant expansion in times of brisk sales.

Little tolerance of work injuries. In most cases, the Japanese factories put great stress on safety and avoiding injuries that can lead to production stoppages. The products are also designed for easy manufacture—with great precision in the manufacturing of all parts and components. This is ergonomically advantageous in assembly since it reduces arduous insertion movements. Nonetheless, the high intensity and repetitiveness of the work and the long work times create considerable health risks, especially for cumulative trauma injuries. For example, an unusually high frequency of carpal tunnel syndrome, a nerve injury of the wrist, was reported at Mazda in 1988. Jim Warren, vice-chairman of Michigan Injured Workers, maintained: "I've never seen as high an intake or as many calls. I believe it's the result of a push for peak performance that disregards safety standards" (*Automotive News*, Feb. 13, 1989).

The overall frequency of work injuries was three times higher at this factory in 1988 than at comparable American installations according to reports in the Detroit press (see, for example, *Detroit Free Press*, July 7, 1990). Yet there appeared to be little tolerance of injuries. The teams had room for only high achievers, and light jobs had been contracted out. Several injured workers were dismissed on the grounds that there was not enough suitable work.

Mazda may represent an extreme case of schedule pressure, but there are other reports of heartless treatment of workers injured in production. Nissan in Tennessee has produced several examples: "As soon as people are injured they have no use for them," says Hardin, a former foreman. "You take the best employee, a hard worker with a good attitude and say an elbow goes out from overwork.

They'll say, 'Get him the hell outta here.' It is hard for me to believe it, and I have seen it" (*Progressive* 5 [1987], no. 6).

At Honda in Ohio, workers were already worried about the rapid pace of work in the mid-1980s. In a 1986 interview in *Washington Monthly* (July–Aug.), a worker summed up the situation: "If it doesn't get you physically, it will mentally sooner or later."

The company was proud that it had never dismissed any workers, but employees wondered what job security was worth if it was not physically possible to work past the age of forty or fifty. During our visit to the engine factory in Anna, Ohio, in 1990, the managers did not acknowledge that the working conditions caused injuries; instead, they claimed, it all depended on the individual: "There are strong and weak persons. There are right and wrong attitudes" (Berggren, Björkman, and Hollander 1991:56).

The unbounded factory regime. By eliminating all reserves, lean production increases management's dependence on the work force. Thus, Womack, Jones, and Roos claim (1990:103) that lean production can "scarcely be more oppressive than mass production." They stress the role of trust and confidence as the foundation of the system: "If management fails to lead and the work force feels that no reciprocal obligations are in force, it is quite predictable that lean production will revert to mass production."

What the authors fail to mention is that management's increased dependence on the workers is more than compensated for by the stricter personnel selection and factory regime, replete with compulsory uniforms, a detailed conduct and discipline code, absolute demands for attendance, detailed regulation of the workplace, and the elimination of all personal attributes. In its ultimate form, this regime calls to mind a well-drilled army and a spirit far removed from the democratic quality associated in the Western European tradition with the concept of teamwork.

How workers could perceive the pressure of this regime was demonstrated by events at the U.S. Mazda plant in 1991. As part of the new contract discussed above, workers were provided with four paid absence allowance (PAA) days, which they could use at their discretion simply by notifying their supervisor a few hours in advance. Despite the alleged trust and feelings of reciprocity in lean production, this new right very quickly became a kind of safety valve for many workers and, as a result, production came to a stop on Fridays in several departments. To guarantee production without having to add workers, the company proposed to restrict the use of PAA days, especially on Fridays, and in exchange offered substantial bonuses. The workers voted no; the right to decide for themselves on one single issue was obviously too important to be substituted for money. (The company subsequently introduced the restrictions unilaterally, which was followed by a new vote in which the tougher proposal was sweetened by a significant "signing bonus" and additional vacation days.)

The German researchers Christoph Deutschmann and Claudia Weber have termed the Japanese company culture a new form of "social heteronomy"—that is, the opposite of autonomy—which is marked by an organized intimacy rather than the traditional instrumentalism of mass work. Referring to Richard Bendix, they warn against "the totalitarian potential contained in the informal collectivism of modern company management" (Deutschmann and Weber 1987:49). A strong work commitment has, in the Western tradition, been identified with the culture of skilled trades and professionals. The former have also been associated with a strong union consciousness. In the transplants, maximum commitment is demanded of the mass-production workers as well but under conditions that weaken the independent standing of trade unions and severely circumscribe the freedom of action enjoyed by the worker collective. Experiences from the unionized transplants nevertheless reveal a remarkable resurgence of union activity and commitment, in several cases strengthened by a sense of disappointment over all the "false promises." The president of the CAW's Local 88 in Ingersoll, Rob Pelletier, described this disappointment in the course of reviewing his own experiences:

> Many of us came to CAMI totally naive as to how a plant functions, and had no reason to question the CAMI plant system. We all wanted CAMI to be the employment Utopia described by the employee handbooks. . . . When I became Vice-President the previous winter I did so because I didn't want a bunch of Union hotheads running the Local, doing nothing but running management down and bad mouthing everything we had worked so hard to establish as "The CAMI way." In the interim, I experienced and heard about as much reality as I could take, until I realized what a smokescreen it all was. I became exactly what I had hoped to protect this Local and this Company from (*Off the Line* 5 [1990]).

The MIT team has attempted to close the debate on the Japanese production system by appointing it the standard global production system and heralding it as vastly more productive as well as beneficial to workers than preceding systems of manufacturing. The argument over its advantages and disadvantages goes on, however, as starkly opposing views are continuously put forward. And inside Japan, where the economy is more dynamic and competitive than ever, criticism of the "regime of long working hours" is mounting in the automotive industry. The same is true of the working conditions, which are frequently referred to as "*san kei*" (3K— *kitsui, kitanai, kiken*), or "hard, dirty, and dangerous."

Japanese automakers have responded to the labor market pressure and recruitment difficulties in two principal ways—by stepping up their international expansion and by sharply increasing their investments in automation in an attempt to find a technological solution to the labor problem. The traditional Toyota model of low-cost rationalization based on continuous shop-floor improvements, which is at the heart of NUMMI's success, is being superseded by a more divided work organization with a much stronger emphasis on professional specialists, such as permanent and specialist *kaizen* teams.[34] But there are also signs of increasing social concerns among the auto manufacturers, which are expressed by, among others, the president of Toyota, Shoichiro Toyoda. The outcome of these considerations is unclear, but lean production is certainly not the ultimate station of industrial development.

3.
The Swedish Automotive Industry: Small-Scale Car Makers, Global Truck Producers

In chapters 1 and 2, we followed the birth and expansion of Fordism and thereafter the development and successful spread of the Toyota system. The Japanese production philosophy may be said to have solved several of the difficulties Fordism met in an ever more changeable market. But other problems, especially those concerning working conditions in auto manufacturing, were largely unaddressed. Because of the social conditions under which Toyotism developed, these issues have not had priority. By contrast, such questions have been central to developments in Swedish auto companies during the 1970s and 1980s. Volvo commenced its pursuit of an alternative production model in Kalmar in 1974; this period of innovation concluded with the bold attempt in Uddevalla, begun in 1989. I shall describe this process by means of six case studies.

Will the fifteen years from 1974 to 1989 be regarded as a parenthesis, a temporary adaptation to particular social conditions, an unsustainable deviation from international normalcy, or will they be seen as a period during which a viable new production concept was born? I shall return to this question in chapter 13.

This chapter describes the overall development of the two Swedish automotive groups Volvo and Saab-Scania. It begins by putting the industry in an international context and follows with a detailed review of the three product lines: cars, trucks, and buses. The purpose is to present the case studies in an industrial framework. Chapter 4 explains the social backdrop to the case studies by describing the Swedish labor market and its special features.

International Perspective

Small-Scale Car Industry

Thirty-four million cars were manufactured in the world in 1988. The three largest car-manufacturing nations were Japan, the United States, and Germany. Swedish car companies produced 400,000 cars, just over 1 percent of world production or roughly one-tenth that of Germany (table 3-1).[1]

Based on the number of cars manufactured, Volvo ranked eighteenth of the world's auto companies, just after Rover and BMW. Saab was in twenty-fifth place, making it the second smallest of all independent manufacturers of standard vehicles outside the Eastern bloc.[2]

At the close of the 1970s, it was thought that small companies like Volvo and Saab were doomed (and with them independent auto manufacturing in small countries). The predicament of Swedish car manufacturers was very difficult at the time. The models were out-of-date. Exports, not least to the United States, had sunk, and home market shares had collapsed. The problem was compounded by the dramatic increase in costs in Sweden in 1975–76.

The crisis produced dynamic results, however. For one, it triggered extensive rationalizations and investments in new production technology. For another, a powerful increase in research and development took place in the car companies. Existing models were refined, and the development of new models was sped up. Thus, when exchange rates changed in a favorable direction, with the Swedish devaluation and the rising American dollar at the beginning of the 1980s, Saab and Volvo were able to double their export of cars to the United States. Volvo became the best-selling European-made car in its class in the American market.

The combination of a small home market and strong specialization yielded an intensive (in a double sense) internationalization of Swedish car manufacture. First, Sweden had a very high import share for an auto-manufacturing nation. Second, Swedish companies sold a very large share of their production outside Sweden. As early as 1970, the import share in Sweden was well over 50 percent. The German market at this time had an import share of only somewhat more than 20 percent. Shares in the French, British, and American markets were just as low. Import shares during the 1970s and 1980s increased on most Western markets, but usually slowly. In Sweden, despite expanding auto production, the import share continued to rise, and at the close of the 1980s it was more than 70 percent. At the same time, the portion of the Swedish companies' production sold abroad rose to more than 80 percent.

The Swedish auto industry was heavily internationalized in a third respect as well. That is, Saab and Volvo were to a great extent dependent on foreign suppliers. This was especially true in the case of components with a high technological

TABLE 3-1. Car Production in Sweden Compared with Major Producers in 1988

Country	Volume
Japan	8,200,000
United States	7,100,000
West Germany	4,350,000
Sweden	410,000

Source: *World Motor Vehicle Data Book* 1990.

content. Car manufacturers in Japan and Germany were surrounded by a strong and research-intensive components industry, which accounted for the majority of new patents in both countries. In contrast, Swedish suppliers retained, with few exceptions such as SKF (the world's leading ball-bearing company) or Autoliv (a subsidiary of Electrolux that produces safety belts), the character of relatively unsophisticated parts manufacturers. From an international perspective, this gave the Swedish auto industry a fragile overall structure.

Large-Scale Manufacturer of Heavy Vehicles

From a global perspective, the Swedish companies were small car manufacturers but large producers of heavy vehicles. Trucks and buses at Volvo and Saab-Scania had a significance unmatched at other auto manufacturers. This was especially so at Saab-Scania, where the production of heavy vehicles at the Scania division had for a long time stood at the center of the company and accounted for the returns.

The world's manufacture of commercial vehicles—buses, delivery vehicles, and trucks—totaled 13.9 million units in 1988. Of these, Swedish companies produced 77,000, less than 1 percent. Within the manufacture of commercial vehicles, however, Volvo and Scania had taken specialization very far and had concentrated almost totally on heavy trucks (16 tons or more) and buses (more than 12 tons).

Within this segment, their position was strong. Both companies very early on developed an export orientation and a commitment to international expansion. In 1970, sales outside Sweden already accounted for 70 percent of the total. By contrast, 50 percent of the trucks manufactured by German companies were sold abroad, and the figure was less than 20 percent for companies in Japan. In the mid-1980s, the foreign share of Volvo's and Scania's sales had risen to more than 90 percent. The German and Japanese manufacturers had stagnated at levels of 60 percent and 40 percent, respectively.

On the car side, Volvo and Saab were doubly exposed to competition, through the combination of high export and import shares. Foreign sales were even more important for the truck divisions. In their respective segments, however, Volvo and Scania had a dominant position in Sweden, where they had 95 percent of the market. This made their position considerably more robust than that of the car divisions.

The Swedish companies' position was also very strong, both internationally and domestically, in the production of buses. Of a total production of more than sixty thousand buses (outside the Eastern bloc) at the close of the 1980s, the Swedish companies accounted for nearly 15 percent. The Swedish companies followed a niche strategy, focusing on upscale markets. In the case of cars, the strategy was to minimize the drawbacks of low annual volumes by changing models infrequently and depending on outsourcing (increasingly from foreign, large-series-producing components manufacturers). In the case of heavy vehicles, the strategy was different and more varied. On the one hand, Volvo strove for high volumes; its objective was to be a world leader in its segment. Scania, on the other hand, invested in specialized expansion on the basis of a strictly defined product concept.

Role in Swedish Industry

If the Swedish auto industry was small internationally, it was indeed large domestically. In 1968, after two decades of strong growth, the auto and auto engine industry still employed only 4 percent (36,000) of all employees in man-ufacturing. Twenty years later, this share had risen to 8 percent (about 80,000 employees, of whom 24 percent were white collar.

In 1988, the year before Saab Automobile was formed together with General Motors, the Volvo and Saab-Scania groups were among Sweden's largest industrial enterprises (measured by turnover), in second and fourth place, respectively. Volvo's turnover was more than twice as high as Saab-Scania's.

Overall, both in Sweden and abroad, Volvo employed seventy-nine thousand persons at the time; Saab-Scania, forty-eight thousand. Both companies had the same overall structure: cars, trucks, buses, and marine and industrial engines. Both also conducted operations in the aviation sector: Saab built civil and military aircraft, Volvo made aircraft engines. (The Volvo Group also had a substantial food division, with nine thousand employees in 1988.)

The strong export orientation of both companies meant that a large part of production, particularly in the truck divisions, was located abroad. Volvo as a whole, however, still had 70 percent of its employees in Sweden; the figure for Saab-Scania was 80 percent. And more than three-quarters of these companies' investments were in Sweden. In these respects the auto groups differed from other large Swedish engineering companies, in which internationalization had pro-ceeded considerably further.

Despite the many similarities between the two groups, there were also consid-erable differences regarding product range, corporate organization, and ownership structure. Volvo was a strongly divisionalized company, in which the divisions for cars, components, trucks, buses, and marine and industrial engines were organized as independent subsidiaries. The ownership philosophy was flexible; Volvo wholly owned some operations, only a fraction of others, and ownership of other operations was in between. In Volvo Car BV in the Netherlands, for example, Volvo's share was only 30 percent. Another example was the manufacture of dumpers. At the start of the 1980s, this operation was severed from the Volvo Group and subsumed in a new company, VME (half owned by Clark Michigan), with headquarters in the Netherlands.

Technically, Saab-Scania had a centralized organization, but it did not entail any real integration or affinity between the divisions. Twenty years after the merger between Saab and Scania (in 1969), Scania still retained a very strong and independent standing, had its own culture, and was influenced very little by the management of the group.

The Saab-Scania group was dominated by one owner, the Wallenberg family. At Volvo, influence was spread among many owners, which gave management a very strong position. During the 1980s, it worked single-mindedly to reinforce its independence by building up a cross-ownership structure with other management-controlled enterprises. By means of this group of "friends of Volvo," Volvo's executives controlled 20 percent of Swedish shares, far more than any other group.

Cars: A Successful Decade That Ended

Swedish car makers have had a dramatic history in the last few decades. In the mid-1970s, the market collapsed in Sweden and abroad, leaving the future very much in doubt. At the end of the 1970s, there was a marshaling of forces and a turnaround involving rationalizations, new production technology, and accelerated product development. The first half of the eighties was a harvest time, characterized by devaluation of the Swedish currency, the increase in the value of the dollar, greatly improved profitability, increased production, and decisions regarding large investments in capacity. Finally, the late 1980s saw sharply increased competition in the exclusive segments, a decrease in the value of the dollar and consequent oversupply in the United States, a steep decline in the British and Swedish markets, acute crisis for Saab, and growing problems for Volvo.

From 1980 to 1986, the Swedish companies' production volume rose by more than 60 percent and by even more reckoned in value. The successes in the American market created a euphoric atmosphere in the industry. The leading Swedish business magazine, *Affärsvärlden* (no. 51–52), for example, wrote in 1986:

> Volvo's and Saab's successes in the American market this year must be judged impressive. The two little Swedish car manufacturers, which do not even have 1.5

percent of the world market, have captured nearly 10 percent of the luxury car segment—the most profitable and least business cycle–sensitive—in the world's largest auto market. Moreover, nothing seems likely in the next two or three years to disturb this market share seriously, or even to stop the continued increase of sales volume in absolute terms.

Saab and Volvo seemed on their way to becoming serious challenges to the German manufacturers of luxury and specialty cars—BMW, Daimler-Benz, and Audi. But by the next year the tide turned, Swedish production fell, and the decline continued. Figure 3-1 shows production for the Swedish companies, compared with their German competitors, between 1970 and 1987. As indicated in the figure, the German champions, BMW and Daimler-Benz, enjoyed a much longer period of stable growth, which to a great extent depended on their strong positions in the highly expansive German market.

Saab 1976–89: From Crisis to Crisis

Saab started as an aircraft company in the 1930s. Auto manufacturing was begun in 1950, but there were constant problems with profitability. The company found itself in an acute crisis in the mid-1970s. The company's main owner, the Wallenberg family, saw a merger between Volvo and Saab-Scania as the only solution. This idea encountered such strong opposition from the executives of both Saab and Scania that it had to be dropped.

In fact, product development was critical for Saab's survival. With the help of Scania's technical expertise, Saab became the first company in the world to furnish series-manufactured cars with turbo-charged engines. Then, in 1983, it launched a new sixteen-valve engine. This technology was subsequently used in the entire auto world. Finally, development work was concluded on a wholly new model, the Saab 9000, introduced in 1984. For a few years the division earned more money than it ever had. Optimism and faith in the future were at a high.

In 1986, a decision was made to open a new factory in Malmö, the first altogether new installation for Saab in many years. But in 1987 profits fell, and 1989 brought catastrophic losses. How could Saab's economic situation deteriorate so dramatically? One cause was the one-sided focus on the U.S. market. During the good years, this focus had yielded important proceeds. But when the tide turned, Saab was left without other large markets against which to balance its American losses.

Another reason was that Saab made a strategic mistake when it attempted, with the 9000 series, to compete against the German high-prestige automakers. Saab lost earlier customers, whose ideal was not a Mercedes or a BMW at all. In 1989, nearly five years after the 9000 series was introduced, only sixty thousand were manufactured each year, clearly less than a break-even level. Furthermore, with

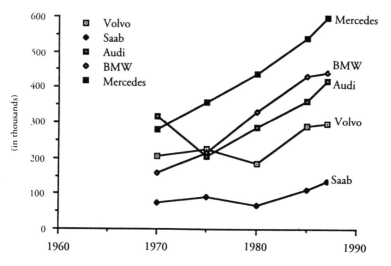

FIGURE 3-1. Car Production at Volvo and Saab Compared with Their German Competitors

this product strategy, Saab bet on a segment all the Japanese manufacturers had entered.

A third cause for the company's decline was the excessive cost of production. Saab had traditionally been the car of drivers and designers, not of industrial engineers. The result was that its cars were markedly more expensive to make than comparable competitive cars (measured in work hours and number of different components); this resulted, among other things, from the low degree of standardization, large array of options in relation to volume, and low manufacturability. The Saab 9000 was the prototype of what MIT researchers have called "fragile product design" (Krafcik 1989). Costs were further increased by inefficiency in the production system, which was not at all adapted to the growing spread of options in the product mix.

Saab had been able to get itself out of the crisis of the 1970s with a relatively small outlay of resources by moving up to a new segment. No such possibilities presented themselves at the close of the 1980s, and in 1989, Saab ceased to exist as an independent manufacturer. A special company was formed, Saab Automobile, Inc., owned half by Saab-Scania and half by GM. Management was in the hands of GM, however.

Volvo Cars: High Profitability throughout the 1980s

Like most other auto manufacturers, Volvo Cars enjoyed a highly expansive period in the first years of the 1970s. Sales in the United States rose especially sharply, and a decision was made in 1973 to start a factory in Chesapeake, Virginia, with the capacity to make 100,000 cars a year. The market situation changed, however, and in just a few years one-third of the sales in the United States had disappeared. The plans for an American plant were shelved and instead the installation in Ghent, Belgium, was modernized. In 1977, the year of Volvo's fiftieth anniversary, the car division showed a heavy loss.

The turnaround at Volvo followed the same pattern as at Saab: heavy investments were made to enhance quality and value in existing products, coincident with the acceleration of a new model. The new car, Volvo 700, came out in 1981–82. Like Saab, Volvo made an impressive comeback in the U.S. market, and in 1985 it was the world's most profitable car manufacturer. A decision was made to expand capacity by opening a new operation in Uddevalla. It was to be Volvo's first new car assembly plant since the Kalmar came on stream in 1974. Saab invested in autos with a "high-tech" image (the same "BMW line" the Japanese companies had chosen). Volvo, by contrast, held to its traditional values—safety, quality, a family orientation (an "upscale family car"). The company tried thereby to reach markets with stable customer groups and less stiff competition. Sharply rising costs for new products, a worsened productivity development, and drastic setbacks in Volvo's three major markets—the United States, the United Kingdom, and Sweden—brought sharply falling profits, however, and in 1990 the division was in the red.

The Swedish groups, and their car divisions in particular, had earlier stressed their "blue-yellow" character. (Blue and yellow are the colors of the Swedish flag.) But during the 1980s Volvo Cars shifted more of its production abroad, above all to Ghent. Of Volvo's total production of 190,000 cars in 1980, 50,000 (26 percent) were made outside Sweden. In 1990, the total volume was 255,000, of which 100,000 (40 percent) were produced outside the country. Production in Ghent during the same period increased from 30,000 to 80,000 per year. Manufacture of the power train, with its considerable economies of scale, continued to be done in Sweden, however, and very large investments were made in other areas of Swedish components manufacture.

A serious weakness of Volvo during the 1980s was that the company failed to increase the efficiency of its product development. This weakness entailed a growing handicap in relation to the ever-quickening pace of development of the Japanese. The new series from the Netherlands, which was introduced in 1986 with the sporty model 480, is an example. This model had considerable similarities to Honda's Aerodeck. At the start, Volvo led in the development work, but Honda passed Volvo by and hit the market earlier. Further, when Volvo finally presented its model, it suffered from a series of deficiencies in quality.

With only a few models and lengthy development times, Volvo remained extremely dependent on the reception of individual products by the market. Mounting economic problems and sharply rising development costs drove Volvo's management to seek collaboration with other car makers. At the start of 1990, management disclosed an agreement on cooperation and co-ownership with French Renault. By the terms of this agreement, Volvo would buy up to 25 percent of the French state-owned parent company and Renault would take 10 percent of the Swedish firm; Renault would acquire 25 percent of Volvo Cars; and both companies would purchase 45 percent of each other's truck and bus operations. In the car division, this far-reaching agreement met with resistance from senior managers, who had had very discouraging experiences in cooperating with Renault.

During the 1980s, the car divisions at Renault and Volvo had collaborated on the so-called PRV engine, which Volvo used in its top-of-the-line models. But the collaboration had been a big disappointment for the Swedes. At the close of the 1980s, therefore, Volvo Cars developed its own six-cylinder engine, and in 1989, less than a year before corporate plans for cooperation were presented, the division called off the agreement with Renault.[3] In 1990, Roger Holtback, the president of the division, accepted the consequences of his opposition to the Renault deal and left the company. The head of U.S. operations, Björn Ahlqvist, did the same.

Truck and Bus Divisions

In contrast to car production, truck manufacture in Sweden, and indeed the world, was exceptionally expansive during the 1970s, and the market hit a high around 1980. A steep decline followed, particularly in the United States and Britain but also in Japan and Germany. Only the Swedish truck makers succeeded in fortifying their positions.

Between the end of the 1970s and the close of the 1980s, Volvo's and Scania's share of the world's heavy-truck production rose from 10 percent to nearly 20 percent (excluding the Eastern bloc). In a ranking list of the world's largest manufacturers of heavy trucks, Volvo came in second and Scania came in fifth. The corporation that structurally most resembled the Swedish companies was the German Daimler-Benz group, the world's biggest producer of heavy trucks and buses; Daimler-Benz was, however, markedly less profitable than the Swedish companies.

The strength of the Swedish companies depended on their ability to turn the particular conditions and stringent demands under which they worked to advantage in the areas of products, technology, and markets.

Early on, truck manufacture at both Volvo and Scania was focused on heavy trucks. The Nordic market was large—for timber transport, for example—and legislation allowed high train weights and vehicle lengths. In the beginning, these trucks were oversized for the rest of Europe, but during the 1960s and 1970s, the growing European truck market moved progressively toward using heavy general-cargo transports. This favored Volvo and Scania, which were specialists in this segment. In contrast to the American manufacturers, Volvo and Saab invested determinedly in the in-house development and production of the power train, which yielded advantages in the form of synchronized product development and a strong grip on the lucrative spare parts and service market.

Volvo was the first series-manufacturing truck maker in the world to introduce turbo engines on its vehicles, which it did in 1954. Volvo could thus produce more powerful engines without investing in costly production facilities. Scania began with turbos on stationary engines, then followed up on trucks in 1960. The trend in Europe and the United States was to increase horsepower by building ever-larger and more fuel-consuming engines. The energy-efficient Swedish approach proved a great advantage during the oil crisis of the 1970s. Scania in particular was very successful in combining fuel efficiency and operating economy with performance.

Volvo and Scania were also pioneers in the development of safer cabins. This was propelled forward by Sweden's tough legal demands for driving safety; these demands later came to benefit the companies in their international expansion.

Volvo and Scania invested early on in foreign sales, since the Swedish (and Nordic) market soon became too small to carry development costs or sustain components production in sufficiently large series. The companies learned thereby to take account of strongly shifting market requirements and to develop rational methods for customer-adapted manufacture. This proved a great asset in the oil crisis at the end of the 1970s, when the large uniform orders from the Middle East nearly disappeared altogether. Volvo and Scania were two of the very few manufacturers who made money during those years. Throughout the 1980s Scania was the most profitable truck manufacturer in the world.

The most important difference between the truck and car markets was that Japan was weak in the heavy-truck market (notwithstanding its leading position in light utility vehicles). The Japanese home market traditionally looked altogether different from the European and trucks over 20 tons were not allowed, but at the end of the 1980s the demand for heavy vehicles started to expand greatly in Japan. The biggest Japanese manufacturer of heavy trucks, Hino (which belongs to the Toyota group), tried to establish itself in Europe—among other means by starting an assembly plant in Ireland—but without notable success.

Volvo Trucks: A Far-Flung International Competitor

Volvo's trucks were designed and manufactured differently, in critical respects, from its cars. First, in the period from 1965 to 1989, not even the most successful truck models were produced in more than 40,000 units. This can be compared with the 140 series, produced by the car division, of which 1.2 million units were built between 1966 and 1974, or the 240 series, of which 1.7 million units were produced during a ten-year period.

Second, there was a wide product range, within the framework of a considerably lower total volume. In 1988, Volvo Trucks marketed four product lines, plus the models that had been developed within White, an American truck producer that Volvo acquired in the early 1980s. Six different cylinder sizes of diesel engine were manufactured—from four to sixteen liters.

Third, both production and design were done throughout the world. In 1988, Volvo Trucks had chassis manufacturing of significance in five countries: Sweden, Belgium, Scotland, Brazil, and the United States. Design operations within Volvo Trucks were also in several countries. Power trains and cabins for the Belgian and Scottish factories were produced in Sweden, while the entire production was local in Brazil and the United States.[4] Lower volume and more widely spread production meant that the assembly plants were much smaller than was standard for making cars. A capacity of 10,000 chassis per year was a high figure for Volvo Trucks; for the car division, ten times this figure, or 100,000, was rather low.

By contrast, Volvo's car division, had only two real production bases, Sweden and Belgium, and one center for design and product engineering. The greater spread of models, markets, and production locations placed hard demands on the truck division's managerial capacity, but at the same time it reduced the division's exposure to risk. Volvo Trucks was not at all dependent, in the same way as the car division, on the reception of one or two platforms in a few markets.

Scania Trucks' Organic Growth

Scania also had shorter series and more widely spread production than the car division. Manufacturing of significance occurred in three countries: Sweden, the Netherlands, and Brazil. The Netherlands was a site for chassis assembly and for the final assembly of cabins and certain engines; in Brazil, all manufacturing—of both chassis and components—was carried out locally, because of Brazilian law.

Volvo Trucks turned all of its efforts during the 1970s and 1980s to attaining a world leadership position. Volume and growth were given top priority. The deal with Renault was part of this strategy of dominance. Scania, by contrast, consistently pursued economies of scale in manufacturing. Instead of spreading design among engineers in several countries, Scania centralized design, product engineering, and production preparation in Södertälje. And instead of having many different product lines, Scania focused on producing modular components with a great number of possible combinations. This concept yielded both a wide product mix and the advantages of long production runs.

As the sole European company in the industry, Scania did not expand by buying up other manufacturers, despite its high profitability and strong finance. The division consistently followed a "strategy of organic growth." Even with a large capacity deficit in 1989, management held fast to this approach. The managers rejected fusions and volume growth attained by acquisitions; they did not believe such a strategy would yield any real economies of scale in production. As Leif Östling, Scania's CEO, put it in 1989, "It takes time to get economies of scale in production. Our production is tailored to individual customers; spare parts must be supplied for fifteen to twenty years. Mergers often result in reduced total volume."[5]

Similarly, Scania refused to enter into any collaborative projects because it feared that this would disturb the products' painstakingly worked-out modular structure. The object was to expand gradually and always maintain high-capacity utilization, regardless of the temporary state of the market. Thus, Scania exploited existing resources to the limit of capacity before making any new investments. The company accepted a lower market share during booms in order to increase its share again during slumps. The advantages of this approach were demonstrated by the fact that the company's profitability was considerably higher than Volvo's throughout the 1980s, despite total volumes of half the size.

At both Volvo and Scania, final assembly became ever more internationalized during the 1980s. Between 1980 and 1988, Volvo Trucks' total production increased from 30,000 to 60,000 vehicles, while production in Sweden, measured in numbers of chassis, stayed constant at about 14,000. At Scania as well, final assembly in Sweden during the 1980s was unchanged, measured in chassis (14,000), while total production outside Sweden—above all, in the Netherlands—increased. In 1990, Scania decided to invest in a large production facility in Angiers, France. In spite of the internationalization, however, turnover and employment in Sweden did not stagnate since the vehicles produced there increased greatly in complexity, work content, and value.

Volvo's and Scania's Buses

A third area covered by the case studies is Volvo's and Scania's manufacture of buses. The similarities in bus manufacture between the two companies and likewise between the product policies of the bus and truck divisions in both groups were marked.

Both companies concentrate on heavy buses (more than 12 tons, or, as defined at Scania, buses for more than thirty passengers). Body work, nearly a handicraft job, is performed in the main by independent companies. Scania supplies finished buses for the Swedish market, however, which correspond to roughly 10 percent of volume.

In common with the truck divisions, the bus divisions have a very strong standing in Sweden, about 75 percent of the market in 1988. At the same time, the majority of production—between 80 and 90 percent—is sold outside Sweden.

As in the truck divisions, the bus divisions locate a considerable part of their production in Latin America; accordingly, 44 percent of Scania's chassis were made there in 1988. Neither have succeeded in establishing themselves in the United States, though both have tried.

Both Scania and Volvo are big bus manufacturers, within their demarcated areas. Volvo was first in volume in Europe and third in the world in 1988; Scania was third in Europe and seventh in the world. Scania's lower volume in large part depends, as in its truck division, on its pursuit of economies of scale in manufacturing. Thus, in contrast to Volvo, Scania has chosen not to develop a bus engine specially adapted to city traffic and refrains thereby from attempting to capture a large part of the city bus market. Scania has instead invested in rear- and front-engine chassis, which use truck engines with a minimum of adaptation.

In the 1970s, both bus divisions enjoyed rapid expansion, during which they more than tripled their output. But in the slump that followed, in the early 1980s, they were severely hit and Volvo management even considered discontinuing the operations. The tide turned, however, and bus production entered another period of expansion. At the close of the 1980s, Volvo and Scania manufactured a total of eight thousand chassis, of which five thousand were made in Sweden. With strong finances and a capacity shortage in Sweden, Volvo went on the offensive in 1988 and acquired Leyland Bus, which among other things gave Volvo access to a complete city bus program. Volvo Buses began thereby to follow the same strategy of global dominance as the truck division had done.

Cars, trucks, and buses represented vastly different levels of production. While the production of cars at Volvo and Saab was counted in the one hundred thousands, the manufacture of heavy trucks was counted in the ten thousands. Bus production occupied yet a lower level on the scale and was counted in the thousands. Because the demands to adapt to the customer were tough (especially in the European bus market), the need for flexibility in production was considerable. To satisfy these demands, both Volvo and Scania invested in new facilities during the expansion period of the 1970s and opened highly flexible assembly systems in Borås and Katrineholm.

During the 1980s these installations were exposed to a double strain. To begin with, the plants entered a period of sharply falling sales and tight economic margins; then, a steep rise in production meant the capacity ceiling was greatly exceeded. As the case studies demonstrate, the new plants—with their new assembly systems—coped with these burdens very well indeed. But these achievements did not lead to any decision to expand production in Sweden. As in truck production, the tendency was to expand abroad. The bus divisions had not come as far, however. In 1988, both Volvo (Leyland included) and Scania still built a good half of their chassis in Sweden.

Summary

Swedish motor vehicle manufacturing has been characterized by dramatic changes. In the first half of the 1970s, all three product branches were expansive and profitable. Moreover, the Swedish labor market was overheated and a severe labor shortage prevailed. Partly as a consequence, new factories were built with distinctive technical and organizational solutions, such as Volvo's Kalmar plant, its Skövde gasoline engine factory (both of these were built in 1974), and its bus factory in Borås.

At the close of the 1970s and the start of the 1980s, car manufacturing went through a difficult period and no new factories were founded. The production of trucks and buses continued to grow, though, and the demands for more flexible production became ever more pressing. Out of these demands were born Volvo's new truck factory LB and Scania's new factory for bus chassis in Katrineholm.

In the mid-1980s, all three business lines were again profitable and expansive. In the case of heavy-vehicle manufacturing, however, the main investments in new capacity occurred outside Sweden. This was particularly true of labor-intensive final assembly. The expansion took place in countries in which unemployment was much higher and trade unions decisively weaker than in Sweden: the Netherlands, Belgium, Britain, and the United States. But except for Britain, auto workers' wages were higher in these countries than in Sweden. This made it easier to recruit and keep personnel in the traditionally organized plants Volvo and Scania operated outside Sweden. No investments in new plants for truck or bus assembly were made in Sweden (except for Volvo Trucks' dock assembly in Gothenburg).

Sweden continued to be the primary base for car production, and profitability at Volvo reached an all-time high in 1985–86. Increasing demands triggered investments in new capacity, both in assembly (Volvo Uddevalla and Saab Malmö) and in gas engine manufacturing (Skövde and Södertälje). At the same time, the companies found it more and more difficult to recruit workers in the overheated Swedish labor market. The new factories thus tried a series of new organizational and technical solutions. Extensive modernization projects were also initiated in the companies' "brownfields" in Gothenburg and Trollhättan.

In 1989–90, car manufacturing entered another crisis period, followed by a deep recession in the entire Swedish economy. Saab ceased to exist as an independent manufacturer, and General Motors assumed control. Continued falling sales led to a decision in 1991 to discontinue the brand new Malmö factory. At Volvo as well, difficulties led to a sharp reduction in capacity utilization, and during 1990 and 1991 the car division decided to reduce its work force of thirty-four thousand employees by more than five thousand. The Swedish plants—the older installations in Gothenburg and Kalmar as well as the new one in Uddevalla— were exposed to severe pressure to raise productivity and profitability. To ensure the long-term survival of the company, Volvo entered a strategic alliance with Renault. For the car divisions, the future was uncertain; for the truck and bus divisions, with their strong international position, the setbacks appeared to be merely part of the normal business cycle, and prospects appeared favorable for continued long-term growth.

4.
Pressures for Change: The Labor Market and Trade Unions

The aim of this chapter is twofold. The first objective is to present some important characteristics of the Swedish economy, labor market, and unions of the 1980s. To this end, the first section highlights a number of particularities of the Swedish economy from an international perspective, while the second analyzes Sweden's union structure and its changing industrial relations.

The second purpose of this chapter is to discuss the set of conditions and pressures for change that forced the auto firms to pursue new strategies for the organization of work. I describe the industrial labor crises that Swedish firms encountered in the second half of the 1980s and the failure of their technological strategies to solve the problems of labor-intensive processes such as assembly. I then highlight the "double pincers" of product complexity and labor shortage facing the Swedish auto firms. In concluding, I describe the company culture and its social preconditions that formed the background for the Volvo trajectory of 1970 to 1990.

The Swedish Economy: High Internalization, Full Employment

Swedish firms, especially in the manufacturing sector, have for a long time engaged in international competition, and they are strongly export oriented. In 1988, 47 percent of Sweden's industrial production was exported, 80 percent to markets other than those in the Nordic countries that are Sweden's closest neighbors.

Rich iron ore-mines and vast forests have historically formed the basis for Swedish manufacturing. By means of advanced methods of exploiting and refining these resources, the forest-related cluster as well as the mining and metals cluster have been able to offset increasingly unfavorable relative factor costs and maintain a central role in the Swedish economy.[1] Another important sector of the economy is the transportation and logistics cluster, which includes firms that produce cars, trucks, automotive components, aircraft, and aircraft engines. The origins of this cluster evolved out of the need of the forest and mining industries to transport natural resources to distant customers. Thus, the manufacture of heavy trucks was encouraged by the massive demand for long-distance transport by the paper and pulp manufacturers. Substantive clusters are also formed by the power-generation industry (its leading firm is ASEA/ABB) and the telecommunications industry (Ericsson is the core firm).

A distinctive feature of the Swedish economy is its high degree of concentration. In 1988, the eighteen largest Swedish firms, including Volvo, Ericsson, and Saab-Scania, accounted for 50 percent of Sweden's exports and for as much as 70 percent of all privately funded research and development. Most of these firms were strongly internationalized, and an increasing share of their operations was outside Sweden. In 1980, Swedish firms in the manufacturing sector employed 330,000 persons outside Sweden. From 1980 to 1990, manufacturing employment in Sweden decreased by 10 percent to approximately 1 million persons but employment in the foreign operations of Swedish firms increased by 50 percent, to 500,000 (Ministry of Industry 1990). Thus, the majority of the employees of most of Sweden's leading firms worked outside Sweden. This accelerated internationalization was a combined result of the small home market and the niche strategies most of these firms pursued. Volvo and Saab-Scania were exceptional among large firms in the engineering sector in that a majority of their employees still worked in Sweden.

During the international recession from 1974 to 1982, unemployment rose significantly in most of Europe and did not return to prerecession levels in the course of the long recovery. Sweden's performance was very different. Unemployment never exceeded 3.5 percent during the period 1970–90, in spite of a high and rising labor force participation rate (see table 4-1).

One of the reasons for this sustained employment rate was the strong position of unions, which, in contrast to the situation in most industrial nations, comprised nearly all employees (table 4-2).

Of all major industrial nations, Germany had the strongest and most cohesive union organization at the end of the 1980s. Yet the overall unionization rate was less than half that of Sweden.

An important characteristic of the German model of labor deployment in manufacturing was its dichotomous structure. Thus, the labor force was composed of highly skilled *Facharbeiter*, nearly always male and German, on the one hand and unskilled *Massenarbeiter*, often foreign or female or both on the other hand (see, for example, Jürgens 1991). *Facharbeiter* had solid, well-respected voca-

TABLE 4-1. Percent Unemployed, 1985 and 1988

Country	1985	1988
Sweden	2.8%	1.6%
Germany	9.3	8.7
United Kingdom	11.8	8.4
United States	7.2	5.5

Source: *ILO Bulletin of Labour Statistics*, May 1990.

tional training and were employed in qualified positions, often in off-line functions. They formed the backbone of the German system of industrial relations, the works councils (*Betriebsräte*), and the unions. By contrast, *Massenarbeiter* were allocated to repetitive production tasks, had few prospects of training and advancement, and normally had a weak voice in the unions.

Sweden also had a division between the skilled and unskilled sectors of the blue-collar work force, but the demarcation was much less important than in Germany. One reason was the absence of an elaborate system of vocational training that could produce the articulated occupational identity the *Facharbeiter* enjoyed. Another reason was that the importation of immigrant workers, quite significant in the 1960s, ceased to be of any practical importance in the 1970s and after. As a consequence of these differences in labor segmentation, Swedish unions were able to organize women and unskilled workers and put their issues on the union agenda to a much larger extent than the German unions could.

From the 1950s to the 1980s, Swedish labor unions pursued a distinctive strategy of egalitarianism, conceptualized in the so-called solidaristic wage policy. According to this policy, jobs requiring the same skills and work loads warrant the same pay, irrespective of the economic situation of the specific firm. One of the results of this policy was that wage differentials between various manufacturing sectors, as well as between manufacturing and service sectors, became quite small. This is illustrated in table 4-3, in which the wage differentials between the automotive sector and manufacturing as a whole are compared for Sweden, Germany, the United Kingdom, and the United States. In 1985, there was a 4 percent differential in Sweden compared to a 40 percent differential in the United States. The decreasing wage differential in the United Kingdom should be seen against the background of the massive layoffs and cutbacks in the British car industry in the early 1980s.

The Swedish solidaristic wage policy resulted in comparatively low wage costs for highly productive industrial sectors, such as the auto industry. At the same time, this policy made it difficult for manufacturing firms to recruit and keep workers when the labor market was tight. This is one of the reasons the large, export-oriented firms started to campaign for decentralized enterprise bargaining, instead of the traditional centralized Swedish model, in the 1980s.

TABLE 4-2. *Union Density at the End of the 1980s*

Country	Percentage*
Sweden	83%
Germany	40
United Kingdom	31
United States	15

Source: Kjellberg 1990 and Bratt 1990.
*As a proportion of all employees.

Features of the Swedish Trade Union Structure

Many of the key features of the Swedish labor market, such as its high levels of employment and individual security against income shortfalls in the event of injury, illness, or unemployment, are closely connected to the influence of the labor movement in the development of Swedish society. Between 1932 and 1976 and again from 1982 to 1991, the Social Democratic party held political power, for the most part as the sole party. Full employment has been, since the economic crisis of the 1930s, a central political objective, as a consequence of the important societal role of the trade union movement.

From an international perspective, the Swedish union movement has several special features, including a high and steady rate of unionization among blue-collar workers; a comparably high rate among white-collar employees, in both the public and the private sectors; and a combination of centralization and decentralization. Thus, there is coordinated national wage bargaining, on the one hand, and highly ramified and active workplace organization, with a strong legal basis, on the other. This strong workplace organization is a central reason for the high rate of unionization.

High Membership Rate among the Working Class

As early as World War II, the majority of Swedish blue-collar workers were affiliated with trade unions. The unionization rate continued to rise in the postwar period, then leveled off in the early 1980s at about 85 percent (more than 90 percent in manufacturing and construction). This figure has remained high in different economic sectors and for various categories of workers. Moreover, as in other Scandinavian countries, the Swedish trade union movement has successfully integrated skilled and unskilled workers: 90 percent of skilled and more than 80 percent of unskilled workers are organized in unions. By contrast, in Germany a mere one-third of semi- and unskilled workers were unionized at the close of the 1970s.

The increase in women's participation in work life in Sweden was accompanied

TABLE 4-3. Hourly Wages in the Motor Vehicles Industry Compared with Manufacturing as a Whole in Selected Countries, 1970–85

Country	1970	1975	1980	1985
Sweden	1.12	1.03	1.00	1.04
Germany	1.27	1.23	1.22	1.15
United Kingdom	1.33	1.16	1.06	1.13
United States	1.27	1.49	1.65	1.41

Source: SAF 1986.

by a rising level of unionization. In 1968, 61 percent of women and 81 percent of men were organized in unions. By 1981, this difference had been more than halved; the figures were 80 percent and 89 percent respectively. In West Germany, by contrast, the rate of unionization among women stagnated at around 20 percent (less than half that of men) throughout the postwar period. Skilled male workers have indeed been overrepresented in the decision-making organs of Swedish unions, from local clubs to national organizations, but the comprehensive integration of women and unskilled workers into trade unions has contributed palpably to the union movement's commitment to reforming repetitive, low-skilled jobs, not least within auto assembly.

In the second half of the 1980s, the international pattern of a weakening trade union appeal began to assert itself in Sweden as well, and the unionization rate sank from 87 percent to 82 percent from 1986 to 1990. The decline was especially marked in the greater Stockholm area, where the service sector was highly significant and the labor market was extremely volatile. Outside the big cities, the unionization rate among workers remains very high—86 percent in 1990 (*LO-tidningen*, no. 33–34, 1990).

High Rate among White-Collar Employees

As in other industrial nations, blue-collar workers in Sweden formed the first trade unions. Between the wars, white-collar employees began, across a broad front, to follow suit. They chose the same organizational structures as the blue-collar workers had done, so that the basic unit was a workplace organization (or club). Their unions were independent of those for the workers, however, and they did not have any connection to social democracy, as the workers' unions in LO, the Swedish trade union federation, did.

The white-collar movement was organized by sector and in some cases by occupation or training as well. The result is that four types of unions are normally represented in the larger Swedish engineering companies (as, for example, in the auto industry): the Metal Workers' Union; the Union of Clerical and Technical Employees in Industry (SIF), which is a general industrial union; the Union of

Foremen and Supervisors (SALF), which organizes first-line management; and one or several unions representing university-trained employees, such as the Union of Civil Engineers. With 300,000 members in 1988, SIF is the largest white-collar union.

The independent organization of white-collar employees in Sweden and the general legitimacy of trade unions in the country have been important reasons for the very high level of unionization. In 1981, 86 percent of all white-collar employees were members of a trade union; among those employed in the public sector, the figure was 93 percent; and among those who were privately employed, the figure was 79 percent.

The unusual extent of white-collar organization in Sweden has contributed to producing a friendly climate for unions and favorable legislation as well. In the matter of workplace reforms, however, the effect of white-collar organization has sometimes been ambiguous. Vertical organizational changes, involving a transfer of work tasks, prerogatives, and responsibility from the office to the shop floor, have been complicated by the fact that white-collar employees and foremen have had abundant opportunities through their separate union organizations to stand guard over existing organizational structures.

Workplace Organization

From an international perspective, the Swedish trade union movement appears, and is widely considered to be, highly centralized. Some of the features usually cited are the strong national organizations, as well as the postwar tradition of centrally coordinated wage negotiations between SAF (the employers' national confederation) and LO (the national trade union confederation). Moreover, research on the Swedish trade unions has contributed greatly to the picture of an ever-more centralized movement, as exemplified in a highly influential study from 1976:

> Few comparable union organizations are centralized to so high a degree. The regulation of members' wages and working conditions—the traditional core of union activities—is today carried out at the highest level within the organization. Another prominent structural tendency is the concentration in large organizational units. Through a series of mergers, the luxuriant flora of unions has been thinned out. The development has been similar on the local level. Here, the so-called big sections have made their entrance, with a consequent drastic reduction in the number of local base organizations (Hadenius 1976).

This research, in which there are detailed statistical analyses of the number of unions and geographical units, has altogether missed the significance of the unions' true base—*the workplace clubs*.[2]

The centralized part of the Swedish system is the negotiations of new wage contracts. The application of these contracts, however, as well as other issues such as members' disputes with their employers, are handled by the clubs. Thus, in practice, there are three levels of negotiations: the central national negotiations between SAF and LO; the negotiations between national industrial unions, for example, the Swedish Metal Workers' Union and the Engineering Employers' Federation; and, finally, local enterprise bargaining. In many cases, local negotiations have considerably greater significance for members than do the central negotiations. This is particularly true in industries such as engineering that have a high proportion of variable wage systems. Legislation in the 1970s further increased the role of the clubs, in so far as it established that they would have specific prerogatives and powers to act as the sole representatives of employees in the codetermination process; to be the exclusive recipients of company information; and to appoint safety stewards, who would be empowered to stop production processes they deemed dangerous.

Parallel with other changes in union structure in the 1960s and 1970s that centralized the structure of the unions, changes of an opposite character occurred. The significance, the areas of competence, and in many unions the number of clubs increased. An example is the Metal Workers' Union. After its congress of 1961, small regions were systematically eliminated. By 1985, there were only 134 regions in all. But at the same time the number of clubs increased, from 1,500 in 1960 to more than 2,340 twenty years later. In 1980, there were clubs at two-thirds of all workplaces with more than ten employees and at more than 95 percent of those with more than fifty employees. At large workplaces, club boards were complemented by group boards, chosen in general elections. At Volvo, for example, in 1969 the group boards were given the task of independently negotiating over piece rates. During the 1970s their tasks became even more extensive; for instance, they were given responsibility for codetermination questions as well.

As the sociologist Anders Kjellberg (1983:77) has pointed out, the other Scandinavian countries are also characterized by a dense organizational presence at the workplace. Moreover, the unions perform significant tasks there. This feature contradicts the picture of centralism pure and simple:

> The Scandinavian system is at the same time decentralized compared with most countries of continental Europe. That is, in the latter countries there has been, or still is, no counterpart to the Scandinavian nations' comprehensive union negotiating activities at the workplaces. . . . The fact that workers in the Scandinavian countries find themselves "near" the union, on account of a well-developed system of union representation on the shop floor and on account of local negotiations, has probably been of great importance for the high unionization rate. Employees have turned to the union when they have had problems, rather than to the enterprise committee or similar organ, as has usually been the case in continental Europe.

The largest LO union in the 1980s was the Municipal Workers' Union, because of the great expansion of public-care services. The leading union in LO, however, was the Metal Workers' Union, the largest within manufacturing (hereafter "Metall," in accordance with Swedish parlance). Metall organized workers in the steel and engineering industries, as well as car mechanics and the like. In 1988, it had 470,000 members.

As a result of alarming reports on the increasing wear and tear suffered by workers in repetitive jobs, plus growing difficulty recruiting young people to vocational training in high school, during the second half of the 1980s work reform, the work environment, and work organization rose to the top of Metall's agenda. The need for change had been underscored in the main reports to the congresses of 1985 and 1989.[3] Thus, as a practical matter, the union's national officers, together with local clubs, engaged in significant projects promoting change.

Codetermination and Increasing Union Participation

To understand the role of the unions in the industrial development of the 1980s, a glance back at the 1970s—the heyday of Social Democratic reformism— is in order. At that time, a series of new labor laws was promulgated, with the intention of strengthening the unions' position. In 1973, a law on board representation for employees came into effect. Other European countries also passed legislation on board representation for wage earners at this time. Sweden was the only country, however, in which the legislation built on the assumption that the trade unions—as the organizations concluding collective agreements—would appoint representatives to the boards.

The following year, a new law on job security was introduced. The law required that dismissal be based on objective grounds and that the employer give notice to the local union organization—in good time—about planned layoffs. The law also introduced rules on precedence and seniority in cases of layoffs arising from lack of sufficient work. The companies' prospects of using dismissal or the threat of dismissal as a disciplinary punishment disappeared almost completely.

Finally, in 1977, the Codetermination Law (MBL) came into force. It required an employer to negotiate with its union before making decisions resulting in significant changes. If no agreement was reached, however, the company could carry out its original plans, after negotiations had been concluded. MBL gave the union the power to postpone decisions—no more. To ensure the union could use its bargaining rights fully, the law contained rules about the company's obligation to provide information. In principle, the union representatives had the right to acquaint themselves with any and all materials needed to judge the company's operations.

MBL came into effect the same year Sweden entered a deep recession. The union agenda abruptly changed: plant closings, layoffs, and company mergers became the dominant concerns. The new law offered the unions few possibilities for defending employee interests regarding such matters. During the boom of the 1980s, however, when the expansion of old factories and the planning of new ones became important issues, the prospects for influence improved markedly. It now became normal for the unions to be engaged early on in the companies' planning processes. When Volvo began planning the Uddevalla factory in 1985, for instance, trade union representatives participated on a full-time basis from the start.

Industrial Relations under Stress

Traditionally, the structure of Swedish unions, both the decentralized and the centralized components, has closely matched the structure of employer organizations. In fact, from the beginning of the century, it was the employers who drove the centralization process, and in the 1950s it was SAF that took the initiative to introduce nationally coordinated, centralized bargaining. Thus, for two decades, SAF and LO exercised a decisive influence on all national negotiations, setting the standards for wage increases for groups in the private as well as the public sector. At the same time, they maintained the tradition of self-regulation of the bargaining parties and avoided state intervention in the industrial relations system, another one of the employers' goals.

This model of coordinated and autonomous bargaining, which was so successful in preserving industrial peace, gradually started to dissolve during the 1970s. LO encouraged and prodded the Labor government to promulgate the new extensive labor legislation on employment protection, codetermination, rights of local union representatives, and so on, signaling a significant departure from the tradition of self-regulation. This was followed, during the 1980s, by recurrent government involvement in the bargaining process, mainly because of the increasing complexity of the pattern of bargaining, brought about by the appearance of a number of new cartels representing various public and private white-collar unions. Kjellberg (1990:48) has stressed this point:

> The top level of bargaining was transformed to a fragmentary arena containing several actors. . . . By that, a state of increased uncertainty occurred, especially with reference to industrial peace/conflict. The big conflict (strike and lockout) in 1980, embracing manual and white-collar workers in all sectors, clearly demonstrated this fact. By that, the conflict gave the employers a powerful impetus to reconsider the model of centralized bargaining.[4]

Even in the period when centralized bargaining was most successful, there was an important element of bargaining at the industry level as well as at the local enterprise level. In the 1980s, the employers, spearheaded by the large engineering firms, turned their interest to these other levels, with the goal of making bargaining fully decentralized and enterprise oriented. Their success was limited, and at the end of the 1980s, there was a—possibly temporary—return to coordinated, centralized bargaining under heavy government orchestration. One important effect of the new employer strategy was a significant reduction in the power and influence of LO, the confederated trade union body for blue-collar workers, and increasing importance for the national industrial unions and especially the Metal Workers, which for some years during the 1980s occupied a strong public position.

Traditional union policies were also under stress because of a profound change in ecónomic policy. In the period from the beginning of the 1950s to the middle of the 1970s, the Labour government generally pursued a tight fiscal policy, combined with selective measures to encourage investments during business downturns and active labor market policies to stimulate retraining and labor mobility. In combination with the solidaristic wage policy, this strategy meant there was continuous pressure on companies to enforce rationalization within firms and transfer resources from less to more productive sectors.

In the economic crises of the late 1970s, the conservative government, which came to power in 1976, embarked on a very different strategy of currency depre-ciation, in an effort to rouse investment and employment by means of a general profit boost. This policy was vigorously continued by the Social Democrats. When they came back to power in 1982, they administered another major depreciation and pressured unions to keep their wage demands low. According to the Social Democrats, the only way to create sustainable growth was to raise capital's share of the national income. From 1979 to 1984, labor's share of the total value added was reduced from 71 percent to 66 percent, despite the favorable outcome for employees of "the big conflict" in 1980. Combined with the strong international recovery of 1983, the result was a virtual profit boom for Swedish firms. The goal of full employment was reached, but, because the new policy relaxed the pressure on firms to rationalize and upgrade, the high profits resulted in only short-term increases in investments and growth. Companies used their expanded revenues for mergers and acquisitions, thereby stepping up their international operations, as well as significantly reducing domestic competition in a number of industries— to the detriment of Sweden's long-term capacity for innovation and development.

In the end, the economic strategy of the 1980s resulted in a slow and decreasing growth in productivity. The yearly growth in labor productivity (value added per hour) in the manufacturing sector for 1985–88 was only 2 percent, compared with 3 percent in Germany and 4.2 percent in the United Kingdom (Erixon 1990:31, 33). In 1989 and 1990, the Swedish growth rate declined even further, exacerbating Sweden's problems in the international recession, which in 1990 succeeded the long boom period.[5]

For unions, the strong political pressure to keep wage demands low at a time when companies were earning unprecedented returns created strong internal tensions and tended to threaten union legitimacy. Specifically, it was one of the reasons for the falling union participation rate in the late 1980s. Unable to pursue an aggressive wage policy because of their political loyalties, the blue-collar unions, and especially the Metal Workers, turned to a strategy of work restructuring, signaled by the benchmarking document "Rewarding Work." For Metall, this was not only a way to attack the problems of repetitive strain injuries or to make manufacturing more attractive for young people. In a time when centralized bargaining had failed to deliver, it was also a way to improve real wages by creating locally negotiated skill and wage ladders, which, according to union policy, would be accessible to all workers. The macroeconomic policy of the 1980s was thus another reason for Swedish unions to focus on work restructuring much more strongly than most other unions in the industrialized world. In this effort, the highly visible automotive industry played a pivotal role.

Industrial Labor Crisis

In 1988, the Swedish labor force was composed of 4.5 million workers between sixteen and sixty-four years of age. More than 90 percent of this labor force were wage and salary earners.

The rate of labor force participation was high: 85 percent of men between sixteen and sixty-four were gainfully employed, as were 80 percent of women. The male participation rate remained constant during the 1970s and 1980s, while the female rate rose continuously from the early 1970s, when the prevailing rate was 70 percent.

One-fourth of the labor force—more than 1 million people—worked in manufacturing (including mining); another 300,000 had jobs in construction. The number employed in manufacturing decreased slightly in absolute terms throughout the 1970s and 1980s; and the proportion in manufacturing fell from 29 percent in 1970 to 23 percent in 1988. The engineering industry increased in importance during this period, however, and in 1986 it accounted for nearly half of those employed in manufacturing.

Throughout the 1970s and 1980s, through the oil crises and the international recession, the Swedish employment rate remained very high (see table 4-4). The favorable labor market also greatly reinforced the position of the unions and strengthened their claims to influence the design of factories and the character of working conditions.

The increase in employment from a level that was already high during the second half of the 1980s sharply limited companies' possibilities to select their personnel and to keep workers in unattractive jobs. Moreover, the short effective work time worsened the labor shortage. The nominal work time was certainly

TABLE 4-4. Relative Unemployment in Sweden, 1970–88

Year	Proportion of population in the labor force[a]	Unemployment as a percentage of the labor force[a]
1970	73.3%	1.5
1971	74.1	2.5
1972	74.4	2.7
1973	74.9	2.5
1974	76.5	2.0
1975	78.2	1.6
1976	79.0	1.6
1977	79.4	1.8
1978	79.9	2.3
1979	80.9	2.1
1980	81.5	2.0
1981	81.5	2.5
1982	81.7	3.2
1983	81.8	3.5
1984	81.9	3.1
1985	82.6	2.8
1986	83.3	2.2
1987	83.4	1.9
1988	84.0	1.6
1989	84.5	1.4
1990	84.8	1.5

Source: SCB (Statistics Sweden), *The Labor Market in Figures, 1970–88; Statistical Report* no. 1, 1991.
[a]Percentage of population between sixteen and sixty-four years of age.

long (leaving absenteeism and overtime out of account), considerably longer than in West Germany, for example, but, because of generous legislation providing the right to leave to study and in the event of parenthood and the high rate of absence caused by sickness, the effective work time per employee was short.[6] If one considers the labor force participation rate, however, and spreads the work hours among all persons between sixteen and sixty-four years of age, the picture appears very different. By this measure, the average Swede worked more than twelve hundred hours per year, compared with one thousand for the average German (see table 4-5).

In 1988, workers in the Swedish engineering industry were absent from work on account of illness an average of twenty-nine days per year. The figures for the Federal Republic and for Britain were eighteen and eleven, respectively. There were many reasons for the very high rate among Swedes. One was the labor shortage. At the end of the 1980s, nearly all persons in the Swedish labor market experienced a demand for their services, including those who, during slumps or

TABLE 4-5. Theoretical and Actual Work Time in the Engineering Industry, 1988

Country	Nominal work time[a]	Actual hours worked[b]
Great Britain	1,780 hours	1,840
West Germany	1,670 hours	1,580
Sweden	1,820 hours	1,500

Sources: *Affärsvärlden* 48 (1989); *Economist* 3 (1990).

[a]Work time is based on the number of workdays, excluding vacations and holidays. The data for Britain are from 1987.

[b]Includes absences and overtime.

in countries with high unemployment, usually could not find work. Another cause was the high and increasing proportion of women in the labor market. In 1988, 86 percent of women with children under school age had gainful employment. Because they still bore the main responsibility for their families, they were absent from work more often than men, among other reasons, to care for sick children.

The high rate of absenteeism among women was also the result of injuries and problems in the work environment. Industrial workplaces were designed for men, and women frequently were assigned the most repetitive, monotonous, and tiring jobs. Among employees in manufacturing, women were absent from work, on average, twice as often as men.

Both short- and long-term absenteeism in Sweden rose during the 1980s, but the greatest increase was in the area of long-term absenteeism. At the end of the 1970s, illness absences of 180 days or longer accounted for 33 percent of all days lost due to illness. Ten years later, the figure had risen to more than 40 percent (Riksförsäkringsverket 1989:24). This occurred in part because of procedural changes in the mid-1980s that made it much easier for workers to obtain sickness benefits for long periods, including for education and retraining lasting several years. Groups that in other countries receive pensions for early retirement or for other reasons are not counted as part of the labor force came to be classified as absent on account of illness.

The rising rate of short-term absenteeism, with its consequences in the form of planning difficulties, need for extra staff, and quality disturbances, was a great concern for the business community. This problem thus furnished the motivation for a growing number of projects in the late 1980s aimed at changing personnel policies and work organization. The rising rate of long-term absenteeism, however, was the central question for the government, because of the soaring social insurance costs, and for the trade unions. Concern over this issue led to an intensive debate, the so-called work load injury debate of 1987–88, about both the structure of the insurance system and the work environment. After the election in 1988, the government appointed a work environment commission with the task of identifying the worst jobs and proposing means for their elimination. In the auto industry, with its extensive ergonomic problems and repetitive trauma injuries, the work load injury debate and the commission had a notable impact.[7]

Young People Turn Their Backs on Industry

Industry's recruiting problems were worsened because young people, in growing numbers, were choosing not to enter manufacturing (the exception being the building industry). Of a total of 126,000 applicants to the senior high school's two- and three-year "lines," just 3,000 or 1 percent, chose the mechanical and industrial technical lines. (A line is roughly equivalent to a major, but it applies to high schools as well as universities in Sweden.) There were twice as many places as first-preference applicants, meaning these lines were last in popularity.[8]

In Gothenburg, Sweden's largest industrial city and the headquarters of Volvo, the number of places in the mechanical and industrial lines was reduced year after year because of the lack of interest. At the close of the 1980s, more than half the places were empty after the first round of admissions. In Södertälje, a city south of Stockholm and Scania's main site, the figures were even more dismal. Despite a sharp reduction in capacity, a mere third of the places were taken after the first round of admissions in 1990. Both Södertälje and Gothenburg are metropolitan labor markets. The same tendency prevailed, however, though more weakly, in other industrial areas. In Uddevalla, traditionally a shipbuilding town and from the close of the 1980s the site of Volvo's new car plant, the number of applicants for the "mechanical" and "industrial technical" lines fell by half between 1980 and 1990.[9]

When the recruiting difficulties first began to grow in earnest in the mid-1980s, industry's first reaction was to see them as an information problem. All that was needed was an information campaign that counteracted the negative image of industrial work. A study of youth and industrial work performed by the opinion institute SIFO, however, showed that it was not that easy. SIFO examined the attitudes of youth with experience in blue-collar industrial work and compared those who stayed with those who had taken other jobs or started to study again. The expectations of both groups were very much alike concerning such matters as job security, development prospects, and social recognition. But, those who had abandoned production work considered their work content and social environment to have improved dramatically. Those who stayed in production work, first and foremost, believed they possessed few other options. Forty-eight percent said they had stayed in their current jobs because they had no choice. The authors of the report summarized their findings as follows:

Manufacturing firms can, by and large, keep only those young people who believe themselves to have no choice. A great majority of the youth who have been in manufacturing but left it consider themselves to have gained by the change. This means industry not only has a bad reputation—young people also think this reputation is well-deserved. . . . This adds up to a big latent problem for industry. That day it needs to expand will be a very difficult day indeed (Crona and Leion 1986:77).[10]

I do not mean to suggest that conditions in, for example, the Swedish auto industry were worse than in other countries. Quite the contrary. Rather, the problem was that Sweden's auto companies, in contrast to such enterprises in most other countries, could not compensate for the arduous work and exacting performance demands with higher wages. As a result of the Swedish unions' solidaristic wage policy, auto workers earned only slightly more than other factory workers, such as those in the textile industry, or workers in the service sector. Nor could the auto companies compensate for the lack of wage differentials by providing generous benefit packages. Because of the universalist Swedish welfare system, with its national health insurance and pension plans, employees were not dependent on their employers for such benefits. This situation contrasted sharply with that in North America, where auto workers were highly privileged in terms of wages and benefits. "People could kill to get a job here," a female taxi driver told me at the Nissan plant in Smyrna, Tennessee, in 1990. In Sweden, such a plant would have had a hard time finding job applicants and an even harder time keeping them.

Failure of the Technological Strategy

At the start of the 1980s, the Swedish auto companies saw comprehensive automation of assembly as a way of drastically reducing the need for staff and of solving the problems associated with repetitive and arduous jobs as well. Automated assembly had existed for a long time, of course, but until the beginning of the 1980s, it was the so-called rigid automation, which consisted of dedicated machinery and was therefore limited to products with very high volumes. During the 1970s, robotic technology had developed quickly and with it the possibility of flexible automated assembly (FAM). Several large auto manufacturers, including GM and Volkswagen, seized on this technology in the hope of developing highly automated assembly plants. At Volvo and Saab as well, great expectations were attached to the FAM concept. After all, the robotization of body work had truly taken a leap in the first half of the 1980s. Why not in assembly as well? Yet, despite great efforts, no breakthrough appeared.

A symposium at the Swedish Academy of Engineering Science held in 1988, summed up some of the problems.[11] One major difficulty was obtaining equipment that combined speed with adjustability. It was hard, in practice, for the flexible, programmable machinery to move as rapidly as the human body. Another difficulty was the low overall flexibility of an automated assembly system, with its multiplicity of different subsystems. Equipment was required to transport and place the base object, to supply additional materials, to handle (grasp, transfer, and insert) additional materials, for communication, and, not least, for supervision and control. The tool carrier (the robot) could be flexible, but many of the subsystems had to be dedicated, which made the total cost per product high. At the symposium, even the mass producer Electrolux, with its strong focus on technology and simple products (compared to the auto industry), stressed how hard it was to find profitable applications for such technology because of the low speed of the robots and the need for costly auxiliary equipment.[12]

The automotive suppliers could point to some successful examples of automated components assembly—of loudspeakers and headlights, for instance. But these cases all involved simple products and high volumes (two thousand to three thousand units per day).[13] Automation was also possible in the more complicated case of gas-engine manufacturing, with its large proportion of high-frequency operations, such as the assembly of valves and valve mechanisms (especially cylinder engine heads with sixteen valves), pistons, and piston rings.

When it came to final assembly, however, the engineers' vision of comprehensive automation failed to come true. Thus, at the close of the 1980s, despite great (and expensive) efforts, there were only scattered and very marginal instances of automated assembly in the auto industry, including mechanized marriage stations at Saab Trollhättan and robotized window assembly at the Volvo plants. The earlier fascination (in 1984–85) with VW's far-reaching assembly automation in its Halle 54 plant in Wolfsburg had vanished, and the same was true for GM's high-tech strategy.

During the second half of the 1980s, the continued restrictions on mechanization in final assembly contributed to a strong sociotechnical renaissance as an alternative approach to solve the personnel and productivity problems. When automation no longer appeared realistic, the argument for using assembly lines in the future were weakened, at least within Volvo Cars. In the bus and truck divisions, with their much lower volumes, automation was never seriously considered even for the assembly of such components as axles or hubs.

Product Complexity and Variation

An important aspect of Swedish auto manufacture during the 1980s was its increased complexity and product variation. In the press and body shops, the introduction of new materials—above all, galvanized plate—made the manufacturing process considerably more difficult. Plants that had been single-type factories became multitype, such as Saab's body and engine shops, Volvo's press plant in Olofström, and Volvo's assembly plant in Gothenburg, TC. New complicated options were introduced, such as antilock brake systems in the bus, truck, and car programs; air springs and rear steering in truck production; and multiple valve products in engine production. The increase in product variation—at a given level of volume—was generally more significant than the increase in production.[14] Demands for manufacturing capability rose further as quality became a paramount issue.

All of this reflected international trends in the industry. One feature that was distinctively Swedish was the companies' focus on the exclusive segments of both the car and commercial vehicles markets. Another special feature was the extremely high degree of internationalization. Thus, the companies had to adapt their products to meet the needs of a great variety of customers. This was especially true for commercial vehicles.

The first great reform wave in the Swedish auto industry had occurred at the beginning of the 1970s and had been caused mainly by social problems, difficulties in recruitment, and so on. The reforms of the 1980s were considerably more wide ranging, because of the changed preconditions of production. In a strongly standardized production system, with relatively low quality requirements and high market demand, high personnel turnover is not a terribly serious problem. When demands for flexibility, precision in delivery, and quality rise, however, the significance of having a stable staff with low rates of absenteeism and high levels of competence and commitment increases. In labor-intensive processes, these qualities can play decisive roles.

The increase in product variation and market fragmentation is a main theme in the "post-Fordist discourse." It is not possible, however, to deduce the development of work and work organization from observations of the marketplace. If one wishes to understand the changes in the Swedish auto industry's assembly methods during the 1980s, one must look to the *interaction* between the sharpened demands on the product market, the failure of the technological strategy, and the labor shortage and consequent improved prospects for union influence. Moreover, it is important to see the entire period from 1970 onward as a period of learning, in which the experiments and experiences of the first reform wave formed the point of departure for the following stages of change.

There Is No "Volvism"!

During the 1980s, Volvo and Saab developed their products in a similar way as they strived to meet the same general forces for change. The transformation of work organization, however, was much more thorough at Volvo. During the 1970s, Saab had no counterpart to Volvo's Kalmar plant, and in the 1980s, Saab's planning for its factory at Malmö (in 1986–89) was a contradictory halfhearted effort compared to Volvo's operation at Uddevalla.

One important reason for the differences between the two companies was the policy and attitude of top management. Gyllenhammar, the CEO at Volvo, demonstrated—in a very different way from the executives at Saab and Scania—an interest in organizational and technical changes designed to meet human demands. This managerial orientation had great significance because of Gyllenhammar's strong independent standing; indeed, it played a decisive role in several new projects. To protect this position, Gyllenhammar strove to achieve a close, long-term collaboration with the trade unions, which, in turn, gave them an increased weight in the decision-making structures of the company. (This position will be much less significant, of course, in the new Volvo-Renault complex.)

The unusually open culture among Volvo's production managers and engineers was promoted by the efforts of executives to encourage new ideas, even from social science researchers. This culture was strengthened during the long series of experiments and attempts with alternative work forms. Not that consensus always prevailed among Volvo's engineers about appropriate forms of production. Rather, the striking feature was the breadth of views and the often sharp disagreements.

The role of the unions was to influence the conception of a problem—what was considered to *be* the problem—and of acceptable solutions, rather than to offer their own alternatives or concrete proposals. As the engineers developed new possibilities, the unions' views of acceptable solutions changed, as did their prospects for influence. Management however, retained the initiative and competence to develop new systems. Three critical features of Volvo, then, were the attitude and role of top management, its alliance with the trade unions, and the open culture in industrial engineering.

It is important not to forget the social preconditions that made possible the "Volvo culture's" capacity for innovation in production and organization. This becomes clear if one considers Volvo's operations in Ghent, Belgium, where Volvo had both a car and truck factory since the 1960s. The auto factory made the same products as in Sweden but in an altogether different labor market and social structure. In 1989, unemployment in the Ghent region stood at 10 percent and the maximum level of unemployment compensation was less than half the ordinary wage. This endowed Volvo with excellent opportunities for selecting personnel, as the head of information explained when interviewed in the trade union journal *Metallarbetaren* (no. 50) in 1989: "When we were going to increase our production in 1984, the news came out on a Friday. . . . On Monday we received 4,000 applications. We take care to choose our people," he added. Another factor was that, although union density in Belgium was high, the trade union movement was split into three factions: liberal, Christian democratic, and socialist.

The significance of Belgium's social conditions for work motivation at Volvo was reflected in an interview with a Ghent worker in *Dagens Nyheter* on November 12, 1989: "You have low employment. We're scared of losing our jobs. It is said we like working, but I don't know if that's true. I think most workers everywhere do their job as well as they can. It's also a difference of mentality. We put up with things more easily; we accept them."

This "acceptance" would seem to be connected to the weak job security. For instance, the workers at the Ghent factory could be dismissed if they were absent from work too often on account of illness, were absent without legitimate cause, or did "bad work." In this setting, Volvo developed a very effective production management, which diligently applied a number of new methods inspired from Japan, such as total productive maintenance (TPM). But no attempt was made to "humanize" the work organization and technology. The social relations seem to have been more important than the "company culture." Thus, the orientation of Volvo management was not, in and of itself, a sufficient factor for change. Rather, Volvo's production strategy, company philosophy, labor-management relations, and engineering culture, in combination with the Swedish social structure and labor market, created the conditions for the Volvo trajectory in the years between 1970 and 1990. At the same time, these conditions did not preclude the possibility of implementing organizational forms or managerial practices developed and proven viable in Sweden in operations in other countries. Indeed, this was done by both Volvo Buses, which implemented its Swedish assembly concept to Britain, and Volvo Trucks, which introduced new managerial practices in its operations in the United States and Brazil.

5.
Organizational and Technical Design of Swedish Automotive Assembly

The preceding chapter outlined conditions in the Swedish auto industry and labor market during the 1970s and 1980s. This chapter is devoted to explaining the concepts and distinctions that are central to understanding the plant studies that follow. The first section discusses the production arrangement and work organization in assembly. Two scales are developed that are joined in a simple model. Thereafter follows a more general discussion of organizational strategies of work and their relation to different types of skill development. The final section is an overview of the case studies and their relation to each other.

From Line to Complete Assembly

The assembly revolution that was begun in Ford's Highland Park factory created a paradigm for mass production that dominated for many decades. Productivity rose immensely. But, at the same time, what had been a handicraft form of production was transformed into a series of divided, repetitive tasks marked by extremely restricted autonomy and great physical burdens.

As long as the assembly line was perceived as a necessity of industrial engineering, these negative (humanly speaking) features were accorded little weight. As early as the 1960s, however, studies performed by the Dutch industrial psychologist Van Beek (carried out within the Philips Group) pointed out the considerable inefficiencies produced by traditional assembly lines (see den Hertog 1978). These analyses contradicted the accepted view of line production as the incarnation of efficiency; however, they reached only a very small audience.

At the start of the 1970s, the British researcher Ray Wild (1975a) did a comprehensive analysis of the industrial engineering losses attendant on manual line assembly; this study had a much greater impact. Wild divided the losses into three types—balancing, handling, and system—which were calculated as per-centage increases in z, the theoretically minimum man-time. Z represented a situation in which all workers were fully occupied, all materials were immediately available for use, and there were no errors of assembly.

According to Wild, *balancing losses* occurred because the work tasks in a serial flow will not require the same amount of time to perform. At all stations except the top (in which 100 percent of the time is used), there are micropauses of unused time. Wild found that balancing losses tended to increase with shorter work cycles because it became ever harder to achieve an even division of tasks. One specific type of balancing loss, variant losses, increase with growing product variation. One way to handle them is to balance the line according to the average complexity of the model mix; this involves adding support staff in the case of heavy variants. Another option is to build the loss directly into time planning, through so-called maxbalancing. This strategy produces the result that the assemblers have extra, unoccupied time in the case of all variants except the most complex.

The time spent in moving materials and tools is known as *handling losses.* The shorter the work cycle, the greater the losses. According to Wild's studies, however, even with long work cycles, such losses cannot be less than 5 percent of z. Moreover, when "making up" (working faster than the norm), workers usually move over larger areas than assumed by industrial engineering (IE) analysis, thus increasing handling losses.

System losses are a result of the human variations in a production system. Their consequence, in the case of a paced line, is sometimes unused time, sometimes a shortage of time (in the latter case the worker releases an uncompleted object). All workers, including experienced ones, exhibit such variations.[1] The size of the adjustments and of the inspection staff is a visible expression of the extent of system losses.

Wild discusses only the effects of the production system; he takes the product design as given. The same applies to his remedies. According to Wild, system losses can be reduced in several ways. One can reduce the number of workers in a series, increase the time the product is at each station, raise the buffer capacity, or widen the system capacity (that is, make more objects available for each worker). Balancing and system losses can be seen as rigidity losses. Another type of rigidity loss arises when the production schedule is changed or new vehicles are introduced. Both entail costs in industrial engineering work (rebalancing). The introduction of new models also usually entails losses of capacity because the speed of produc-tion in conventional car assembly is much lower than usual at such times.

In Saab's assembly of the 9000 cars in Trollhättan, the industrial engineering losses were as follows in 1987: balancing losses: 50 to 55 percent, of which about half were variant losses; handling losses: 20 to 25 percent; and system losses: 95 to 100 percent. These losses came to about 175 percent in toto. Thus, final assembly of a Saab 9000 took nearly three times the theoretical minimum. Some of the reasons for the losses were the difficulty of coping with the variant spread and the irrational system of materials provision.

The figures for Volvo's 740, assembled in Torslanda, were better but still excessive: balancing losses: 30 percent; handling losses: 15 to 20 percent; and system losses: about 70 percent, for a total of 115 to 120 percent (Bergdahl and Johansson 1987:70).[2]

During the 1970s, industrial engineers in the Swedish auto industry began to realize the extent of these losses. This was especially true at Volvo Trucks, where product variation and thereby variant losses in assembly began to rise sharply. Because of the difficulties of "mixed-model assembly" in a rigid line system, the development of variants also contributed to increasing the rate of capital tied up in inventory. The increasing emphasis on quality ("right from the beginning") also encouraged reconsideration of the rationality of the line. From having been self-evident, the technical organization of the assembly process became an open question during the 1980s. The case studies that follow reveal a great variation, with significant implications for both the economy and working conditions.

The assembly design, the way in which equipment and work stations are grouped and the physical flow is organized, was one central dimension of analysis. Theoretically, the number of grouping plans or layout options is great. In practice, however, the range of configurations is smaller. The different ways of arranging assembly in the Swedish auto industry from 1970 to 1990 can be placed along a dimension that I shall call the assembly system's x-axis. This axis is closely related to the horizontal division of labor. The x-axis indicates the technical framework for horizontal division or integration in the assembly process. The starting point corresponds to the traditional line system; the points along the line correspond to how much of the product's final assembly is performed by one assembler or assembly group.[3] Five levels, or steps, can be discerned. "Half-steps" between steps 2, 3, and 4 are also distinguished; they represent variations between factories (Volvo LB and Volvo at Borås, for example) in their development from flexible line to complete assembly.

1. *Orthodox line assembly.* Production layout is of a strictly serial type, and jobs are highly repetitive. Work cycles in car manufacture are normally one to three minutes, fifteen minutes in heavy truck assembly (in which the total volume is lower).

2. *Flexible line assembly.* This is usually a series flow with buffers. Technically, it can consist of elastically linked conveyor sections, but it can also have an individualized transport system with centrally controlled carriers (AGVs). Workers in this system can follow the base object a ways, so that the work cycles can be somewhat longer (ten to twenty minutes in car assembly).

3. *The parallel series system.* There are two main forms of this system. One kind consists of several short parallel flows. The other has parallel sections in a single overarching serial flow, possibly with concentrations or "waists" for facilitating mechanization or the addition of materials. In that case, the structure is parallel section, line assembly, parallel section, line assembly. The work cycles can range from fifteen to twenty minutes to a couple of hours in complex assembly.

4. *Complete assembly.* In this system, one or two individuals, or a group, perform the entire assembly, sometimes because the operators follow their base object through a short flow. In this case, the overall system consists of a collection of parallel flows. The most consistent version is wholly parallel stationary construction—pure dock assembly. The work cycles are long—hours or days—depending on the product.

5. *Integrated assembly.* This system integrates an even longer section of the flow, including not just assembly but also inspection, testing, and adjustment. The assemblers, at the individual or team level, are responsible for completed, ready-to-drive products. Such integration normally presupposes certain technical conditions, as does complete assembly. For example, decentralized testing equipment is needed. The organizational structure and qualification level are of great importance in how these technical conditions are utilized.

There is a connection between the production layout and the way the work stations are linked. This connection is a matter of technical control. A pure, "orthodox" line requires mechanical pacing of the sort provided by a conveyor belt for all heavy base objects. This was one of Ford's basic principles.[4] In an unpaced serial system with operator pacing, lighter objects might be moved by the assemblers themselves. And in flexibilized lines and in parallel series systems with a main flow, the technical conditions exist for control of the base object to be decentralized. For instance, the assemblers can instruct the carrier to move the object when the work has been completed. Such autonomy often comes into conflict, however, with the synchronizing demands of the larger system. Thus, the technical control of production tends to become centralized, and the autonomy enjoyed by the assemblers can be as insignificant as on a line. In long-cycle parallel assembly and complete assembly, central control of the base object's movement is not possible as a practical matter. Complete assembly arranged in a flow requires some coordination of the operators' pacing; by contrast, dock assembly allows in principle for completely individualized pacing.

Organization of Work

Another central dimension is the organization of work. This concerns how different work tasks are joined in work roles (positions) and how prerogatives, information, and responsibilities are distributed. Ideally and typically, the Taylorist work organization has four basic features: (1) a high degree of specialization of positions and functions; (2) a strict hierarchical structure throughout the organization and usually a hierarchy among blue-collar positions, according to the pattern subforeman, adjuster/inspector, assembler; (3) control by means of detailed instructions and the giving of orders through a chain of command; and (4) individualized and "verticalized" relations. The workers are related as individuals to their superiors, who bear exclusive responsibility for all *coordination*. This coordination occurs in an individual and hierachical manner, rather than through horizontal *cooperation* within groups or work teams.

As with the assembly line, this form of organization, which was originally very efficient, came to entail significant drawbacks for companies over time. Costs of administration rose, while feelings of responsibility and motivation among workers decreased.

Since the 1970s, the organization of the shop floor has been changed in Swedish auto factories, and various forms of group work have been introduced. Several different aspects of this development could be analyzed. I have chosen to concentrate on one—namely, how the vertical division of labor and the distribution of prerogatives have been changed. This dimension is represented by a y-axis. Levels 2 and higher on the axis assume organizationally developed forms of cooperation between the workers over and above those arising directly out of the production process. The higher the value, the more integrated the shop-floor organization and the more numerous the issues the groups can influence. Four levels can be distinguished in the case studies:

1. Conventional hierarchy, which is strictly individually based. The room for worker influence is very small, except possibly over matters of work rotation.

2. Group organization within the framework of a traditional shop-floor managerial structure, or what may here be called hierarchically circumscribed group organization. The groups can influence short-term matters such as the planning of the workday and the distribution of their own work. The role of the group representative or leader, if there is one, tends to be fixed and linked to the organizational hierarchy.

3. Strong group organization, with a high degree of decentralization. The production groups perform a good deal of the traditional tasks of first-line management and some industrial engineering work besides. Group representatives and such are selected by the groups themselves.

4. Integrated teamwork. There is no first-line management of the traditional kind. The groups' areas of responsibility include working with staff employees responsible for such functions as product preparation and engineering.

"Integrated assembly" on the x-axis means the work area includes more tasks than merely assembly. Analogously, "integrated teamwork" on the y-axis means the groups' tasks and prerogatives extend outside the immediate production function and its organizational hierarchy.

There is a connection between the structure of the organization and the administrative control, just as there is between the arrangement of production and technical control. Detailed monitoring of workers' conduct usually occurs in plants at the lowest level on the y-axis; in plants at the highest level, the pattern of administrative control tends to merge into management by objectives instead of detailed control. As we shall see, however, inconsistent forms—with contradictory patterns of control—also occur. The axis does not directly indicate the degree of collaboration between the workers. At the same time, strong groups with a high degree of influence (y > 2) are scarcely thinkable without developed relations of cooperation.

Self-Management versus Partial Self-Management

Researchers within the sociotechnical tradition, especially as it developed in Norway, have analyzed the vertical division of labor from a self-management perspective. In the most structured analysis of different industrial work groups, Norwegian researcher Jon Gulowsen (1971) found that the degree of autonomy was determined by whether the group could do the following: (1) influence its qualitative goals (the choice of product); (2) influence its quantitative goals (the number of units produced); (3) choose if it shall have a leader and, if so, who (to handle the group's relations to its surroundings); (4) determine which extra activities shall be undertaken; (5) decide when it shall work; (6) select the method of production; (7) determine its internal distribution of work; (8) decide questions concerning recruitment; (9) choose if it shall have a leader and, if so, who (to handle the group's internal questions); and (10) determine how particular work operations shall be carried out.

Gulowsen found no groups that had any influence over the choice of product, but he did find several that fulfilled criteria 2 and 3. These groups worked on various time-limited contracts, and management did not intervene so long as the agreed-upon production level was maintained. In these cases, self-management was grounded in genuine independence. In all the other groups Gulowsen studied, the measure of self-administration was strongly dependent on the attitude of management. For example, changes in first-line management could entail substantially reduced autonomy by the group.

Gulowsen concluded that the concept of self-management should be reserved for groups that have negotiated contracts that specify mutual obligations and that apply for demarcated periods. For other kinds of groups, which fulfill certain minimum criteria for stability, autonomy, and efficiency, he preferred the term *partial self-management* ("semiautonomous groups"). The distinction is qualitatively important. A self-managing group, according to Gulowsen, is one that participates in determining the framework under which it works. The conditions for the group's performance of its task, and its internal self-administration, are guaranteed for a demarcated period. Of course, even partial self-management may be considered a great step forward compared to an organization in which work is controlled in detail. But in contradistinction to "genuine" self-managed groups, such groups can lose their autonomy on short notice as a result of company restructuring, production transfers, or new production programs.

A problem with this analysis is that the role of unions in the development of group organization is not discussed at all. Gulowsen did not analyze the possibility of employing union power to reinforce the independence of partially autonomous groups or of using union contracts as a partial substitute for the time-demarcated contract he considered a condition for true self-administration. As we shall see, the local union at Volvo LB played a critical role in prolonging the survival of the group organization.[5]

For the groups Gulowsen studied, the ten criteria listed above formed, in the order given, a simple scale. Groups that fulfilled the criteria for self-management to a certain degree thereby also met all the less demanding criteria. Gulowsen's material was limited, however. Modern mass production of the kind examined in this book was not the focus of his study. For this type of production, Gulowsen's criteria yield no one-dimensional measure of self-management. For example, some production groups can determine their external leadership and make decisions about extra activities (criteria 3 and 4) but select the method of production (criterion 6) only in a very narrow sense. This should not in itself be considered proof that these criteria are not relevant (that is, that the production method follows absolutely from the product choice). The concrete shaping of the technology and the specification of the work methods occur during the stages of product engineering. A lack of shop-floor influence in this case means that organizational development has been restricted to changes in the production function.

Model for Describing Production Design and Organization

If combined, the x- and y-axes create a simple model for describing the production design and organization in assembly workshops[6] (see fig. 5-1). This model emerged in the course of trying to chart the course of Sweden's experiences. What I have called production design, the x-axis, represents various forms of technical and physical organization, while the y-axis represents the hierarchical organization

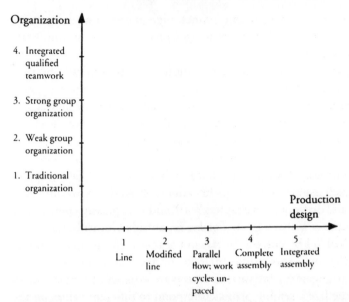

FIGURE 5-1. Model for Analyzing Production Design and Work Organization

of workers. The division emphasized by sociotechnical analysis—that between the social and technical system—is another point of reference. It is crucial here, however, to explain the meaning of "technical system." As Ulf Karlsson has pointed out (1979: 35), this concept can stand for either "a collection of machines, apparatuses and such—that is to say, a collection without defined relations—or an already structured collection of these things—that is to say, a concrete layout with specified geographical and functional relations." My x-axis represents the technical system in the latter sense. Thus, this model cannot be generalized from here. In particular, the organizational dimension, which combines integration and influence, is strongly rooted in the Swedish situation. It would be difficult to apply, for example, to Japanese production, in which a frequently high degree of functional integration is not accompanied by increased influence for the workers and the role system is discoupled from the technical system (the work process). Therefore, high values on the y-axis cannot be assumed unambiguously to carry the same meaning across national boundaries. (Perhaps "paradigm boundaries" is the more appropriate expression).

A movement to the right on the x-axis corresponds to a reduction in the costs that traditionally are attendant on the division of labor: industrial engineering losses, sensitivity to disturbances, quality problems (difficulties of building right from the beginning), and high personnel turnover. Against these advantages stand the classical gains of the division of labor that were so important in the development of the Ford system: short instruction times, high and even work intensity, standardization, and visibility. Which advantages predominate is an important question in the case studies.

A movement upward on the y-axis can be motivated economically by such social gains as increased commitment and taking of responsibility on the part of the workers and reduction of administrative costs. Against this must be weighed the more fragile structure (viewed from a traditional organizational perspective), with reduced possibilities for direct control "in case of need."

Likewise, in the case of working conditions, it is reasonable to suppose that movements in a "northeast direction" (upward on both axes) can have palpable positive effects on such issues as variety, qualifications, physical and psychological strains, automony, and discretion. In chapters 9, 10, and 11, I present comparative data from five factories—Volvo TC, in Torslanda, outside Gothenburg; its satellite plant, TUN; Volvo LB; Volvo at Borås; and Scania at Katrineholm. In that each of these factories represents a different value on the x-axis, the significance of the production arrangement for various aspects of work can be analyzed. In addition, three of the five assembly plants correspond to different values on the y-axis. Chapter 12 is devoted to a discussion of the relation between work organization and worker autonomy (in the sense of power and influence) in these plants.

Multitasking or Reskilling?

Organizational form is closely connected to qualification policy. Two principal "skill strategies" can be discerned. One is skill development within the framework of a largely traditional organizational hierarchy and division of labor. The most restricted form is competence development for career-selected groups, in line with a strategy strictly oriented to career enlargement within an established organizational structure. A more comprehensive form entails training of all the production workers, in what remain fragmented work tasks through, for example, systematic work rotation. This is often what is meant by the diffuse concept multiskilling. A more accurate term would be multitasking. Alternation between positions is encouraged, but the job structure is unchanged. Reskilling beyond the level of narrowly specified tasks scarcely occurs.

The other main skill strategy is linked to changes in the organization and the production arrangement and amounts to a flanking strategy that is coupled to these structural reforms. As the case studies show, there are a range of variants in this area:

One variant is the *depth* of the qualifications. The minimum type entails purely operative instruction in the new tasks (the new operations, for example). A more comprehensive version involves the conveying of functional understanding, such as product knowledge and genuine understanding of the production technology. Only in the case of the latter does reskilling seem an appropriate term.

Another variant is the *nature* of the new qualifications. They can be product- or process-specific, or they can be general and marketable, of the sort that distinguishes the skilled trades.

Finally, another variant is the *form* of training. This is closely linked to the nature of the qualifications. Learning at the work station, under the pressure of production, results in mainly product-specific skills. To develop the general and cohesive skills traditionally associated with skilled work, a significant amount of training outside production, in training workshops or production schools, is normally required. In a study by Norbert Altmann and others (1982) of new work forms in German industry at the close of the 1970s, it was found that scarcely any of the companies investigated had developed their training methods. The usual practice, as earlier, was for production workers to learn on the job. Workers who had acquired long-cycled tasks saw this as a serious deficiency: only with a proper training workshop could they obtain basic professional qualifications and escape the burdensome link between training and performance. A training workshop was viewed as a "refuge" from the social conflicts and tensions arising in connection with learning at the place of work, where new employees were a disturbance and a burden for the workers. Important questions for the Swedish case studies therefore concern not only which organizational strategies are developed but also *how consistent the attempt at change is* and whether it is linked to a comprehensive qualification policy or just a quantitative extension of existing training practices.

Introduction to the Case Studies

Chapters 6, 7, and 8 present six case studies of organizational and technical change in the Swedish auto industry between 1970 and 1990. Two main questions are raised in these studies: is it possible to discern a specific Swedish trajectory in the technology and organization of auto assembly, and, if so, which forces drove these changes onward, what forces hindered them, and what were the effects?

Chapter 6 reviews the production experiences of the two units with the most extensive experience with long-cycle assembly with rich work content: Scania and Volvo Buses. Volvo's Borås plant was so efficient during the 1980s that the company decided to introduce the same assembly concept when it acquired the British subsidiary, Leyland Bus. Such a step would have been far from self-evident in the years immediately following the startup of the factory in Borås.

Chapter 7 focuses on Volvo's Kalmar plant, the main attempt during the 1970s to reform car assembly. Volvo Trucks' LB plant is also analyzed. In the early 1980s, it was a flagship among plants aspiring to reform the organization of work.

Chapter 8 contrasts the original planning of Volvo's remarkable greenfield operation, Uddevalla, with the aborted process of reform at the main brownfield site in Gothenburg, TC.

These six cases are a sample from a comprehensive study in which twenty plants were followed for ten years. The goal was to attain as complete coverage of developments in the Swedish auto industry as possible and thereby to avoid resting the entire analysis on a few selected "pioneers" or purported trend setters.

The case studies in the following chapters discuss the assembly stage only. Of the production cost of a Volvo car, the value added within the car division (press, body, painting, assembly, and seat production) came to about 20 percent in 1989. To this may be added about 5 percent in value added from the operations of Volvo Components, above all for engine manufacture. Purchased materials were therefore the most costly item by far.

Assembly accounted for about 40 percent of Volvo Cars' labor costs in 1989. The share increased during the 1980s as more complex products were produced in the still low-mechanized systems. Of the production cost that can be affected, then, assembly comprises a very important part. This is also clear from a British comparison of manufacturing times for various production processes in 1980 and 1986. According to this analysis, which examined only the manufacturing process in car companies, assembly time in 1986 was 35 percent of total time, compared with 27 percent six years earlier.

Taken together, the case studies weave a fabric in which one may discern a complicated interplay between different factors in the industry's technical and organizational transformation and both important driving forces from without (technology, products, and the labor market) and significant learning processes within.

6.
Competitive "Craft Work" in Two Bus Plants

A t the end of the 1970s, both Volvo's and Scania's bus divisions built new plants for chassis assembly, which entailed a comprehensive shift from line assembly to group-based work in parallel assembly. The new facilities were sharply questioned at the start, in part because their capacity to manage fluctuations in production and personnel was doubted. During the 1980s, however, both factories proved that they were able to handle the pressures of tight capacity utilization, and they thereby became forerunners in the development of modern long-cycle assembly. (Their principal production design and work organization are shown in fig. 6-1.)

Scania Katrineholm

Scania Katrineholm develops, designs, and builds heavy bus chassis and bodies. Approximately two thousand chassis were assembled in 1987, as well as two hundred complete buses. The plant had about seven hundred employees and included the following production operations: a component shop for pressing and machining; a chassis workshop; a bus shop with body and outfitting work; and a paint shop.

This chapter principally concerns assembly at the chassis workshop, the chassis flows. Of the 150 workers in this shop in 1987, 60 worked in preassembly, 40 in chassis assembly (frame jobs), and 20 in adjustment and outfitting work. Others were employed in undersealing and materials handling. Two main types of chassis were manufactured, both for rear motors: K chassis, with straight-mounted engines, and N chassis, with transverse-mounted engines (city bus chassis). The variant spread was great and had increased sharply during the 1980s on account of the introduction of a series of new chassis for double buses and buses with

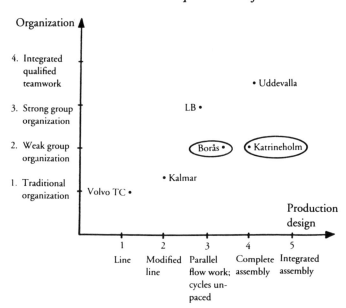

FIGURE 6-1. Production Design and Work Organization of Borås and Katrineholm

trailing axle bogies, computer-controlled transmissions, antilock brakes (ABS), and electronically controlled brakes. In addition, a growing number of chassis were being built according to special designs tailored to individual customer requests.

The total direct-assembly work for a single chassis took about fifty hours, of which twenty were spent in final assembly (in the chassis flows, that is).

1981: The Big Step

For several decades, Scania manufactured buses in direct association with its production of trucks in Södertälje. In 1969, however, bus production was moved to Katrineholm, where bus and chassis production was carried out in a common workshop until 1981. The chassis were assembled on two unpaced lines.

During the 1970s, problems mounted at this facility. A growing variant mix increased the IE losses, and the feedback from adjustment and inspection to assembly functioned in an unsatisfactory manner, which created quality problems. The work cycles were long—about 1.5 hours—compared with car manufacturing. Nonetheless, chassis assembly had a paced character, a bad reputation, and a high turnover. By contrast, bus manufacturing enjoyed a better status. It was characterized by low volume, an older work crew, and craft-type work with high piece-rate earnings.

Scania started a new chassis workshop in 1981. The assembly was done in three unpaced flows, in which the chassis were moved on air-cushion platforms through five steps to a common start station. Bus manufacturing as well as rolling tests, adjustment, and customer-ordered additions for both chassis and complete buses were done in the older shop (see fig. 6-2).

At each flow, there was a work team with a common piece rate. Within this team, the assemblers strove for "complete competence"—building the entire chassis. This approach worked well during the breaking-in phase, during which no time demands were applied. But there was reason to believe it would be difficult for the assemblers to master more than a couple of stations as the performance demands grew more severe. According to the shop management, in 1982 it took about three months for a group to come up to full pace and at least a year longer for it to learn all the stations.

A team piece rate had long been applied in assembly at Scania. At the new shop, the rates were extended to embrace more tasks. Thus, the workers at the last assembly station would follow the chassis out to the start station, fill it with oil, and so on and do various adjustments. The object was to improve the feedback from adjustment and inspection that had been lacking in the former shop. The assembly workers were also assigned, in exchange for a wage increment, responsibility for quality, which meant that, after his station, each worker would inspect his work and sign a check list. The company also established leading hand positions in two of the chassis flows. In the city bus group (N chassis), however, the group itself attended to administrative responsibilities.

The changes that occurred at Scania in the form and content of the work can be summarized as follows:

The work content was enlarged significantly. Station times were lengthened (to two to four hours), and the assemblers sought to learn how to build the entire chassis ("complete competence").

Quality control was incorporated directly in the flows, eliminating the need for adjustment and control stations in the assembly shop.

There was a conspicuous improvement in the level of cooperation between workers in the flows.

There was increased participation in IE work. The assignment of tasks within the teams was managed in large measure by the assemblers themselves.

There was a kind of experimental self-management in one of the flows.

The breaking-in phase was carried out by experienced assemblers during a period of low volume. One question was how well the new system would be able to handle higher production pressure. Another was whether it could cope with

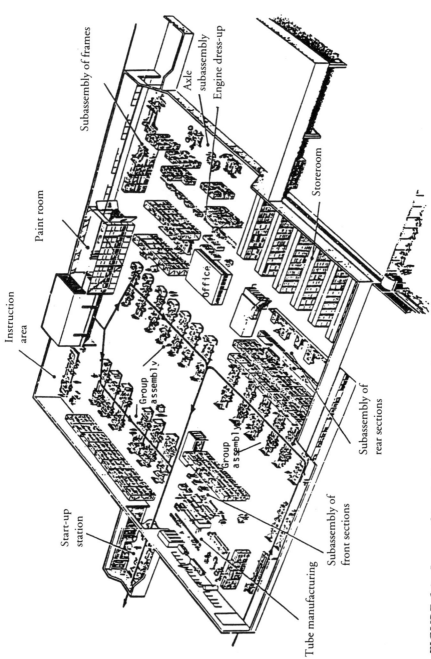

Instruction area

Start-up station

Tube manufacturing

Subassembly of front sections

Group assembly

Group assembly

Subassembly of rear sections

Office

Paint room

Subassembly of frames

Axle subassembly

Engine dress-up

Storeroom

FIGURE 6-2. Layout of Scania Bus Plant at Katrineholm

personnel turnover and the training of new workers. These questions would be answered in a new investigation five years later.

1987: The Chassis Shop Revisited

By 1987, capacity utilization had been very high for a year, which had necessitated hiring a large number of new employees. In 1982, the chassis shop employed 70 persons; in 1987, the figure was 130 (excluding adjustment). In addition, the product variation had increased greatly, putting the shop's flexibility and competence to a test.

The shop passed the test very well indeed. As in 1982, the chassis were assembled in three unpaced flows, in five steps. But at that time, the goal of reaching complete competence had not been tried at full pace. From the start, some of the assemblers had been skeptical of this way of working since they did not want to be on training pay but wanted to earn the full piece rate as soon as possible. The shop management and the union together urged that all the assemblers try the new work forms, however, and by 1987 they were the obvious routine. In each flow, two assemblers built the entire chassis together, by following it from the first station all the way through to the start station. The total cycle times were therefore long—ten to twelve hours.

When a large group of new employees was hired in 1986, experienced workers operated two of the flows, while the new arrivals worked, under the guidance of "godfathers," at a more relaxed pace in the third flow. This way of training new workers functioned very well, in the view of the shop manager.

Productivity had increased significantly. Thus, there was no longer any need for a separate staff to assist in the assembly of particularly complex chassis.

Opinions were divided, however, over whether the new production arrangement and work forms had truly brought about an assembly without any efficiency losses as defined by IE analysis. A team leader said in an interview that variant losses remained—even if the company did not pay for them—since assembly still took place in series-dependent flows (in contrast to pure dock assembly). But the industrial engineers maintained that variant losses had in practice been eliminated. As proof, they pointed to the assemblers' versatile skills and prospects for cooperation and to the fact that many operations were not station-bound but rather could be moved in case of need. Flexibility had increased, in general, and it was much easier than before to cope with swings in volume and staff; for instance, it was possible to make productive use of "overattendance."

The work was much more integrated with the new assembly system than it was before. The teams not only did complete assembly (including quality control), but they also balanced and distributed work within their teams. The work arrangement, in which pairs of workers followed the chassis, made it easy to cope with absenteeism. For example, if a worker was absent, his partner stayed at the first work station the whole day, while the other pairs followed the chassis through the other stations and in case of need assisted at the first work station as well. If two assemblers were gone, the other pairs worked precisely as they would have in the case of full attendance, the only consequence being that production fell in proportion to the degree of absenteeism. In the line assembly of the 1970s, it was often difficult to get production going in the morning because all stations had to be staffed before anything could be done. These difficulties largely disappeared in the 1980s.

In summary, then, the shop had established resistant work patterns characterized by a low sensitivity to disturbances. As the head of the shop emphasized, this made for simple control, without the need for reserves. It also made high-quality assembly possible, as one assembly worker testified: "By following the chassis, you can correct things that went wrong yourself. If you miss a console or install it wrong at the first station [a critical operation for the continued assembly], you can correct it at the next station. If you forgot a PVC hose you can cut open a clamp, install the missing hose, and clamp the bundle together again."

With a work pace of one chassis per day and pair, it was easy for the assemblers to get an overview of the workday and, with the help of the order chart (the "pick chart"), the workweek as well. Thus, despite the profusion of variants, by the standards of assembly work at least, the workers were provided with an unusually good overview of planning.

Compared with work on the old line, the jobs in final assembly now enjoyed a much better reputation. The work was brisk and varied, and the physical burdens were relatively tolerable, despite the weight of some of the components. At the old chassis shop, personnel turnover had been high, and the jobs in bus manufacturing had been more highly regarded and better paying. This was no longer the case in 1987. Turnover was now very low; the majority of those in the chassis flows had worked in the shop longer than five years. This was an unusually high figure for a Swedish assembly plant during the 1980s. When new jobs had arisen in other parts of the factory in connection with the big upswing in production in 1986, only a few workers had left chassis assembly. Moreover, the rate of unemployment in Katrineholm had been low throughout the 1980s; thus, the stability was not the result of a lack of alternative industrial jobs with comparable pay.

Ambiguities of the Change

The development of the new work forms and content at Katrineholm was considerable. Yet the new assembly design was not part of a larger organizational transformation. This resulted in limitations in four critical areas: skill policy; the relation between assembly, IE, and product engineering; the teams' administrative autonomy; and the wage system.

The new work mode involved extensive on-the-job training of new hirees, most of whom had a technical education. Otherwise, the company made no special efforts to develop the workers' technical skills and theoretical understanding of the products, despite the significance of quality awareness in the chassis flows. Nor did the company try in any systematic way to make use of the assemblers' competence outside production, by encouraging broad collaboration in product preparation between assemblers, industrial engineers, and designers. In an opinion survey conducted in 1987, the experienced assemblers expressed strong interest in taking part in the preparation of new products, which were introduced into the shop in quick succession. The established routines, however, left little room for meeting these wishes. The most significant design changes were examined in the development workshop by the chassis shop manager, the industrial engineers, and the leading hands. The leading hands built a trial chassis, using the new design, together with engineers and sometimes with the assistance of selected assemblers. Broad forms of cooperation—in which, for instance, whole teams of experienced assemblers work through new designs—were not to be found. The lack of prospects for influencing the design of new vehicles was a source of considerable dissatisfaction among the experienced assemblers, who considered themselves capable of preventing many production problems.

In 1982, many of the pioneers of the new shop had aspired to combine the more qualified work content with new organizational forms, especially in the assembly of the so-called N chassis. But the company had no such plans. Self-management was never integrated into a larger organizational transformation. It was more a "local deviation" that depended on there being strong leaders in the team. When these leaders moved on to other jobs, the system of self-management withered.

The union club strove during the 1980s to extend team work to the entire plant and urged its coupling with enhanced decision-making prerogatives and the abolition of traditional first-line management. In several cases, the club took its opposition to the appointment of foremen all the way to the level of central negotiating between the Metal Workers' Union and the Engineering Industry Employers, but without success.

The dominant form of control at the Katrineholm factory, outside the chassis shop, was focused on individual work operations, rather than on the rationalization of the production flow as a whole. One of the consequences was that a high proportion of capital was tied up in inventory. The rate of materials turnover was just four to five times per year in 1987.[1] The wage system did not encourage a higher rate of turnover, as it could have, for instance, by awarding premiums for delivery precision or for zero-defect chassis.

Despite the new work forms in chassis assembly, a traditional piece rate calculated on worker-time was applied, based on a unit price per chassis. This wage system was a simple means of performance control, but it produced problems in other areas. According to the club chairman, for instance, it created conflicts between the assemblers and the industrial engineers. The emphasis on capital rationalization and more rapid materials turnover increased significantly at the end of the 1980s. It was not, however, coupled with any change in the wage system.

Summary

At the start of the 1980s, Scania Katrineholm took a big step away from line assembly and Taylorized production toward complete assembly with long cycle times and much higher skill demands. Between 1982 and 1987, the plant proved that this arrangement was viable by coping successfully with both record-high capacity utilization and a heavy influx of new employees. Compared with the earlier line assembly, the new structure had great advantages in terms of productivity, flexibility, and capacity to cope with disturbances. Moreover, working conditions and the reputation of assembly jobs had markedly improved.

The horizontal division of labor had also been diminished greatly. But the vertical hierarchy, the functional specialization, and the wage system stayed much the same. The union club pressed for decentralization of responsibilities and granting decision-making prerogatives to the work teams. The company maintained a reserved attitude, however. The seeds of self-management that had existed in 1982 did not survive. Yet, from the larger perspective of the Katrineholm plant, the jobs in the chassis shop had come a long way indeed. In 1987, therefore, both the company and the club concentrated their efforts on other areas, such as establishing flow groups in component production.

Volvo Borås

Borås is the main site for Volvo's bus chassis manufacturing operation, while product development is done in Gothenburg.[2] In contrast to Katrineholm, no body work was done in Borås.

In 1987, the plant's 300 employees (of whom 60 were white collar) produced about three thousand chassis. Assembly had 140 workers in all: 60 in subassembly, 50 in chassis assembly (in four parallel docks), and 30 in the adjustment and equipment shop.

Borås manufactured the mid-motor chassis B10M, which accounted for 80 percent of volume, and front- and rear-motor chassis as well. The product variation was great. Forty percent of the units were manufactured on the basis of "market-adapted" designs drawn to match a particular customer's specifications. The total direct work required for a simple chassis, leaving out painting and materials handling, was about sixty hours. Of this, thirty hours were accounted for by subassembly and twenty by chassis assembly. The total demand for assembly knowledge in a chassis dock team (expressed in quantitative terms) was forty to forty-five hours because of the variant spread; the rate of increase was about 10 percent per year.

As in Katrineholm, chassis assembly (the docks) was the focus of my interest. It was in this part of assembly that the changes were greatest, and it was the most critical sector besides (in the view of the head of engineering): "It is there we measure, it is there the number of variants is greatest, it is there the risk for disturbances is greatest."

A Rocky Start

Until 1976, Volvo had assembled its bus chassis at the truck assembly plant in Gothenburg, on an intermittently paced mechanical line. The station times were comparatively long—fifty-three minutes—on account of the low production volume.

In 1977, bus chassis manufacturing was moved to a new factory in Borås. In contrast to Katrineholm, where Scania had been operating long before chassis assembly was transferred there, Borås was a greenfield site. The assembly configuration in Borås was inspired by the dock system Volvo Trucks operated at Arendal in the mid-1970s. (This is discussed further in chapter 7.)

A fundamental requirement in the planning of the Borås facility was that the plant not be based on a traditional line. Chassis assembly was therefore organized in four parallel docks, with subsequent stations for inspection, adjustment, and test driving (see fig. 6-3). This was not pure dock construction, however, which assumes stationary assembly; rather, each dock consisted of three steps. In practice, therefore, assembly took place in short parallel flows, just as at Katrineholm. The assemblers moved the chassis on air-cushion platforms. The division into several parallel flows had the consequence of lengthening the cycle times from one hour to between two and four (depending on variants and production pace).

Work was organized in teams, in a total of seventeen team areas. A "typical" work team at each dock could have the following structure: eight assemblers, one replacement, one adjuster, and one coordinator. The idea at the start was that the role of coordinator would be rotated among the workers, but this never happened. Instead, the coordinators became permanent team leaders, whose duties were to report times, check payments, maintain contacts with other sections, manage rebalancings (redistribution of assembly tasks because of changes in volume on the introduction of new product features), and train new employees.

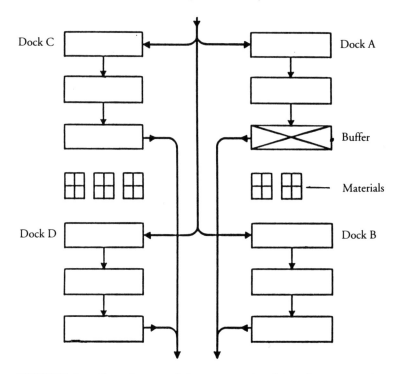

Dock C

Dock A

Buffer

Materials

Dock D

Dock B

FIGURE 6-3. *Basic Layout of the Four Docks of the Chassis-Assembly Operation at Borås*

The plant's breaking-in phase was very difficult. Yet as early as 1979, an economic assessment of Borås indicated a marked improvement in productivity (Eckerström and Södahl 1980). IE losses at the old line in Gothenburg had been heavy—36 percent, in the form of balancing losses, variant losses, and disturbances. The figure at Borås was a mere 10 percent. This represented a personnel rationalization of more than 20 percent.

Four years after the start, in 1981, both levels of productivity and quality were high, and there was a significant amount of flexibility. The system of four parallel flows meant that a special variant needed to take up only one-fourth of the chassis assembly, and it also facilitated rapid rebalancing. Earlier, the industrial engineers had had to do an individual balance for every assembly worker. Now, they needed only to specify a total time per vehicle; the work teams then decided how to distribute this total within their own ranks.

The changes in working conditions were more ambiguous. Opportunities for the assemblers in each team to push common demands had increased as a result of the new work organization, and the work content was richer and more varied than on the old line. Yet, as in the line system, each assembler worked on his own balance. There were no plans to have the workers follow the chassis through the docks, as was done in Katrineholm. In addition, the new dock assembly entailed heavy work loads. In interviews in 1982, the assemblers emphasized three problems: (1) The intensity of the work, which was much greater than in line assembly since there were no balancing losses. (2) The stressful interdependencies within the docks. The absence of buffers in the flow (except in Dock A) meant the three chassis in the dock had to be moved simultaneously. Accordingly, the assemblers had to coordinate their efforts fully, which entailed severe time control. (3) A lack of cooperation and collaboration in the teams. Those who fell behind got no support from the others. One of the coordinators stressed that in large part this was a consequence of the pace: "It makes for stress; everybody pushes everybody else, because everything has to be done at the same time. Slow workers get sneered at. If the pace were slower, it'd be possible for us to help each other. As it is now, everyone works individually."

Because of these problems, chassis assembly at Borås was the least attractive work in the plant, as line assembly always had been in traditional plants. The shop manager doubted the staying power and stability of the system of dock assembly:

> When all stations are manned, this system works better than others; it makes for high quality and short lead times. However, it is highly sensitive to staff disturbances, because of the long station times and the variant spread. When workers are absent, it's hard to put adjusters in the assembly or use substitutes from one dock in another. And it will be a big problem if we have a heavy staff turnover.

The training time for an assembler was calculated at three to four months. If half the workers in a dock were replaced, it would take a year for the situation to stabilize, in the estimation of the shop manager: "No stabilization of personnel in the docks has occurred as yet. When the labor market improves, personnel turnover will increase. The inherent sensitivity of the system will be thereby revealed."

1987: Efficiency Proven

Between 1982 and 1987, both the volume and the number of employees increased by about 20 percent. Product variation increased markedly as well. Together, these changes put the production system under increasing strain. Contrary to fears, however, the personnel situation stabilized noticeably, so that from 1982 to 1986, the annual labor turnover was just 3 to 7 percent. Internal mobility in chassis assembly was high, however. When the central warehouse was transferred to Borås in 1986 and a number of new positions were opened up in the plant, nearly half the dock workers applied for the new jobs. This was the trial by fire the head of the shop had feared. Fortunately, his fears were not realized. The shift took less than half a year to stabilize, and the quality index stayed at a high level the entire time. An important condition for this stability, however, was that the turnover was internal. Those who took new jobs outside the docks had to stay in dock assembly while they trained new employees; only after this was done could they assume their new positions.

The stabilization of personnel and the continued streamlining of production meant that, between 1982 and 1987, Borås could persistently maintain good performance in several important areas. The quality level was high and very stable; moreover, it was achieved, to an increasing degree, by building right from the beginning. Adjustment times fell, despite the rapidly growing complexity of production, and in 1987, a new system was introduced for measuring the proportion of "zero-defect vehicles." This referred to those chassis that were ready for delivery immediately after test driving. The proportion was still low in the first year—5 to 6 percent on average—principally because of shortages of materials, which meant that the chassis had to be sent to the equipment shop after test driving.

A high rate of capital tied up in inventory was the only negative feature in the economic assessment of 1979. Since that time, capital rationalization has been intensive. A big step was taken when central responsibility for all bus parts was shifted from the truck division in Gothenburg to the plant in Borås. Traditional arguments of scale—volume and specialist competence—supported joint storage of parts for the trucks and buses. At the same time, unified responsibility for one's product—from supplier to customer—spoke for the transfer to Borås.

The advantages of integration predominated and soon revealed their practical value. So-called synchronized control of materials was introduced, resulting in much more frequent deliveries from the twenty biggest suppliers, many of them German. The high-quality work in assembly and the increasing share of chassis also contributed to reducing the rate of capital tied up in inventory, as did the introduction of delivery precision (calculated as the share of vehicles delivered during the right week) as a control instrument. The rate of materials turnover grew from eight to nine times per year in the early 1980s to twenty times per year in 1987.

A broader approach to rationalization was reflected in the wage system. During the plant's first years, the assembly workers were paid on the basis of an MTM piece rate. (MTM is a method of analyzing repetitive work before it is actually performed.) By the 1980s, however, because of the increased significance of quality and of capital tied up in inventory, bonuses were introduced for productivity (number of chassis per worker and year), quality, share of immediately OK vehicles, and delivery precision.

Continued Development of the Technical Design

When the factory was being planned, little attention was devoted to subassembly, which was organized altogether conventionally. Accordingly, engine dress up was arranged in a four-station unpaced line. This arrangement led, with the increasing variant spread, to numerous disturbances in relation to the docks. Thus, in 1985, the engine line was replaced by four parallel assembly areas and a common materials store. The work cycles were two to three hours.

This arrangement was much more flexible than the preceding one, and it facilitated the rapid production of engines for which the need was particularly pressing. In addition, the design yielded great advantages in the area of training. New employees were granted the possibility of working at their own pace, without being dependent on or disturbing coworkers. They could begin with the simplest engines and then move on to successively more complicated tasks. Further, the work patterns were robust. If a worker was sick, it did not affect the others. In the view of the team coordinator, there was "a difference of night and day" between the old system and the new: "The engine station is now the best job in the section. It was pure trash before. Compared with the docks, it's easier to make the quota for the piece rate. We help each other more, too."

In chassis assembly, the industrial engineers strove to reduce the burdensome dependence in the docks by changing from three to two assembly steps. This required a transfer of work to the predock stations. With just two assembly steps, there would be a space in the docks that could be used either as a buffer for coping with variant spreads or for inspection and adjustment. These alternatives were tried in 1987.

Development of the Work Organization

At the same time as the industrial engineers were trying to make the technical design more flexible, the company was seeking a more integrated work organization. These changes were limited mainly to horizontal development, however. Accordingly, materials handling was integrated with assembly. This meant the assembly teams were assigned full- or part-time positions in materials handling. In the chassis docks, these were fixed positions; in other teams, these roles were rotated among the members. With such integrated work methods, the company successfully coped with the stringent demands on materials handling, which were a consequence of the reduced time margins allowed by the system of synchronized control.

Another step toward more integrated organization was taken with the introduction of "intact teams" in dock assembly in 1987. From then on, instead of maintaining a fixed pace, teams distributed tasks and chose the pace of work according to how many workers were present. The teams would always consist of the same people; no one was added temporarily in cases of absenteeism. The company's objective was to reduce sensitivity to disturbances and to increase reliability.

A condition for intact teams was that every worker had to master work stations other than his normal station, since in cases of lower attendance he might need to do some work at the stations before or after his own. The point of departure was thus a work arrangement that was strictly divided into stations. And, in contrast to the robust pattern of engine assembly, the use of intact teams entailed frequent rebalancings.

In 1987, dock assemblers also began discussing the possibility of following the chassis (as in Katrineholm), and the foreman supported the idea. The production director did not consider the idea realistic, however, because of the long training times that would result.

In 1984–85, negotiations had been conducted between the company and the union club regarding the delegation of administrative responsibility to the teams. The idea, which was to be coupled to a new wage system, was to pay the teams for such tasks as scheduling, task allocation, participation in planning groups, inspection and quality reporting, the handling of altered orders, and budget assistance. This system was tested in one team. The parties never reached an agreement about the wage system, however, so the test was discontinued, just as a similar project had been in 1982. The company wanted to count downward from the existing wage level—that is, to change part of the wage into a bonus. The union club considered it appropriate to calculate upward instead—that is, to add the bonus to the existing wage. It appears the incentive to change was not so strong on the company side. If it had been, the test would not have come undone over the pay issue. One of the reasons for discontinuing the test, according to the production manager, was that the teams already had so much responsibility.

As the assemblers pointed out, this was a big difference from a traditional plant: "Here you decide things for yourself far more than at any other workplace. We don't see the foreman so much. It's enough to talk to the coordinator about taking a leave and such."

Instead of delegating prerogatives to the team as a collective, the company concentrated on strengthening the position of the coordinator and integrating him into the organizational hierarchy. Accordingly, the dock assembly foreman emphasized: "The coordinator should be my man. If I don't believe in a guy in the team [as a coordinator], I go in and select another. The guys can be surprised at first, but usually not for long." Both assemblers and coordinators, however, saw the coordinator first and foremost as a member of the team, and this made the role contradictory.

The company's focus on "horizontal transformation" was combined with an investment in "horizontal competence development." The individual skill rates introduced in 1986 were based only on assembly skills. This meant, in principle, that each worker would receive extra pay for learning how to perform different assembly tasks and would earn the maximum pay if he or she mastered the entire work task of the team (which corresponded to more than twenty hours' work content in chassis assembly).

Working Conditions

Despite the considerable improvements in the levels of competence and co-operation within the teams, dock assembly in 1987 was still the least attractive work in the factory. One coordinator, who had been employed at the plant since it opened, summarized the reasons the work was so unattractive: "The foreman makes a hassle about the times, for rests and such. The coordinator makes a hassle about moving the chassis at the right moment. The inspector makes a hassle about mistakes. Taken together, it makes for heavy pressure on the assembly workers."

The pressure was caused by the process of wage setting and performance control or, to use the terms of German industrial sociology, the relation between *Lohn und Leistung*. Despite the new features in the wage system, such as the qualification bonuses, the control system was still based on MTM piece rates. These had created great dissatisfaction in assembly in 1982 and in 1987 as well. The demand for an MTM performance level of 115 was considered severe by both the assemblers and the foremen.

To maintain the necessary low level of balancing losses required much more intensive work than on a traditional line. In addition, the variant spread in the docks was great, which produced constant shifts in work assignments between the steps in the docks. The variant spread also made it hard for the assemblers to develop quick and smooth ways of building a certain type of chassis. In subassembly work, which had more standardized jobs, such as axle assembly, the demand for an MTM of 115 was much easier to satisfy. These workers could earn more than the chassis workers while working less hard.

The MTM method assumes that production is standardized and well prepared. In Borås, however, the share of chassis without detailed production preparation increased. For example, the IE department often did not have the time to build a production prototype of the so-called market-adapted vehicles. A foreman in dock assembly, interviewed in 1987, summed up the situation: "It's a tough job, it's hard to find better methods when there's so much new. Lots of workers just fall into bed when they get home. Dock assembly is the toughest job in the whole factory—but even so it's not paid extra."

To summarize, the wage system in the docks was a mismatch between, on the one hand, a performance-control system rooted in the logic of standardized mass production and, on the other, a production design and product flora that increasingly departed from that logic. Why, then, did the company persist with this system? It appears above all to have been a question of managerial control, as so often is the case in labor-intensive production: the toughly applied piece rate had replaced the line as an instrument of control.

The focus of the wage system on performance control made cooperation between engineers and assemblers in developing work methods and preparing new vehicles more difficult, precisely when this had become increasingly critical. In the words of the club chairman:

> There are such big differences in judgment between the industrial engineers and the [assembly] guys about how long it takes to do different things, and when disturbances occur you have to turn in piece-rate notices [specifying the reasons for the problems and the failure to attain normal production quotas], which always leads to the same nagging. . . . There are a lot of guys in the docks, and there can be hot-headed discussions with all those people. It's happened that both paper and other things have been snatched out of the industrial engineers' hands.

Summary

When the Borås plant began operating in 1977, its parallelized production design and team organization were controversial innovations. By 1982, productivity and quality had reached a high level, but there were serious questions about the plant's stability. Did the long cycle time mean that things had "gone too far" and that it would be impossible to manage higher personnel turnover? The experiences in 1986 showed that this was not the case; although turnover was high that year, the chassis docks continued to deliver consistently high quality.

There were also questions in 1982 concerning the limitations in the plant, such as the stressful sequence dependencies in chassis assembly, the fragmented work organization (the team principle notwithstanding), and the lack of fit between the method of performance control and the new principles of production. Between 1982 and 1987, the production design was modified to allow greater technical autonomy and flexibility, two-step assembly was tried out in the docks, and the system of engine assembly was changed from line to complete assembly. The horizontal division of labor was reduced. Finally, materials handling was integrated with assembly (this had been a goal in 1982 but had not been considered practical).

The vertical division of labor and the distribution of decision-making powers were not changed, however, notwithstanding negotiations and discussions between the company and the union on several occasions. Capital tied up in inventory and quality were taken account of in the wage system, but the performance control in assembly was the same as in 1982; thus, an MTM piece-rate system was used that had no direct connection to production targets. The company's motive for retaining this system was that, despite its drawbacks, it "has given a reliable output" (just as line assembly had done).

Achievements and Limitations: Borås versus Katrineholm

The long-cycle, parallelized assembly at Scania in Katrineholm and at Volvo in Borås represents a radical contrast to car production in both its Fordist and "lean" forms. Both Volvo and Scania had produced chassis on traditional lines during the 1960s and 1970s, but because of the low volume, the work was less repetitive than in car manufacturing. Moreover, Scania never introduced the MTM method.

Both manufacturers experienced great demands for change during the 1970s. The growing product variation became ever harder to handle, and there was strong dissatisfaction among workers in line assembly, especially at Katrineholm. Both manufacturers also expanded extensively during that decade. The need for increased capacity was the factor that triggered the introduction of new production designs and organizational forms. The most radical change took place at Scania, where assemblers acquired "complete competence" by following the chassis through the entire flow and building complete objects. This also made it possible to integrate inspection duties with assembly.

In the beginning, many managers doubted the new plants' stability and capacity to cope with future staff turnover. The performance during the 1980s put these doubts to rest. Both plants proved themselves capable of excellent economic performance, even in the midst of personnel changes produced by the rise in volume.

The new forms of production embodied an advance chiefly on the horizontal level. First-line management and IE continued in rather traditional forms, and performance controls were based on a quantity-oriented piece-rate system. This supplied management with a simple control instrument to replace the line's mechanical pacing; however, it also rendered more difficult extensive cooperation between engineers and assemblers in the preparation of new products. Such cooperation is potentially of great significance for low-volume manufacturers without large technical staffs.

At Katrineholm, the production arrangement and work forms in chassis assembly made possible a stable staff with considerable productive skills. Yet the company felt no impetus toward continued "vertical" development, precisely because the situation regarding production and personnel had become so much better. Such a change would have required restructuring of the large organization and of the wage system and training policy as well.[3] There was no tradition favoring such innovations in Scania's conservative company culture, and there were no examples to point to.

At the Borås plant, by contrast, company-union negotiations took place on several occasions regarding delegating increased responsibility to the teams and instituting a new wage system to match. But these negotiations produced no results. As at Katrineholm, the fact that much had already been achieved worked as a brake on continued progress.

Despite the many similarities, working conditions in chassis assembly at Volvo's and Scania's bus factories also differed in important respects. For instance, the structure of the performance measuring system was very different in the two plants. At Scania, teams were paid a straightforward price for each chassis. At Borås, the performance measuring system was based, in classical mass-production fashion, on MTM. The latter system made for great strains, in view of the profusion of variants and the large share of products that were not prepared in detail before assembly. These strains had no counterpart at Katrineholm.

Another critical difference was the work pattern in assembly: at Borås, workers were divided into stations with fixed balances; at Katrineholm, workers had overall responsibility for complete assembly. The latter arrangement produced more robust patterns of collaboration, higher skill requirements, and more varied physical activity. As a result, workers at Katrineholm evaluated chassis assembly far more favorably than did workers at Borås, and the former shop had an exceedingly high level of stability among its personnel.

7.
Pioneers in Car and Truck Assembly: Volvo Kalmar and Volvo LB

This chapter focuses on two pioneers of the 1970s and early 1980s. The first pioneer I consider is Volvo's Kalmar plant, whose innovations set in motion the Volvo trajectory of sociotechnical design. This account covers the period between 1974, when the factory opened, and 1985, when the next major innovation within Volvo Cars—the Uddevalla project—began.

The second pioneer I consider is Volvo Trucks' LB factory for heavy-chassis assembly. During the 1980s, this plant developed an organizational concept founded on group organization and a high degree of delegation and collective assumption of responsibility. For much of the 1980s, it was the model of the new organization of work within Volvo.

LB is also one of the factories examined in chapters 11 and 12, in regard to both the effects of production design on working conditions and the significance of group organization on workers' prospects for exercising power and influence. This chapter describes the development of the LB factory from the initial planning stages at the close of the 1970s to the situation in 1990. By the latter date, a certain organizational retreat had occurred in the main plant, while a new operation carried the innovation process further (introducing whole-vehicle construction in a system of integrated assembly). The case of LB illuminates both the tensions in the organizational transformation of assembly work and the contradictory effects of "flexible specialization." (The production design and work organization of the two plants are shown in figure 7-1.)

Volvo Kalmar

The Volvo factory VKAV in Kalmar is a small auto-assembly plant by international standards. Since the mid-1980s, it has specialized in Volvo's top-of-the-

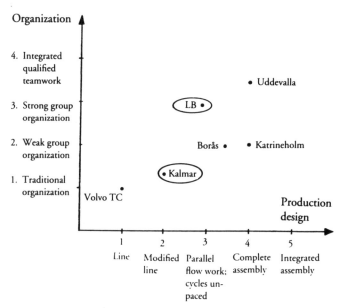

FIGURE 7-1. Production Design and Work Organization of LB and Kalmar

line models, the 760, and, since 1990, the 960. The factory's capacity is about thirty thousand cars per year, which are produced during one shift. Production in the mid-1980s was about thirty-three thousand cars. At that time, the plant had 850 employees (80 white collar and 770 blue collar), 475 of whom worked in assembly, 60 in materials handling, and 160 in adjustment, inspection, and revision.

The significance of the plant has been far greater than its physical size. When the plant opened in 1974, it was a true pathbreaker—"the world's first auto assembly plant without mechanically driven assembly lines."[1]

Planning and Design

Volvo at Kalmar was conceived as the answer to the severe personnel problem plaguing the auto industry at the start of the 1970s, when turnover rates of 100 percent and higher were not uncommon. The goal of being an innovator was not obvious from the outset, however. In fact, the engineers began to design a traditional auto factory. It was only after top management intervened that efforts were directed to designing an original plant. In this respect, there is a striking parallel between this plant and the Uddevalla factory, described in chapter 8. In contrast to Uddevalla however, Kalmar was, as Jonas Pontusson has correctly pointed out (1990:315), almost completely a product of management thinking. In no way did the unions influence or even participate in the decisions pertaining to its design and technology. In the early 1970s, such issues had not entered the union agenda.

The most striking manifestation of Kalmar's "different character" was the design of its building, which captured the imagination of industrial architects throughout the world (see, for example, Törnqvist and Ullmark 1989:119). One of the central ideas was that the building's construction should facilitate working in teams. The Kalmar plant was thus designed to have many walls and corners so that each team could work close to outer windows and have its own lounge. This solution contributed as well to creating a better physical environment; rooms were bright and airy, and the noise level was generally low.

A precondition for such a construction—distinct as it was from the traditional way of building plants as big warehouses—was a transport system that was more flexible than a mechanical conveyor belt. Here—in the battery-powered, automatically guided vehicles (AGVs or "carriers") and the production layout—lay Kalmar's greatest technical innovation. The carriers were arranged in a series-connected main flow through the factory, but this flow was divided (with the help of buffers) into twenty work areas, or teams, with fifteen to twenty assemblers in each. Thanks to the buffers, the teams enjoyed temporal autonomy from each other. The carriers were not controlled by the assembly teams, however, but rather by a central computer that automatically transferred one AGV to the next station as soon as the *takt* time (three to four minutes) was up (see fig. 7-2).

When the factory began operations, one of the central ideas was that it should be possible in certain areas for a team to perform its entire assembly on stationary carriers, in so-called docks. Instead of four to five stations in succession within the team area, there would be four to five parallel stations. An important restriction, however, was that the sequence had to be maintained—the AGVs had to leave the area in the same order that they came in.

A further goal of the factory was to improve assembly ergonomics. The AGVs were therefore equipped with a tilting contrivance—that is, the car body could be rotated by 90 degrees, which is still very rare in the international auto industry. After the marriage stations (where the body and the motor were "wedded"), tilting was no longer considered practicable; the AGVs were thereafter furnished with columns that enabled those working on the underbody to adjust their work level.

The novelties in the design of the building and in the production flow became the basis for a series of other features of the plant: the team culture, extensive prospects for job rotation, and the functional assembly (in principle, each team was responsible for a clearly demarcated function, such as the dashboard). Together, these features expressed the core idea of the project: efficient production by motivated, capable co-workers. In the words of the head of the company, Gyllenhammar:

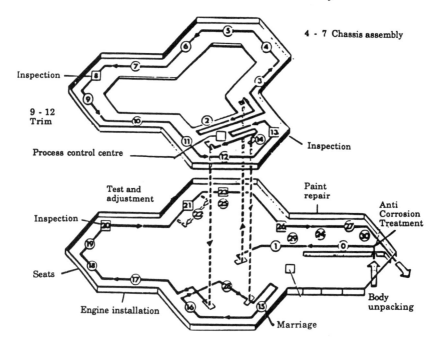

FIGURE 7-2. *Layout of Volvo's Two-Story Factory at Kalmar*

The objective at Kalmar will be to arrange auto production in such a way that each employee will be able to find meaning and satisfaction in his work. This will be a factory which, without any sacrifice of efficiency or the company's financial objectives, will give employees opportunities to work in groups, to communicate freely among themselves, to switch from one job assignment to another, to vary their work pace, to identify with the product, to be conscious of a responsibility for quality, and to influence their own working environment. When a product is made by people who find meaning in their work, it must inevitably be a product of high quality (quoted in Agurén, Hansson, and Karlsson 1976:5).

Crisis and Intensive Rationalization

By 1976, the factory had been broken in, and SAF's and LO's joint Rationalization Council carried out an official evaluation. The report emphasized that the assembly workers appreciated the team-based work organization and the possibility of varying the work pace and considered the physical work environment to be good in most respects. The plant had not achieved any exceptional level of efficiency, however. Both direct and indirect time per vehicle were the same as in Gothenburg, while investment costs had been higher than for a conventional plant. Moreover, adjustment work was as extensive in Kalmar as at the TC plant in Torslanda, Gothenburg.

In 1977, one year after this evaluation, Swedish auto production suffered a powerful setback. Kalmar's production fell to seventeen thousand cars, nearly half its capacity. In the interests of survival, a sharp rationalization of direct labor hours was introduced. All assembly stations were analyzed with the help of a new balancing system, the so-called MOST system. Using this system, the company was able to squeeze nearly all the idle time out of the work cycles. Further, quality was made a top priority. By introducing inspection and adjustment stations into the team areas, it was possible to follow up each assembler's work. As part of this process, the managerial structure—in which the foreman was in the center—was strengthened, and each foreman got clearly defined goals for personnel, materials, quality (with zero defects being the object), quantity, hours per car, and other costs. "The foreman is measured in length and breadth," in the words of the head of production. Moreover, in 1980, the company introduced a results-based wage for all employees. Bonuses were based on assembly hours per car, scrapping and adjustment, consumed materials and tools, inventory level, and a quality index.

At the same time, monitoring and control of the production flow were intensified. A special control center was established in 1977. Earlier, the work teams had been able, via a terminal in their work areas, to change the pace at which the AGVs were transferred from one area to another. The company considered that this led to "mischief"; for example, "for fun," a team would change the pace for another. This prerogative was therefore removed from the work teams and lodged exclusively in the control center. No AGV could be kept in one place, or removed from the flow, without the control center's approval. The central computer checked the status of the AGVs every five seconds. As soon as any AGV had stayed at a station beyond the allotted time (e.g., three minutes), this was registered on one of the screens at the control center. A "time-out" message was printed, and the control center alerted a team leader or foreman in the work area, via a staff locator.

Kalmar in 1984

Ten years after the factory opened, it was time for the next official evaluation. This time, Kalmar's economic results were much better. Assembly hours per car were 25 percent lower than in Torslanda (a differential that has since persisted), quality was high, and overhead costs were very competitive.

There were three explanations for this improvement in efficiency. First, Kalmar, a small and exposed unit at the margins of Volvo Cars, was able to carry out a considerably tougher rationalization program than was possible in Gothenburg. When the new system for balancing the assembly tasks (the MOST system) was

introduced, the company was able to reduce the assembly time per car by about
1.5 hours. In Gothenburg, by contrast, the trade union local had rejected this
system.

Second, the more elastic technical system was used to raise work intensity,
reduce the consequences of mistakes, and achieve a high degree of efficiency. In
1985, assembly workers at Kalmar were productively occupied 95 percent of the
time, compared to 80 percent at Torslanda. One reason was the MOST balancing
system. Another was the longer work cycles at Kalmar (the assemblers usually
kept pace with the car for four to five stations, reducing the balancing losses
considerably). The carrier system also made it possible to introduce inspection
and adjustment stations into the team areas. Cars requiring especially extensive
adjustment could be removed from the flow, thus ensuring that the fault was not
built in. As a result, in 1985, the total time for mechanical adjustment was 2.5
hours in Kalmar, versus 4 hours in Gothenburg. The combination of elasticity
and meticulous supervision had the effect of raising the up time from 96 percent
in 1976 to 99 percent in 1985. The buffers were used to pick up disturbances
and, when needed, to drive one section faster than another.

Third, the technical system at Kalmar also entailed flexibility in product
changes. The head of the engineering department emphasized that rebalancing
the line could be achieved over two weekends in Kalmar, whereas the same task
required 4 weeks in Gothenburg. For example, when antilock brakes (ABS) were
introduced at Kalmar, all that was required was the insertion of another loop (a
planned-sequence interruption), whereby the ABS cars were removed from the
main flow.

In sum, by 1985, Kalmar's technical system possessed a series of advantages
from the standpoint of efficiency. It was expensive, however. Because all assembly
on the base object occurred in a series-connected main flow with brief station
times, the carriers had to function as both assembly fixtures and transport vehicles.
The investment in carriers was therefore heavy. In 1985, with car production at
more than thirty thousand, 240 carriers were used, each at a cost of 100,000 U.S.
dollars.

Return of Line Pacing and Control

An important question, particularly in 1985 when planning for the Uddevalla
project was begun, was, What does Kalmar's system mean for working conditions?
The official evaluation in 1984 described the changes in euphemistic terms: "The
harsh economic climate, with declining car sales in 1980, increased understanding
of the need to rationalize production. . . . The result [of introducing the MOST
system] was a considerably reduced assembly time, as well as a more even pace in
assembly work" (Agurén et al. 1985:36).

In a 1985 interview, the plant's personnel manager went more to the point: "One should not let oneself be deceived because the work seems pleasant enough. That is just because the assemblers have developed tremendous skills. In actual fact, this work is hard, and it has gotten harder in the last few years. When people look for a job here we stress that the work is tough. This is necessary, especially in view of all that scribbling about a 'dream factory.' "

Moreover, some of the innovations in job content and design were eliminated or modified in connection with the rationalization program at the close of the 1970s. The buffers were the focus of one such change.

The buffers were originally meant to be work load buffers. The idea was that a team would be able to have a longer break by working more intensively for a time and thus filling the forward buffers. But this did not happen in practice since the teams were series-connected in a single long chain. If all teams worked faster simultaneously, it was impossible to fill any buffers. If every team took a rest at the same time, the result was a waiting period before any new carriers arrived. Accordingly, a number of buffer zones were removed in connection with product changes, which increased the need for more space for materials and work places. No longer was it possible for the assemblers to influence the speed of the AGVs through their work areas. The remaining buffers were used exclusively to compensate for technical disturbances.

At the time the factory opened, a parallelized assembly system existed that enabled a team to perform its entire assembly task at a single station—in so-called partial dock assembly. This was considered a critical innovation. Yet in 1984, the official evaluation said only that "the original dock system has been taken away, but it is not missed" (Agurén et al. 1985:22).

The problem was that parallel assembly was incorporated into the main flow, in which the movement of a carrier in and out of a dock was controlled by a central computer. This meant that the carrier was on its way out of the dock as soon as the allotted time had been consumed, regardless of whether or not the assembly work had been completed. On the one hand, this produced stress, since the assemblers could not easily ascertain the status of the AGV (i.e., how much time was left before the AGV would leave the dock). On the other hand, if a carrier was removed from the flow and directed manually, "disorder" would arise in the flow, making it difficult to install the correct optional articles in the stations that followed.

As the demand for options increased over time, the synchronization problems became ever harder to handle. Management therefore demanded that a given sequence of carriers be maintained, both before and after the team areas. This resulted in queues if, for example, one assembly dock worked faster than another in the area.

Another problem was the plant's traditional system for materials provision, which required surfaces for materials at each dock. With increasing variation in options, these space requirements were more and more difficult to accommodate.

Yet another problem was the technical design of the main flow, which included only one workplace in a dock. This was another source of waiting-time losses if, for example, several docks had worked ahead for a rest and required simultaneous refilling.

Finally, the dock principle was not equal to the demands for flow control posed during the intensive rationalization. As the manager of engineering said in 1985, "With dock assembly one cannot easily see what is happening. For about fifteen minutes the car stands still, with no indications coming. With straight assembly, the car goes to a new station every third minute."

After ten years, the last docks were removed in 1984. Only straight assembly remained except in subassembly work. The system in use in the 1980s was an intermittent line; it was technically flexible but as rigid as a typical assembly line from the viewpoint of the assembler. Compared with a traditional line however, the job content at Kalmar was considerably larger in that the assemblers usually followed the car through one or two team areas, which could be up to eight stations, or for twenty-five minutes. The desire for long work cycles was strong among the assembly workers.

Despite this job enlargement, the work was repetitive, and after the tough rationalization of the 1970s, the work intensity was high. Together, this caused considerable physical strains. In 1985, only 9 to 10 percent of the workers were women, and the company's health office advised against employing more since the risk of wearing them out or their being injured was too great.

Importance of Socially Defined Terms

"The team is the basis. The team—including the work area, the rest area, and the total work assignment—is the little factory within the factory. For the team members, this is home. The workers have an overwhelmingly positive view of the team approach" (Agurén et al. 1985:39). This comment summarizes the team concept at Kalmar.

The factory had a number of sections, each headed by a supervisor. Sections, in turn, were divided into two to three team areas. Each such area was responsible for assembly, inspection and adjustment, and materials handling. These tasks were strictly divided by job classification, with no rotation. Utility and relief persons (replacement employees) were in a pool, subject to the foreman.

Physically and spatially, the team areas were clear units within the plant, but this geography could easily deceive the visitor, for the distinctive building design and production arrangement were not matched by real organizational renewal, decentralization of responsibility, and integration of work tasks. Thus, in 1985, a team could not work independently vis-à-vis other teams since the buffers did not allow disengagement between areas. Further, the team did not constitute a decision level within the organization, with the right to decide such questions as the distribution of work and leaves. Changes in the pace of the AGV—such as increases to compensate for disturbances—were decided by the foreman in consultation with the control center. Industrial engineers, possibly together with team leaders, prescribed work arrangements, methods, and times. The foreman or team leader determined the distribution of work. The foreman also handled such matters as vacations and transfers, as well as all budget-related tasks.

On the team level, there were certain production targets but no shared all-team tasks other than housekeeping. The original thought was that each team would assemble a complete function, such as the electrical system; this could not be held to, however, because product changes unevenly affected the job content of different subsystems. The content of the team's work came to be defined, in conventional fashion, as a number of minutes, rather than functionally.

Finally, the wage system in 1985 bore no relation to teamwork. It consisted of a job assessment for different positions (a kind of skill rate), attendance and seniority allowances, and a productivity bonus. There were neither individual competence steps within positions nor any group bonuses for increased responsibility.

From "Ceiling" to "Floor"

When the Uddevalla project began in 1985, Kalmar, with its high efficiency and reliability in production, was Volvo Cars' "best-practice plant" in Sweden. The production system, especially the carriers, was relatively expensive, however. Compared with an ordinary line, the work was richer in content, but it was still very restricted and permitted no real autonomy. In the words of Gyllenhammar, "Volvo Kalmar is no final solution. It is the first step on the road. But much remains to be done in the matter of work organization. I could imagine much greater freedom and independence at work" (*Ny Teknik* 1984).

More or less consciously, the plant management had changed its fundamental view of the factory since the mid-1970s. The original personnel focus—employee motivation and identification with the product as productive forces—was replaced by a different profile: technical exploitation of the system's elasticity, combined with computerized control with the aim of accomplishing a stringently rationalized assembly. The causes of this conservative shift were twofold.

First, the Kalmar plant was supposed to be the first in a series of new Volvo plants, but because of the acute economic crisis in 1977–78, this did not happen. The result was that the factory was alone in an industry that strongly doubted the plant's productive capacity and efficiency. Proving its economic viability became a condition of survival.

The discretion enjoyed by the plant's management in regard to rationalization methods was narrowly circumscribed with the result that the rationalization was directed largely at exploiting the new system for increasing work intensity, control, and quality supervision. The factory had very little input on design changes affecting the manufacturability of new products since product engineering was wholly confined to Gothenburg. There was no comprehensive use for the plant's impressive workshop competence (at times including, among other things, a considerable number of engineers among the assemblers).

Second, the original production design contained contradictory elements. On the one hand, the teams had the possibility of working in docks and using the zones between teams as work buffers to vary the work pace. On the other hand, the teams were connected in a single long (if crooked) flow in which a completed car had to be released every three or four minutes. In addition, a central computer controlled the movement of the AGVs.

In the resulting "conflicts" between these elements, the straight-flow principle won the day so that the overall system was not as flexible as it had seemed at the start. A rational parallel assembly system requires, for instance, that the AGVs be able to drive past each other, change sequence, and, in relatively large part, follow an individual timetable. This was not possible. Furthermore, in that the provision of materials at Kalmar was altogether traditional, a series of problems arose in the parallel assembly, because of the increased number of options, which led to a greater need for space and more places for materials. Long-cycle assembly required a new way of handling materials; this was a central lesson for the Uddevalla project, which directed much effort to designing new methods in this area.

The setbacks at the end of the 1970s encouraged a conservative orientation at Kalmar: "Assembly without centralized control does not work." As a consequence of this conservatism, coupled with the plant's status as Volvo Cars' "best-practice plant," opportunities for changes were not exploited, at least not until 1989, when methods to renew the production system, away from the line system, gained currency. In anticipation of the new 960 model, a parallel system for motor-axle assembly was installed, with the purpose of both increasing operating efficiency and improving working conditions. In this change, the union was actively and eagerly involved.

Kalmar had to wait a long time before similar changes occurred elsewhere in Swedish car manufacturing. A turning point was reached in the mid-1980s. Kalmar's role changed from being the "ceiling" to being the "floor"—the minimum standard for changes. Accordingly, Volvo's senior executives criticized the 1984 general plan of the management at TC for setting lower goals than Kalmar's.

And in 1985, the company decided that the Uddevalla project would depart from the principle of line assembly to a much greater extent than had Kalmar.

Its limitations notwithstanding, Volvo Kalmar has a place of honor in the development of new production systems. It showed, as the first factory of its kind in the world, that there were feasible alternatives to the traditional rigid assembly line. The plant also demonstrated that a small factory can produce efficiently. For example, productivity throughout the 1980s was higher than at Torslanda, where the volume was five times as great. This confutes notions of economies of scale in manufacturing. Kalmar also set a new record for quality, most notably in 1991, when its cars had the highest standards in the history of Volvo.

Volvo Trucks' LB Plant

Volvo Trucks is centered in Gothenburg, which is the prime site for design and development. During the 1980s, production in Gothenburg included the manufacture of frames, axles, and wheels, as well as two plants for assembling heavy chassis: the X plant in Gothenburg itself and the LB factory in Tuve, outside the city. The X plant was established in the 1950s, LB at the start of the 1980s. In 1988, these plants produced eight thousand and six thousand trucks respectively. LB specialized in vehicles with the most complex equipment, such as antilock brakes and overall air suspension. The plant had 450 employees in all, of whom about 30 were white collar. Of the blue-collar workers, about 300 worked in assembly and preassembly; 80 in adjustment, control, and special vehicles; and 50 in painting and materials. More extensive custom outfitting of the chassis was performed at a special factory in Gothenburg (the TLA shop). Assembly time at LB in 1988 on average was thirty-six hours per vehicle, of which twenty were devoted to assembling the chassis. The factory also built special chassis for S trucks according to customer specification. These trucks, which had special features, could require considerable extra assembly work; in extreme cases, they needed twice as much work as a standard truck.

Planning under Pressure

At the close of the 1970s, after a lengthy period of expanding sales, Volvo began planning a new truck factory. At the time the problems in the old X plant's manufacturing system were alarming. In particular, productivity was very unsatisfactory. The pilot study for LB pointed out that more than every third worker was an inspector or an adjuster and that there were considerable balancing and variant losses related to the increasing variations in products. Moreover, a major investigation documented considerable deficiencies in the physical environment, with the result that workers were doing heavy lifting and working in ergonomically stressful positions along the entire line, inflicting numerous back injuries.

The investigation also indicated a series of other problems (Volvo Trucks 1981). First, workers felt there was very little stimulation from the work itself. "The questionaire as well as interviews present the picture of a job which for many has little stimulation or variation, and which places few demands for talent or knowledge. The job gives a feeling of expendibility; all that's needed is to put another guy in your place." Second, workers felt their jobs lacked purpose, meaning, and significance. An operator described this feeling in the following way: "It feels like Volvo doesn't give a damn about me and I don't give a damn about Volvo." Third, workers had an extremely negative view of the industrial engineers: "They go around with their damned papers and don't understand a thing," "you can't talk to them, they must be brainwashed."

The problems at the X plant formed the backdrop when the new factory was discussed. The project leader for the Tuve factory emphasized this in an interview in 1984: "It was clear to the top management that the company couldn't keep building factories in the old way. People won't want to work on a line in the future!"

Another objective was to avoid a colossus like the auto plant in Torslanda and instead to have small units with at most two hundred workers. The paramount problem at this time concerned personnel: it was hard to recruit people to work in the assembly plants. Turnover was very high. Absenteeism was also considerable, but it was believed it would decline if the jobs were less rigidly controlled. Moreover, a theme frequently discussed in the press at this time concerned granting employees greater freedom and autonomy at work. Volvo had a bad reputation: working there was thought to involve doing one- to two-minute operations on an assembly line.

Since the mid-1970s, Volvo Trucks had been developing new ways of making vehicles. The operation in Arendal played a key role in this connection. It was there that new assembly arrangements were tried out, during two periods: 1974–77 and 1977–79. In the first phase, twenty men assembled complete vehicles in a two-step dock. The pace of production was two trucks a day, performed in work cycles of about four hours. Despite the long work cycles, Arendal quickly reached the same productivity as the X plant, and quality was much higher. Further, it was easy to outfit the trucks according to customer orders without disturbing production, and the assemblers' knowledge and initiative could be used and developed in a wholly different way than in traditional line assembly. Volvo's new bus factory in Borås, which commenced operations in 1976, had been planned at first as a conventional plant with mechanically paced lines. Instead, inspired by Arendal, it introduced assembly in four parallel docks.

The management of Volvo Trucks in Gothenburg was very suspicious about the experiment, however. The head of the X plant considered Arendal a "devil's invention," and X plant's union organization, which could negotiate about the line speed and wages but not work forms, largely shared management's views. This negative environment helped explain why the great successes of Arendal's first period did not prove lasting. As the organization researcher Åke Philips pointed out (1986:19): "To be held out as a successful example can, in a longer-term perspective, create a recoil effect, because nuances in the degree of success relative to failure are lost in descriptions of the unit. . . . In order to 'balance' the successes of the first period at Arendal, some setbacks in the organizations were 'needed.' "

In Arendal's second phase, 1977–79, the product as well as the way of working were changed. Demands on work intensity were greatly raised. Yet, even with the new product and the more severe demands, quality at Arendal remained 20 percent higher than at the X plant. The workers found it hard to turn out the required number of trucks, however, and relative to the X plant, productivity fell.

The assemblers at Arendal endeavored to hold on to and develop the basic idea of dock assembly, but for the company, Arendal was classified as a "failure." The long cycles and lack of line control were seen as responsible for the difficulties in achieving a reliable output and high productivity. Alternative explanations were not discussed, such as the lack of support from the organization as a whole, the constant deficiencies in Arendal's materials provision, or the minimal scale—a single dock, without prospects for support in case of absenteeism.

At the same time as these problems were arising in Arendal, the new bus factory in Borås was encountering considerable difficulties getting on track. Together, these problems contributed to a "Taylorist backlash" in Volvo Trucks' production management.

From Radical Designs to Cautious Compromises

The planning for LB, which began in 1978, came to reflect strong cross-pressures. On the one hand, there were the well-known problems in the old plants. On the other, radical departures from line assembly seemed very risky. These tensions were clearly expressed in the pilot study for the LB factory. After a long survey of the problems of the assembly line came a diametrically opposed conclusion: "We can state that the paced line is altogether superior to other assembly designs when it comes to giving a constant output."

The planning of LB initially involved a radically small-scale alternative to traditional assembly: two "modules," each with two parallel buffered assembly flows; a yearly capacity of forty-two hundred vehicles; and 150 employees. There were also plans to commission a special development dock capable of making three hundred vehicles per year. The purpose of this dock was partly to prepare the assemblers for further development of this way of organizing work at the plant and partly to be able to build special vehicles. Senior managers in Gothenburg were doubtful, however, if it was right to abandon the traditional paced line in any way. They had several arguments against dock assembly: the costs involved in doubling the tools in parallel special stations, for instance, when the motor is built in; the long learning times; the impossibility of converting the system to line assembly "if required," as management demanded; and the bad experiences in the first years of the bus factory in Borås.

No attempt was made to develop appropriate conditions for dock assembly, such as by formulating assembly instructions and systems for materials provision to facilitate learning and efficiency in long-cycle assembly. The module idea was dropped in favor of a single factory with a higher volume. Moreover, management abandoned the idea of a development dock, on the grounds that no activities of an "experimental character" were desirable in the factory.

The outcome of these deliberations was a chassis assembly arranged as two parallel and buffered flows, where the chassis are transported by specially developed AGVs controlled by the assemblers (and not by a central computer as in Kalmar). The layout is illustrated in figure 7-3.

In principle, two buffer areas divide each assembly group in the chassis flows from the others. After chassis assembly comes adjustment and, in a separate building, roll testing and inspection. The cabins and engines are dressed up in separate short flows before they are "married together" with the frames in the main flows. Between these flows are materials areas, where the assemblers in the flows can fetch additional materials. These areas are also used to subassemble items such as valves, radiators, tanks, and headlights. During the 1980s, typical cycle times in the two chassis flows and in motor and cabin assembly were thirty-seven and forty-four minutes respectively (corresponding to thirteen and eleven vehicles per day).

This arrangement, in which there are two parallel chassis flows in the final assembly, can be seen as a compromise between line and nonline assembly. On the one hand, it allows the assemblers to control the transport of work objects, and thanks to the buffers, it gives the groups some possibility of varying their work pace. On the other hand, the design fundamentally retains a series layout and thereby the possibility of centralized control.

Relative to Arendal and the Borås factory, LB signified a retreat, grounded in a rather hasty judgment of the new experiences. The bus factory in Borås certainly had problems coming on stream, with its four parallel assembly docks and cycle times of two to four hours. But, as we have seen, during the 1980s both the productivity and quality were considerably higher than in any of Volvo Trucks' Gothenburg factories. In planning LB, management gave priority to security ("line assembly gives a reliable output") ahead of qualitatively enhancing the

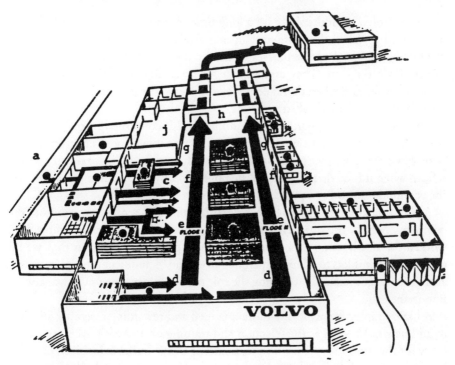

a. Materials delivery
b. Engine dress-up
c. Cabin dress-up
d. Frame and axle assembly
e. Engine mount
f. Cabin installation
g. Final Assembly
h. "On-line" inspection
i. Roll test and final inspection
j. Adjustment

FIGURE 7-3. Volvo Trucks' Chassis Plant LB

content of assembly work and increasing the flexibility of the productive apparatus. They believed the limited changes in LB's production design would suffice
in achieving decisive improvements in quality and personnel turnover. The LB
compromise was insufficient for reaching these targets, however, and in the end,
this risk-averse approach in the planning stage cost the factory dearly.

Organizational Structure

Kalmar, as well as Borås, were greenfield sites where there were no local unions
before the start of the plants. In contrast, the strong Metal Workers' Union had

existed at Volvo in Gothenburg for a long time. At the close of the 1970s, Metall had started to take a keen interest in issues related to work organization and production design. Representatives of the union club were involved in the LB project from early on. They argued first for arranging all of the production as dock assembly, and when that failed, they supported the idea of the development dock, with a similar lack of success.

The most innovative part of the planning for LB concerned its organizational structure, and in this area union participation was much more effective. At the same time, the subsequent experience of LB indicates the limits of organizational reform when it is carried out within the bounds set by the production design and the economic control system.

A planning group focused on work organization, with representatives from the company, Metall, the foremen's union, SALF, and the white-collar union, SIF, worked for nearly two years developing a new group organization that would enable the assemblers to do more qualified work and include a new training system and a new wage system. Developing the role of first-line management was also an important issue.

A basic strategy for achieving more qualified and rewarding assembly jobs was to add new tasks, such as the selection and training of new employees, responsibility for the utilization of work time, handling of the buffers, decisions on short leave periods, and responsibility for the group's budget. A special role, that of the group representative, would involve taking care of most of these tasks, as well as inspection, time reporting, and so on. This role would rotate among competent assemblers. The traditional assistant foremen and on-line quality inspectors were eliminated.

For the assemblers in general, the work content was not to change very much, other than that the cycle times would become longer and the work could be performed on a stationary object. The big change was the organizational form— group work—with the better prospects it allowed of changing tasks and influencing everyday decisions (such as the distribution of work within the group and the allocation of short leave periods).

Management Structure

In the new organization, a number of tasks that used to be supervisory prerogatives were delegated to the production groups. The foremen were relieved of some of the stressful parts of their old role, such as chasing after people to man the lines every morning. In exchange, they were assigned greater responsibility for economy and planning.

The union club desired the greatest possible leeway for the groups and therefore wanted few foremen and limited possibilities for behavioral monitoring (such as by time clocks). The company's original staff plan did not differ from that of similar conventional units. The result was compromise with a rather sparse management structure.

To fit the new work organization, a new wage system was formulated, which featured an individual and a group element. Steps 1 and 2 of the individual part represented different levels of assembly skill; step 3 corresponded to a group representative's competence. The bonus was based on the group's degree of responsibility and competence in five areas: personnel, industrial engineering (such as work allocation within the group), planning, maintenance, and economy (time reporting, budget for incidental materials, and so on).

Simultaneously, the balancing principles were changed. At the X plant, individual station balancing was applied on the basis of the most complex variant. From the viewpoint of the company, this had two drawbacks. First, because of the difficulty of balancing the line, it was hard to achieve an even distribution of the work load; second, time losses occurred in the case of all variants that required less time than the most complex (variant losses). At LB, balancing on the group level was introduced instead. Each group therefore was given an aggregate time per vehicle. With this system, work intensity increased a good 10 percent. The new organization and wage system was codified in a special contract and an organization handbook for the plant.

Successes and Failures

Both labor and management had high hopes for the new LB factory when it o pened in 1982. The breaking-in phase was tough, marked as it was by a series of rapid raises in the production targets. In just a few months the size of the staff was nearly doubled (compared to the budgeted level). The senior management in Gothenburg gave priority to attaining the output requirement, and with great effort, the factory met both the rising output demands and the productivity goals. But under the heavy pressure for quantity, quality became deficient, adjustment times increased, and the number of unfinished vehicles piled up. The management of Volvo Trucks had expected "superb" quality, meaning that no vehicles would be waiting for rework. Now the factory's organization appeared to be a failure. In an interview in 1985, the vice-president of Volvo Trucks declared that LB had not attained its goals. LB certainly had lower variable costs than other units, but, overall, manufacturing was considered too expensive, the quality too low, and the personnel turnover too high.

The factory also seemed to be a failure from the viewpoint of the workers. According to an opinion poll presented in a company newspaper in 1985, almost all LB workers had been looking for another job.[2] A couple of years after LB began—envisioned then as the flagship plant within Volvo—the serious question arose of whether the new ideas had been shipwrecked. Was it time therefore to return to a traditional organization? Volvo Cars' large assembly plant, TC, was about to begin a process of change, and the new project at Uddevalla had just begun. In 1984, the Royal Institute of Technology in Stockholm had been given the task, which I subsequently performed, of carrying out an extensive evaluation of LB's economy, production methods, and organization, within the framework of a larger research project within the Volvo Group. The discussion of "failure" gave this work a special significance.

With an eye to the goals the enterprise had laid out in the planning stages, I compared the results for LB from 1983–85 with the performance of the X plant.[3] The results demonstrated, to the surprise of many in management, that in four respects LB's results were more favorable. First, worker time per vehicle at LB was a good 10 percent lower than at the X plant. Second, less capital was tied up in inventory. LB's elastic flows could release a large share of the trucks fully equipped according to customer specifications, while the X plant sent all chassis to the outfitting workshop TLA. Third, there was reduced sensitivity to disturbances. Despite markedly higher capacity utilization, LB had fewer production losses caused by interruptions and disturbances. Fourth, there was considerably more mixed manufacturing; very different types of vehicles were assembled during the same production week, instead of maximizing the production runs within every six-week period.

LB had succeeded in those areas in which the factory and organization had truly undertaken a process renewal in comparison to traditional production and work designs. But where the LB compromise was too modest, the improvements were small.

First, it was difficult, with the chosen production design, to reach the quality goals for the complex products without a significant amount of rework. As a consequence of the series links, the groups often were forced to release unfinished vehicles when difficult models rich in options were being constructed. The significance of the buffers for easing the series links proved to be very limited because the buffers tended to be transformed, for a variety of reasons, into workplaces. The higher the output and the greater the range of options, the stronger this tendency became. The objective of the factory was a considerably enhanced level of quality. The evaluation showed that the level was in fact about the same as for the X plant and for the truck factory in Ghent.

Second, the "LB compromise" limited the possibilities of qualitatively changing the content of assembly work. Personnel turnover was lower than in the old lines at the X plant, where at the start of the 1980s it had been 30 to 40 percent, but it was still high; on average, 16 percent of the work force left the chassis flows and the factory every year from 1983 to 1985. The personnel manager offered the following reflection in an interview three years after the plant opened: "We believed the difference from a typical assembly workshop would be very great. But the assembly work is not so different. Already, after a month on the same job, a guy is dissatisfied he hasn't been able to learn other things. Assembly work is never stimulating or rewarding in itself."

My 1985 evaluation indicated that workers with assembly-line experience at other Volvo factories thought that working at LB was considerably better than working at TC or the X plant but that deficiencies in the working conditions and work content were still great. Eighty percent of the line assemblers at TC considered the work degrading. At LB this figure had been reduced by half, but 40 percent still viewed the work as degrading. The greatest change brought about by the "LB model" was that workers had greater influence over their workday, job rotation, planning, work assignments, and training.

In short, my evaluation of LB provided a picture of clear improvements in economy and in work compared with traditional assembly. At the same time, the LB model appeared to be a compromise in several respects. The production design was a compromise in that senior management's traditionally framed demand for stable output limited the possibilities of developing the work. This contributed to an instability of personnel, which weakened the group organization and made it difficult to achieve consistently high quality. Furthermore, the work organization was a social compromise, between management's desire to keep the possibilities of detailed control ("just in case") and the determined effort of the union club to gain maximum worker autonomy and discretionary power at the team level. Finally, LB was stamped by a growing tension between the product program's rapid increase in complexity on the one hand and the limited potential for flexibility and the use of traditional economic forms of control on the other.

Between Fordism and Custom Building

Over a long period, Volvo Trucks' assembly system had increasingly developed custom building. At the start of the 1970s, customers could choose between different options for 30 components of the truck chassis. In 1985, it was possible to choose options for 140 components on the most common of the LB-assembled vehicles. Further, the number of options increased for each of these components. For example, there were increasing numbers of power trains, suspension systems, and axle configurations from which to choose. Moreover, the number of vehicles designed according to customer specification over and above the option program also increased. To keep delivery times short, it became ever more important for production to be done in small batches. A 1982 investigation of options in Volvo Trucks described this development and emphasized the importance of drawing the appropriate conclusions:

The options are a very important part of the operations. They are what mark out our products, and so they concern everyone in the company. The question of options should not be regarded as a problem which concerns only certain sections; instead, it usually has to be solved throughout the whole company. . . . The production strategy must be adapted to the great number of options and option combinations existing today and must be able to handle future increases.

No such strategic connection was made in the planning of LB. Compared with earlier rigid production systems, the factory had greater flexibility, on a level with the product changes that had already occurred during the 1970s. But it was not sufficient for developments in the late 1980s. With respect to its production design, method of economic control, and organizational structure, in many ways the factory had a transitional character. I shall begin with the method of economic control and then proceed to the relation between design, industrial engineering, and assembly.

As in other companies, the management of Volvo Trucks during the 1980s focused increasingly on the significance of reducing capital tied up in inventory. In 1984, the total lead time from component to customer was forty weeks; nearly half of this time was after assembly. The assembly plants affected tied-up capital above all indirectly by their ability or inability to deliver orders on time. To reduce inventories in the distribution system, the truck dealers in and outside Volvo had to be able to count on short and sure delivery times. Thus, at the close of the 1980s, precision of delivery became an important parameter for the assembly plants. It was added to the old demands, which remained as before. Within the company, a discussion had been conducted about changing these demands in line with the new needs and budgeting the utilization of staff at a lower level—about 90 percent—to improve the prospects of achieving secure and reliable production. Nothing came of this, however. As LB's head of planning said in a 1985 interview: "This idea fell victim to the moral repugnance felt at the notion that the hourly people maybe would not need to work every Friday afternoon, and to the fact, or appearance at least, that [production] would entail higher fixed costs."

As it had done earlier, Volvo tried to reduce the calculated manufacturing costs (fixed as well as variable) by means of a budgeted maximal utilization of staff and equipment. According to theoretical calculations, this yielded the lowest manufacturing costs. But this method denied production any margins for handling difficult options and complexity. Problems in assembly tended to increase the need for adjustment after assembly, to increase the numbers of incomplete trucks awaiting rework, and to lengthen the time from component to customer. The traditional methods of holding down costs contributed to making the wide range of options a burden both for production management and for the assemblers' working conditions. The new balancing principles in LB's assembly worsened the problem. In a standardized manufacturing system, a high work intensity would have been relatively easy to handle. With growing product differentiation, however, it resulted in increased sensitivity, a lack of time for the assemblers to keep up with options information (especially in the case of one-vehicle orders), and small margins for coping with disturbances.

The transitional character of the LB of the 1980s is also reflected in the relations between assembly and industrial engineering. My evaluation in 1985–86 revealed widespread discontent, especially among the experienced utility and repair men. In manual production there are often conflicts between workers and industrial engineers. The traditional criticism of industrial engineers, which was well represented among workers at the X plant, concerns in large measure the relation between compensation and performance, as well as the work intensity and times allotted for different operations. The subassembly workers in particular expressed these criticisms at LB. As one of them put it in a 1985 interview, "I'd like to see the industrial engineers work at our station for a month and hold the pace that we've got to. That's been my dream ever since I started here. They'd cry their eyes out."

But the LB workers' main criticism concerned something else: the massive deficiencies (in the assemblers' eyes) of the industrial engineers' way of functioning as the liaison between design and production. One cause of this criticism was the insufficient interplay between production engineering and product design. A constant stream of more or less incompletely prepared options flowed into the factory from the design department; this left little chance for the industrial engineers to bring about any changes in the design.[4] Another reason for the discontent was the strict division of labor between assembly and industrial engineering. With the introduction of the new organization of work, the assemblers' skills and demands rose. Many assemblers considered themselves able to perform industrial engineering work. As a team leader in engine assembly said in an interview: "If we had the training and the time, we could manage the industrial engineering work ourselves. The IE guy scarcely teaches us the frills; he just sends us papers. We often have to make the tools ourselves. We could also make the computer calculations if we got training."

The industrial engineering department at LB had neither the interest nor the ability to use and work with the assembly groups in a new way. The assemblers usually received information about new options late and had few prospects of participating in the work of preparing them for assembly. A former foreman at LB who had transferred to another plant stressed that the introduction of group organization had heightened the assemblers' aspirations: "That things seem sluggish at LB also depends on the level of the guys. Here [in the old plant] you don't ask questions; it's just a question of putting in your time and getting your money. It's different at LB. The guys there have a higher development level; they make demands about tools, layout, and so on."

The LB workers' more developed and constructive criticism of production planning, including their ideas about what was wrong and how production could be improved, could have been an asset to the factory. Instead, their ideas were seen as a burden. To quote the head of the IE department: "When 250 men come at you with opinions it can be a nuisance."

Another expression of the lack of interplay between industrial engineering and the shop floor was the character of the technical information in assembly. Assembly instructions and operation manuals were not formulated according to what, from the workers' perspective, was important and problematic about the assembly work itself. Two researchers in vocational training, Lennart Nilsson and Bengt Pettersson, gave this problem special attention (1986:6):

> One must be careful not to mix up different organizational models. If, as in this case, the assembly is group-based, the information should be group-based as well. It should be added that, in certain cases, details and components should be renamed, so as to spare the workers the present labeling, which does not build on any daily associations and is hard to communicate. Now, by means of computer technology, it is possible to put labels on components which are rich in associations, easy to understand, and desirable for the assembly workers. For these same components, IE or design can have their own terms, without translation problems thereby arising.[5]

This proposal got a cool reception from LB's industrial engineers.

Contradictions of the New Work Organization

The greatest change at LB, compared with traditional plants, was the palpable increase in the workers' decision-making rights. An overwhelming majority of LB's employees felt positive about this change (see also chapter 12). The foremen also saw advantages in the group organization. Accordingly, two foremen on the flows said:

> At the X plant the foreman had to run around all the time and check the vehicles on the line. Here it's enough to contact the group representative. The guys here are more conscious of costs. It's also good they take care of training within the group itself.

A former foreman at LB, who at the time of the interview was back at a traditional factory (the G plant), made the following comparison:

> At LB the foreman is more of a teacher, and he works more with long-term questions like planning, following up the budget, checking training plans, and such. He can make more important decisions, especially in budget work and training, and can discuss goals and objectives with the group. Here, at the G plant, all his time is taken up with daily things, practical matters like going and fetching this or that. He doesn't have time to work in a long-term way. There's also, among the guys, very little inclination to take initiative.

But the group organization also entailed difficulties for the foremen, who lost control over the status of production. In a traditional organization, foremen had the privilege of handling staffing, assigning tasks, and contacting other departments. In LB, foremen all but lost these prerogatives. The foremen therefore no longer performed any central function for the workers. The assembly workers usually went to the group leader to solve problems such as mistakes in the calculation of wages or to discuss the possibility of taking a leave.

Plant management thought the foreman should develop the group organization but also be "out on the shop floor," "making daily contacts" with the workers and "keeping control" of operations. These demands were contradictory. On the one hand, the foreman was supposed to manage the group in a general way, with the focus on whether or not the group attained its output goals with high quality and low cost. On the other hand, plant management required, especially in case of difficulties, that the foreman direct the *conduct* of the workers, for example, by keeping a close watch on their time cards and work times. Generally, supervisors resent this obligation to surveil their subordinates. At LB it was especially burdensome because the groups were granted considerable responsibility. The work organization, moreover, had been formed in such a way that regular contact was between the foreman and the group representative. The average assembler had no need for many contacts with the foreman, as an assembler at LB noted: "At TC you saw the foreman very often. It's better here. We don't have much contact with first-line management, and that's good."

Why were there such contradictory demands at LB? One reason was that the new organization lacked decisive support from the senior managers of Volvo Trucks. The company had delegated considerably greater responsibility to the plant manager at LB than shop managers generally enjoyed. But instead of giving the plant manager support and respecting his increased responsibility, top management demonstrated mistrust of the fundamental ideas of LB and intervened in conduct and discipline issues. This made it difficult for the management of the plant to apply the new organization's principles consistently inside the factory.

Another reason for the contradictory demands was a series of problems in the group organization that had not been foreseen in the planning stages. Coming on line was much harder than expected, and labor turnover was considerably higher. This had consequences for quality, competence, and stability. Because of pressure from top management, the managers at LB demanded behavioral monitoring "until the organization began to function again."

The lack of a fine-meshed control net, in the form of supervisors and foremen as well as specialized quality inspectors on the line, led Volvo Trucks to view LB as less reliable than a traditional plant, even if statistical evidence for this view was lacking. This points to a more fundamental problem in reforming labor-intensive assembly, in which productivity to a high degree is determined by the intensity of the manual labor. In an automated work process, both workers and management have a strong interest in ensuring that operations proceed free of disturbances. In repetitive manual production, this *mutual* interest is much more limited. Demands for supervision and direct control, to ensure stability and high productivity, have therefore shown a strong tendency to recur, sooner or later, in assembly.

In the mid-1980s, production volume at LB increased markedly, and the size of the assembly departments grew (each foreman in assembly had fifty to sixty men under him in 1986). This gave fuel to management's demands for an expanded supervisory apparatus. Metall's group board saw this as a threat to the group organization. The conflicts over managerial prerogatives and team autonomy, which existed already in the planning stages, surfaced again.

Organizational Changes

In 1987, an attempt was made to "get around" the conflict over first-line management by raising the competence of the assembly groups. In a settlement between the company and Metall's club and group board, a considerable increase in training was agreed upon. All assembly workers would be trained in product knowledge. A plan was formulated for a three-week introduction for new employees and the pay-for-knowledge system was expanded. Training cards were introduced for all employees in which knowledge prerequisites, training, and the person in charge of training for the different development steps were specified. The objective was first and foremost to enhance development possibilities for workers in final assembly and thereby to reduce the "flight from the flows."

The overall organization of Volvo Trucks was also changed. Chassis design was placed under the head of production in Gothenburg to increase the manufacturability of the expanding product range.

These attempts to develop the LB model were obstructed, however, by changes in production volume and product structure. A very powerful truck boom brought with it a heavy production program, considerably over the plant's limit for rational assembly. The number of blue-collar workers increased by 50 percent during the three years 1986–88, primarily because of the exploding number of sophisticated new options. Thus, during 1988, for example, the average assembly time per vehicle rose by 9 percent in only six months. This development had several important consequences.

First, the assembly groups became larger. A typical group in 1988 was twenty men: twelve assemblers, one group representative, one adjuster, and two trainees and two replacement employees to cover in case of absences.

Second, the differences in the times required to manufacture various vehicles became harder for the groups to handle. This required an increased use of special options operators, working outside the group structure. For example, full-air suspended vehicles, which in 1988 comprised 10 percent of the volume, required fourteen hours of extra work, of which five hours were performed in the assembly groups. Two extra men per group were needed for every such vehicle.

Third, the heavy use and need of options operators had the ultimate consequence of transforming the buffers into workplaces. While the product program became ever less standardized, the conditions in the flows became, paradoxically, more akin to those in line assembly. The work cycles got shorter and rigidity worsened. Personnel turnover in the flows rose to 24 percent, which nullified much of the effects of the investment in training. The combination of high personnel turnover and large assembly groups with an unstable composition made it very difficult to maintain competence and efficient coordination between the groups.

Economic comparisons between LB and the X plant, carried out in 1988, produced less favorable results from LB's point of view than earlier comparisons. Production losses because of disturbances were greater, and adjustment time per vehicle was higher. Labor turnover was about the same in the two factories, but because of the greater interchangeability of personnel in the X plant, training costs there were lower. According to LB's head (appointed in 1988), the problems were occurring because LB's work organization no longer functioned. He emphasized three problems in particular. First, there was unclear allocation of responsibility in the groups: "The rotation of additional tasks must occur in a controlled manner. Today it can happen that people don't give a damn about their inspection or group representative responsibilities." Second, coordination was inadequate between the groups: "If there is a surplus of workers in one group and a shortage in another, no evening-out is done." And third, consistently ensuring high quality in assembly was extremely difficult: "Right from the beginning requires that one stop and clear things up right away; it assumes someone with authority and responsibility."

Management's approach was to make the control net more tight by adding more levels to the organizational hierarchy, having more foremen, and assigning each foreman fewer workers. It also wanted to introduce full-time, professional inspectors into the flows, according to the model that had always prevailed at the X plant. The group board opposed these proposals, but after fruitless negotiations, the organizational changes were introduced. As of 1990, management had succeeded in raising quality and delivery precision but partly at the cost of a high worker time per vehicle. Within the framework of LB's flows, it was no longer possible to cope with the complex options structure at a 114 MTM work speed without considerable balancing and system losses.

Renaissance for Dock Assembly?

The increased product variation within Volvo Trucks, with its spread of assembly times from 50 hours for simple basic vehicles to 120 for the most complex chassis, also triggered innovations. A development project was begun in 1988 that featured a two-step dock on which two chassis could be assembled per day. The purpose was, first, to handle some of LB's most complex vehicles and, second, to test new methods of assembly, including building whole vehicles in a single work team in long work cycles (four to five hours). This design had many similarities to the one used in Arendal and to the development dock management had rejected in the early planning of LB (with the justification that no operations of an "experimental character" were desirable). The new dock was given overall responsibility for planning, assembly, testing, and adjustment and was staffed by twenty assemblers, one production leader, and one industrial engineer.

In less than one year, the dock came up to full production speed and had a lower worker time per chassis than had been expected. The results during 1990 were excellent in other respects as well: personnel was stable, delivery precision was high, quality was rising rapidly, and the capacity to build complete, ready-to-buy vehicles was impressive.

The dock specialized in the manufacture of the very demanding "many-wheelers" (chassis with four axles), which LB had great difficulties in handling. A product engineer was assigned to the dock to take care of design-induced problems. Volvo's newspaper, *Volvo Now,* wrote in August 1990: "The first dock in Tuve has been going for over two years. In the last few days they built the 500th vehicle, a jubilee which shows that Volvo Trucks' whole-vehicle project is coming through."

A special wage system was introduced whereby workers received a job evaluation based on their individual knowledge, an all-group qualification bonus, and a considerable team performance bonus based on quantity and quality. Senior managers asserted the value of having a driving first-line management and rejected the idea of introducing a rotating group representative. At the same time, they stressed the importance of a vertically flexible organization in which there are no dividing lines between different positions. As a result, both foremen and assemblers worked on industrial engineering problems.

In 1990, another new dock began operations, in which technical aids, assembly instructions, and materials provision were further developed. This dock was part of an extensive yet cautious expansion plan. In all, eight chassis assembly docks were planned to come on stream in 1993. As part of the plan, the old X plant in Gothenburg would finally be taken out of production.

Contradictory Effects of "Flexible Specialization"

The "case of LB" demonstrates the contradictory effects produced when there is a significant increase in product variation. In the first phase, the planning of the factory, this variation contributed to a renewal of the organization and production arrangement. In the next phase, however, when the variation continued to increase well beyond the factory's capacity to handle it, the result was increased rigidity, constraints, and inefficiencies in the assembly groups. Eventually, management decided to resort in part to traditional organizational mechanisms in an attempt to compensate, with the aid of an extended control system, for an ever harder-to-master product flora and labor market. The group organization was retained, albeit in a more circumscribed version.

At the same time, the increased complexity of the products contributed to an impressive renaissance for dock assembly with the goals being to raise efficiency in the manufacture of particularly demanding products and reduce the strains at LB. The first dock was begun in 1988, the second in 1990. The results were well above expectations. In this operation, new forms of close co-working between designers, industrial engineers, and the skilled vehicle assemblers were introduced as well.

Production in Sweden during the 1980s expanded very slowly to reach slightly more than fourteen thousand vehicles in 1989. The number assembled in Belgium increased to seventeen thousand in the same year (of which ten thousand were heavy vehicles), and further increases were planned for the 1990s. Volvo Trucks thus developed a plurality of assembly concepts within its European operations. In Belgium, with its abundant labor supply, the company continued to invest in assembly-line plants where it could manufacture a simpler product mix cost effectively. In Sweden, with its less disciplined but more change-oriented labor force, Volvo invested in flexible and holistic forms of production for the assembly of complex and customized products. The plan was to expand both the LB plant and the new dock operations and to phase out the traditional assembly lines completely.

8.
Innovations in Uddevalla, Stalemate in Gothenburg

In 1985, for the first time in more than a decade, Volvo Cars began planning a completely new auto factory. A greenfield site was chosen for the new facility, as it was in Kalmar in the early 1970s. The project started with the aim of copying Kalmar's production design. This option was rejected, however, by Volvo's corporate executives and the unions, as well as by the project's many innovative engineers. Several of these engineers had been personally involved in the planning and/or operation of installations such as Kalmar, Arendal, LB, and Borås, and now they wanted a consistent alternative. In contrast to Kalmar, the unions were involved on a full-time basis from the start, and the local representatives of the Metal Workers also got significant support from their national research department.

A series of factors reinforced Volvo's commitment to instituting fundamental innovations. For one thing, the labor market situation made it crucial for the company to offer attractive jobs. For another, mechanized assembly had proved altogether unworkable for the manufacture of existing product lines. In addition, in 1987, a joint labor-management group at the Uddevalla plant had studied an example of the latest "Japan wave" firsthand: Nissan in the United Kingdom. This strengthened a common conviction that the Japanese solutions were not possible in Sweden and that Volvo had to find its own way. The interest of Volvo's CEO, P. G. Gyllenhammar, in the renewal of work also contributed to the desire to experiment.

The result was a wholly new concept—long-cycle parallel final assembly with partly mechanized and individualized materials provision. The plant attracted great international interest when it opened in 1989—350 journalists attended the inauguration—but it also met with considerable skepticism. Accordingly,

MIT researcher John Krafcik declared in *Business Week* (August 28, 1991) that "Uddevalla can achieve high quality but there is no way it can match the productivity of a reasonably efficient mass-production system, Japanese or American."

Nor was the commitment to radical reform unanimous within Volvo. Management, as well as the unions at Volvo's main plant in Gothenburg, were split in their opinions during both the planning period and after the plant started operating. There were ardent supporters but also critics who expected the experiment to be either a dismal failure or an irrelevant episode of no significance to Volvo's main operations.

At the same time Uddevalla was being planned, the company's main assembly plant, TC, in Gothenburg was being pressured to change because of its great difficulties in coping with productivity demands and personnel problems. Technological changes and motivational campaigns were tried, then increasingly radical sociotechnical strategies. In 1989–90, TC even organized an experimental workshop where small teams built complete cars à la Uddevalla. This step proved to be antithetical to the plant's basic Fordist culture, however, and the experiment was interrupted before the workshop reached any of its productivity targets.

The experiences of TC demonstrate the difficulties of transforming work in a brownfield site. When the company began a severe downturn in 1990, during which there was drastically reduced capital for modernization efforts, very few of the plans of the 1980s had been realized. (Figure 8-1 marks the positions of the Uddevalla and TC plants in terms of production design and work organization.)

Volvo Uddevalla: The Death of the Assembly Line?

From the beginning, the intention with Uddevalla was to build a complete facility with body and paint shops, trim, and final assembly. When it was shown this would entail some intricate environmental problems, the plans were restricted to constructing an assembly plant pure and simple with the capacity of making forty thousand cars per year (it operated with only one shift). Breaking in was commenced in 1989, and in 1990 sixteen thousand cars were produced. The factory had eight hundred blue-collar and one hundred white-collar employees in that year. The original objective was to reach full capacity in 1992, but sluggish sales forced the target for this year to be reduced to twenty-five thousand cars.

The factory was placed in a former shipbuilding area. The materials shop used a large building from when the shipyard was operational; the shop was responsible for supplying assembly with individually prepared building kits. Six new so-called product shops were erected, in two groups of three; they had a common roll-testing installation in the middle (see fig. 8-2). Five of these product shops were in operation in 1991.

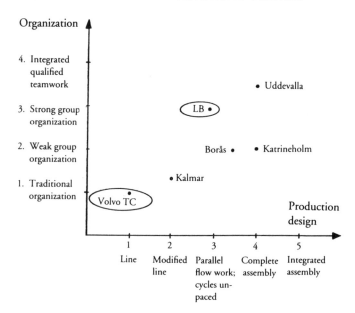

FIGURE 8-1. Production Design and Work Organization of TC and Uddevalla

Major Stages in the Project's Development

The Uddevalla project began in a period when demands for new approaches, especially in assembly, had increased sharply and Volvo's profitability was very high. Conventional ideas were proposed at the start of the planning process, but thereafter came a steady stream of "concept shifts," layout changes, and replanning phases even after production began. This complex development consisted of four main stages.

Phase I. In 1984, a public evaluation had shown that Kalmar was Volvo's best-practice plant in Sweden. (The company's own comparison showed the same.) Further, Kalmar's director of engineering became the first project leader for Uddevalla's assembly unit. Thus, not surprisingly, as at Kalmar, assembly was initially arranged as a carrier line. In an interview in 1985, the project leader maintained that qualitative improvements in assembly work were not possible at the existing technological level:

> A radical departure from line assembly requires parallelization, and that is expensive, in both space and equipment. Besides which, a marked increase in leeway makes for heavy demands on the buffers. To attain a more flexible flow than at Kalmar— that is to say, a flow in which the carriers follow individual timetables—a new type of control and information system would be required. However, the development time for new systems is much longer than the planning time for a new factory. A genuine change in assembly work requires mechanization. The limits are severe in

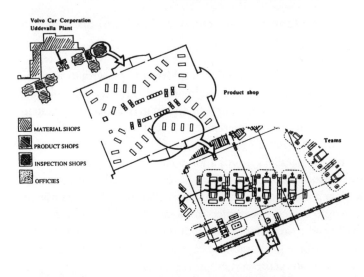

FIGURE 8-2. *Sketch of the buildings at the Uddevalla Plant. Used with permission from Ellegård, Engström, and Nilsson 1991:24.*

this area, with the products of today. It is necessary to improve the work by other means—by giving people good work times, for example.

The top management of Volvo did not see replicating Kalmar as the solution at Uddevalla, and some engineers had already begun to sketch other solutions. At the start, the unions had no alternative to the "Kalmar strategy," but the opportunity to influence a decision as important as the design of Volvo's "plant of the future," which was bound to influence the rest of Swedish industry, started a process of internal union discussions in which Metall's research department participated actively. The result was that Metall rejected the Kalmar concept and formulated four demands of its own. First, assembly should be done on stationary objects instead of on a moving line; second, job cycles should be extended to at least twenty minutes; third, there should be no machine pacing; and fourth, all assembly workers should perform indirect tasks as a significant part of their regular duties. These were Metall's maximum demands; in practice it restricted its agenda to what had been achieved at LB (which was discussed extensively at this time). The union did not envision any possibility of transforming assembly operations to genuinely skilled work, so that the final solution at Uddevalla was way beyond the most radical demands of the union.

Most of management also had a narrow perspective on the possibilities for reform, even after it had rejected the Kalmar model. In the meantime, innovative engineers and researchers had the opportunity to pursue far more radical alternatives, and, most important, to develop the entirely new support systems (materials handling, technical informations structures, and so forth) that would be required by a transformed assembly operation.

Phase II. The next concept in the history of the project—"Model Ultra"— was an attempt to realize the *original* Kalmar concept from 1974, with its sectional parallel assembly. This did not function at Kalmar as it was originally planned because of, among other reasons, the design of the materials-handling system. "Uddevalla Ultra" learned from this experience and coupled the idea of parallelization with a new form of materials provision, in which the storeroom would collect the materials for the parallel stations and "serve the assembler on a tray."

"Uddevalla Ultra" introduced some innovations into the production system as well. In place of Kalmar's line carriers, taxi carriers would fetch and deposit the base objects, which would then be assembled in so-called double docks. As with the company's overall production strategy, mechanization was seen as a strategic solution. When the costs of the proposal were calculated, however, the suggested serial parallel system proved altogether too expensive. No definitive decision about the production design was made in 1985. In fact, the entire project came to shift character: from implementing existing alternatives to discovering and developing fundamentally new ideas. This endowed the process with an open-ended character and created an unusually large space for exploring the fundamental conditions for change.

Volvo had gotten very generous support from the government for locating the new plant at Uddevalla, in large part because a big state-owned shipyard had been closed there. Now the company was being prodded to create new jobs as fast as possible. Thus, even before the construction of the factory was begun, the company decided to start a new training workshop.

In the intensive discussions concerning the objectives of the workshop, Lennart Nilsson, a researcher in occupational pedagogy who was engaged as a consultant, formulated a new view of training as containing potential rather than as a mere residual expenditure: "Training as an independent means, and a point of departure in the design of work, instead of the usual view—in which training is designed after the fact, to fit already given jobs, and in which it is merely a question of simple instruction according to the model—'one day is enough for your cycle time.'"[1]

When the training shop opened in 1986, the manager in charge of training formulated the goal as follows: "In the training shop we learn how to make complete cars. Both manual and intellectual functions are required: planning, organizing equipment and materials, assembling, following up, and reporting. Assembly here involves more than just mounting screws; it's also a matter of functional know-how."

The training shop came to function as a sort of laboratory for production development, in which changes in production design were tested before being introduced into the product shops. Accordingly, practical tests in the training shop showed it was possible, with an appropriate materials arrangement and administrative system, to learn how to build cars in considerably longer cycles than twenty minutes—which earlier had been considered the absolute upper limit for car assembly. Thereby, a critical restriction on further development was overcome.

A conventional assembly design is based on the balancing of—that is, the distribution of parts along—a given line. The number of stations and the content of work are wholly determined administratively by the demands of volume. This leads to a division of labor that is unrelated to the functional structure of the car. Fragmentation is reinforced by the administrative representation of the car and its components, with its abstract digitalized structure in which the numbers on parts transmit no information about their functions. It is therefore very difficult to create holistic jobs simply by fusing existing line operations.

In 1985, researchers from Chalmers Institute of Technology were engaged by Volvo to create a basis for functional assembly by means of an impartial (system-independent) design analysis. They demonstrated that the car consisted, in assembly terms, of four natural parts. This division became the basis for Volvo's continued work in production design, which by now had begun to depart definitively from the line model. It also became the point of departure for the development of a new system of materials handling.

Phase III. In 1986, an assembly arrangement was sketched that deviated significantly from the Kalmar concept of the previous year. In the words of the new project leader:

> We shall produce two hundred cars a day, which comes to twenty-four an hour. Two extremes can therefore be set against each other:
> —total parallelization, which requires ninety-six "garages," each of which assemble one-quarter of a car every hour and which therefore have a station time of four hours.
> —pure line assembly, with a cycle time of 2.5 minutes. This also yields twenty-four cars an hour.
> After many and long discussions we have chosen to put ourselves on a one-hour station time, consequently a twenty-four fold parallelization.

The idea was to achieve optimal balance between the costs for quality and balancing (which were assumed to increase with pure line assembly) and the costs for training and equipment (which were assumed to decrease with line assembly). Six identical parallel shops were therefore proposed, each with four flows. At certain points these flows would be joined together in waists (for operations requiring expensive equipment, such as polyurethane (PUR) adhesing of windows). For longer transport needs, taxi carriers would be used. Inside the product shops, manual moving would be cheapest, but many industrial engineers opposed this since they thought it would increase the risk of paint damage. Rolling tests and final inspection would be centralized. The basic design of the building was fixed according to this pattern in 1986, and the purchase of heavy equipment was begun.

This design was a significant change from traditional car assembly, but it was still not fully consistent with the assumptions of the project in the area of vocational pedagogy, for instance. The notion that cycle times could not exceed a certain limit was still one of the bases of the design, as opposed to the idea that function and task were the central issues and that time was a dependent variable. The major innovation was at the level of the factory, with the division into parallel subfactories (product shops). Within each product shop, the production design resembled the flow structure of the truck plant LB: in both cases, assembly in unpaced flows was divided into four main steps, and the volume of production was roughly the same (twenty-six to twenty-seven hundred vehicles per year and flow at LB, seventeen hundred at Uddevalla). LB's design was an improvement compared to a conventional assembly plant, but, as we have seen, it was basically a compromise (and it had the weaknesses characteristic of a compromise). Experiences from LB, and from the development work proceeding simultaneously on other fronts in the project, such as the training shop, indicated the need to break much more radically from assembly-line principles. This was facilitated by Uddevalla's parallel factory concept, which yielded the possibility of testing new ideas on a small scale without being locked into a single design for the entire production system.

Phase IV. After a time, the idea of concentrated sections with sophisticated equipment (waists) common for all the flows in a product shop was abandoned. The possibility of switching to an organization *along* the flows was thereby opened in which team areas (about twenty workers) would be responsible for an entire car. Assembly would still take place in four distinct steps, and the cycle time would be an hour, as before. In 1987, construction of the training shop was begun, in preparation for the start of production.

Only a few months later, however, the managers of the project, supported by the union, decided to take the last step from line to whole-car assembly. This entailed a forty-eight–fold parallelization in which each work team (eight to ten men and women) would make an entire car in two steps. The new design was tested in the training shop first. Assembly shops 1, 2, and 3 were thereafter rebuilt according to the same principles.

This "final step" was of critical importance, as emphasized by one of the project's innovative engineers, Bertil Johansson, a veteran of the planning phases at both LB and Borås:

> The project leaders had had a tough job selling Uddevalla's ideas upward in the organization, and they had been badgered by the pace argument—"how can the

production pace be handled with extensive parallelization and free flows?" We had worked for two years without a vacation, and we didn't want any more half-measures. Now, with this step, the investment in change became wholehearted. The support from the top is much stronger now, including from the production executive of the car division and from the group management.

The "long march through the layouts" was still not over, however. After tests in the training shop with wholly tilted assembly (in which the car body is tilted 90 degrees throughout the assembly process), assembly shops 4 through 6 were replanned to accommodate this way of working. The result was completely stationary assembly. This change—carried out during the breaking-in phase—illustrates the advantages of the 1986 decision to build the workshops so that they were parallel to one another.

Qualitative Development of Work

For many years, mechanization has been held out as a central strategy for solving work and production problems in assembly. When this has not been an immediate prospect, the need for mechanization has been used as an argument for keeping the line system with all its human problems, so as to be prepared for the more or less distant future, when technology will liberate assembly work once and for all. This old "pie-in-the-sky" argument has recently been reiterated by MIT's auto researchers in *The Machine That Changed the World.* They assert that one advantage of lean production is that it is so propitious for automation, while the alleged "craft systems," involving long-cycle and autonomous work, will never be able to automate.[2]

From the engineering perspective, all human work is residual, waiting for automation in the next technological wave. Thus, everything depends on the time perspective and on how much one generation ought to sacrifice for the next one. Lean assembly may be suited for automation, but visiting the Japanese transplants in North America in 1990, most of which were only a few years old (some had just started operating), I was struck by the massive amount of repetitive, restricted, and stressful manual jobs in virtually all of the final-assembly shops.

The mechanization debate was raging in Volvo, as elsewhere, in the mid-1980s. But in view of the largely unsuccessful installations in final assembly (not only at TC but at General Motors plants in the United States), the planning team at Uddevalla determined in 1986 that Volvo could not wait for the technologies of a nonspecific future to solve current problems.

The use of parallel product shops was a very conscious break with the conventional engineering outlook, but not in order to revert to traditional craft methods (as used by British luxury car makers). For example, Uddevalla invested in new advanced technologies for maximum mechanization of materials handling. This centralized process included a number of subassemblies, which it was not feasible to allocate to the parallel teams. Thus, opportunities for future automation in the assembly field were created without enforcing this perspective as a constraint on the whole process and layout.

The rejection of the traditional mechanization perspective made it mentally and materially possible for the plant to focus all of its efforts on developing manual assembly in its own terms. Qualitative development of work, instead of quantitative reduction, came to be the fundamental idea of the project. This made for a pronounced impulse toward small-scale solutions in final assembly.

Throughout the 1980s, Volvo's installation in Halifax, Canada, which manufactured 10,000 vehicles per year, was considerably more efficient than TC, with 150,000. The Canadian plant, like Volvo's small-scale plants in Asia, was not based on any production strategy, however. Rather, it was dictated by local market conditions or political agreements. Uddevalla was the first example of a thought-through attempt to build a large factory based on small-scale production in an essential part of the process.

One of several obstacles to reaching this solution lay in the expensive equipment used in traditional assembly. According to conventional wisdom, such machinery had to be multiplied many times over (with a matching increase in costs) if consistent parallelization was to be achieved. The Uddevalla project sought to overcome this problem by adapting the technology according to the principle that low frequency requires less technical sophistication.

Material and Intellectual Innovations

The planning for the Uddevalla plant resulted in several innovative features, including the following:

1. Parallelized production design for whole-car assembly, within a building designed to facilitate small-scale production.
2. Centralized materials provision based on individual building kits.
3. Combined technological development: simple, duplicatable solutions in assembly and high technology in small materials handling (kitting) in the materials shop.
4. A new product analysis and information structure for functional, holistic assembly and materials handling.
5. A comprehensive ergonomic effort, from new hand tools adaptable to different sizes and strengths to tilted assembly.
6. A compressed hierarchy without traditional first-line management and an extensive team organization (white-collar and blue-collar demarcations were retained, however).

The production design. The first three assembly shops each had eight assembly teams. Each team occupied four workplaces—two with tilting equipment, two with lifting platforms. In IE terms, assembly was arranged as a seven-man balance, so that the car moved after half the assembly was completed. Each team was also responsible for three major subassemblies: the engine dress-up, the doors, and the instrument panel. At full pace, one car was produced every other hour, or twenty per week. There were no permanently employed repair people at the testing shop. If the test drivers discovered any mistakes, the representative of the team involved was contacted, and one of the team's assemblers was sent to correct the problem.

Assembly shops 4 and 5, which began operating at the end of 1989, were formed differently: twelve parallel small teams performed wholly tilted assembly. The entire car was assembled in one place. Four assemblers were normally required to build a car, but at times only two were needed (as at Katrineholm). Although this demanded greater knowledge on the assemblers' part, it was not considered a big problem. In the words of the union club chairman: "You learn half the car here just as fast as you learn one-fourth of the car in product shops 1 to 3. You also get a better overview of the production situation here than in the other shops."

Cycle times at Uddevalla were unique in the world for standard cars. Yet, in comparison to those of heavy vehicles, they were by no means outstanding. At Scania Buses, for example, pairs of assemblers built the entire chassis in cycle times of ten to twelve hours. Volume, however, was just a twentieth of Uddevalla's at full pace; this made the system at Scania much simpler, since it did not require nearly the same development of materials handling and assembly support.

Traditional auto-assembly buildings are basically storehouses in which the assembly takes place between walls of materials. It is thus hard to receive light from and to maintain contact with the outside world. In contrast, Kalmar's building design entailed moving the line to the outer wall and bending it as well (with the help of carriers). The design also involved placing materials in the middle. The result was a bright and airy workplace.

The distinctive form—composed in principle of folded-up honeycombs—was a manifestation of new thinking. The form was also intended to facilitate the new way of working. Thus, teams worked in spatially determined sections, each of them responsible for one function. The close coupling of the assembly structure and the building design proved only temporary, however. When the product was changed, the previously unified work content decomposed. More complex products required more work to assemble (the dashboard, for example) and these additional tasks fell to workers further down the line. The spatially determined division into team areas thus became increasingly administrative, as opposed to functional.

The design of the building at Uddevalla was an important part of the new concept as well. The six separate assembly shops there underlined the commitment to small-scale final assembly and made returning to traditional models considerably more difficult than at Kalmar.

Materials provision. Early on at Uddevalla it became clear that batch supply had to be replaced by individualized materials supply. The question was the degree to which this would occur. As early as 1981–82, Scania's cab plant in Oskarshamn had introduced individualized supply of medium-sized articles—an innovation that at one time had been controversial in the materials department. The purpose was primarily to reduce the need for space for option materials in a series–parallel assembly system, rather than to make complete assembly possible or to facilitate the learning of long work cycles. By 1986 in Uddevalla, when the model featured a four-step flow, it became clear, because of the need for space, that individual collection of large and medium-sized articles was required. With the orientation to whole-car assembly, this principle was extended to nearly all materials, down to the smallest lock washer.

The argument against the Uddevalla model was that it would be too expensive, since everything would need to be handled twice, first by the materials handlers in the storeroom and then by the assemblers. The argument for the model was that, if it were not introduced, there would be too many materials addresses and supply areas in the shop. Furthermore, it would be impossible to use the feeding of materials as a form of instruction in assembly. Besides, the advocates claimed, conventional materials handling was not nearly as efficient as was assumed. This position was underscored by one of the engineers who most energetically supported the change:

> Handling losses in assembly are much greater than the MTM analysis shows. That analysis assumes the assembler works in the most suitable position vis-à-vis the base object and materials. In practice, however, the assemblers are seldom there, on account of variants, disruptions, and the periodic need to work faster in order to make up time. This means greater distances and a lot of running, much more than is visible in the analysis. In our system, the materials are handled twice, but for a short time per article. There's a lot of waste on the line, furthermore. The worker takes a handful of nails, for example, often loses some of them, and then throws out those he doesn't use. At a special station at the end of the line, workers have to vacuum the coupé for loose screws.[3]

As a consequence of the introduction of the new principles in combination with the use of both old and new buildings, materials handling at Uddevalla was completely separated from assembly, both organizationally and geographically. All collection was done in the materials shop, as was the subassembly of the exhaust system, the front members, and the rear axles. On average, thirteen hundred to seventeen hundred different parts and components were handled per car.

Assembly at Uddevalla was technically simple. Producing the "car building kit," however, was a complicated process with three main steps: the bagging of small materials ("the kit"), which embraced roughly half the number of parts, the collection in crates of medium-sized articles plus the bags of small articles, and the loading onto kitting racks of the crates plus large objects, such as the exhaust system, the propeller shaft, and the engine. Finally, the prepared kitting racks were placed in exit areas from which they were fetched automatically by AGVs for delivery to the assembly shops.

The bagging of small materials was the step requiring the most work and the one with the greatest risk of mistakes. The process started with mechanized feeding, counting, and filling of the materials, complemented by manual filling, whereupon the materials were collected in bags by special-purpose machines with the capacity of handling twenty thousand bags per day. Approximately one hundred bags were used for each car. After being filled, the bags were weighed (a checking step) and placed in boxes that went to a storeroom. The kits (or bags) were produced according to weekly plans. The timetable for the collection and delivery of crates and kitting racks was determined by orders posted by the assembly teams.

The major technical demands on the materials-handling system were for reliability and high packing density. Thus, the mechanization of small materials handling required solving a series of intricate inspection problems.[4] Certain articles—rubber plugs and clamps, for example—which created difficulties in the materials shop because of their variation in weight, had to be removed and delivered separately to the assembly teams. High packing density was very important for holding down the number of kitting racks and carriers. With fewer carriers, the intensity of the flow and the risk of traffic disruptions could be reduced. In 1989, six kitting racks loaded on three materials carriers (AGVs) were used per car (plus one for the car body). Thirteen car body carriers and about thirty-five materials carriers were required for the factory as a whole—a surprisingly low figure, especially considering that Kalmar used more than one hundred carriers just to move the car bodies. Even so, the total flow of materials in the Uddevalla plant was intensive.

When the principles of the new materials-handling system were outlined in 1986, managers from the materials department at TC thought it was altogether impossible and that it would require twenty hours of materials handling per car. The development engineers at Uddevalla replied that they would make it work in only two hours. Four years later, in 1990, they had come a long way and were close to the level at Kalmar (three hours per car).

The Uddevalla system was sensitive, however. The quality of the materials handling was extremely dependent on the competence and sense of responsibility of the individual materials handlers. Another problem lay in the sharp boundary between materials handling and assembly. The planning system in 1990 required the assembly teams to have several days' advance planning, which was often impossible. When orders were changed, the materials shop found it difficult to deliver on time. It was also hard to satisfy demands for complementary articles on short notice.

A dual technological strategy. For small-scale assembly to be feasible, the expensive and complicated features of a high-volume line had to be replaced with technology that could easily be diffused to a great many assemblers. An example was the new tilting equipment. The technical demands on these tilters were severe: rapid handling, vertical adjustability, no protruding parts, and great stability. At the same time, the price could not be too high since every team had to be equipped with two tilters, for a total of nearly one hundred.

Another example was window assembly. The idea at the start was for each shop to have the same type of sophisticated, automated PUR facility as had been installed at TC in 1986. The final solution was to adhere rear windows in the materials shop. A robot applied an adhesive strip to the window, which was then affixed manually to the car body. The total cost for the equipment was just a tenth as high as at TC. Yet, despite the relatively low cost, this work had to be centralized since a large area was needed to carry out the process. The windscreens, however, would be installed in the assembly shop. This was done in traditional fashion, using windscreen presses shared by two to four teams.

Technological developments in the factory's "large-scale" materials-handling system were of another character. Mechanized collection of kits had been used earlier by the furniture company IKEA; Uddevalla introduced flexible automation. Whereas IKEA's equipment collected in batches of 20,000 to 200,000, Uddevalla had to handle batch sizes of 300 to 400 bags. At Volvo, it was also necessary to combine mechanical with manual collection (the latter for cases in which counting could not be mechanized). For both these reasons, wholly new solutions had to be found.

New technical language. A manufacturing system with increasing product variation and frequent changes in components and parts requires the flow of considerable amounts of technical information. If cycle times are long and no-fault production (which necessitates combining instructions for assembly and inspection) is a must, then the mass of information per car and assembler becomes very large—reckoned in operations, part numbers, and tools. The Uddevalla project therefore developed a new way of handling technical information. The purpose was twofold: to support holistic assembly on stationary cars and to contribute to the development of a new "culture of assembly" in which the language would be capable of expressing nuances and the assemblers would have a knowledge level that was relatively stable, even if there were changes in auto variants and yearly models.

The typical way of presenting technical information in short-cycle assembly and materials handling, using part lists and operation sheets at the level of the individual balances, affords no overview of the assembly of the *car*. This has no import in such a production design, however. All employees, engineers as well as operators, work with just a small piece of the product. The work is treated in a strictly mechanical manner—for the assembler, it is a matter of learning to do a fragmented job as quickly as possible.

In contrast, in long-cycle assembly, getting an overview of the work process is critical. The model for providing technical information developed at Uddevalla can be described as a hierarchical menu model with a geographical structure. Tomas Engström, a Chalmers researcher engaged in the project, described the problem as follows:

> An assembly atlas is needed which includes everything from continent to country, from capital city to village and local district. . . . The problem today is that assembly is so broken into pieces that, even in its technical-administrative representation, it is impossible in this system to move between different parts of a functional unit— between, for example, the parts having to do with the steering shaft. There has simply been no interest.

The new technical descriptions and language had to satisfy many different demands: for functional grouping; symmetry (right should be directly matched by left and so on); and variant clarity: any given variant should be related in a simple manner to a base variant, with the help of categories such as omit, replace, and add.[5]

Engström and other researchers engaged in the project ascribed great importance to the development and consolidation of a rich and nuanced language. First, it would facilitate assembly, since proper names in full-text printouts would provide much better guidance than part numbers and acronyms. Second, such a language would become the basis for communication and the transfer of knowledge—in other words, for a stable, group-based way of working.

"October Verses," by the Swedish poet Lars Forsell, summarizes the issue perfectly:

> I must use words
> when I speak to you!
> Imagine the captain
> of a ketch, a freighter,
> a schooner, a brigantine,
> a frigate, a corvette, a brig,
> with the cloud of canvas above:
> gaff and boomsail,
> topsail, staysail,
> clew, head, tack
> When blows the storm
> he cannot simply point his finger
> and shout: Take down those there!

Physical strains of assembly work. The Uddevalla project early on had as
objectives high personnel stability and a balanced work force; the goal was that
40 percent of the blue-collar workers would be women. This meant that the
traditionally heavy physical strains of assembly work could not be accepted. At
both Volvo in Kalmar and Saab in Trollhättan, the company health offices had
advocated the opposite—reducing the share of women—precisely because of the
risk of strains and cumulative trauma disorders.

Whole-car design, with its great autonomy and long cycle times (and thereby
considerable variation) in itself reduced much of the risk of the CTD injuries
associated with excessively repetitive motions. The need for mechanization or
complicated equipment for handling heavy components (such as heating units)
also disappeared because individual employees had to work with such items for
only a short portion of their work time. Not all ergonomic problems disappear
with an altered production design, however, especially if the share of female
workers increases at the same time.

Efforts at Uddevalla in the area of ergonomics were focused principally on
measures to prevent two types of strains. One was strains at specific spots—in
the wrist, for example. These arise because the worker uses his or her hand as a
dolly, a fixture, or a tool. To reduce such strains, efforts were made to persuade
the tool manufacturers to develop tools capable of being adapted to grip size and
power requirements. This idea met with a very cool reception. The Japanese
suppliers, for instance, which otherwise stress their flexibility, were not interested
in accommodating in the slightest, since other markets had not made similar
demands. As of 1990, no tools of the new type were being used in production.

The other main type of strain Uddevalla sought to prevent is produced by the
weight of the worker's own body as a result of doing a job in a stooping position
(in engine-compartment assembly, for instance). This static strain tends to increase with long-cycle work if no countermeasures are taken. Four different so-
called whole-body positions were identified by the project's ergonomists: standing
upright, standing in a stooped or twisted position, crouching outside the car body,
and crouching inside the car body.

Ideally, as much of the work as possible should be done standing upright. Only
12 percent of the work time is spent in this position in conventional assembly,
even if one includes tilting in some of the trim and chassis sections. Practical tests
in Uddevalla's training shop in 1988 demonstrated that this percentage could be
drastically increased if the entire assembly—even work in the passenger com-
partment—were performed on a tilted car body. Instead of sitting inside the
coupé, the assembler would stand in the door opening of the tilted car; materials
would be supplied through the window opening. This way of working demanded
changes in both layout and technical equipment; more powerful tilters were
needed, as well as another "marriage" technique and specially designed tables for

tools and materials. The project had just gone through the transition phase to whole-car assembly and all efforts needed to be devoted to starting production. The advantages of tilted production were so evident, however, that the next set of assembly shops was replanned to incorporate this technique.

Organization. The integrated assembly, signifying a low horizontal division of labor, had its counterpart in a decentralized organization: plant manager, shop managers, and work teams (low vertical division of labor). The principle was adopted early on that the factory organization should not include traditional first-line management. The foremen's union, SALF, later criticized this idea at the national level and recommended instead Nissan's foreman-centered British factory at Sunderland as a model.

Within each team, matters such as quality, economy, and maintenance were handled by the team representative and by members specially selected for these tasks. The goal was to rotate these functions monthly. There were no U & R men as such. Production goals were defined at the level of the assembly shop, and in principle each team's output would vary according to its staffing level (although it was possible to borrow assemblers from other teams in cases of acute staffing shortfalls).

The first contract for Uddevalla's metal workers was signed in 1988. New employees would begin with a "trainee's wage," which would increase in stages before the standard wage was reached. This wage could then be augmented with a qualification bonus depending on how large a portion of the car's assembly the worker had mastered. Workers at the highest competence level would be able to build an entire car.

The process of reaching whole-car competence was designed to be a true test of skill and knowledge. The requirement in 1990 was that a worker had to be able to make a complete car with a maximum of four small defects in at most twenty hours. Workers were required to have undergone training and then built cars for at least sixteen months before they could take the test at all. In 1990, there were a dozen whole-car builders among Uddevalla's five hundred or so assemblers. (All of these were men, but in May 1991 the first woman passed the test.)

Bonuses were paid for achieving competence as a team representative and in tasks in industrial engineering, personnel, and quality control. These bonuses were paid both to the individual performing the task and to the team as a whole.

There was also a productivity bonus. Initially, this was based on the productivity of the plant and bore no relation to the results achieved by teams. In 1991, however, a revised system was introduced featuring productivity bonuses based on team achievement.

The new organization flattened the hierarchy and brought management and labor close together, but it did not eliminate the white-collar/blue-collar distinction. This limitation was shared by the other work-reform exercises within Volvo, in spite of some attempts on the part of the project head to campaign for a one-union agreement at Uddevalla.[6]

Working Conditions

From the worker's point of view, Uddevalla's distinctive production design yielded a series of advantages compared with a traditional assembly line. First, the work content was holistic, and the production process could be grasped in its entirety. This created the basis for transcendent understanding and reflection supported by a nuanced language and a broad functional knowledge on the assemblers' part. Second, there were unique conditions for the development of an upgraded assembly culture, with the whole-car test as a modern "craftsman's diploma." Third, there was an appreciable reduction of physical strains, thanks to the production design and efforts in the area of ergonomics, and fourth, group cooperation was the basis for administrative delegation and self-regulation of the work but also a means of exerting peer pressure to reach production targets and be given the productivity bonus.

One of the points of departure for Uddevalla's production design was that the assemblers were able to control the pace of work; they were therefore freed from detailed administrative or technical control. Since the base object was moved just one time within the teams in assembly shops 1, 2, and 3 (and not at all within the teams at assembly shops 4 and 5), Uddevalla had no queue system and so was spared the often severe operator pacing such systems create. The teams were highly dependent on external materials provision, however. For the work to proceed without losses (time spent waiting for materials) or stress (when the materials arrived), the teams had to be able to plan their work on the basis of a stable rhythm. They also needed an overview of the workday—an effective planning horizon, in other words.

During the planning stages, the training shop played an important role in building up competence, trying out different solutions, and training the new assembly teams. The training shop was later discontinued, however. In the future, new employees would be trained directly on the job.

Discontinuing training was considered justified since the work now included a "learning" aspect; moreover, the training shop had become so isolated from the factory that new assemblers needed retraining when they came out on the shop floor. But as a consequence of closing the training shop, new employees had to acquire their skills under social pressure to achieve a high work output. The difficulties with this system were compounded in 1989–90, when the factory hired a large number of women who were unaccustomed to working with power tools. During 1990, therefore, a one-month introductory course for new employees was prepared. The object was to impart an understanding of the work's holistic character and to train the new arrivals in quality control, ergonomics, and the information system. Moreover, since the low sales figures meant that a sixth assembly shop would not be required for production, management decided to use it as a training center instead.

The Breaking-in Phase

The Uddevalla project began during a time of transition at Volvo. In 1986, when time-honored concepts were abandoned and virgin ground was broken in such areas as technology, materials handling, and assembly structure, the introduction of other innovative projects within Volvo also increased. Enthusiasm and faith in the future spread.[7] Yet Uddevalla also met with strong opposition from the company's guardians of the sanctity of industrial engineering.

The production targets were low in the first year of operations (1989), but productivity measured in worker hours per car in assembly developed "surprisingly well," according to Volvo's top management. It was more sluggish in 1990, however, when both staffing and volume doubled. Uddevalla certainly made the transition from the 700 to the 900 series much more smoothly than did Volvo's other assembly plants in Sweden. Intermittently, the product shops also reached high levels for quality. The results lacked stability, however; great variation occurred from week to week. Productivity development was also slow. Finally, personnel turnover was 15 percent and absenteeism due to sickness about 10 percent; these figures were better than at Torslanda, yet far from the factory's goals.

The problems had many causes. In the mid-1980s, the Uddevalla area was considered a crisis zone after the closing of the shipyard. It was easy for Volvo to recruit workers. At the close of the 1980s, however, the regional labor market was overheated; the unemployment rate dipped to a mere 1 percent. Furthermore, because of the long training period, the starting pay was lower than at Saab's assembly lines in neighboring Trollhättan. This made it especially hard to recruit men over thirty. It also meant that Volvo could not engage in the careful selection of staff required to ensure that the skilled and demanding work was performed properly.

Earlier examples of long-cycle assembly had been characterized by their low production volume and small number of parallel teams. The scale at Uddevalla was altogether different: forty parallel teams in final assembly where Borås had four. A decentralized organization with many work teams can exhibit both conservative tendencies (teams that stubbornly keep to established methods and work patterns) and dynamic tendencies (innovative and competent teams constantly finding new and better ways of performing their job). The variation between teams was very great at Uddevalla in 1990, even in light of their different levels of experience. Some teams had no difficulty attaining high rates of quality and productivity, while others fell far behind.

"Noble Experiment" or "Noble Failure"?

The media's enthusiasm for the plant when it first opened was soon replaced by scathing criticism. "It is a nightmare plant," a Swedish business magazine (*Veckans Affärer*) exclaimed on November 28, 1990, pointing to Volvo's costly excess capacity and the low productivity of the new plant. The message was that Swedish manufacturers must learn from Japan. This criticism was reiterated eight months later in the *New York Times* (July 7, 1991): "The idea was to return dignity to the worker. But assembly lines are just more efficient. . . . Uddevalla has been hailed around the world as one of the boldest gambles in what is known as humanistic manufacturing. But this noble experiment is increasingly looking like a noble failure, its productivity nowhere near the exacting standard of world competition."

All this criticism merely strengthened the commitment of both management and the workers to make the new operation a success, and in the middle of 1991 they made an important breakthrough. The *New York Times* article had asserted, without qualification, that "assembly lines are just more efficient." Even before the article was published, Uddevalla falsified that statement by reaching the productivity level of the assembly lines in Volvo's main Swedish operation. During a visit in May 1991, I saw an organization in which, compared to a year before, everyone had a much stronger morale and determination to continue improving performance. Further, there were a wealth of ideas about how to do so. Turnover had fallen to 4 percent, and the workers took great pride in their jobs. A new wage system, with team-based bonuses for productivity and quality, was being implemented; it was thought this would motivate workers to learn from the most efficient teams and improve their methods constantly. During 1991, the quality level stabilized around the corporate target (which was index 910, according to Volvo's measurement system, in which 1,000 signifies an absolutely perfect car). This performance was better than that achieved at TC, which had also improved significantly during 1991.

Compared with the Ghent plant, Volvo's most efficient assembly operation and, according to MIT studies, one of the best-performing plants in its segment in Europe, Uddevalla was still far behind. But the long-term potential for increases in productivity was high on account of the low balancing and variant losses in the long work cycles, the integration of tasks into complete assembly functions, the supportive materials provision system, and the optimized working positions. Reaching the goal of Ghent did not seem to be an impossible task given sufficient time. The Borås plant, which was a much less comprehensive innovation, had also had a very hard breaking-in phase and had taken five years from the time it opened to reach a consistently high level of performance. (For Uddevalla, the corresponding time would be in 1994.)

Compared with the Japanese, even Ghent was lagging. For a Volvo plant, be it Belgian or Swedish, to match the performance of the Japanese, the products must be as easy to manufacture as Japanese cars. Unfortunately, *The Machine That Changed the World* focuses too much on plant productivity but reports only one manufacturability analysis, made by GM (Womack, Jones, and Roos 1990:97). According to this study, the "design factor" contributed up to 41 percent of the productivity differential between a GM and a Ford plant. In 1988, product engineers at Saab selected doors from equivalent Honda and Saab models to perform comparative assembly, using the same methods and technology. They found that the Honda doors could be built in a quarter of the time it took to assemble the Saab doors.

Equally important, for a Volvo plant to be equivalent to a Japanese one, the supplier system (accounting for 75 percent of the value of a car) must be of the same quality and commitment as the formidable Japanese components industry. This is unfortunately far from the case.

Without considering these basic conditions, unqualified comparisons of assembly hours are misleading. Naive observers, such as the author of the *New York Times* article mentioned above, have interpreted the differences in worker hours between various plants as a direct indicator of relative plant productivity. But even if they are properly conducted, these comparisons give us only a proxy of the total performance gap between manufacturers; they do not account for the different factors behind this gap and thus do not demonstrate the relative efficiency of different assembly concepts.

Driving Alone

The Uddevalla plant took form, as did the Kalmar factory, during an economic boom characterized by acute recruiting problems, high profitability, and great optimism about the future. In 1990, however, the company's situation was worse than it had been in the years following Kalmar's inauguration. Falling sales, production cuts, personnel retrenchment, and heavy pressures to cut costs were the order of the day. As a result of excess capacity, the Swedish assembly structure, which had one large and two small plants, became an issue on Volvo's corporate agenda; one of the small plants was, in fact, superfluous if sales did not recover. Management made the plants compete intensively against one another but denied intentions to close down any of them. Nonetheless, the discussion created an agonizing atmosphere of insecurity.

Corporate management commissioned the innovative design process in Uddevalla. It then adopted a conspicuous standby attitude however, which in part could be explained by the deep divisions within management concerning the viability of the concept. The very committed plant management were thus left without any public executive support.

Uddevalla had been conceived too much as a strategic response to Sweden's labor market problems. As a result, there was a lack of aggressive performance targets for the plant. All the goals—productivity, quality, cost—were framed as part of a catch-up strategy, that is, to reach the levels of the company's best-performing plants. Furthermore there was no corporate strategy for capitalizing on its advantages to improve company performance in other vital areas.

The Uddevalla operation had unique qualities as a potentially productive point of interaction between design, product engineering, and production. Such an interaction was highly needed to upgrade Volvo's painfully slow process of product development. But because of the lack of an integrating corporate strategy, this potential was left to plant management and individual designers to realize, just as the Uddevalla concept itself was largely the result of innovative engineers working from the bottom up. In hard times, a much more distinct management profile and support were needed. Here Volvo management fell far behind the record of the often criticized GM leadership. In spite of severe economic difficulties and internal debate, GM executives time and again repeated their backing of the innovative but highly controversial Saturn project, with its new product, integrated production system, and team-based work organization. They made perfectly clear that they did not expect short-term profitability but long-term innovation. Uddevalla had to drive alone.

The Fight over TC

Volvo at Torslanda, just outside Gothenburg, was the car division's main installation for many years. A press works, body shop, painting shop, and central materials store were located there, as well as TC, the trim and final-assembly plant. The facility was part of Volvo Cars' production division, together with Halifax, Ghent, and Olofström (the latter was the principal site for producing pressed parts and body subassemblies for all assembly plants). A central engineering staff for preparing new products was also headquartered in Gothenburg, close to the design department. This staff worked with all of Volvo's plants but had especially strong ties to the factory at Torslanda, since this plant traditionally bore the responsibility for breaking in new products.

In the early 1980s, TC was a one-series factory: it produced only the 200 series. In 1984, with the introduction of the 700 series, TC became a two-series plant (Volvo's only one). The majority of the assembly took place on two conventional assembly lines. Line 1 operated in the daytime and built the 700 series; line 2 operated in two shifts. In 1987, the pace was thirty cars per hour on both lines. Some of the work was done in the form of subassemblies; the share for the 200-series vehicles was 20 percent, 30 percent for the 700 series. Subassembly was done mainly in special workplaces or on short, unpaced lines.

Ten thousand persons were employed at the Torslanda facility as a whole. TC had 280 white-collar and 3,800 blue-collar employees, of whom 2,500 worked in assembly, 900 in inspection and adjustment, and the remaining 400 in equipment, materials handling, and maintenance. The total production of vehicles that year was about 160,000. (The principal layout of the plant is shown in figure 8-3.)

Proposals for Change

When TC was inaugurated in 1964, it embodied the large-scale industrial ideal of the time, both in the design of the building and in the IE techniques applied there (the factory was based on long, paced lines). It was considered a sign of modernity that, with the help of MTM, jobs could be specified and organized in detail even before any workers had been employed.

The Kalmar plant—with its entirely different physical design—was opened ten years later. By comparison, TC now appeared very old-fashioned. Yet, in 1976, at the height of an economic boom, as commentaries on the Kalmar plant noted at the time, the new concept did not spread to Gothenburg. Nonetheless, TC began to experiment with different production methods. Dock assembly was tried out on a small scale: a team of workers was given the task of building complete cars from start to finish. According to the company's evaluation, the results were good in many respects: greater variation, more coherence in work, and increased freedom, responsibility, and influence. But it was not possible with dock assembly to exceed half the planned production pace. Moreover, the union club and the company had not reached any agreement on wage rates. Finally, the preconditions for dock assembly—in technical equipment and assembly instructions—had not been properly worked out. The attempt was discontinued after half a year. Both the company and the club deemed it a failure, and neither sought to take advantage of the experiment's positive aspects. When production dropped sharply in 1977–78, moreover, the interest in reforms cooled further.

In 1979, production planning for the 700 series began. At TUN, the special factory built for breaking in the new series, trying out new ideas was considered urgent. One motivation was to reduce Volvo's increasing personnel turnover. Another was to reduce the large share of adjustment work on the lines. The hope was that new forms of work organization would make it easier to build in quality right from the beginning. The changes could not be too great, however, since the

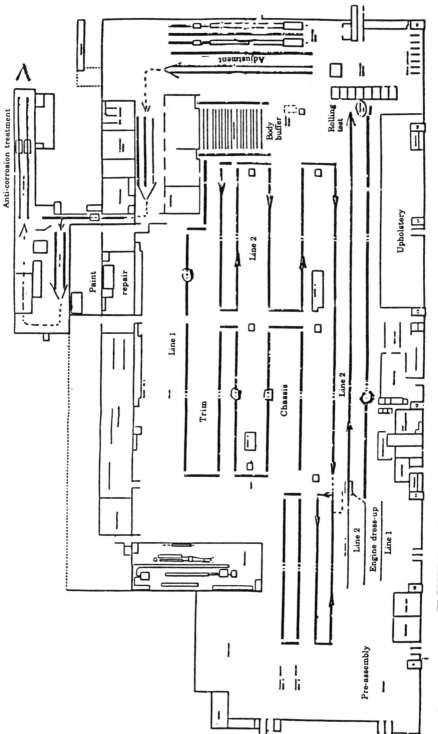

FIGURE 8-3. Trim and Final Assembly at Volvo's Car Assembly Plant in Torslanda

new type of assembly had to be applicable at the main plant. Three production designs were considered: pure line assembly, buffered line assembly (that is, a sectionally divided elastic line), and dock assembly. The last alternative found no advocates in either the company or the union. A buffered line system was considered reliable; it was also thought that it would make considerable improvements in both production and working conditions possible.

The implementation of this concept at TUN resulted in a production system that was much less sophisticated than the one at Kalmar. But in contrast to Kalmar, TUN invested in organizational development; responsibility for quality, materials handling, and the assignment of tasks were delegated to groups of assembly workers. A critical factor contributing to this experimental approach was the connection of the project to a new robotized body plant that was applying advanced organizational ideas.

Although some reforms were introduced at TUN, the main factory largely retained a 1960s-style production design, technological level, and managerial organization. There was a shortage of both money and ideas for change. Among Volvo Cars' product engineering and planning staffs, however, the realization was growing that sweeping changes would soon be needed. These ideas were presented in a 1982 report "Production Project 90." This was to be the first in a long series of such investigations. The report analyzed TC's problems exhaustively:

> The most critical problem is that productivity is too low, which in turn depends on a production process which is inflexible, yields losses, and is sensitive to disruption. The RFB (right from the beginning) result is too low, and the climate is unfavorable for change. . . . The process yields:
> —large variant losses;
> —inefficient utilization of personnel (balancing, handling, and system losses);
> —low efficiency during peaks of both absence and attendance;
> —low motivation among a large portion of the work force, on account of the monotonous, machine-paced, short-cycle work operations.

The proposals for change were intended to reduce manual line assembly by increasing mechanization and the proportion of preassembly work. The remaining line assembly would be successively converted from individual line balances with 2- to 6-minute cycle times to developed teamwork with cycle times of 1 to 1.5 hours. Buffers and parallel assembly would be introduced, thereby reducing variant losses.

At TC, however, there were no champions for this comprehensive strategy of reform. The TUN plant was just being broken in, and TUN's production design embodied a much more cautious reform—a sort of miniline system. The heavy staff turnover from 1979 to 1980 (23 to 25 percent) was halved in 1982–83. This also weakened the interest in radical changes.

Attempts to Change Attitudes

Instead of sweeping reforms, the next few years brought rationalizations of line assembly and campaigns to influence employee attitudes. This approach was the core of the "General TC Plan 90," formulated by management in 1983. It fit in well with the "Japan wave" that was reaching Swedish industry. In 1982, two engineers from Volvo Cars had studied Japanese industry—Toyota especially—for six months. The views of management were captured in a 1983 article in *Stockholmstidningen:* "Volvo's production director believes in a wholly new Volvo spirit inspired by the Japanese. 'They bow and smile, propose rationalizations and work overtime. We want the same mentality here.' "[8]

In 1984, the so-called MATCH campaign began, with the message to employees that "we all play in the same game." The campaign spread such slogans as "The operator in focus" and "People are our most important resource." Much was said about improving communication, expanding the introduction of new employees, upgrading procedures for receiving suggestions from employees, and the need for new attitudes toward the company. A company song was composed. Yet changes in work design and organization were conspicuous in their absence. Nor were there any demonstrable changes in personnel turnover, job satisfaction, or product quality. On the contrary, in certain cases the campaign actually provoked negative reactions, by building up expectations that were not followed up by concrete changes.[9]

Personnel policies were another instrument of the conservative arsenal. The company tried to recruit more assemblers over twenty-five years of age and to cut down on leaves for study. But Volvo did not control the labor market in Gothenburg (the second largest city in Sweden), so these methods were unsuccessful in practice. The general manager of line 1 stressed this in an interview in 1987: "We can't handle future challenges with personnel policies alone—changes are needed in the work itself. Work content has to be enlarged, autonomy has to be increased, etc."

In 1986, the company switched tactics. In place of the attitude campaign, attempts were made to change the organization of work without changing the production design. The assemblers would be divided into groups with responsibility for inspection and adjustment, which had earlier rested with the foreman. The idea was to hand over responsibility for all inspection to the groups and then to follow up by transferring such tasks as materials handling and participation in drawing up the budget. Plans were made to train group representatives and the other assemblers in these tasks. The management of the assembly section believed these changes would lead to an increased commitment, lower turnover, and much reduced adjustment work. The only measurable effect after some years, however, was an expansion of the training budget.

Changing first-line management's responsibilities within the framework of the established organizational structure also proved difficult. The company tried in 1986 to increase the responsibility for results within the chain of command by introducing contracts between managers at different levels and in different functions. General Motors was the inspiration. Thus, the general manager would sign a contract with the superintendent, who would do the same with the foremen and personnel in areas such as materials and industrial engineering. Follow-up of the contracts, which specified requirements for quality, quantity, personnel, and costs, would take place every month. But here too, no practical results were evident.

The most significant change on the main lines during the first half of the 1980s was the broad extension of job rotation. In a 1986 survey, 83 percent of the assemblers reported that they changed work stations several times a day, and 44 percent said they did more than fifteen balances. This rotation helped reduce CTD injuries. For first-line management, however, it became more difficult to use substitutes in cases of absence since an entire series of balances had to be mastered. The frequent switching of tasks was also thought to produce quality problems; it made it hard, in any case, to trace who was responsible for a mistake. Volvo tried to reduce job rotation in 1986, but this aroused great discontent at TC. (In the majority of cases, the foremen simply reported one rotation schedule while allowing the assemblers to follow a wholly different one.) Thus, even modest work changes came up against serious restrictions.

The planning of TUN in 1979–81 had held out the promise of great improvements with the introduction of a buffered line system: delegated responsibility for results, prospects for varying the work pace, reduced sensitivity to disruptions, and higher quality. A 1985 assessment of TUN showed, however, that the factory's economic performance was about the same as that of the corresponding lines at TC. The assemblers considered the working conditions somewhat better, but the difference was not great and personnel turnover was not much lower.

"Production Strategy P 90"

In the mid-1980s, Volvo Cars' economic situation improved dramatically. Criticism of Torslanda, of the assembly plant especially, grew more severe among top managers both in the car division and at the level of the corporate group. It was thought unacceptable that TC, with its general plan, had lower goals than Kalmar. In 1985, the product engineering and planning staff presented a report entitled "Production Strategy P 90—Final Assembly." The purpose was to achieve a uniform development of Volvo Cars' manufacturing units in time for production of the next line of cars.

P 90's goals were aggressive, especially the demands for a reduction of worker time. Assembly time per car for instance, would be reduced by 60 percent between 1985 and 1995. The strategic perspective favored mechanization, both for raising productivity and for improving assembly work. It assumed a continued serial flow. The main source of inspiration, as the project director stressed, was the big mechanization project presented by Volkswagen and GM during this period:

> It is with mechanization that the problems of assembly work will be definitively solved: the short work cycles, the constant performance of the same standardized job under pressure of time, etc. . . . The object is to reach a level between 10 and 25 percent mechanization. Compare that with VW, which has 16 percent mechanization in Wolfsburg these days, and figure on coming up to 25 percent in the second stage.

The P 90 project was pursued single-mindedly during 1985. Two years later, however, the idea of a uniform production strategy for mechanization common to the entire division had withered away. This was the result of both a shift in concept at Uddevalla and TC's own dearly bought experience with resistance to the mechanization of assembly.

Obstacles to Mechanization

A 1983 report on TC's future included a long list of operations fit for mechanization: marriage points; seat installation; media filling, including inspection; leak testing on finished cars; tube bending; roof hatch and head lining; handling of PUR windows, including the application of polyurethane adhesive to the glass; and anticorrosion treatment. Five years later, only one of these operations had been mechanized: the PUR adhesing of windows on the P 70. This involved some costly equipment, which also had very serious break-in problems. Some of the other items on the list were pursued at various stages of pilot studies.

The P 90 plan included a demand, pushed by the product engineering staff, for 5 percent mechanization, to be attained from 1986 to 1990. Yet TC proved unable to reach even 1 percent. The gap between the visions of the central engineering staff and the actual possibilities presented by production were obviously wider than the planners had realized. Even the long-term potential of the mechanization strategy appeared very limited. In the view of TC's management, no significant advances in automation would be possible in the manufacture of the expected new platform (the Volvo 800 series) either, except for the introduction of automated "marriage."

Thus, in the mid-1980s, all strategies based on continued line manufacturing—the attitude campaign, efforts to change personnel recruitment, organizational experiments, and mechanization efforts—had proved insufficient. At the same time, the pressure on TC to change had increased sharply.

Crises in Productivity and Personnel

Volvo Cars' most important demands on assembly were for customer quality, short assembly times, and reliability in delivery. Ever since the launch in 1984 of the 700 series (the P 70), demands for quality had increased in significance. The quality index was rather low during the first years of production—around 750 (wholly fault-free assembly is assigned the value of 1,000). Volvo's factory in Ghent, Belgium, held the lead in improvement and reached 900 early on. This increased the pressure on TC, which had to work very hard to reach roughly the same level in 1987. TC's problem was that it could not improve both its quality and its productivity as rapidly as the company's other factories could. In 1987, TC budgeted thirty-four hours for each vehicle in the 700 series; Kalmar required nine hours less and Ghent twelve hours less (a difference of 40 percent).

A critical cause of TC's difficulties was the high personnel turnover at the factory. As shown in table 8-1, the values varied over the years, reflecting both the general state of the labor market and changes in the volume of production. Turnover increased continuously between 1982 and 1989, however, to a new record high. At the same time, the increasing quality demands made it ever more important for the plant to retain stable personnel. (The exceptionally high stability at Ghent was one of the reasons for its success.)

Another important personnel cost at TC was absenteeism due to sickness. This stayed rather constant, at 15 to 16 percent of all employees, from 1980 to 1987. (Total absenteeism, including those taking various kinds of leave, was 27 to 29 percent.) Absenteeism due to sickness became increasingly costly during the 1980s, in step with the raised quality requirements. Thus, future planning for TC, from the mid-1980s onward, focused more on improving the recruitment and retention of workers. A significant reduction in staff turnover was considered a condition for achieving future productivity and quality goals.

Plant management had long believed that the high rates of turnover and absenteeism were a result of the way mass media had portrayed the jobs on the line and that this had given them their bad reputation and low status. In a 1984 interview, Torslanda's plant manager had the following to say: "It's important that the majority like their jobs, so they stay. It's also important that the notion of the assembly line as something ugly be expunged from the public consciousness. The assembly line is here to stay. This is because [mass auto production] is necessarily a centrally controlled process."

A series of investigations of the working conditions on the line showed that these negative attitudes could scarcely be ascribed to the mass media. A study in the early 1980s, for example revealed that only 12 percent of the workers on the line said their jobs gave them a feeling of personal satisfaction, and only 10 percent reported that they had used their talents and skills some of the time. In an analysis

TABLE 8-1. Personnel Turnover at TC, 1975–89[a]

Year	Turnover
1975	23.8%
1976	20.5
1977	13.5
1978	14.0
1979	23.2
1980	24.9
1981	18.4
1982	12.0
1983	13.2
1984	16.3
1985	16.1
1986	19.7
1987	21.6
1988	25.2
1989	27.3

[a]Based on shares of all employees within TC's organization. (The departments for materials handling and quality assurance are not counted.) The table includes only net turnover—that is, cases in which the employees themselves gave notice. Vacation workers, holders of youth places, and so on are consequently excluded. If internal transfers within the Volvo group are included in the calculation, the figures become about 4 percent higher for the late 1980s. Turnover on the lines was even higher.

of workers who quit their jobs in 1986 (carried out by Torslanda's health office for the assembly section), more than 80 percent said they had no prospects of developing skills in their work, and as many said they felt dissatisfaction when coming to work. In the mid-1980s, the realization grew among production managers that these "negative attitudes" had arisen because the working conditions really were inferior.

Project TC 90

The productivity and personnel crises combined with the failures of line rationalization and purely technical solutions led to a sociotechnical renaissance. In 1986, management at TC produced its own modernization plan, Project TC 90. In many respects, the plan represented a return to the product engineering staff's "Project Production 90" from 1982, which had attracted no support at the time. The essential idea was to replace the line system step by step over a period of five years with a more flexible transport technology, so as to make possible the establishment of a number of product shops with a clear-cut responsibility for their results. As suggested in "Production Strategy P 90," the workshops would each produce part of the car. Within each product shop, different layouts, with varying degrees of parallelization, would be possible. All work and responsibility inside the product shops would rest on a group-based organization, and the technical system would be flexible at the group level. The groups would be granted resources both for administrative tasks and production service. Training would be a natural part of the work and would be oriented to professional training and the attainment of higher skill levels.

TC 90 assumed, as did P 90, a fundamentally serial structure in which each product shop would constitute a high-volume factory. TC 90 lacked P 90's focus on mechanization, however, and it stressed personnel matters a great deal more. This was emphasized by the director of investment and construction:

> Earlier projects were technology projects. TC 90 is much more an organizational project, in which the object is to shape the technology so as to alter the organization, and by that means to compete for the work force of the 1990s. We've got to get people to stay longer, and that requires changes in the design. We can't develop the organization with the present line system.

By 1986, then, TC had begun to abandon the P 90 concept. Uddevalla took the decisive step toward small-scale assembly that same year. Ghent retained its line organization, however, though it modernized and made it more flexible with the partial installation of AGVs in conjunction with the introduction of the 700 series in 1984. Accordingly, the goal of the product engineering staff to achieve uniform development within the division had failed. The idea was a sound one in terms of economies of scale. But in a time of transition, marked by powerful demands for change and a great need for experimentation to find new solutions, it proved impossible to "install" a common model from above.

The rebuilding prescribed by TC 90 was planned to take place without altering production output and within existing buildings. It thus fragmented the process of renovation, since it was necessary first to prepare space and then to reconstruct a section.

The first stage of TC 90 was the MAX project, whereby the engine dress-up, which earlier had been done on two sublines, was to be organized as an assembly shop with a new production design. Another components shop was designed in Project Door. The next stage would be Project Chassis, which involved removing so-called tilt assembly (the work on the underbody) from the lines; this would become the basis for another product shop.

Experiences of MAX

The new motor axle shop, which was responsible for the assembly of front axles and the power train (engine and transmission) for the 200 and 700 series, began operating in 1987 with 250 employees. The pace of production was eight hundred trains per day. The shop was the first real test of the TC 90 concept. The experiences of this shop came to affect the entire planning process, and so I shall examine them in some detail.

MAX was designed as a series-parallel system with a total of ten steps. First came a row of stations directly tied to the serial flow, for the installation of front axles and engine intakes and for mounting the transmission on the engine. Engine dress-up was done in a large number of parallel booths. The cycle times increased from two minutes to fifteen to twenty-five. Thereafter came a series of other stations, for the assembly of the exhaust system and media filling (oil and so forth), among other things. All moving of the base object (the engine) was done by carrier. In the engine dress-up, the taxi principle was applied; that is, the assemblers ordered the carriers to deposit "raw engines" and then fetch completed engines after the assembly was done.

The purpose of MAX was both to change the assembly work itself and to lay the foundation for a group-based organization. The goals were high. Production groups would be responsible for quality and quantity, and they could increase their participation in such extra tasks as planning, economy, maintenance, industrial engineering, and the hiring of new employees. Group representatives would function as coordinators and substitutes.

When the product shop began in 1987, however, it became clear the system design had not at all given the assemblers the freedom assumed in the plans for group development. The combination of line and dock principles created a series of unforeseen problems. On-line stations, for the engine intake, for instance, grew into bottlenecks from which disruptions quickly spread, both backward and forward, in the flow. The taxi system in the engine dress-up led to unexpected waiting time; this meant MAX had great difficulty reaching planned capacity. For one thing, the depositing and fetching of the engines took a long time in itself. For another, the carrier line section following the engine booths was badly adapted to coping with the varying output of the parallel assembly system. Queues of carriers easily arose in the loops outside the engine booths, which meant complete engines could not be fetched and new ones deposited. Waiting times in engine dress-up were difficult to use for such activities as materials handling and subassembly since the assemblers could not know which engine variant would be assembled next.

War between Managers and Assemblers

These problems in the design required management to focus all of its efforts on the most elementary matter: ensuring that the prescribed number of engines was produced. In the planning phases of the project, group work had represented organizational development and work integration, and the union was the driving force. Group work now came instead to signify management's efforts to increase work intensity. With wholly individualized work in assembly (one assembler, one booth), the up time fell to a mere 80 percent. If the assemblers at three stations worked together, however, so that two stations were always occupied, the engine dress-up system could reach 99 percent availability.

There were no benefits for the assemblers, however, in helping one another in order to compensate for the waiting time produced by the system when they worked alone. Because of deficiencies in the system's functioning, the reward for collective effort—made-up time in the form of a "bank" or filled buffer—was very uncertain. The assemblers could not generally judge how much time they could make up, and even when they could, there were not any economic incentives to work more efficiently.

Management's attempts to get the assemblers to do "group work" thus led to strong antagonisms. In the words of the MAX general foreman in 1988:

> It's been war all year between management and the assemblers. In order to get them to work in groups—that is, more than they think they need to—constant supervision and pressure from the foreman is required. This has also led to tensions among the assemblers: "He doesn't help me. Why should I help him then?"
>
> The group representative has to stress to his colleagues that "you're employed to work in a group," an unrewarding job he doesn't get paid extra for. It's very hard to compensate for disturbances. The theoretical capacity is far above the program. In practice, it's hard every single day to reach the production target.

Stabilization and Competence Enhancement

The problems in MAX initially led top management to consider halting the entire project and returning to the old system. That idea was abandoned, however, and thereafter a "commission of inquiry" was given the task of planning a reconstruction of the workshop. It proposed an entirely different design, based on integrated parallel groups with overall responsibility for assembly. But after production at TC fell in 1989–90 (due to sluggish sales) and the personnel in MAX achieved more experience and competence, performance improved decisively without the reconstruction. Production stoppages, which in 1987–88 had required hours to clear up, took just a couple of minutes in 1990. At the same time, waiting time losses in the engine dress-up booths were eliminated: first, by performing assembly in pairs in some of the booths; second, on account of technical overcapacity (as a result of the lower production program, several engine booths were unused under normal operating conditions). Thus, the assemblers could, after finishing work in one booth, switch to another booth and do the assembly there, without having to wait for the completed object to be removed. Consequently, reaching the production targets was much easier than before. The engine assemblers also got the opportunity to work ahead and thereby acquired some of the technical autonomy promised by the project. This contributed to increased satisfaction and personnel stability. In 1990, several of the shop's sections had much lower staff turnover and sickness absenteeism than did the factory's line sections. The overall system was still considered much too complex and expensive, however. Simple parallel systems with long-cycle jobs were preferred over both line assembly and complex series-parallel systems.

The general conclusion many engineers drew in 1987–88 was that bolder departures from line assembly were needed—toward compact assembly systems with few steps and base object transfers and thereby much greater work content. During the planning of MAX, it had been feared that increased work cycles would prove troublesome. When the shop began operations, it became obvious that long work cycles were not the problem at all. According to production managers, interviewed in 1990 after three years of operations, there was widespread discontent with the remaining short-cycle stations, despite systematic work rotation. A small fraction of the workers were not suited to the more complex long-cycle work in the engine booths, but it was altogether clear that the vast majority of assemblers preferred these jobs.

Project Door

Project Door, the other of TC 90's component shops, was based on an old idea: that it was better to detach the doors from the body and assemble them outside the line, as Kalmar had always done. Assembling the doors on the main car line, as was done at TC, made for ergonomic difficulties in assembly, crowding on the line, and paint damage. Within the framework of TC 90, a proposal was presented in 1987 that had many similarities to the thinking behind MAX. Project Door contained, among other things, an automated warehouse for buffering and sorting, carriers for the transport of doors inside the product shop, and a conveyor system for transport back to the line.

Experiences with MAX motivated management to avoid complex flows and equipment at all costs. The planning work had to begin again on the basis of different assumptions. When the decision to build a new shop was finally taken in 1988, the orientation was altogether different from before. The project's main study emphasized this:

> The proposal now before us is in many ways wholly different from the earlier proposals, and it is above all the much lower technical level that makes it possible for the project to be profitable now. . . . The social part will gain an ever greater significance, which means work organization must also be ascribed an ever greater importance. . . . The sociotechnical part should be given priority.

The new door shop was designed as a wholly manual system with forty-eight parallel one-worker workplaces plus some preassembly jobs with special equipment. Each assembler would build a complete set of doors (all the doors to a car, that is). The task included fetching materials, assembly, inspection, function testing, and adjustment—in all, a job of about eighty minutes per set at full speed. The work tasks would be performed, inspected, and, when applicable, adjusted by the same individual. The so-called one-car concept—one assembler, one door set—meant the product shop would be able to cope with changes in sequence of the car bodies; this was important for increasing flexibility in the overall production flow. According to the plans, the work would be group organized, with the group as the smallest planning point. In practice, however, the design implied a thorough individualizing of the work, which later on was reinforced by a new wage system with virtually no group components.

Chassis Project

Both MAX and Project Door were in principle simple to start within the framework of TC 90 in that they concerned components assembly and did not interfere with the main line. With the Chassis Project, however (which was planned to follow directly after MAX), the idea was to remove a large part of the final line assembly. In 1987, 160 persons worked with chassis on line 1 (P 90) and 270 on line 2. The work included the mounting of brake and fuel pipes, fuel tanks, steering shafts, spring struts, propeller shafts, rear axles, rear exhaust pipes, bumpers, and so on. The Chassis Project's main study described the existing system as "problematic, static, and inefficient"—a split-up assembly line with short station times (1.5 to 2 minutes), expensive materials handling, and a high share of capital tied up in inventory.

The first modernization plan was produced in 1987. It proposed that a new shop be built with four series-connected sections plus a few central subassembly areas. Within each section, assembly would take place in up to thirteen to fourteen parallel workplaces. Accordingly, the plan proposed, as did MAX, a combination of serial and parallel principles. The object was to attain a more productive design less sensitive to disruption and more attractive workplaces and thereby more stable personnel. This was justified with a broadened "socioeconomic cost estimate," in accordance with the guidelines of TC 90. Thus, the plan assumed that the high costs for personnel turnover and absenteeism would be reduced by 50 percent in the new shop. It was also assumed that inspection and adjustment costs would be halved since the longer cycle times and more elastic flows would yield greater possibilities of building right from the beginning. Finally, in IE terms, the assembly system would be more integrated and have longer work cycles; this would allow reduced balancing losses and simpler rebalancing. A considerable improvement in up time compared to line assembly was also expected.

The cost estimate produced a much better picture of the total costs of the existing production system than did earlier methods. The revenue side was problematic, however. The optimistic assumption that turnover and absenteeism could be reduced by 50 percent if the projected changes were carried through was not substantiated to the slightest degree.

The 1987 plan for the new chassis shop was never carried out. First, the new equipment required by the plan made the cost too high. Second, plant management considered the MAX-type design (with its large number of base object transfers within the shop and its many "dock steps" in succession) too sensitive to disruptions. A much more compact design was worked out in 1988: the entire chassis assembly would be done in a single step with a cycle time of one hour. The new concept was simpler and safer than the first proposal. Since it required fewer movements of the base object and therefore fewer carriers and pallets, it was also much cheaper. With the increased need for space and more products in process, however, it nonetheless involved higher costs than the existing line.

The new chassis concept, with its no fewer than forty parallel double docks, was the most radical parallelization possible within the TC 90 structure. It was not just a change of layout; it also required development of handling equipment for heavy components and of new types of assembly tools, since the planned shop would involve marked parallelization in the main flow, necessitating simple, duplicatable technology and manual transports. The concept had far-reaching consequences for the whole assembly process since it would make mechanization—at least of the conventional variety based on the use of heavy stationary equipment—impossible in a critical section for the foreseeable future.

At the same time, the product engineering staff worked intensively to realize the dream of mechanized marriage (the joining of the body and the power train) for the new product platform. This project included chassis assembly, marriage, and the transport system. Carriers would bring pallets to various loading stations and then enter a mechanized marriage section. With this solution, the precise tightening of critical joints would be ensured, and the variation between the front and rear axles would be reduced. TC's engineers were worried about the accessibility of a system with more than thirty dedicated assembly machines. The equipment would be entirely model-specific and therefore costly. Besides, the project contradicted "the sociotechnical renaissance" at the factory. The manual work (which was still the lion's share) would be done in a fragmented structure, with a series of repetitive and one-sided loading and subassembly jobs.

The intense conflict in 1988 surrounding mechanized versus manual marriage brought to the fore fundamental questions about the future of the TC assembly plant. On the one side, the product engineering staff championed a strategy of

retaining the high-flow structure. On the other, the idea of fundamental parallelization was raised for the first time—along the lines of the whole-car concept
at Uddevalla. The new Chassis Project fell between these two basic perspectives
and was therefore dropped, as its predecessor had been. The entire TC 90 plan,
thereby, in practice, ceased to apply.

After TC 90

TC 90 had been launched as a modernization project in which changes were
introduced in one shop at a time. Thus, despite the plan's large-scale orientation
and TC's resources as Volvo's high-volume factory, the work of restructuring was
marked by the drawbacks of small scale. TC's management proceeded on the
basis of series-parallel assembly since it considered that this would make successive
reforms possible with minimum risk and within existing space. When tested in
practice, however, this seemingly safe compromise between straight and parallel
assembly instead produced a high sensitivity to disruption and low efficiency.
Investment costs were also prohibitive. This led first to radical rethinking on the
level of the product shop. The next step was to apply these experiences to TC as
a whole; thus, in 1988, the future structure as a whole was called into question.
This opened up new perspectives, but in practical terms a demobilization occurred. With the TC 90 plan now impossible, there was no longer any common
strategy for change. These uncertainties convinced company management not to
break in the next car model (the 800 series) at TC but instead to choose Ghent.
The deadline that had kept up the pressure for change thereby disappeared.

In 1989, a new perspective on the development of TC as a whole was presented
in the form of a pilot study entitled "New Assembly TC." This study expressed
the polarization following the failure of the TC compromise. On the one hand,
it proposed the construction of three whole-car shops, with a total capacity of
30,000 cars per year. On the other, it proposed that 110,000 cars (or 80 percent
still be assembled on the lines.

An experimental operation was begun in 1988 around the concept of whole-
car construction. This had not been possible before because of the TC project's
fragmented planning. The head of the operation had earlier been a full-time
officer in Metall's factory club.

The operation introduced a new and controversial style based more on cooperation between experienced assemblers and academic researchers than on expert
IE reports. The objectives were two fold: first, to gain experience in working with
equipment, assembly manuals, and methods for whole-car assembly; and second,
to formulate a plan for the rebuilding of TC.

The operation moved into TC's main factory in 1989, to prove that the whole-
car concept was not only technically feasible but also economically reasonable

from TC's standpoint. A secondary purpose of this transfer was to awaken the work force to the idea that a broad process of change was unavoidably being set in motion. Instead, because of TC's basically Fordist tradition, which permeated the plant's industrial engineering, materials-handling, and data systems, as well as the majority of the trade union officers, the new assembly shop was expelled as an alien body. After scarcely a year, the "whole-car project" was discontinued, the justification being that worker times were too high and materials handling too expensive. The decision to suspend the experiment was supported by Metall's union club.

In the absence of a common approach laid down by top management, the plans for change at TC swung back again toward conservative solutions. Falling sales and the company's worsening economic situation radically reduced the leeway for investments in modernization. Plant management again shifted its focus to changes within the framework of the existing system.

The Agony of Change: TC from 1964 to 1990

In 1964, Volvo proudly inaugurated its new large-scale car factory, Torslandaverken, outside Gothenburg, with final assembly taking place in the TC plant. Ten years later, when the Kalmar facility was opened, the assembly lines at TC were suddenly out of fashion. But before any serious reform efforts were made, Volvo was hit by the car crisis of the late 1970s.

In 1984, the plant was very much the same as twenty years before. Pressures for change began to mount. Both Ghent, which in 1980 had produced only thirty thousand cars, and Kalmar outperformed TC. Labor turnover soared, rising from 12 percent in 1982 to 27 percent in 1989. At first, plant management tried to attack this problem by streamlining the existing technical system. Lengthy visits to Toyota inspired a set of measures to rationalize line operations as well as materials deliveries. This was accompanied by an attitude campaign to make workers identify more closely with the company. Attempts to change the recruitment practices to attract more experienced and stable workers were also made. Inspired by General Motors, plant management sought to create more dynamic first-line foremen by means of so-called internal contracts outlining personal responsibility for specified targets. But turnover continued to rise and productivity to drag.

The next major attempt to get the plant back in shape was spearheaded by product and process engineers, who promoted a technological solution. This too was inspired by GM but even more by VW, which in 1983 opened a highly automated final-assembly plant in Wolfsburg. But the results of various attempts at robotization in TC were an economic disaster.

Now TC turned to a sociotechnical strategy. In 1986, a grand modernization plan was launched. The assembly lines were to be converted to a series of assembly shops, each featuring group-based and parallelized assembly. This series-parallel layout was theoretically a safe alternative to Uddevalla's risky strategy of scrapping the cherished line altogether. The reality turned out to be different, and the first new shop, which was implemented for components assembly, had enormous problems. Pushed by the creative atmosphere at Uddevalla, the younger industrial engineers favored compact and simple systems, with a much more expanded work content and cycle times of hours instead of minutes. Thus, in 1989, an experimental shop for whole-car assembly was opened at TC. But this clashed with the entrenched Fordist culture of the plant and failed to deliver.

At the same time, Uddevalla was proceeding from the happy period of planning and innovation to the difficult task of realization. The problems at this stage contributed to a backlash and stalemate at TC. In 1990, the factory was back to square one.

In the wake of a central unifying idea for modernizing the plant, management emphasized incremental improvements in areas such as quality assurance and employee involvement. From 1985 to 1990, the volume produced at the plant decreased from 160,000 to 120,000. The destiny and direction of the plant were highly dependent on future sales and the relative successes of the concepts applied at other plants. On its own, TC had no cohesive model.

9.
Methodological Problems in Comparing Working Conditions

The great range of technical and organizational forms in the Swedish car industry during the 1980s makes possible a detailed analysis of the effects of production design and work organization on working conditions in auto assembly. Does the abandonment of traditional line assembly in favor of integrated assembly—with long work cycles and decentralized, self-managing work groups—bring about qualitative improvements in such areas as physical strains, skill development, and worker influence? This has been strongly disputed by MIT's auto researchers, who argue that changes in assembly design have no essential influence on working conditions and specifically that integrated, long-cycle assembly does not contribute to worker satisfaction. Womack, Jones, and Roos (1990) do not even mention work-related injuries, such as CTDs. No data are provided to support these claims.

Ambiguous Effects of New Work Forms

The following analysis has been inspired by German industrial sociology. A central contribution here is Horst Kern and Michael Schumann's classic study from the 1960s, *Industriearbeit und Arbeiterbewusstsein* (1977), the point of departure of which was the long postwar debate on the consequences of technological change on industrial jobs and worker consciousness. One of the major questions was whether technological development leads to a leveling of working conditions or, on the contrary, to greater differentiation. The study was designed to capture the *differences* in various dimensions of industrial work, as well as to answer the following questions: What degree of autonomy characterizes the jobs, and how have workers' prospects of exercising discretion changed? What qualifications are required, and what changes in qualifications have occurred? What are the physical and sensory demands? What cooperative ties exist, and what are the prospects for social contacts and communication? (Kern and Schumann 1977:69).

Grenzen neuer Arbeitsformen by Norbert Altmann and others (1982) is another relevant contribution. In this study, a group of researchers in Munich examined working conditions in the context of a series of new work designs within manual mass production. In their analysis, they used the same basic categories as Kern and Schumann did, with a few additions, especially concerning such topics as the relation between wages and performance, on-the-job training and working up to speed, and the position of different worker categories in the factory and on the labor market. In general, Altmann et al. found that the new organizational forms had *ambiguous* effects on working conditions. They identified three causes of such ambiguities: discrepancies, disparities, and deficiencies.

By discrepancies the researchers meant the redistribution of work burdens— for example, physical strains may be reduced, but at the same time the work is intensified. This occurs if the potential for improved working conditions is found precisely in those areas where management seeks enhanced performance. An example is the stimulation of the capacity for performance by means of individualized workplace organization. This has the potential of increasing the technical autonomy of the workers and of allowing them greater possibilities of varying the pace of work. In almost all of the cases analyzed, however, the pressures for performance were so great (because of quantity demands or wage systems) that it was difficult to take advantage of the technical autonomy. Reforms aimed at improving cooperation often encountered difficulties as well, because of quantitative pressures. According to the researchers, the potential for more cooperative relations between workers was realized only in jobs that required consistently high skill levels; this allowed for informal bargaining over performance norms.

Disparities were another cause of ambiguity. The point in this case is that changes can have different effects on different parts of the work force. For example, when newly developed workplaces are allocated to the most qualified workers instead of to former (retrained) job holders, those not chosen face worse conditions than before the changes and become marginalized.

Finally, deficiencies appear when complementary (or "flanking") measures for decreasing work burdens were absent. Such is the case, for example, when job enlargement is not combined with measures for systematic retraining. Other deficiences might concern a lack of development of the physical work environment or in the company's organizational hierarchy.

Areas Investigated

The main instrument for comparing the five Swedish assembly plants in my study was a series of surveys done between 1985 and 1987. These included the following topics: work content, the degree of responsibility required, and prospects for skill development; autonomy and influence; ergonomic design (working positions, for example); physical effects of work (pain and weariness) and psychosomatic symptoms; pace and intensity of work; and desired changes in work content, influence, and so on.

The skill dimension was measured essentially subjectively based on questions about work content: respondents were asked to assess their jobs with respect to monotony, prospects for learning and personal development, and so on. Autonomy, in the investigations of Kern and Schumann, is based on the degree to which such features as the quality and quantity of production, the timing of operations, work methods, the work pace, and physical movements are determined in advance. My survey questions on "technical autonomy" have been limited to the pace of production and work strictures (the timing of operations).

The section on influence takes up autonomy in another and broader respect: as the extent of self-determination and room for maneuver enjoyed by the worker groups. The questions in this section have been inspired by the sociotechnical tradition, with its interest in autonomy (in the sense of self-managing groups) and by Scandinavian research on participation and workplace democracy (Jon Gulowsen, Thomas Sandberg, Lars-Erik Karlsson, and others). The focus of my investigation is workplace organization and direct worker influence. I have not tried to measure the distribution of influence between different actors and groups concerning such long-term questions as product innovation, investments, and plant localization. The positions of different categories of workers in the company and in the labor market were important questions in Altmann's study, but it was not possible to investigate them with my instruments.

Methodological Problems with Surveys

Extensive sociological research has shown that individuals' views of their jobs are determined both by their actual working conditions and earlier experiences and by their living conditions in general. Is it possible nonetheless with surveys to obtain reliable data on conditions in different workplaces such that the results can be meaningfully compared? The question is important as well in regard to sections in the questionnaire that seek to chart different groups' expectations and desires for influence (precision and reliability are critical here), in that I want to compare expectations (and not an unclear mixture of expectations and actual conditions). This problem requires further methodological discussion.

In recent decades, it has become common to use questionnaires for studying the work environment and working conditions. This method has met with heavy criticism, however. It has been held to be insufficiently precise (in contrast to technical measurements) or too subjective (i.e., questionnaires give more information about individuals' values than about their actual conditions). Several studies have shown a clear connection between respondents' expectations and their answers. Torsten Björkman and Karin Lundqvist's studies of ASEA (the Swedish partner in the multinational ABB group) during the 1970s showed that correlations between answers about working conditions and the actual work environment were weak and that answers varied greatly from individuals who "in reality" had identical work environments. Workers in departments with a high frequency of problems tended to underreport them, while those in divisions with few problems greatly exaggerated them. The worst working conditions were consequently underestimated, as were the differences between different work environments.

At workshops and offices performing routine tasks, the same tendency arose with respect to the skills thought to be necessary for the work. A majority of the workers reported that their work was more qualified (i.e., less monotonous, with greater prospects for learning and so on) than one might have expected in view of the actual skill requirements (Björkman and Lundqvist 1981).

One consequence of the heavy influence of expectations on results was that the various studies conducted by ASEA produced plainly contradictory findings. On the one hand, a comparison between studies from 1974 and 1977 showed a general increase in the proportion of workers claming to suffer from various problems related to the work environment. On the other, a majority in 1977 thought working conditions either were unchanged or had improved in recent years.

Precisely the same pattern was obtained in a comparison of LO's investigations of working conditions in 1969 and in 1979. In both investigations, LO members were asked if anything at their workplace caused problems. Because a higher number in 1979 claimed there were problems, the researchers had the impression that the work environment had worsened during the 1970s. But the 1979 study also asked the workers how their conditions had changed over the years, and many more claimed they had improved than that they had deteriorated (see Bolinder et al. 1981).

As a result, many surveys have had great difficulties comparing groups over time. Björkman and Lundqvist's solution was to emphasize the importance of ex post interpretation based on an in-depth theory of the "mediation stage" between the "human psyche and the environment." This is hardly a satisfactory solution. During the 1980s, researchers at the Central Bureau of Statistics (SCB) in Stockholm showed it is possible in many cases to develop the methods of questionnaires (i.e., their design) further. The methods are neither subjective nor objective in themselves. Rather, what is decisive is the wording of the questions—their precision or lack thereof—with regard to concepts, reference points, the types of answer scales, and so on.

In a number of methodological studies, SCB tested three types of questions about the physical working environment against different objective evaluations. The first type included questions about work strains, such as "Are you bothered by noise?" This type of question contains a large subjective element, both in the formulation of the question and in the alternative answers, often of the type "Very often, Often, Seldom," and so on. The second type of questions classified working conditions in a general way: "Is your work noisy?" or "Is your work normally physically exhausting?"[1] The third type, finally, consisted of newly designed questions with great precision and distinct reference points, such as, "Is it so noisy that you cannot conduct a conversation in a normal tone when the machines are on? If so, during what proportion of the day is this the case: at most one-fourth, at most half, etc.?"

The different types of questions produced great differences in validity. The first two types yielded results diverging from objective measurements for a good 20 percent of the respondents. With the third type, however, the share fell to a mere 10 percent.[2] The correlation coefficient (which expresses the relation between the objective measurements and the survey results) was 0.53 for the first type of question, 0.66 for the second, and 0.83 for the third. The last figure represents a very marked improvement (see Wikman 1982 and Statistiska Centralbyrån 1985:96).

Questions about Physical Effort and Ease

Vague formulations of questions and alternative answers are very common in studies of the work environment. They dominate in Björkman and Lundqvist's studies of ASEA, as well as in LO's environmental studies of 1969 and 1979 (which contained questions such as "Are you bothered by . . ."). This is probably the main reason for the contradictory outcomes when the results from different periods were compared.

Questions about mental effort or mental strain on the job deserve a special comment, first, because they are so common, and, second, because they exemplify the profound problems contained in surveys using items with a weak methodological and theoretical basis. As early as 1974, the SCB observed in a report on living conditions and employment that the distribution of answers was strongly correlated with the job's educational demands. Not surprisingly, therefore, the study appeared to show that white-collar employees had mentally more demanding work than did blue-collar workers; at the top were the teaching professions. The respondents had obviously thought questions about mental strain concerned whether or not they had to "use their brains."

An altogether different definition of mental strain is produced from a combination of monotony and stress. This definition has been used in the surveys of living standards carried out by the Institute for Social Research at the University of Stockholm. The proportion of "mentally heavy work," if measured in this manner, was found to be lowest among teachers. In other words, this definition led to diametrically opposing results.

Mental strain can also be interpreted in a much narrower way—as the demand for sensory performance and quickness of response. This is Kern and Schumann's definition. According to this usage, work that is both monotonous and intensive can still be characterized by a low level of strain if the workers are able to become completely habituated in their body movements and thus devote their thoughts to other matters. If these conditions are lacking, however, monotonous work causes great psychic strain. Kern and Schumann use the example of the inspection of bottles on an assembly line, a repetitive job requiring intensive use of the senses. In terms of content, it is totally impoverished, but the worker's mind must still be continuously focused on the work; the job therefore combines maximum concentration with minimum intellectual freedom (1977:84). In view of the range of definitions of mental strain, it is not very meaningful to use it in a direct survey question. It nonetheless recurs constantly.

The same is true of the question "Are you satisfied with your job?" It is used often and leads to a response distribution with a strongly positive bias (with an exception to be discussed later). In Björkman and Lundqvist's study of ASEA, nearly everyone claimed to be satisfied with his or her colleagues, work tasks, company, and neighborhood—regardless of the actual living and working conditions. Further, in a national study from 1981, the SCB found that, in general, only 5 percent of the gainfully employed were dissatisfied with their work. An important reason for these highly positive responses is that work normally comprises an important part of a person's identity; there are therefore strong psychological mechanisms that make a person defend her or his job before herself or himself and others. The same tendency may be observed when people are asked if they are satisfied or dissatisfied with their private lives, their friends and acquaintances, and so on.

Surveys purchased by companies often use the problematic type of question discussed here. In certain cases, as when questions with a strongly positive bias are used, the result can be apologetic. In other cases, genuinely positive changes can be impossible to discern (as in the studies referred to above of the development of the work environment during the 1970s). When hierarchical and authoritarian organizations undergo change, so that prospects arise for the employees to develop their skills and their jobs, the demands of the workers tend to grow as well. Indeed, the growth of demands may outpace the actual changes (i.e., the gap between the actual and desired state of affairs gets larger in the new organization). As a result, the work force may be more dissatisfied about certain issues after the changes than before—even while they consider the new work better than the old. With a survey instrument focused on the attitudes of individuals, then, the responses can be more negative in the "new" factory than in the "old," although the working conditions in various respects are actually better.[3]

Two Examples from Volvo

Two attitude studies carried out at Volvo in the mid-1980s provide a textbook example of vague and ambiguous questions that appear resistant to theoretical and methodological criticism.[4] One of the studies, "Attitude 85," was developed by Sigvard Rubenowitz and others at the University of Gothenburg. It was a survey of all employees at Volvo Trucks in 1985 (see Volvo Trucks 1986). Two examples from the section entitled "Surveying the Physical Work Environment" give an indication of its character: "How satisfied are you with the lighting at your workplace? Very satisfied/Rather satisfied/Neither satisfied nor dissatisfied/ Rather dissatisfied/Very dissatisfied;" "Are you bothered during your work by gas, dust, smoke, or haze? No, never/No, only on rare occasions/Yes, sometimes." As is evident, both the questions and the alternative answers leave much room for different expectation levels and reference systems among the respondents.

The section on the "psychosocial work environment" is no less problematic. It contains questions such as the following: "Do you think your work is mentally demanding?" and "Are you satisfied working here at the company?"

Other questions in "Attitude 85" were intended to yield a description of the individuals' prospects for influencing different conditions. The alternative answers were of the following type: very great possibilities, rather great possibilities, certain possibilities, rather small possibilities, very small possibilities. Again, the respondents' expectation levels showed up strongly in the results. Not surprisingly, it was difficult in "Attitude 85" to detect any pronounced differences between the two truck factories LB with its decentralized group organization and the X plant with its traditional form of organization (Volvo Trucks 1986).[5]

Another problematic study is "Volvo Monitor," which the polling firm SIFO carries out repeatedly within the entire corporate group. It also contains questions with strongly subjective features, about "mental strain" and "job satisfaction," for example, that are similar to those in "Attitude 85." A report on the 1985 survey in the company newspaper *VTV-nytt* (October 1985) illustrates the apologetic character such questionnaires can have. The report notes that "most employees at the Torslanda plant are satisfied with their work in most respects. Seventy-five percent are content with their jobs either most or a large part of the time."

Some problems were noted: "The employees feel a certain stress in their jobs sometimes. Nineteen percent say their work is mentally demanding. . . . Nineteen percent say they are often afraid of health hazards. [But] the great majority of the employees still think it is fun to go to work, and a majority think things go really well at the job." It is difficult to understand from the Monitor's picture of the situation why acute staff problems drove the firm to launch TC 90, the biggest project for change in the history of the plant, in the following year.

Technical Design of the Five-Plant Questionnaire

The purpose of the questionnaire used in my investigation was to make comparisons possible between the plants. It was therefore important to minimize measuring mistakes arising from the effects of expectations. It was also critical to formulate questions and alternative answers in a discriminating manner—in other words, to avoid questions with highly skewed response distributions. Each questionnaire was preceded by qualitative interviews with workers in different positions, preferably assemblers. The idea was to get an overview of the different conditions at work and how they had changed, as well as to obtain a more profound understanding of certain issues, such as the structure and planning horizon of long-cycle assembly work. In all, about one hundred one-hour interviews with workers were carried out; these were complemented by extensive plant visits and interviews with management.

In designing the questionnaire, I made use of results from the SCB's methodological studies, which at this time mainly included questions about physical strains. I was also inspired in formulating my questions on influence by a technique used in the project "Industrial Democracy in Europe," (see Björklund, Molin, and Sandberg 1979).[6]

A later project at the SCB focusing on the psychosocial work environment sought to obtain more precise survey items on such issues as work content and responsibility. Anders Wikman's final report on this project (1989) indicates both the possibility of improvement and the difficulty of developing as rigorous validity criteria in this area as for questions about the physical environment (i.e., to obtain data on the psychosocial environment independently of the respondents). After many attempts, however, SCB constructed a number of precise items concerning time pressures, concentration demands, and monotony. They would have been valuable to include in my studies had they been available at that time.[7]

After testing several versions of pilot questionnaires at two factories, I carried out the final version of my survey at the five plants from 1985 to 1987. The results were presented for management and the union at each factory. In addition, at Volvo LB and at Scania in Katrineholm, the findings were discussed with all the participating workers. These discussions showed the questions to be quite satisfactory.

The surveys at TC, LB, Borås, and Katrineholm were carried out on company time and on company premises. The proportion not responding was low (ap-

TABLE 9-1. Basic Data on the Surveys

Factory	Number of respondents	Sample	Number of final assemblers among respondents
TC	283	35% of the day-shift workers on Line 1	127
TUN	136	Entire factory	86
LB	236	Entire factory	128
Borås	32	All of the dock assemblers	26
Katrineholm	73	All sub- and chassis assemblers	28

proximately 15 percent of the total sample). At TUN, where no company time was set aside for participating in the survey, 55 percent of the workers took part. (Table 9-1 provides data on the number of respondents at the five plants.) Despite the relatively high nonresponse rate, the distribution of actual respondents according to positions, skill levels, age, and sex closely matched that of the population as a whole.

At all of the factories the questionnaire included questions on work intensity and autonomy, symptoms of physical and mental strain, assessment of the job, and desires for change. At the three Gothenburg plants, questions about actual and desired influence were added. Finally, the LB and TUN questionnaires included questions in which respondents compared their current job with previous work they had had at Volvo.

The survey results are presented below in tables, diagrams, and simple statistical analyses. Three different types of analysis are used, based on each questions' scale level: correlation analyses for interval scales; nonparametric tests (such as the gamma type) for ordinal and nominal scales; and variance analyses for combinations of interval and nominal scales. The correlation coefficient has a well-defined meaning, which is not true for nonparametric measurements.[8] Ordinal scales can be converted to interval scales by means of dichotomization and a correlation analysis can then be done, but this conversion entails a considerable loss of information.

There is a contradiction between different demands in survey analyses. The questions that are statistically easy to process are based on data at an interval or quotient scale level. They have various numerical estimation scales, which is probably why questions of this kind are popular. At the same time, such questions have, in my survey, yielded relatively less precision and validity. Questions with answers on the ordinal scale (given in time measurements, such as all of the day, half of the day, one or a few hours each day, and very seldom) make greater precision possible but are harder to process statistically.

All of these efforts to secure reliable and comparative survey data on the actual working conditions in different plants could not eliminate a significant limitation—the small numbers of workers in the operations with the most advanced work content. This was a limitation in the real world, not just in the data. The bus plants were small, but they had been in operation for several years, which was a major advantage. At the time of the study, the larger Uddevalla plant was just about to start its long breaking-in process and thus could not be included. Nonetheless, the data are sufficient to compare work in different organizational settings, to elucidate important ambiguities of the new production concept, and to identify general patterns, such as workers reactions to repetitive jobs. The latter issue is the focus of the following chapter.

10.
The Degrading Monotony of the Assembly Line

It is natural to begin the analysis of my data with Volvo TC in that it well represents the production design that for so long has dominated the auto industry and that is still vigorous internationally. The Japanese transplants, for example, apply the same basic technical design in their long, mechanically paced lines.

At the time of my survey, in 1986, auto assembly at TC was done on two assembly lines, both of the conventional conveyor type. The work organization was strictly hierarchical, with a clear chain of command: assembler, subforeman ("instructor"), foreman, general foreman, line manager. Training times in assembly were short—normally one to a few days (up to a week if the training covered a number of stations at the same time).

The sample for my survey was selected from line 1—the daytime line—to facilitate comparisons with the other factories, all of which had daytime production. The survey included assemblers on the line and in subassembly, utility and repair (U & R) men, inspectors, and material handlers. I focus here on the assemblers, who accounted for somewhat less than half the respondents (127 of 283).[1] The average assembler was young. Thirty-four percent were twenty years of age or younger; 75 percent were less than twenty-six. The average time of employment on the line was extremely short—52 percent had held their current job for less than a year. Just 17 percent of the assemblers were women.

Physical Strains

I will first consider three basic issues affecting the assemblers' working conditions: work content, measured in station time (I shall treat enhancement through rotation later); work strictures and autonomy; and time pressure and work intensity. Ninety-four percent of the assemblers stated that their cycle time was two to three minutes or less. The inspectors along the line also had short cycle times in the main, while subassembly workers and U & R men reported that their times were somewhat longer (the median was between four and ten minutes).

The combination of the short cycle times and mechanical pacing yielded a high degree of confinement. Two-thirds of the assembly workers said they could not leave their work stations without having a replacement (they could not visit the restroom, for example), and only a fifth (22 percent) could leave their work stations for longer than two minutes without a replacement.

Generally, the possibilities of influencing the work pace were limited. More than 60 percent of the assemblers stated that they were held for the entire day to a work pace they could not affect; 74 percent said they were confined in this way for at least half the day. Only the subassembly workers reported markedly less confinement than the line assemblers, and this was because they worked off line and as yet without any JIT control. In the terms of Womack, Jones, and Roos (1990), the subassembly workers worked under conditions of old-fashioned mass production.

The least negative factor for the assemblers was the time pressure. To the question "Do you work part of the day under such heavy time pressure that you have to work as fast as you can?" 20 percent replied that they did so for at least half the day. The pressure enforced by the pace of the line appears to have been compensated for to a considerable extent: first, in that the workers learned to perform their brief operations quickly and habitually; and, second, in that there was unused work time because of balancing and variant losses. Figure 10-1 summarizes the assemblers' working conditions in the areas considered above.

Despite the short average employment time and the youthfulness of the workers, symptoms of physical strain were common among TC workers. An overview of the problem is shown in figure 10-2.

One cause of these strains was the line's repetitiveness. Seventy-four percent of the assemblers reported that their work time was characterized by one-sided, monotonous physical movements. Another cause was the design of the assembly tools, which did not allow any adjustment to accommodate for varying hand and grip sizes. This contributed to a high incidence of wrist injuries, especially among the women. Yet another cause of the physical difficulties was the design of the product. Half the workers spent at least half their work time in a forward-stooping position without physical support (assembling components in the baggage and engine compartments, for example).

The connection between working position on the one hand and one-sided movements and physical strains on the other is palpably illustrated in figure 10-3. The longer the time spent in a awkward working position or in performing monotonous operations, the higher the incidence of physical strains. The fre-

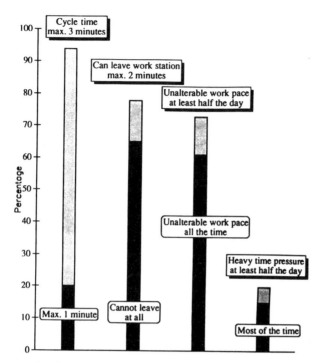

FIGURE 10-1. *Incidence of Severe Restrictions, Unalterable Work Pace, and Heavy Time Pressures among Assemblers at TC*

quency of back and neck problems was strongly correlated with working in a stooping position; a clear causal relation would seem to be discernible here. That the incidence of wrist and hand aches was also correlated with such working positions is perhaps more an expression of covariation than evidence of a direct connection.

The data on cycle times does not give the whole picture of the TC assemblers' work content in that job rotation was widely practiced. More than 80 percent of the assemblers switched assembly stations several times a day. During the week studied, 27 percent changed between two and five stations; another 27 percent switched between six and fifteen stations; and 35 percent worked at more than fifteen stations. Just 11 percent stated that they took part in no rotation at all. Without this extensive rotation, the physical strains would have been even worse. The proportion of workers with aches in their shoulders and arms diminished with increased rotation, as did the proportion with aches in their wrists and hands. The share of assembly workers with long-lasting physical difficulties that arose during their time at TC appeared to decrease with increased rotation as well.

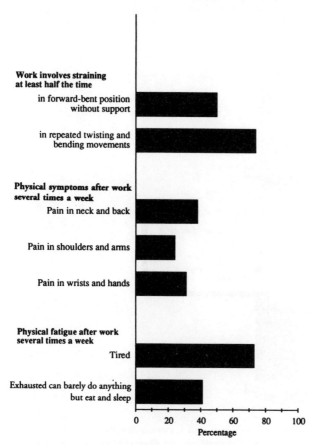

FIGURE 10-2. Physical Effects of Assembly Work

Nonetheless, the overall level of physical strain remained high. The work operations in the areas in which job rotation occurred (typically, within the same supervisor's unit) were all too similar to offer any genuine alternative or relief. Rotating jobs did not change the essential conditions of work. Rather, it was probably the heavy personnel turnover that really limited the extent to which the workers suffered from work-related injuries.

Uddevalla had as a goal a much lower turnover. This required a drastic reduction of the physical burdens so as to avoid increasing the incidence of injuries. Likewise, the physical stress at TC contributed radically to the drive to change work arrangements at Uddevalla. There were three main ways of doing this: introducing parallel, long-cycle assembly, which greatly reduced the repetitiveness of the work and the extent of one-sided motions; devel-

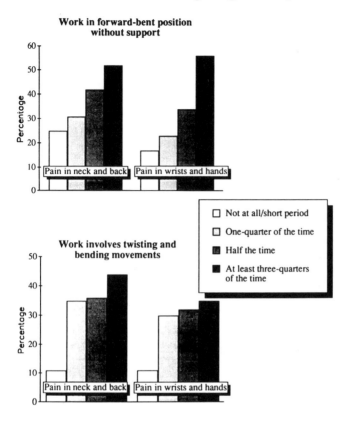

The correlation is statistically significant at the following levels: work in forward-bent position and pain in neck and back, .001; pain in wrists and hands, .004; work in monotonous movements and pain in neck and back, .001; pain in wrists and hands, .04.

FIGURE 10-3. Share of Assemblers Who Suffer Physical Difficulties from the Strains of Their Work

oping assembly tools with new hand grips, which reduced the risk of wrist injuries; and changing to wholly tilted assembly (with raising and lowering capabilities), to eliminate work performed in a stooping position. It thereby became possible to carry out assembly in the coupé and the baggage and engine compartments in an upright position.

Mental Strains

Physical strains are but one aspect of working conditions. Another feature, and, as revealed in the interviews, an even more important one, is the effect of the minute division of labor on work content and development prospects. To quote

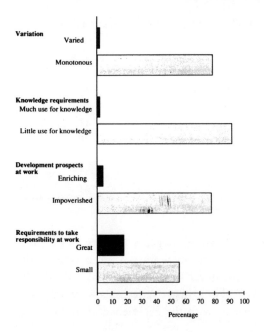

Jobs were placed on a five-step scale. Values 1 and 2 have been combined here as have values 4 and 5. Answers at level 3 (neither varied, nor monotonous) have been omitted.

FIGURE 10-4. Variation, Knowledge Requirements, Development Prospects, and Responsibility of Assembly-Line Workers

one of the engine assemblers: "People outside Volvo think I know everything about engines now—but in fact I only know about the few operations I do, nothing else."

Fifty-six percent of the assembly workers considered the work *very* monotonous, and 52 percent considered it *very* degrading. Figure 10-4 provides an overview of the work content and prospects for skill development in assembly.

There was no connection between these negative assessments and educational background. Assemblers with only grade-school education considered the work to be as monotonous as did assemblers who had studied social science in high school. The extensive work rotation also had very little effect on the experience of monotony; an analysis of the relation between job rotation and the assessment of variation in work revealed no significant connection. Again, the extent of the rotation proved too limited to change the basic character of the work.

The repetitive and unskilled work also produced mental strains, which found

TABLE 10-1. Psychic and Psychosomatic Reactions and Feelings about Work

Symptom	
Headaches on the job several times a week	17%
Stomach aches on the job several times a week	24
Hard to sleep because of thoughts of work	13
Satisfied with the day's work	
Daily / several times a week	17
Some time each month or not at all	76
Distaste at the prospect of work	
Daily / several times a week	33
Some time each month or not at all	61

N = 127. Response rate: 93–98%.

expression in psychosomatic symptoms and strongly negative feelings about work (see table 10-1). Less than one-fifth of the assembly workers were satisfied with their work, while three-quarters seldom or never were. As many as a third felt distaste at the thought of going to work. These negative feelings were strongly associated with the job's character—that is, with the experience of monotony, degradation, and lack of responsibility.

Among the TC workers with the most monotonous jobs, one-quarter had head and stomach aches on the job daily or several times a week. Among workers with skilled jobs, the corresponding figures were a mere 13 percent and 6 percent.[2] Why did the assemblers dislike work so much? The following random sample of quotes suggest several of the reasons (the emphases are mine):

Because it's not much fun being *bound like a slave* to the line.

Boring and *monotonous,* you go around the cars day in and day out and nobody cares.

A sick feeling of *never really accomplishing anything.*

The total *meaninglessness.* No matter how well you work and how little you're absent from work, the greatest reward is getting to sweep up for a couple of hours. It's horrible seeing how many people get broken down by this monotonous, uncalled-for job.

The job is *physically heavy* and monotonous at the same time. Your work is completely empty.

Stress, monotony and the total lack of responsibility and personal work planning.

Equally interesting are the explanations offered by workers who said they felt satisfied with their work (only assemblers are quoted):

Maybe got to *try some interesting new balances.* Got responsibility, maybe as a replacement. Helped a workmate who had problems.

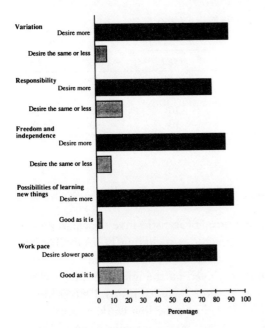

FIGURE 10-5. Desire for Change among Assemblers

Had luck and got a job that takes a long time [a so-called *long balance,* that is]. Had fun with some of the mates.

Got to *use my head* a bit.

If I *had been assistant foreman* one of the days and quality had been high.

Did a good job with no mistakes.

I survived another day and it makes me proud!

The press broke down (a break in work, that is).

The answers reflect two aspects of the job. The first is the importance of being given responsible and interesting tasks, from long balances to being assistant foreman. The other is the importance many workers attach, despite the dull and repetitive work, to doing a good job and maintaining high quality. On the one hand, the alienation expressed in the answer "the press broke down" (the line stood still) was very rare. On the other hand, a large proportion reported they were never satisfied.

The reasons workers gave for why they were never satisfied are reflected in the desire they expressed for change. Figure 10-5 shows that this wish was widespread. Almost all the workers wanted more variation, freedom, and possibilities to learn; 67 percent wanted *much* greater variation, 75 percent wanted *much* greater freedom, and 79 percent wanted *much* greater possibilities for learning new things.

TABLE 10-2. *Conditions at Volvo TC, 1982 and 1986*

	Skilled workers	Assembly workers	
Condition	1982	1982	1986
Bound by a work pace one cannot influence[a]	15%	92%	74%
Work is tedious	20	69	79
Only meaningful thing is the money[b]	20	69	—
Seldom or never any use for knowledge or talent	10	90	92

[a]1982: "Most of the time"; 1986: "Half the time or more."
[b]This question was not asked in 1986.

Results from 1982 versus 1986

In 1982, researchers from the Central Bureau of Statistics investigated industrial working conditions at several Gothenburg factories, including TC. A total of 237 Volvo workers took part. They were grouped into three occupational categories: skilled workers, unskilled workers not employed on the line, and line workers. Many items in this survey were similar to those included in my 1986 study, so comparing the results is useful. Table 10-2 shows the line workers' answers to some similar questions asked in 1982 and 1986, as well as replies given by skilled workers in 1982.

The distribution of replies given by the assembly workers was very similar in 1982 and in 1986, despite differences in sampling, response rate, and the precise formulation of the questions. This strengthens the picture of the working conditions presented above; it indicates, moreover, that worker attitudes have been strikingly stable over the years.

The discontent on the assembly line was basically the same in 1986, when labor turnover reached 20 percent, as it was in 1982, when turnover was at a record low, 12 percent (the lowest figure for TC in the entire period 1970–90).

The table also reveals dramatic differences between assemblers and skilled workers. While 90 percent of the skilled workers said they often had use for their talents and knowledge, the corresponding share among assemblers was only 10 percent. The differences are also reflected in replies to the question "Are you satisfied or unsatisfied with your job, on the whole?" As discussed earlier, questions concerning job satisfaction generally have a strongly positive skew. This is reinforced by the data in the righthand column of table 10-3. It is highly unusual for the proportion of dissatisfied workers to exceed the share of satisfied workers. That this was the case with TC's line workers is a clear sign of their severe discontentment with their jobs.

TABLE 10-3. Job Satisfaction Among Workers at Volvo in 1982 and of the Swedish Labor Force[a]

	Volvo			Labor force
Response	Assemblers	Other unskilled	Skilled	
Satisfied	27%	55%	80%	70%
Unsatisfied	41	11	5	5

[a]Those answering "neither/nor" are not included.

Managerial Argument for Repetitive Jobs

The classic defense companies offer for repetitive jobs is that such work matches the wishes of many workers. Henry Ford, for example, wrote (1924:103):

Repetitive labour—the doing of one thing over and over again and always in the same way—is a terrifying prospect to a certain kind of mind. It is terrifying to me. I could not possibly do the same thing day in and day out, but to other minds, perhaps I might say to the majority of minds, repetitive operations hold no terrors. In fact, to some types of mind thought is absolutely appalling. To them the ideal job is one where the creative instinct need not be expressed. The jobs where it is necessary to put in mind as well as muscle have very few takers—we always need men who like a job because it is difficult. The average worker, I am sorry to say, wants a job in which he does not have to put forth much physical exertion—above all, he wants a job in which he does not have to think.

In the years between the wars, as well as in the immediate postwar period, Swedish advocates of scientific management seized on the notion of the blessings for workers to be had from repetitive and restricted work. They excepted persons, certainly, "who by nature have a strong need for variety and are therefore not suited for repetitive work." Others, however, were considered well endowed for the performance of such tasks: "They happily perform the [monotonous mechanical work] in an automatic sort of way, by devoting their thoughts to other things. They talk or sing while they work, they think of pleasant things (like the film the night before), they build castles in the air, etc. . . . A majority of women [workers] are of this type" (Sällfors 1939:80).

In somewhat different versions, this argument has constantly recurred. The personnel director at Saab Trollhättan, for instance, claimed the following in 1987: "It's tedious standing on the line. But remember—many people like monotonous jobs, since that way they can think about other things."[3] A feature common to these statements is a cocksure assertion of what "workers" think; these confident claims are not based on any studies, however, in which the workers themselves were able to express their views.

My study of TC and other assembly plants yields a wholly different picture. *In*

TABLE 10-4. *Correlation among Monotony, Physical Symptoms, and Exhaustion among TC Workers*

Symptom	All TC workers	Workers older than 30
Aches in wrists or hands	.24[a]	.40
Aches in hips, legs, or knees	.22	.56
Exhausted after work	.33	.48

[a]The majority of correlations were significant at the .001 level. The relation between monotony and aches in the hips, legs, and knees (for all TC workers) had a significance level of 0.01, as did the relation between monotony and aches in the wrists and hands (TC workers over 30 years of age). "Monotony" was defined as answers 1 or 2 to the question about monotony and variation ("very or rather monotonous"). The base sums in the "all" column varied between 212 and 245; in the "older than 30" column, they varied between 47 and 60 (far fewer, on account of the skewed age distribution of the TC workers). The correlations may seem rather weak. The analysis has been done with the dichotomization of ordinal variables, however, and a considerable loss of information is the consequence.

all factories and age groups and at all educational levels, workers with monotonous jobs expressed a strong desire for more variety and better prospects for development. Switching between fragmented jobs did not solve the problem; despite very extensive job rotation, 80 percent of the assemblers at TC considered their work monotonous and degrading.

Another tendency that is clearly visible from the results of the study is that *repetitive work has a series of negative effects,* over and beyond being a burden in itself. Thus, among the workers at TC there was a clear correlation between monotonous work and physical strains, such as aches in various parts of the body and exhaustion. This connection became more and more evident with advancing years: older workers suffered more from the monotonous work than did their younger colleagues (table 10-4).

Monotony coexisted with psychosomatic reactions as well, such as stomach aches and feelings of distaste before going to work (table 10-5). Those who had worked at TC longer appeared to suffer from the monotony more than did those who had worked there a shorter time; one cannot assume people adapt to impoverishing work with passing years.

Repetitive jobs are still the norm in the world's auto industry, especially in assembly (in which cycle times of one to two minutes are standard). The global tendency during the 1980s, moreover, has been to strengthen such work. This arises in large part from the successes enjoyed by the Japanese production system and its transplants, with their strong emphasis on high-speed assembly lines (cycle times are about sixty seconds), minimum staffing, and the contracting out of service and maintenance work. The high productivity of the transplants has in its turn affected production design in Western car companies. More than seventy years after the breakthrough of Fordism at Highland Park, a strict division of labor is still associated with high productivity and quality.[4] A critical question is

Table 10-5. *Correlation between Monotony and Psychosomatic Symptoms among TC Workers with 5 or More Years of Service and among All TC Workers in Monotonous Jobs*

	All	At least 5 years of service
Stomach aches at work	.23[a]	.41
Distaste before work	.30	.36

[a]All correlations were significant at the .001 level. The base sums in the "all" column varied between 245 and 248 individuals and between 92 and 93 individuals in the "at least 5 years" column.

whether the distinctive Swedish developments between 1970 and 1990, aimed at reducing the dominance of repetitive jobs, have resulted in a decrease in the strains associated with assembly work. These are the central issues to which I now turn in the comparison between the working conditions in the five assembly plants.

11.
Assembly Designs and Working Conditions: A Five-Plant Comparison

This chapter analyzes the relation between assembly design and working conditions (physical and mental strains, job content, development prospects, and so on) by comparing the five different factories in the study. Table 11-1 summarizes some basic facts about the factories.

A compressed picture of the character of the plants is shown in figure 11-1, in which I use Uddevalla as a reference point. It builds on the model presented in chapter 5 for describing production design and work organization in Swedish assembly plants.

Each of the five factories represents a distinct value on the x-axis (production design).[1] The axis for work organization has three points, with LB at the highest. In the next chapter I treat the relation between organizational design and direct worker influence on the basis of a comparison of this plant with two other Gothenburg factories, TC and TUN.[2]

An important characteristic that is not included in either table 11-1 or figure 11-1 is the performance policy and wage system. All four Volvo plants used MTM and performance agreements, but there were essential differences between the Gothenburg factories (TC, TUN, and LB) and Borås. The wage system at the Gothenburg installations was in practice fixed (performance was set by the pace of the line and the number of workers). Thus, it was the task of the industrial engineers to assign work for the assemblers so that performance would be as near to the level agreed upon as possible. At TC and TUN, these possibilities were limited because the work pace was not allowed to exceed 115 MTM at any work station. At LB, a group balancing system was applied, which was calculated as an average over a certain period of time. This entailed a sharpening of performance demands compared with traditional line assembly. The assembly groups aimed

Table 11-1. Production Design and Work Organization of Five Swedish Assembly Plants, 1986–87

Plant	Product	Volume/yr.	Assembly design	Cycle time	Work organization
TC	cars	160,000	mechanical line	about 2 minutes	traditional
TUN	cars	12,000	line-buffer system	about 10 minutes	groups with limited responsibility
LB	trucks	6,000	unpaced carrier flows with buffers	30–40 minutes	groups with great responsibility
Borås	bus chassis	3,000	four parallel three-step docks, with assembly divided between stations	2–3 hours	groups with some responsibility
Katrineholm	bus chassis	3,000	three parallel flows; pairs of assemblers build whole chassis	10–12 hours	groups with some responsibility

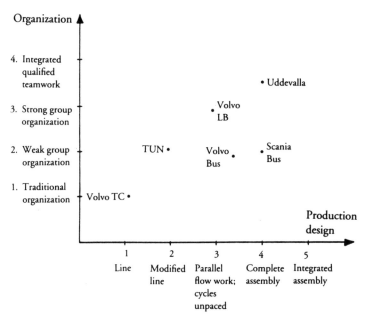

FIGURE 11-1. *Production Design and Work Organization of Six Swedish*
Automotive Plants

at quantitative goals—a certain number of cabins, engines, chassis, and so on per day.

Borås, by contrast, had a higher MTM performance level than prescribed by the production plan to allow for a margin. The performance demand of 115 MTM made for a high work intensity in the factory's long-cycle assembly. First, there was less unutilized time in the docks than on the short-cycle lines at, for example, TUN or TC. Second, the large variant spread necessitated continual redistribution of work tasks between the steps in the docks; this caused losses that had to be compensated for by a more rapid work pace.

Finally, Katrineholm had purely team-based piece rates, based on time studies. The standardized MTM system had never been applied. The team's payment was calculated as a certain price per chassis. Direct comparisons with Borås are not possible, but it seems the combination of the wage system and the high skill level at Katrineholm resulted in lower work intensity than at the Volvo plant.

The assembly systems of the five plants differ considerably in the qualifications required and in the length of on-the-job training, from barely one week at TC to half a year at Katrineholm. In the bus factories—Borås especially—the differences in working conditions (the pace demanded, time pressure, and so on) were considerable between new hires still in training and those who worked on

TABLE 11-2. *Age Distribution, Educational Level, and Length of Service of Personnel in Five Swedish Assembly Plants.*

Characteristic	TC	TUN	LB	Borås	Katrineholm
Share 25 or younger	75	76	64	31	29
Share with no more than elementary school education	22	17	29	54	46
Share with vocational or technical training	15	21	26	27	39
Share with at most two years in their position	78	70	77	62	36
N	127	86	128	26	28

piece rates. Only fully trained workers, therefore, have been included in the comparisons.

Composition of the Five Factories

The three plants producing commercial vehicles (LB, Borås, and Katrineholm) had practically no women workers in final assembly. At the car factories, by contrast, there were a fair number of female assemblers: 13 percent at TUN and 17 percent at TC. The incidence of work strains was somewhat higher among the women. There was no reason to break down the TC respondents according to sex, however, and only include the male workers in the comparison with the other plants. For example, the proportion of TC assemblers suffering from pain in the wrists or hands, which were the most common complaints, decreases by only about 2 percent if women are excluded. Nor was there reason to divide the work force according to nationality. At three of the factories—TUN, Borås, and Katrineholm—almost all of the workers in final assembly were Swedish. Approximately 13 percent at TC and LB were of other nationalities (Finnish especially). No significant differences between Swedes and Finns could be observed, however, in their evaluation of the job. Differences in length of service, age, and educational level are more significant (see table 11-2).

The personnel in the three Gothenburg plants (TC, TUN, and LB) had a very similar profile: they were young, well educated, and employed a short time. In the two bus shops, the average age was higher and the proportion of well-educated personnel lower. The latter plants had significantly more workers with technical training (in, for example, automotive repair and maintenance), which was much more relevant than general high school for the actual work. This was especially true for Katrineholm, where skill demands in assembly work were highest. The length of service was also clearly higher at Katrineholm than at the other units. While 55 percent of the assemblers at TC had worked less than one year in their positions, 64 percent of those at Katrineholm had at least five years of experience.

TABLE 11-3. General Work Content at Five Assembly Plants

Items	TC	TUN	LB	Borås	Katrineholm
Variety	1.7	2.1	2.5	2.9	3.1
Knowledge demanded	1.3	1.6	2.4	2.8	2.2
Impoverishment/development	1.7	2.1	2.7	2.7	2.7
Responsibility	2.4	3.0	3.3	3.3	3.6
N	127	86	128	26	28

Mean values were calculated on scales from 1 to 5, where 1 = very monotonous, 5 = high degree of variety, and so on. The differences between the plants are highly significant for all variables. The correlation R in the variance analysis varies between 0.32 and 0.41, with variety having the highest value.

Workers' Assessments of Their Jobs

I begin my comparison with the assemblers' assessments of the job content and qualifications demanded at the five factories. These have been estimated on scales for variety, the possibility of using knowledge on the job, work impoverishment versus development, and degree of responsibility. Table 11-3 shows the average values for each plant.

From the table, it can be seen that the five plants form a clear ladder with five steps. TC consistently has the lowest values, followed by TUN. The bus factories have higher values and are rather similar to each other. Variety and responsibility increase monotonically from TC to Scania in Katrineholm, while Borås has the highest value for the use of knowledge on the job.[3]

Figure 11-2 shows the proportions of assemblers at each factory who rated their jobs as highly negative. TC consistently ranked worst and TUN the next worst. In three of four categories, the majority of the assemblers at TC were very negative toward their jobs. The lowest negative proportion was found at Borås. Not a single person there thought the work was very monotonous, compared with a majority at TC. At Katrineholm, by contrast, where average values were very high, a relatively high share were dissatisfied. As we shall see, this was because Katrineholm, in contrast to the other factories, had a considerable proportion of assemblers with a long length of service (at least five years) who felt there were too few challenges and opportunities for them to apply their skills except in direct assembly work.

The next comparison concerns the incidence of weariness and physical strains. Katrineholm had the best results overall, although the average length of service, and consequently the risks for cumulative trauma injuries, was much greater there than at any of the other installations. It is noteworthy that Katrineholm had a large proportion of workers who had no symptoms at all (see fig. 11-3). This suggests that long work cycles, which allow for greater variety and freedom of

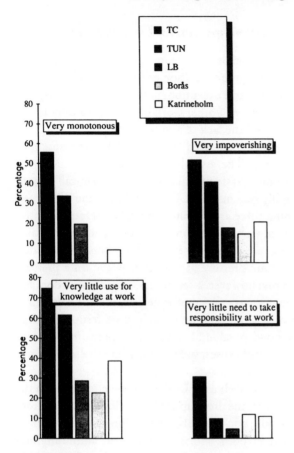

FIGURE 11-2. *Percentage of Assemblers Who Rated the Work Content of Their Jobs Negatively*

movement, have a great effect on bodily wear and tear. But how then does one explain Borås? Clearly, the proportion of tired and exhausted workers there was relatively low—about the same as at Katrineholm. The frequency of physical strains, however, was greatest. Thus, Borås breaks the otherwise clear pattern of a declining incidence of strains with increasing cycle times. This can hardly be related to the fact that Borås workers were older on average than workers at the Gothenburg plants, since in that case Katrineholm would have had the second worst values instead of the best. The explanation probably lies in the performance demands and time pressures at Borås, which, as we shall see, were more exacting than in the other factories. Ergonomic research has shown that time pressure entailing the continuous exertion of muscles increases the risks of physical strains.[4]

The Ambiguities of Change: Autonomy versus Time Pressure

There appears to be a clear connection between work content and skill requirements and assembly design; a lower degree of division of labor has highly positive effects. This has also proven true, with one exception, of the incidence of physical strains. What then are the results with two other work burdens classically found in assembly work—time pressure and the lack of autonomy?

At TC, 74 percent of the assemblers reported that at least half the time they could not influence their work pace. The assemblers themselves associated the lack of autonomy with the technical system—that is, the mechanically paced assembly line. Two of the assembly systems in the five plants (TC and TUN) use mechanical pacing; the remaining three are operator controlled. Does the latter system make for a higher degree of technical autonomy? As we shall see, no such clear pattern emerges. This is because autonomy is strongly influenced by other factors, one of them being the time pressure at work.[5] A heavy time pressure results in a severe lack of autonomy; however, a severe lack of autonomy does not necessarily coincide with an intense experience of time pressure. The assembly workers at TC suffered from a lack of autonomy much more frequently than from a heavy time pressure. As shown in table 11-4, both time pressure and a lack of autonomy in turn reflect a variety of causes, such as organizational and "workshop culture" factors.

No pure cases of parallel assembly, such as at Uddevalla, were included in the comparison. In 1985, however, an engine dress-up section at Borås changed from short, nonpaced line assembly to pure dock assembly. According to the assemblers interviewed, the change resulted in both noticeably increased autonomy and reduced stress, while flexibility rose at the same time. The number of assemblers in the section, however, was not sufficient to allow for statistically significant comparisons.

Both the product variation and the time horizon affect the transparency of the working day. In a flow with completely standardized products, the work is monotonous but easy to grasp. If the product variation is great, however, the assemblers often lack a planning horizon, the working day loses its transparency, and the work pace tends to become uneven. Heavy performance demands from the company have an obvious impact on the time pressure and lack of autonomy that charactererize these types of manual production. Performance demands can also be generated by the workers themselves, however, in the form of pressure to work ahead. Finally, good cooperative relations can work in the opposite direction and alleviate performance pressures.

Figure 11-4 shows the incidence of time pressure at the five plants. As is clear from the figure, it has not been possible to fit the plants into any simple pattern. Borås had high values for time pressure in that 69 percent of the assemblers

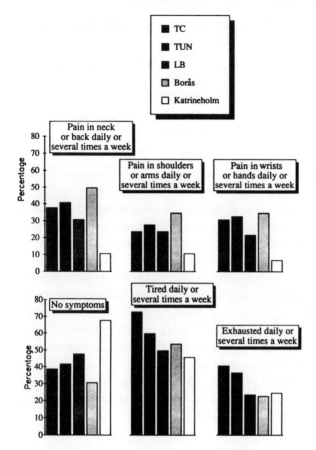

FIGURE 11-3. Percentage of Assemblers Who Have Physical Strains

claimed they were forced to work as fast as they could for at least half the working day. A major reason for this pressure was the performance demands previously described. The time pressure also made its presence felt through the low degree of autonomy, which was even more restricted than in the two factories with traditional assembly lines. Borås is thus a clear example of a discrepancy, in which improvements in one area (work content and assembly design) are hampered by changes in another area (the stricter performance policy). As indicated above, this is also probably an important reason for the high incidence of physical strains at this factory.

After Borås, TUN and TC showed the lowest degree of autonomy, while LB and Katrineholm had the best results. But even in the latter two facilities, the majority of assemblers felt they were bound by an inexorable working pace at

TABLE 11-4. Conditions That Influence Technical Autonomy and Time Pressure

Conditions that directly influence technical autonomy	Conditions that influence time pressure
Control of work: centralized or operator-controlled pacing	Management-induced performance demands (wage system)
Production layout: series or parallel system, use of buffers	Worker-induced performance demands (to work ahead)
Product structure, time horizon, and planning possibilities	Cooperative relations; presence or absence of mutual aid and support

least half the time. The improvements in relation to the conventional factories (TUN and TC) were not very striking. At LB and Katrineholm as well, assembly was arranged in serial fashion, with the consequent requirement to work at the same pace. Furthermore, the objective performance demands at both plants were higher than at TC (i.e., there was a lower proportion of unbalanced time). Another factor leading to stress at LB was the combination of great product variation with the workers' limited possibilities of efficiently planning their work. Accordingly, in interviews the assemblers described the work rhythm as highly uneven: "Sometimes it's very relaxed, sometimes really stressful (if difficult variants come)."

The production design and work pattern at LB were not sufficiently flexible to satisfy the highly varied product program, which thus resulted in new work burdens. Similar effects in assembly systems with great product variation have been observed in another context by Altmann et al. (1982).

Degree of Satisfaction

Figure 11-5 illustrates three psychosomatic reactions and work attitudes in the five factories: the incidence of head and stomach aches on the job, feelings of satisfaction with the day's work, and distaste at the prospect of going to work. Workers on the highly repetitive jobs on TC's assembly lines had the most symptoms and worst attitudes, while those at Scania in most cases had the fewest symptoms and the best attitudes. The differences are statistically significant;[6] 17 percent of the assemblers at TC had headaches daily or several times a week, whereas none of the workers at Katrineholm mentioned this problem. Half the assemblers at the bus plants felt satisfied with their work at least a few days a week, while this was true for less than one-fifth at TC.[7] The high values for Borås are especially noteworthy in view of the contradictory working conditions there. Compared with TC and TUN, the assemblers at Borås seem less focused on such drawbacks as the time pressure and lack of autonomy than on the positive features of the assembly system—the high degree of variation and responsibility.

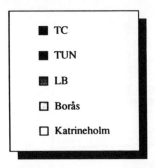

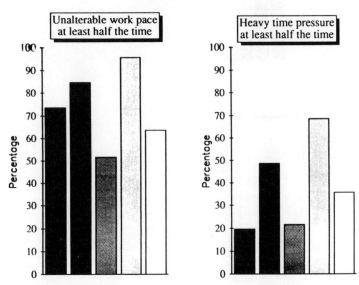

FIGURE 11-4. *Percentage of Assemblers Who Suffer from Time Pressure and Lack of Autonomy*

It is also useful to compare the differences in the responses of those who felt distaste at the prospect of work at TC and at Borås. The reactions at Borås were closely connected to the time pressure and physical burdens. This is evident from the following sample of replies:

Fatigue, pain in my arms and shoulders.

The work pace is too fast.

The stress and the fact that in the dock we're not allowed to control and arrange the work.

You get so much damned back pain after a day's work.

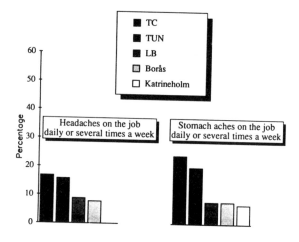

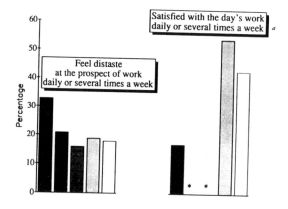

a This question was not asked at TUN and LB.

FIGURE 11-5. *Psychosomatic Reactions and Feelings about Work among Assemblers*

At TC, by contrast, the reactions of distaste arose largely because the work was experienced as boring, degrading, and deadening. Such responses were not elicited at Borås.

Desire for Improvement

The assemblers' desire for improvement also reflects their assessment of their working conditions. To estimate the direction and strength of this desire, a five-grade scale was used in which 1 = desires much less (variety, for instance), 3 =

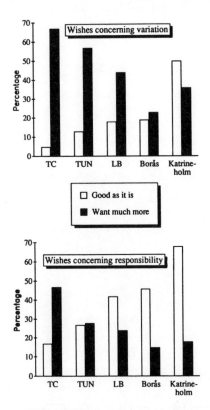

FIGURE 11-6. *Desire for Change in Work Content among Assemblers*

good as it is now, and 5 = desires much more. The differences between the plants were statistically highly significant and formed a distinct monotonic pattern. Thus, the weakest desire for improvement was expressed by workers at Scania. Desire was somewhat stronger at Borås, still stronger at LB, second strongest at TUN, and strongest of all at TC. Exceptions were the desire for greater freedom and independence and for a slower work tempo. The desire for change in these areas was very strong at Borås.

Figure 11-6 shows the proportions of workers desiring marked improvements. Concerning variety, responsibility, and the possibility of using one's knowledge, the majority at Scania at Katrineholm felt the situation was "good as it is." At TC, by contrast, a majority desired *much* greater opportunities in these areas. Borås assemblers were also fairly satisfied about these issues, while those at LB took a middle position. In interviews at LB, a recurring theme was the wish to work with a much larger portion of the vehicle. (These workers had obviously not read *The Machine That Changed the World*, which rejects contemptuously the

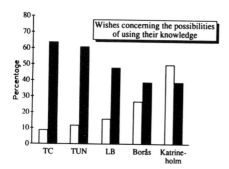

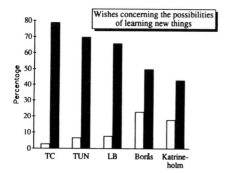

FIGURE 11-7. Desire for Change in Work Content among Assemblers

idea that integrated assembly jobs contribute to job satisfaction.) The following comments from LB workers were typical:

> It's been my dream to assemble a complete vehicle—to learn more, to see how everything is connected. (Subassembler)
>
> I wish the group built a whole vehicle. Only the group would be responsible. Then everyone would do his best. For example, we could follow the vehicle through the flow—as a group. If we could only decide what to do with the subassemblies, it could work. (Group representative)
>
> You ought to work with the same vehicle from start to finish, instead of working thirty minutes on one and then running over to the next. There should be ten guys who build it from start to finish, including test driving—in other words, build 100 percent of the vehicle. It's important to get away from the monotonous assembly work that wears out both your body and your soul. (Utility man)

Workers at all of the factories expressed a great desire to learn more new things at work (see fig. 11-7), but the differences were large in this area as well. The greatest dissatisfaction was at TC, where 80 percent desired much greater learning opportunities; by contrast, the proportion at Katrineholm was 40 percent.

Desires regarding the work pace diverged from the general pattern: Borås and not TC had the lowest share of satisfied workers. As many as 88 percent of the chassis assemblers at Borås wanted a slower work pace.

In all areas, the desire for change, on average, was weakest at Katrineholm. But even there a considerable number of workers wanted greater independence and opportunities for development. This brings us to the next section—the significance of the length of service.

Length of Service and Job Satisfaction

A common belief is that the longer one works at a job, the better adapted one becomes. A long period of service is thought to correlate with greater acceptance and lower expectations. Gunnela Westlander (1978) has described such an adaptive process, which is reflected in two interviews with a factory worker (Berit) conducted within an interval of one year. In the first interview, Berit complained about her monotonous work as a machine operator and said she intended to quit as soon as possible. When asked about the job in the next interview a year later, she replied that it was "altogether in order. The work is OK; what counts now is to provide for my family." She could not even remember that she had talked earlier about monotony or that she had had plans to quit. Berit had given birth to a child between the two interviews, and it was difficult to find work in the area. Her living situation had changed, her freedom of choice had become more restricted, and her perception of the job had changed.

If the "Berit case" is generally applicable, we may expect industrial workers with longer periods of service to be more "adapted"—in the sense of being less expressly dissatisfied—than those with a briefer length of employment. This tendency should also be visible in a cross-sectional investigation. The burden of providing for a child in Berit's case should accordingly be just one of many possible events that could create tendencies to adapt.

In four of the five plants in my investigation, the number of assemblers who had long periods of service was too small to make possible an assessment of this factor. Scania at Katrineholm was an exception, however. At the time of the study, there were two clearly distinct groups there: those who had worked at the plant for at most two years (36 percent) and those who had worked there for at least five years (64 percent). These two groups differed from each other both in their evaluation of the work and in their desire for change.

Assemblers who had been employed for a relatively short time (two years or less) generally had a very positive attitude toward their jobs, the work content, and the demands for responsibility. By contrast, the experienced assemblers were much more critical. On average, 80 percent of the assembly workers at TC and 40 percent at LB felt their work was impoverishing, whereas only 20 percent of the less experienced assemblers at Katrineholm shared this view. This proportion was more than twice as high among experienced assemblers—44 percent. Further, while all "new" assemblers were satisfied with the distribution of responsibility, almost half the experienced workers wanted greater responsibility.

The symptoms of physical strain—pain in various parts of the body—were no more frequent among the experienced than among the less experienced workers. The absence of an increase of such symptoms are a good indication of the varied and all-around character of the work. Nonetheless, in the long run, the work appeared to cause wear and tear on the body. Despite their elaborated routine, the proportion of workers who were tired after work was twice as high among the experienced workers as among the "new" ones (60 percent and 30 percent). The desire for a slower work pace was also clearly greater among the more experienced workers.

Katrineholm's chassis assembly provides an example of a development that evolved in the opposite direction from that posited by the thesis that increased length of service leads to increased adaptation. The jobs in chassis assembly were sufficiently holistic and responsible that the assemblers felt satisfaction and a feeling of having "done something" for the first few years. The opportunities of advancing beyond pure assembly work were few, however, because the plant organization as a whole had retained a conventional structure, with a strict division of labor between assembly and industrial as well as product engineering, and traditional demarcations between blue- and white-collar positions. As a result, a large proportion of the experienced assemblers were dissatisfied with their prospects for using their knowledge on the job. Their criticism was directed particularly at the product engineers, planners, and industrial engineers. These assemblers strongly desired a greater role in the preparation of new products and options. The limited opportunities for doing so were an important reason many workers, even in Katrineholm's holistic assembly system, perceived their work as monotonous, as including too little responsibility, and as offering too few prospects for learning.

In sum, the plant comparisons provide a strong refutation of the view, propagated by the uncritical adherents of the Japanese production system, that the progressive reduction of repetitive and subdivided work structures contributes nothing to worker satisfaction and well-being. A recurrent theme among assemblers performing short-cycle labor is the desire for holistic work. As one female subassembler stated, "It's been my dream to assemble a complete vehicle—to learn more, to see how everything is connected." The evidence from the plants proves that she is not alone in her feelings. Assembly design really makes a difference in the work, in experiences of meaning and purpose, and in the wear and tear on the body.

12.

Shop-Floor Power and the Dynamics of Group Work

The preceding chapter focused on the relation between production design and working conditions. This chapter explores the significance of altered forms of organization for workers' prospects of influencing various aspects of their job. I shall treat only the Gothenburg factories—TC, TUN, and LB. Each represents a value on the "organizational axis": TC ($y = 1$), a traditional hierarchical organization, TUN ($y = 2$), a group organization within the framework of a conventional first-line management structure, and LB ($y = 3$), a group organization with a considerable delegation of prerogatives to work teams. The bus plants are not included in the comparison. Their organization may be seen as a variant on the theme: there is a team organization on the shop floor but no significant changes in management hierarchy.

The comparisons are based on the responses of all the workers from each factory, including the assemblers, U & R men, inspectors, and so on. A central question is the extent to which the new organizational forms produce clear differences in the prerogatives and prospects for influence enjoyed by rank-and-file workers. Another important issue is the effect such differences have (to the degree they are found) on the claims for influence workers advance on their own or their union's behalf.

A total of thirteen questions was included in the survey; they concern influence in a range of areas, from daily job planning to influence over the pace of production. In each one of these questions, it was asked "Who decides in the first place: everyone, the group, the group representative, the foreman, management, or others outside the section?" The purpose of this technique was to measure direct influence in a differentiated manner—that is, to determine the extent to which the workers themselves could be said to decide different issues.[1]

Another type of influence is the indirect, representative influence exerted

TABLE 12-1. Allocation of Survey Questions by Category

Group questions	Section questions	Management questions
Rotation between work tasks	Leaves	Changes in production design (e.g., equipment, space, flow)
Assignment of work tasks	Hiring	Production pace
Daily job planning	Staffing schemes	Whether to make up for lost production
Selection of group representative	Two- to three-week planning	
Use of utility people		

through unions. This is not measured here. Twelve of the questions in the survey may be placed in three different categories: "group-level questions," "section-level questions," and "management-level questions" (table 12-1). The specific allocation of these items to these three levels varies depending on the work culture and management style, but the distinctions made below are highly relevant in the Swedish context. Similar structures have been applied by other researchers in the industrial democracy tradition (see, for example, Björklund, Molin, and Sandberg 1979 and Karlsson 1985).

Workers' Influence at the Three Factories

Actual Influence

Figure 12-1 compares workers' direct influence on different levels of the three factories. For all three categories of questions, the plants form a scale in which workers at LB have the greatest direct influence, workers at TC the least, and TUN is in the middle. The differences are especially striking for the group-level questions. At LB, 80 percent responded that the workers determined such matters. At TC, 80 percent said first-line management did. The workers at TUN—whose work organization was more developed than at TC but who worked on a more traditional flow than at LB—took the middle position: 50 percent said the workers decided such issues.

The same difference could be noted in replies to the section-level questions. Workers at LB enjoyed much less direct influence at the section level than at the group level; nevertheless, their influence was greater than that exercised by workers at TC (who had virtually no influence at all). TUN workers also had very little power to decide section-level issues.

Finally, the differences between the factories essentially disappeared on matters at the managerial level; such matters were largely outside the purview of the workers' group organization.

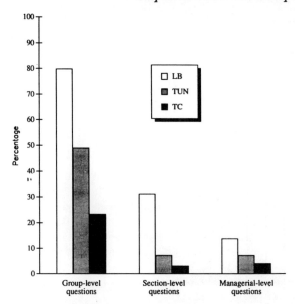

FIGURE 12-1. Actual Direct Influence at LB, TUN, and TC

These results support my ranking of the plants on the organizational dimension. Palpable differences existed between these facilities in the employees' influence over work. Figure 12-1 also illustrates the great differences in influence at the three different levels. While the overwhelming majority of LB workers stated that they made daily decisions about such matters as task assignment and work rotation, a mere 30 percent judged workers to enjoy decisive influence in section-level matters. And for management-level issues, such as the pace of production, decisions to make up lost production, and production design, this share was halved again. Just 14 percent said workers determined such matters. (At TC, the influence over even group-level questions was so restricted that the spread between the levels was small.)

Figure 12-2 shows the differences between the plants, question by question. Even at this level of disaggregation, the pattern is crystal clear. LB workers had the most influence throughout, TC workers the least, and TUN was in between. At TC, the workers enjoyed significant influence only over job rotation.[2] In contrast, the significance of delegation and direct influence was evident at LB, as illustrated by the following from the interviews:

> At TA [a traditionally organized body plant], it was always "You there! You there!" A huge difference from here. The foreman decided everything. Here you can influence things. There, the foreman had his favorites who got the good jobs, while others got the shit jobs. (Engine assembler)

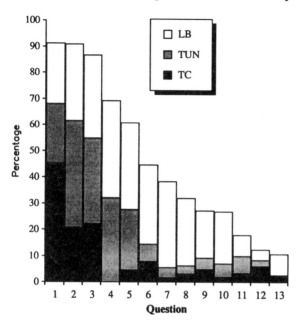

1 = Rotation between work tasks, 2 = assignment of work tasks, 3 = daily job planning, 4 = selection of group representative (does not apply at TC), 5 = use of utility men, 6 = repairs, 7 = leaves, 8 = new hirings, 9 = staffing schemes, 10 = two- to three-week planning, 11 = changes in production design (e.g., equipment, space, flow), 12 = production pace, 13 = if lost production should be made up.

FIGURE 12-2. Actual Direct Influence of Blue-Collar Workers at LB, TUN, and TC

At the X plant [Volvo's other truck factory in Gothenburg], you couldn't affect things in any way. You always stood at the same balance. If the foreman didn't let you go, you didn't learn a thing. (Adjuster)

At TC, the foreman had all the responsibility. If there was something, you always had to go to him. That's not needed here. Here we don't have any middlemen, which means more responsibility for us. At TC you had no say: "Do this and do that and keep quiet." Here you can affect things, you've got a little more freedom. (Assembler on the flow)

There, at the X plant, they told you nothing at all, you just stood at your station. We didn't know anything about how we were doing, about the budget, etc. It's a damned big difference. (Adjuster)

Actual versus Desired Influence

The interplay betwen actual and desired influence at the three plants is represented in figure 12-3, which has the same categories of issues as figure 12-1. Three interesting observations emerge.

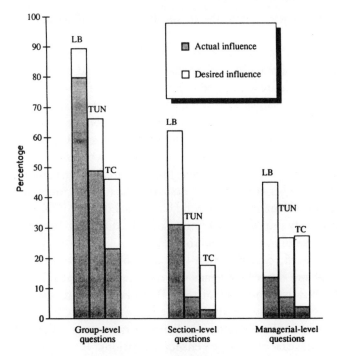

FIGURE 12-3. Percentage of Blue-Collar Workers with Actual and Desired Direct Influence at LB, TUN, and TC

The first observation is that in all cases the workers wanted more influence. This was true at LB, where the real influence was already fairly large, as well as at TUN and TC. A detailed analysis shows that this applied to all issues at the three plants.

The second observation is that there is a remarkably consistent correlation between actual influence and desired influence. The rank order of the three factories is almost as clear in the case of desired influence as in the case of real influence. The desired influence was accordingly strongest at LB, next strongest at TUN, and weakest at TC. Management-level issues are a partial exception. In this area, the desire for influence was as great at TUN and TC as at LB. Relevant here is that the differences between the factories concerning workers' direct influence at this level were very small.

A question-by-question comparison of the desire for influence shows that at LB a majority thought that ten of the thirteen issues should be determined by the workers affected. This was twice the number they felt they actually influenced. A majority felt that only matters concerning the pace of production and whether or not lost production should be made up were not appropriate for the workers directly affected to decide. (They thought the union should have influence over such issues, however.)

There was a strong desire for greater influence at TUN as well, but the level was much lower. In this case, a majority replied that workers should decide five out of the thirteen issues. The figure was halved again in the case of TC; a majority wished to decide only two matters: daily planning and task assignments.

A third observation reflected in figure 12-3 concerns the difference between desired and actual influence at the three levels. In chapters 10 and 11, which concerned working conditions, I noted that the TC assembly workers insisted most strongly on change. That pattern applied here only in the case of the group-level questions: the difference between real and desired influence was most significant at TC and least significant at LB. It should be recalled that the influence of the LB workers was already near the maximum; thus, the difference between real and desired influence could not have been too great.

The pattern is reversed in the case of section-level questions. In this case, the difference between actual and desired influence was most significant at LB and least significant at TC. Nearly two-thirds of the LB workers thought groups should be able to decide section-level matters, while just a third of the TUN workers thought they should. The difference in desired versus actual influence was also greatest at LB in the case of management-level questions.

One may interpret these findings in the following way. The group organization at LB resulted in a considerable decentralization of prerogatives and responsibilities. The workers considered themselves equal to the task, and they found their jobs improved when they were able to exercise influence. Competence and self-confidence increased, which created demands to influence matters the assemblers at TC considered absolutely impossible to influence. This dynamic was verified by supervisors, who found the LB workers significantly more demanding and enterprising than employees at traditionally organized plants.

On group- and section-level matters, workers at TC desired the same level of influence workers at TUN already enjoyed. The desired influence level at TUN, in turn, was roughly the same as the actual influence level at LB, where the desired level of influence was accordingly one notch higher. In other words, the organizational changes triggered an interesting dynamic of rising claims of influence.

A high degree of direct influence over one's own work is a good in itself, as many workers have said in interviews. An interesting question is whether it affects other working conditions as well—physical and mental strains, for instance. If we attempt to correlate assembly workers' influence with their conditions of work as reviewed earlier—work content, development prospects, strains, and desire for change—we find a number of connections (all of them are statistically significant at the 0.001 level). For example, both stomach aches on the job and difficulties in sleeping caused by thoughts of work fall significantly with rising influence.

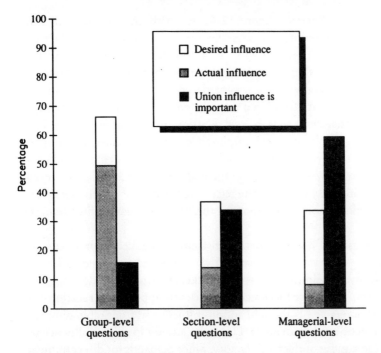

The scales for direct influence and for interest in the union are not wholly comparable. For individual influence, the value of 100 = all workers state that they themselves decide the matter in the first instance (or wish to decide it). The value = no workers say they decide (or wish to). For interest in union influence, the value 100 = all workers think union influence is important. The value 0 = no workers think this is important.

FIGURE 12-4. Percentage of Blue-Collar Workers with Actual and Desired Direct Influence and the Importance of Union Influence at LB, TUN, and TC

Insofar as this expresses an independent connection, it may be seen as supportive of the hypothesis that influence at work is both valuable in its own right and contributes to reducing physical and psychic strains. It is hard to say, however, whether these correlations have any independent significance since systematic differences exist between the factories in both influence and other independent variables. The correlations can therefore be interpreted, at least in part, as another way of describing the differences that exist in a range of respects between the plants.

Desire for Union Influence

The desire for influence discussed so far has concerned possibilities for exerting direct influence at either the individual or the group level. How is this related to the desire for union influence? Figure 12-4, in which answers from all three factories are represented, points to a generally inverse relation between real influence and the desire for union influence. In areas where workers enjoyed high levels of direct influence, there was, for rather obvious reasons, low interest in union intervention. Generally, workers wanted to take care of group-level matters themselves; these were not considered a union concern. A majority, though a smaller one, favored handling section-level questions directly as well. Here, however, the proportion emphasizing the importance of union influence rose markedly. Finally, on management-level questions such as the pace and design of production, the pattern was the opposite: the majority favored union rather than direct influence. This was especially true regarding the pace of production: three-quarters of the workers thought it important that the union have influence in this area.

This pattern persists if one considers each factory separately. For group- and section-level issues, however, certain critical variations can be observed (see fig. 12-5). At LB, the overwhelming majority of workers wished to decide group-level matters themselves. The desire for direct influence was important for section-level issues as well. Workers at LB thought union influence was desirable only concerning management-level matters. At TUN, the interest in union influence was almost exactly the same as at the truck factory. Since demands for direct influence were weaker, however, the interest in union influence played a relatively larger role. At TC, where both real and desired direct influence were much lower than at the other plants, the interest in union influence was, as if to compensate, much greater.

On the one hand, a correlational analysis reveals no direct connection between *actual* direct influence and *the desire for union influence* when each factory is taken separately. On the other hand, when the material is analyzed as a whole, several significant—if weak—negative correlations appear between actual direct influence and the wish for union influence. No such connections, either positive or negative, appear, however, in the case of management-level issues. The dynamic of claims visible between actual and desired direct influence therefore appears not to embrace the interest in union influence. The latter probably occupies another dimension.

A correlational analysis of desired direct influence and the wish for union influence illustrates the differences between the plants at the shop-floor level. At TC, which had little actual influence, there was a greater interest in union influence at the group and section levels than at the other plants. This found expression in a positive covariation between the desires for union influence and for increased direct influence. At LB, which had a great deal of direct influence at the group and section levels, the connections tended to be opposite in character. Here, a continued increase in direct influence held the greatest interest for the workers.

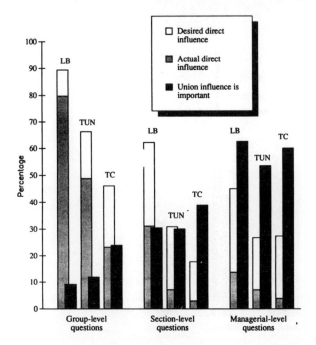

FIGURE 12-5. *Percentage of Blue-Collar Workers at LB, TUN, and TC with Actual and Desired Direct Influence and the Importance of Union Influence in Three Major Areas*

The desire for union influence over managerial questions was at almost exactly the same level in all three factories. Increases in real direct influence had no effect in either a positive or a negative direction on the desire for union influence over management-level questions.

Within each factory, there were considerable differences in views on these questions. Workers in different sections within LB held highly varied opinions about the importance of union influence at the managerial level. The assembly sections had the highest proportion of "yes" answers; the lowest were found in the quality assurance and materials departments. (It should be borne in mind that the latter two sections are outside direct production and its demands for performance.)

Some Swedish studies have found that the desire for increased influence through production groups is tied not to the experience of working conditions but rather to the strength of union consciousness. This may be true of workplaces with a traditional work organization and little direct influence by workers (as at TC).

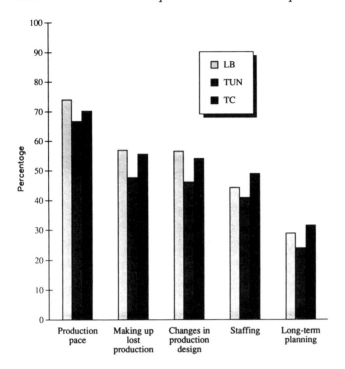

FIGURE 12-6. Issues on Which Workers at LB, TUN, and TC Consider Union Influence Is Very or Rather Important

The results from plants with a different type of organization point in another direction, however: the desire for direct influence is not coupled to an interest in union strength. Rather, the former is strongly connected to actual direct influence, which, of course, is an aspect of working conditions.

Issues That Should Be Important for the Unions

In earlier comparisons, I attached special attention to the differences between the three factories. I shall conclude with a comparison that underlines some of their similarities. This concerns which issues, in the view of the workers, should be important for the union (see fig. 12-6). Workers in all three factories considered the same five questions most important. They also rank-ordered the five in precisely the same way. Decisions over the pace of production were ranked first, followed (in order of declining importance) by decisions to make up lost production, changes in production design, staffing, and long-term planning.[3]

In spite of the organizational differences, the work in these plants has fundamental similarities. Human beings are still the most important factor of production in all three, and, for the workers, the intensity and pace of work remain central union concerns. There is, nevertheless, a fundamental difference, from the standpoint of the union, between a traditional factory (TC) and a plant based on a new organization of work (LB). At LB, the union had clearly expanded its agenda; during the 1980s, the local plant section of the Metal Workers' Union was considerably more actively involved in issues of long-term significance related to the work organization, such as training and the structure and staffing of first-line management, than was usual in conventional plants.

13.
Toward Postlean Production

This chapter summarizes my empirical findings and contrasts them with the arguments for lean production. It also deepens the analysis of some specific aspects of the Swedish trajectory, the renaissance of holistic assembly, and the interdependence between technical design and organizational change. In the final sections I discuss the contributions and shortcomings of Japanese production, as well as the contributions and drawbacks of the Swedish experience, in order to assess the possibilities of achieving a synthesis—human-centered postlean production.

Importance of Social and Technical Forces in Creating Change

Throughout the Western industrial world the early 1970s were characterized by a revolt against Taylorism and degrading work in mass production. In Sweden, as in other countries, this movement fostered widespread interest in organizational reform and sociotechnical engineering. In Sweden, however, unlike many other nations, this interest became permanent and gained new momentum in the second half of the 1980s. One reason for this sustained interest was the nature of the labor market. Unemployment overall practically never exceeded 3 percent, while most European countries had rates of 10 percent. Another reason was the high and even union density; more than 80 percent of all employees belonged to unions. As a result, it became increasingly difficult to recruit and keep young people in manufacturing jobs.

These problems were exacerbated by the product strategy of the Swedish auto producers, which focused on the demanding up-market segments of both the truck and car businesses. Moreover, the extraordinary dependence on foreign sales meant that products had to be adapted to customers in a great variety of ways. In a strongly standardized production system, with relatively low quality requirements and soaring demand, a high personnel turnover is not necessarily a serious problem for companies. When demands for flexibility, delivery precision, and quality rise, however, the significance of having a stable staff with low absenteeism and high levels of competence and commitment increases. Together, the requirements of the marketplace, the pressure from the labor market, and the unions' increasingly strong demands created intense pressure on firms to innovate, especially such labor-intensive processes as assembly.

The Japanese personnel policy developed as a very different form of adaptation, when organized labor was defeated and the idea of national industrial unions was dead. Management had a free hand in shop-floor organization and worker utilization, but in return the (male) work force expected job security, predictable seniority-linked wages, and "full membership" in the enterprise community.

During the 1980s, the Japanese-style personnel regime was applied in other countries. One important reason for the success of this transplantation was the ability of Japanese firms to select their own work forces with utmost care. To do so required an abundance of applicants, which has been possible in the United States because of the large wage differentials between auto jobs and other unskilled jobs and in the United Kingdom because of the high level of unemployment. But the Japanese firms have also had to make adaptations to render the transplants more attractive, such as establishing a much more egalitarian profile than in Japan and applying a basically flat wage structure and not the elaborate Japanese personnel evaluation system (*satei*).

Womack, Jones, and Roos (1990) discard all concern for particularities in favor of extreme homogenization, asserting that one organizational form—lean production—will supplant all other forms and become the standard industrial production system for all manufacturing. In that this prediction is based only on studies in one of the world's most scale-intensive production systems, the car industry, the empirical basis is weak. The basic notion is that Japanese management is superior in all kinds of manufacturing. But, as Michael Porter has emphasized, "like all nations, Japan has achieved national competitive advantage in some industries, but has failed in many others. Whatever is happening in Japan clearly does not work equally well in all industries. Management practice alone cannot explain all it has been credited with" (1990: 384).

Innovative Bus Plants versus Problematic Car Factories

In this and the following section, the six case studies are summarized. I also discuss some developments within Saab.

Bus Plants

In the late 1970s and early 1980s, Volvo Buses and Scania Buses expanded their capacity by opening new plants. Because of their sharply increasing product variety, both companies had efficiency problems in their traditional facilities that became more and more difficult to master. Scania especially also experienced severe personnel problems, since workers perceived the old plant as a very unattractive workplace. When the firms planned new plants, they seized the opportunity to introduce new design principles, which they did by substituting integrated parallel assembly for the fragmented line work and making teams responsible for complete products.

Volvo had a hard time breaking in its controversial operation at Borås, but after a few years this plant as well as Scania's proved to be highly competitive. These good results persuaded Volvo Buses to introduce the Borås concept to British Leyland, which was acquired in 1988. Volvo in Britain had no need to make jobs more attractive; rather, management expected quality advantages to result from the application of the Swedish concept.

Both Volvo's and Scania's new plants entailed a significant upgrading of worker competencies, raising technical as well as social skills. At Borås, the new work forms could be described as skilled but rather stressful as a result of a tight performance measurement and wage-setting system. At Scania, however, where the change from fragmented to holistic assembly was more thorough, the gains in working conditions were unequivocal. This was reflected in an impressive stabilization of the work force, further contributing to the rising skill level.

Car Factories

Volvo's and Saab's brownfield plants in Gothenburg and Trollhättan stand out in stark contrast to the innovations in bus assembly. Compared with the bus plants, these factories were large-scale operations with an entrenched Fordist culture and the product-derived demands for flexibility were weak. Personnel problems were the paramount forces creating interest in change. The significance of the labor market was also reflected in the dramatic decline of any interest in human-centered reform, which occurred when the economy entered a downturn in 1990 and unemployment started to rise and turnover to decrease.

At Saab in Trollhättan, the production engineers during the good years of the company (1982–87) attempted to solve the factory's problems through a combination of mechanization and technical modification of existing lines to make the system more elastic ("mini-lines"). The results were modest. The sociotechnical tradition (with advanced group work), developed at the body shop as early as the mid-1970s, was not built upon. Traditional rationalization work was also neglected. When more cars had to be produced, the work force was simply enlarged. Above all, indirect activities, such as inspection and adjustment, were expanded.

The assembly plant of the late 1980s may be described as an example of low-efficiency, laissez-faire Fordism. The company entered a deep crisis in 1989, which resulted in GM assuming control. A shift of cultures took place within management, and the pressure to change increased drastically. With the express goal of emulating "the best global practice," a Toyota-inspired strategy was developed, with line rationalization and strict inventory and quality control as the basic elements. The crisis, the staff cuts, and the radically reduced personnel turnover that resulted made it possible to tighten the factory regime and the control over work times and attendance. Indirect activities were reduced, and production was streamlined by means of JIT control. All attempts at dispensing with line assembly ceased.

The many omissions and sloppy leadership of earlier years made it easy for the new committed and determined management to reach considerable productivity improvements by means of simple but consistently applied methods. The long-term tenability of this strategy was uncertain, however, since unattractive working conditions would scarcely enable the company to maintain personnel stability during the next economic upturn.

Since the early 1970s, Volvo TC had been plagued by massive discontent with working conditions on the assembly line. Qualitative changes were rejected by plant management, however, in favor of attempts to reform operations within the bounds of line assembly. These attempts failed altogether. In 1986, a major modernization plan was launched. The goal was to wind down the line and introduce a comprehensive group organization.

In contrast to Saab, Volvo actually began to operate product shops on the basis of series-parallel assembly. But this way of organizing production proved so difficult to master that all thoughts of changing TC as a whole to such a system had to be abandoned. This had the result, for a time, of increasing the leeway for experimentation with radically different alternatives. Developments proceeded so far that, at the close of the 1980s, whole-car construction—the antithesis of the assembly line—appeared to be a genuine alternative. At that point, however, the prospect of change became so risky and dramatic that the entire process was postponed. In 1990, after a decade of engineering reports, experiments, and practical attempts at technical and organizational renewal, TC was marked by great uncertainty about the future. Earlier obstacles to change—in the form of rigid notions about "maximum possible" cycle times or about assembly equipment, materials-handling systems, and so on—had been partly broken down. Yet the traditional model had not been replaced by a new one except in a few components shops.

In the early 1990s, recession and retrenchments reduced personnel turnover significantly at TC, and quality improved. Management no longer subscribed to any single solution or strategy but tried to adopt different methods to boost productivity and personnel commitment, such as line-rationalization techniques from Belgium and ergonomic innovations from Uddevalla. The factory worked hard to improve, but it had no cohesive strategy for how to shift attention from the Ghent plant, which was increasingly favored by Volvo's management.

From Kalmar to Uddevalla

Kalmar: The First Stage of the Volvo Trajectory

From Volvo's start in the mid-1960s, Volvo Torslandaverken (with the final-assembly plant TC) was the main operation of the company, and it was still so in 1990. But the frontier of development had long since ceased to be there. To evolve, new plants needed to be built with alternative assembly designs that rendered autonomous and skilled group work possible.

The Kalmar plant of 1974 embodied the first stage of the Volvo trajectory. With its socially elaborated team structure, new flexible transport technology, and ergonomic adaptation, Volvo Kalmar constituted an ambitious response to the intensive labor market pressures of the early 1970s as perceived by management. The plant quickly acquired international fame and contributed to enhancing the brand name of Volvo.

Enhancing productivity took much longer, and the first years after its inauguration Kalmar reached only the level at TC. In the crises of the late 1970s, the plant was subjected to an intense rationalization program. The new technology was exploited to raise work intensity, to facilitate quality control "at the spot," and to accommodate new and more complex products more efficiently. In 1984, after ten years, the plant was acknowledged to be Volvo's best operation in terms of overall productivity and low overhead. Three years later, Kalmar acquired the sole responsibility for Volvo's top-of-the-line model, 760 (later 960).

Working conditions improved compared with the traditional line, but not as much as was intended at the start. Being a pioneer, Kalmar came to discover several of the technical restraints inherent in any attempt to reform assembly work without breaking radically with flow-line principles. Thus, it proved very difficult to increase worker autonomy by inserting buffers between series-connected teams without disturbing the overall process; it also was difficult to combine serial and parallel principles in a high-volume flow. As a result of the rationalization program, management retreated from some of its original goals for reform and tightened control of the work process considerably. From an international perspective, however, Kalmar still represented an innovative plant. At the end of the 1980s, the interest in reform was revived and new technical systems were introduced in the chassis assembly, creating the basis for a more integrated and autonomous work environment.

LB: The Second Stage

The LB plant for heavy-truck assembly, which opened in 1981, represents the second stage of the Volvo trajectory. In contrast to Kalmar, there was significant union input, both in the planning process and in the actual running of the work organization. The production design at LB, using buffered flows and operator-controlled AGVs, was a compromise between a traditional line system and the integrated assembly in the bus plants. The work organization was more sophisticated than at these plants, however, and work groups at LB had considerably more decision-making powers.

The making of the Kalmar plant was basically labor market derived. The possibility of exploiting the sociotechnically motivated design to handle the growing variation in options was utilized long after the plant was started, when Volvo Cars started to move up-market. In contrast, the LB plant from the very beginning was conceived in terms of a dual reform need: the difficulties of coping with an expanding product mix and the perceived need to make assembly work much more attractive.

For several years, LB achieved good results. In the second half of the 1980s, the complexity of the product program rose sharply and made it difficult to perform efficient assembly within the limits of the "LB compromise." And, as a result of the very tight labor market, personnel turnover soared, which made the group organization fragile and unstable. To cope with these strains, management strengthened shop-floor supervision, circumscribing but not abandoning the fundamental concept. At the same time, the company started a dock assembly shop where one team built complete trucks. This relieved LB of the most complex vehicles and established a venue for workers demanding more challenging tasks. The move was supported by the union, which strongly had opposed the tightening of control at LB. The plans for Volvo Trucks in Gothenburg called for an expansion of LB's capacity, combined with a step-by-step process whereby new dock assembly shops would be broken in. Together, this amounted to a flexible and dynamic structure, in both its product structure and work force demands.

Uddevalla

In a trial run, Roger Holtback, president of Volvo Car Corp., exchanged his usual Saville Row suit for overalls and assembled a car all by himself at a new plant in Uddevalla, Sweden. Holtback managed to drive off in the finished Volvo 740, though it was by no means free of defects. . . . Still, this 1987 experiment reinforced Volvo's radical decision to mass-produce the midline 740 at Uddevalla without using assembly lines.

With this story, *Business Week* (August 28, 1989) introduced the Uddevalla plant, the third stage of the Volvo trajectory. When planning for the new plant started, there were few indications of this outcome. The initial idea was to make a modernized version of the Kalmar plant. But neither corporate management nor unions, which participated with full-time officials from the start, viewed this as a viable response to the growing labor market problems. Project engineers with experience in alternative production design in other Volvo companies (trucks and buses) emphasized the inconsistencies of these earlier exercises and the importance of developing a comprehensive and cohesive alternative. Further, the Japanese revival of the assembly line, represented by the newly started Nissan operation in the United Kingdom, was seen by both managers and unionists in the project as neither desirable nor possible in Sweden. Altogether, these factors contributed to an unusually creative planning process. The result was a radical production design in which about fifty parallel teams made complete cars. The flat plant organization, without any traditional foremen, transferred important prerogatives and responsibilities to the assembly teams. On a conventional assembly line, the jobs are designed according to the requirement of making even use of the different assembly stations (or balancing the line); as a result, each work cycle consists of a number of subdivided operations. By contrast, in whole-car assembly, the work is coherent and the inner logic of the product is apparent. At Uddevalla, this quality of *transcendent production,* in which worker reflection is not confined to fragmented tasks but spans the whole production process, was reinforced by a new assembly-oriented product analysis and information structure.

Uddevalla's whole-car assembly is reminiscent of craft work in some respects, which has enticed MIT researchers Womack, Jones, and Roos and others to label it as "neocraft." But the context is very different from any craft culture. Materials are collected in individual kits in a largely automated process. Planning and coordination are based on an advanced computerized information system. And a number of technical aids have been developed to make small-scale assembly efficient and at the same time ergonomically vastly superior to line asembly. Furthermore, the holistic assembly and its upgraded intellectual quality support a greater collaboration between assemblers, industrial engineers, designers, and product engineers. In contrast to the static character of traditional craft work, the work organization thus has a dynamic potential.

When the plant started its operations in 1989, the overheated labor market was a serious problem, making it impossible to select a work force suited for the demanding tasks. The result was an unexpectedly high turnover. Initially, the plant was much praised, but with a deepening recession, mass media quickly lost interest in work improvement and started to criticize the plant sharply for its lagging performance. A widely disseminated article in the *New York Times* (July 7, 1991) stated that "assembly lines are just more efficient." In the same article, James Womack from MIT declared that "Uddevalla is not in the ballpark. . . . It's not even in the outer parking lot of the stadium. Frankly, it's a dead horse."

The denunciations galvanized the "dead horse" and in 1991 productivity rose 25 percent in less than nine months. Two principal problems confronted the plant at this time. One was Volvo's plummeting sales, which created a substantial excess capacity in its assembly plants. In relation to volume, Volvo had a scattered and expensive production structure (in 1990, its five so-called volume plants, three Swedish, one Belgian, and one Canadian, produced only 255,000 cars in all). Many worried that without a substantial improvement in the market this structure would lead to a Darwinian struggle between the Swedish plants. The other problem was the public attitude adopted by corporate management vis-à-vis the innovative process it had initiated at Uddevalla. Deeply divided in its assessment of the concept, management did not develop an integrative strategy that could exploit its unique potentials. The plant had been conceived as a "noble experiment in humanistic manufacturing." In recessionary times, this was not necessarily an advantage.

Economic Performance of New Assembly Systems

The economic performance of the Swedish assembly systems has been widely disputed. Here, I will draw together evidence from bus, truck, and car production. According to Womack, Jones, and Roos (1990), any attempt to replace the established short-cycle line systems with integrated assembly in long working cycles represents a "craft nostalgia" that is doomed to be a dismal failure. The authors' empirical studies are squarely confined to car production, but they assert that their conclusions hold true for all automotive production. My study of the Swedish heavy-bus manufacturers Volvo and Scania, ranked number one and three respectively in Europe, provides a different picture. In these cases, the insurmountable problems in line assembly were successfully solved by adopting what the MIT authors so misleadingly refer to as "craft principles." As early as 1979, two years after its start, Borås had reduced assembly hours per chassis by 20 percent compared with the previous line assembly. In the 1980s, the plant maintained high productivity combined with superior quality. This was increasingly achieved by building right from the beginning. Adjustment times fell despite the rapidly growing complexity of assembly. During the 1980s, the plant also pursued an intensive policy of capital rationalization, reducing the lead times of vital components significantly.

Within Volvo Trucks, the less radical "LB compromise" worked well during most of the 1980s. The plant achieved higher productivity, had less capital tied up in inventory, reduced sensitivity to disturbances, and had a much greater capacity to produce customized vehicles than did Volvo Truck's traditional line plant in Gothenburg. At the end of the 1980s, LB grew less efficient, mainly because of an overwhelming increase in product variation. A new dock assembly was started to take care of the most complex chassis. It reached full production speed in less than one year, and its assembly hours per chassis were actually lower than calculated. The results during 1990 included high delivery precision, rapidly rising quality, and an impressive capacity to build complete ready-to-buy vehicles. To make the products more easy to manufacture, the integrated assembly facilitated close cooperation with design and product engineering.

Volvo also used dock assembly in its cabin plant in Umeå, which supplied all the company's European plants. Starting with the most heavily equipped cabins, the results were clearly positive, especially for flexibility and capacity to utilize worker skills. As a consequence, this form of assembly expanded to comprise 40 percent of the total output (thirty-three thousand cabins in 1988).

Volvo Kalmar had some disappointing years after its start in 1974 but then surpassed the productivity of TC in Gothenburg with a vengeance. In 1987, the last years both plants built the same basic model, Kalmar budgeted 25 percent fewer assembly hours per car than TC did. In 1991, the plant set a new quality record by building the best cars in the history of Volvo, a feat that was repeated in 1992. Yet it was not able to reach the productivity level of Ghent, which had made remarkable improvements during the 1980s. There were two main reasons for this failure. One was the considerably lower personnel stability at Kalmar (an effect of the different labor market situation and social legislation in Sweden compared with Belgium). Another reason was that Kalmar exercised less control over its vital components. As a pure final-assembly plant, Kalmar got its car bodies from Gothenburg. Ghent produced its own, applying a much stricter quality control than Volvo Gothenburg in this process. Ghent also pursued a more exacting quality policy toward its suppliers, including Volvo's Swedish engine operation, than the assembly plants in Sweden.

During the 1980s, integrated manual assembly was successfully applied in the manufacture of commercial vehicles for highly differentiated markets, such as heavy buses, complex truck cabs, and heavily equipped truck chassis. Most of these cases represented relatively small-scale production with a simple technological structure. Uddevalla introduced this principle of complete assembly on a large scale for car manufacture, which required a set of new support systems, such as materials handling and information systems.

In the first full year of production, 1990, the plant proved its capacity to be flexible by making the transition from the 700 to the 900 series much more smoothly than did Volvo's other assembly plants. But an inexperienced and rather unstable personnel and a lot of system "bugs" resulted in a painfully low productivity. Womack, Jones, and Roos (1990:102) assert that "the productivity of the Uddevalla system is almost certain to be uncompetitive even with mass production, much less lean production."

During 1991, however, the personnel situation stabilized markedly. Turnover fell from 15 to less than 5 percent, and the average skill level rose significantly. In this year Uddevalla reached the same productivity as TC—and boasted higher quality. Uddevalla had proven that indeed it could match a traditional mass-production plant. Absenteeism remained relatively high, though (about 10 percent), which in part was attributable to the large proportion of female workers— 40 percent. (On average, women were absent from work twice as often as men in Swedish manufacturing industry.)

Nonetheless, the performance level at Uddevalla was far from that of Ghent. To close that gap, the plant required much more experience, including a systematic fine-tuning of its technology, quality-control procedures, and management systems. And, like Kalmar, it would also need to enforce more exacting standards on its suppliers. Compared with the Japanese, Ghent's productivity was also lagging. For a Volvo plant, be it Ghent or Uddevalla, to match the Japanese performance, the products had to be designed for as easy manufacture as the Japanese were, but the Volvo cars were definitely not. Equally important, the supplier system had to be of the same excellent quality as the world-leading Japanese components industry. Without these basic conditions, Uddevalla could aspire to become a first-class European plant, but it could certainly not reach world-class productivity.

Working Conditions on Assembly Lines versus "Neocraft" Systems

A main result of the survey of working conditions, reported in chapters 10 and 11, was the importance of the production design and work content for workers' satisfaction and well-being. From the lines of TC, the study in 1986 reported massive dissatisfaction. An overwhelming majority, 80 percent, perceived their work to be monotonous and degrading, and one-third felt distaste at the thought of the job every morning or several times a week. Another reason for the discontent was the heavy physical strains. The widespread feelings of boredom and impoverished work content existed in spite of extensive job rotation. The rotation ameliorated some of the physical strains, but it did not change the overall perception of the work as dull, dreary, and degrading.

The same broad pattern of dissatisfaction had been observed in studies performed four years earlier, when the visible expression of discontent—the labor turnover—had been only half that in 1986. This testifies to the consistency of worker resentment toward line work and to the risk of using high personnel stability as a measure of job satisfaction.

Another important finding of the assembly survey was that all the plants workers with monotonous jobs in all age groups and at all educational levels expressed a strong desire for more variety and better development prospects. According to a notion often propagated by management, a majority of workers prefer and are quite happy to perform monotonous work. This view is obviously not shared by the workers themselves.

What happens when short-cycle line jobs are replaced with integrated assembly, consisting of work cycles extending to several hours? Does this significantly improve the quality of the working conditions? Womack, Jones, and Roos "strongly disagree" that a system of the Uddevalla type provides "a working environment that is much more humane" and argue instead that "simply bolting and screwing together a large number of parts in a long cycle rather than a small number in a short cycle is a very limited version of job enrichment" (1990:101). No studies are quoted to support their defense of short-cycle line work.

The five-plant comparison of working conditions reported in chapter 11 shows, however, that the content of basic production tasks is of decisive importance for workers. The results are clear-cut. The further from traditional line assembly a plant moves, the better the outcomes in terms of variation, prospects for personal growth, the taking of responsibility, and the opportunity to use one's skills. TC consistently had the lowest values, followed by TUN, while the bus factories, where teams were responsible for the assembly of complete vehicles, consistently had the highest scores. At Borås, for example, not a single person thought the work was very monotonous versus the majority at TC.

Moreover, the share of assemblers suffering from physical strains and severe fatigue after work, problems that were never mentioned in *The Machine That Changed the World,* was lowest in the plant with the longest work cycles. And, also contrary to the argument of Womack, Jones, and Roos, in all the subdivided and fragmented assembly systems, workers displayed a strong desire for integrated work, very often framed as a desire to work in groups responsible for building complete objects (engines, trucks, cars, or buses). To quote an assembler at the LB plant: "You ought to work with the same vehicle from start to finish. There should be ten guys who build it from start to finish, including test driving—in other words, build 100 percent of the vehicle. It's important to get away from the monotonous assembly work that wears out both your body and your soul."

The positive potential of integrated production can be limited and in some cases directly counteracted by strategies aimed at the maximum extraction of performance. Borås was a clear case of such a discrepancy. A considerable enrichment of the work content was accompanied by exacting performance demands. The Borås assemblers were strongly positive when evaluating the work content, compared with their counterparts in traditional assembly plants. At the same time, the heavy performance demands meant that the time pressure at Borås was considered tougher than at other factories.

Taken together, the investigations showed the great potential in abandoning fragmented line assembly in favor of holistic, long-cycle assembly. From the workers' point of view, this implied much more than just increasing the number of parts to be screwed or bolted: it enhanced functional understanding and the sense of purpose and meaning, it created possibilities to vary the work pace and the working positions, and it increased their opportunities for social cooperation and interaction. Even when cycle times were as long as several hours, further expansion yielded positive results since such a lengthening made it possible to switch from subdivided to complete assembly and from a work organization divided into stations (with constant rebalancings) to very flexible and resistant forms of work.

My investigations also showed that organizational design significantly affects the character of daily work. In cases of highly developed team organization, the direct influence exercised by a majority of the workers was much greater than under traditional organizational forms. Claims of more influence and participation also markedly increased. Together, the results indicate the great potential for developing assembly work by means of both organizational and technical redesign.

According to Womack, Jones, and Roos (1990:102), lean production offers "creative problem-solving," while "neocraft" long work cycles present only the meager prospect of satisfaction from "reworking and adjusting every little part so that it fits properly" (an activity that is completely unnecessary in lean production). This is a doubly flawed argument. First, it glosses over the fact that the basic tasks on lean lines do not require problem solving but the execution of standardized tasks in an intense tempo. Second, integrated assembly with long work cycles does not require more fitting as opposed to problem solving. On the contrary, when properly organized and supported by a committed management, integrated assembly creates opportunities for vastly extended problem solving, by enhancing the intellectual quality of the work and the transcendent reflection of the workers, which are not confined to the continuous improvement (*"kaizening"*) of fragmented suboperations.

Renaissance of Holistic Assembly

The principle of complete assembly has a long history in the Swedish auto industry. As early as the 1970s, Volvo and Saab began to experiment with the assembly of complete objects in docks. None of these experiments outlasted the decade, however. At Volvo Skövde, the complete assembly of gasoline and diesel engines was tested on a small scale in the mid-1970s, in the last years of the long postwar boom. The results as far as the efficiency were good, but no changes in the regular production system resulted. Problems in materials handling, among other things, were deemed insoluble.

Dock assembly was also an important ingredient of Kalmar's production design, but in a limited form: parallelized assembly in certain sections along the flow. The assemblers in the "docks" could perform only a small part of the work on the car, and sections based on line assembly came both before and after. It was hard to carry on parallel assembly within the framework of the larger serial-control system; it was discontinued, therefore, in the early 1980s. Partial dock assembly was reintroduced at Kalmar at the close of the 1980s, but with a much more efficient technical design.

TC also tested dock assembly of whole cars, in 1976–77. The technological conditions were primitive, however, and labor and management could not agree on criteria for setting wages and performance demands. During the short period the experiment lasted, the level of efficiency was only half that of TC's assembly lines.

At Arendal, Volvo Cars introduced "genuine" dock assembly in 1974 on a somewhat larger scale. The results were excellent in the first years, and Volvo Buses' new factory in Borås took inspiration from Arendal. Despite these successes, or because of them, Arendal met with entrenched resistance from the champions of the established production paradigm. In a later phase, Arendal's relative productivity declined, and at the end of the 1970s it was also in the category of failed attempts. At the same time, the Borås plant had considerable breaking-in problems and was called sharply into question, as was the comparable workshop at Scania in Katrineholm.

At the end of the 1970s, then, dock assembly was considered without a future as a realistic alternative to the assembly line. It made a remarkable renaissance in the mid-1980s, however. Borås and Katrineholm had by that time demonstrated they could maintain, with their long-cycle final assembly, high quality, productivity, and flexibility in the face of powerful swings in both production and personnel. Volvo Trucks' plant in Umeå also attained good results in the dock assembly of heavy cabs.

At the same time, the seemingly reliable and efficient compromise between serial and parallel assembly forming the basis for TC's modernization plan proved in practice difficult to master. As illustrated by the MAX workshop, this compromise led to both expensive and complicated systems for transporting, buffering, and sequencing assembly objects. With this in the background, the Uddevalla project came, after some agonizing, to choose a whole-car concept. In contrast to the experiments of the 1970s, however, Uddevalla applied the whole-car principle in its full form. With the support of Volvo's top management, a wholehearted effort was made to develop the prerequisites—materials handling, advanced occupational training, assembly technology, and so on—for integrated assembly on a much larger scale than before. At the close of the 1980s, moreover, renewed efforts were made to develop dock assembly design at Volvo Trucks.

Matching New Production Systems with New Products

For decades, the development of technical equipment, work methods, production control, and logistics in the auto industry has been based on the model of the assembly line. (Compare the totally dominant role of the Otto cycle engine as the basic concept in the development of engines in the last one hundred years.) This stable mono-paradigmatic regime has entailed a number of advantages in economic scale, including the following: First, new vehicles are prepared and adapted for production on the basis of a single concept. The same is true for all subsequent changes within a model series. Second, similar equipment can be acquired for all the factories in a company. Since the basic concept is the same for the entire industry, there is also a rich offering of standard technology. And third, the sharing of experiences between different units is facilitated, since all the plants of a company have the same basic design. In short, the assembly line has been and is an exceedingly large-scale and thorough application of Taylor's "one-best-way" principle.

The Japanese car companies have been the most consistent in standardizing their production system. They have been scrupulous, throughout their international expansion, in applying exactly the same production design, management methods, organization, and supplier system to all their transplants, whether Toyota NUMMI, or Honda Alliston.[1]

Since 1974, Volvo Cars has embarked on another road, from standardization to multiplicity. The first step was taken when the Kalmar plant began to depart from the dominant model of assembly. From the standpoint of encouraging innovations in production organization, this was very important. The new solution entailed added long-term costs for industrial engineering and product preparation, however, since it was not possible to duplicate the methods used at TC. The production function was therefore subjected to a "penalty fee." The intention was for the other plants to shift to the same concept as well. The American operation planned for Chesapeake in the mid–1970s, was to be built according to the model of Kalmar. This project was shelved, however. Instead, the main issue for Kalmar in the crisis years of the late 1970s was to demonstrate its economic viability. The divergence of production concepts at Volvo was to last.

In 1985, Volvo's production executives saw the possibility of recreating uniformity in assembly by means of a companywide application of a central production strategy: P 90. P 90 was based on Kalmar's assembly design, complemented with mechanization in specific areas. The objective was for all the plants, including TC and Ghent, to reorganize their production systems in this direction. In this way, the company would have restored uniformity and eliminated the penalty fee in good time before introducing the next car generation.

Unfortunately, this attempt at centrally implementing a factory model from the 1970s was not at all equal to the accumulated needs for innovation. Instead, Volvo Cars' assembly plants—Ghent, TC, Kalmar, and Uddevalla—each developed in its own direction. This multiplicity triggered considerable creativity, but in the contest with "monolithic" competitors, it entailed a marked increase in the penalty fee already brought by Kalmar.

For production management, it was a strategic task to begin a process of convergence. The Uddevalla concept, however, was so revolutionary that it could not provide the basis for a new strategy without first being tested for a longer period, especially since the Ghent plant had succeeded in improving the efficiency of its line-based manufacturing during the 1980s, selectively picking up Japanese methods, such as total productive maintenance.

In short, despite the great value for the company of having a common strategy, the gap between the different production concepts within Volvo has widened in the face of the challenges of the 1990s. This illustrates well the difficulties of radically shifting production paradigms in an established international mass-production industry.

For Volvo Trucks the situation was different. This division also had a composite production strategy, characterized by the plurality of assembly concepts within its European operations. But at Volvo Trucks, with its much more decentralized and less technology-intensive production, management perceived this strategy not as a problem but as an asset. It considered the composite production strategy well suited both to the diversified product structure and to divergent labor market demands. In Belgium, with its abundance of disciplined workers and strongly traditional industrial culture, Volvo Trucks continued to use the assembly line for cost-effective manufacturing of a simpler product mix. In Sweden, with its more demanding, less well disciplined, but also more change-oriented labor force, Volvo invested in flexible and holistic forms of production for complex and customized manufacturing. Both the LB plant and the dock assembly operations were expanded to create a flexible and adaptable production structure.

Limits of Organizational Choice

A common notion, since the publication of the famous work *Organizational Choice*, by E. Trist et al. (1963), is that work organization can be "chosen" and shaped independently of technological conditions and the character of the work process.[2] This view can easily find support in studies with a short time horizon, such as cross-sectional studies or case studies of workplaces over a few years.

The case studies presented in this book had a time perspective of eight to ten years, embracing periods of both expansion and contraction, unemployment, and overly full employment. They demonstrate the strong interplay and mutual interdependence between organizational development and the technical design of production. Other studies carried out at the Royal Institute of Technology in Stockholm have also indicated that over the long term there is a close connection between technical design, working conditions, and possible ways of organizing work (see, for example, Bengtsson et al. 1991). These results provide reason to qualify the notion of organizational choice in other manufacturing industries as well.

To overstate the point slightly, it is difficult to "choose" a Taylorist organization for certain types of work, while it is hard to avoid so doing for others. In chemical process industries with nonstandardized jobs and demands for immediate and accurate operator reactions and close cooperation, the operators cannot be divided hierarchically without impairing the efficiency of the process. The shift team is a social collective of such significance for production that administrative interventions and transfers are hazardous. A highly fragmented type of organization is simply inadequate for such work. The prevalence of non-Taylorized work organizations in such processes need not, then, be the expression of a conscious organizational "choice." It may rather be a more or less enlightened adaptation to the special demands of the production process.

At the same time, there are jobs in which Taylorist forms of organization tend constantly to reappear. For example, there are strictly standardized and restricted jobs in which, in theory, there is a choice concerning the level at which to arrange coordination. The restrictive character of the work and the absence of stable conditions for group interaction make it very difficult in practice, however, to find an enduring alternative to hierarchical management and control of such work. Consequently, most attempts at developing and maintaining decentralized forms of group work within existing line systems have failed. Both TC and Saab Trollhättan employed this strategy in the mid-1980s, without lasting results. The work content was too limited, the autonomy too restricted, the basis for cooperation too fragile, and the labor turnover too high to allow room for genuine vertical integration within the organization.

Similarly, it has proved difficult to construct new forms of organization based on integrated positions (combining production and maintenance, for instance) in those areas of body manufacturing in which the work has remained especially repetitive and machine paced. For this type of process, it is in advances in the level of technology that solid organizational innovations have become possible. Thus, a genuine basis for qualitative organizational development exists only on advanced lines, in which the larger part of materials handling has been automated. In assembly, in which automation has not been possible, repetitive and restricted work must be overcome by other means—parallelization and complete assembly—if a new organizational culture is to be consolidated.

Assignment of Prerogatives and Organizational Policy

Process industries, such as oil refining or chemical processing, and the assembly line represent the polar extremes of work organization. Between these two extremes are a series of jobs in which both Taylorized and non-Taylorized forms of work are possible over the long term. These jobs are characterized by a sufficient work content and degree of autonomy for successful decentralization of decision making and responsibility to be possible. Coordination and planning are not, however, directly tied to production work; they can be detached and lodged in special levels of the organization. The distribution of prerogatives is therefore to a high degree a matter of organizational policy.

Advancement on the x-axis in my model, representing the expansion of work content and responsibility in direct production, creates the potential for vertical integration; other forms of organization, however, are also possible. Two examples reviewed above are Scania at Katrineholm and Volvo at Borås. At the former, each chassis flow was organized as a work team with responsibility for balancing and the assignment of tasks; a similar model was applied at Borås. The leeway of the worker collective was limited, however. The further decentralization of responsibilities and prerogatives to the team level had been an important topic of discussion in both factories between the company and the union, but no lasting agreement had been reached. The company and union at Borås had negotiated a number of times over vertical delegation and an altered wage system, but without result. Already achieved results functioned as a brake on continued development (especially since there was the potential for the overall system of managerial control to become endangered).

Team Autonomy

This leads to two other important questions regarding organizational development in manual mass production: How should the intensity of work be regulated? And who benefits from new methods invented by the workers? The managerial perspective in Swedish companies has been split on these points: on the one hand, managers have an interest in delegating responsibility for such tasks as quality control, group balancing, and job assignment; on the other, they are wary of abandoning the traditional hierarchy, with the control over work intensity and individual performance it makes possible. The Metal Workers' Union has strongly committed itself, both locally and centrally, to achieving a team-based organization with maximum decentralization and self-management.

In contrast to the "team concept" prevalent in Japanized British and American auto plants, the Swedish model of teamwork is a *compromise* between different social interests; the degree of team autonomy has consequently varied, according to the state of production, the managerial policy, the labor situation, and other factors affecting the local balance of forces. A critical question has concerned the position of group leader: Should it be permanent, with the occupant appointed by the foreman? Or should the work team itself select the representative and thereby shift the position among competent team members? This problem has constantly recurred. The union clubs have strongly supported the latter procedure, management the former.

The LB plant rotated group representatives. This entailed a clear shift in the balance of power to the advantage of the assemblers. The same principle was originally going to be applied at Borås, but the position of coordinator soon became permanent and the company tried to strengthen it as a link in the chain of command. Both assemblers and coordinators, however, still considered the coordinator first and foremost a member of the team; this made the role a contradictory one.

During organizational negotiations at Volvo Trucks' plant in Umeå in the mid-1980s, these differences of perspective found expression in a struggle over the titles given to different positions. The company favored "leading hand"; the union wanted a "group representative." The resulting compromise was "coach."

Uddevalla's assembly concept aimed at far-reaching decentralization, including the abolition of traditional first-line management. The group representative was chosen by the team itself. The position rotated among competent members, but during the difficult breaking-in phase, management attempted to limit the rotation to ensure continuity and competence. More consistently than other plants, Uddevalla tried to design the process as true team production, matched to the organizational concept of team working. The factory therefore amounts to a test of the leeway for autonomous group work and of how far technical control and hierarchical supervision can be eliminated in a manual assembly system with exacting performance demands.

Strengths and Shortcomings of the "Japanese Machine"

During the 1980s, the fight between the world's car makers was played out in the United States, and the victors were the Japanese. They captured 25 percent of the market and established considerable local production. The Europeans initially enjoyed great success but were then pushed back; they failed to maintain their American production and lost market share.

The great battle of the 1990s will be in Europe, which has become the world's largest market for cars. In 1985, sales in Europe and the United States were roughly the same. The difference has become considerable since then: in 1989, 10 million cars were sold in the United States, compared with 13.4 million in

Europe. The share of the Japanese companies was limited to 11 percent, but they were fiercely determined to increase it, by building up considerable local production (as in North America). Nissan came to Britain as early as 1984, Honda and Toyota five years later. In the mid-1990s, their yearly European production is expected to be about 500,000 cars; by 1998, it may well be 1 million (*Fortune*, Jan. 29, 1990).

The German car makers were very successful during the 1980s. On the strength of their engineering competence and advance design, Daimler-Benz and BMW could set the world standard within the luxury segment, without needing to worry much about costs. The customers paid. In the late 1980s, however, the Germans became sensitive to their cost-effective Japanese competition, which started applying its sophisticated mass-production principles to the luxury segments. Toyota's Lexus and Nissan's Infiniti, launched in the United States in 1989, quickly outcompeted Daimler-Benz and BMW in the American market.

By 1990, the Japanese automotive sector had developed into a most formidable industrial cluster, in a continuous process of upgrading, triggered by the intense rivalry between the competing firms on the large and sophisticated home market. In this process the auto firms benefited from Japan's world-leading manufacturers of materials and general inputs, such as steel and semiconductors. They purchased their equipment from an outstanding machinery industry, where Japan was number one in such products as industrial robots, press dies, and body welding jigs. They were supported by an immense number of specialized supplier firms, several of them gaining global technological leadership in their own right (the most prominent being Nippondenso). Auto firms and suppliers alike benefited from the long-term commitment and perspectives of capital owners, management, and employees.

The Machine That Changed the World must be acknowledged for the breadth of its analysis of Japan's competitive strategies not only in manufacturing but in the design process, the collaboration between car makers and suppliers, and manufacturers' dealings with customers. In many of these fields, the Japanese automakers have developed new world standards. For the Western, and especially the European firms (including Volvo), it has become imperative to learn and to learn thoroughly. One area targeted for increases in efficiency is product design. European GM figured on reducing development times to three years in the first half of the 1990s, after previously having required five years. In the good years of the 1980s, when Volvo Cars was the world's most profitable automaker, the company did little to make its product development more efficient or its lead times shorter. Volvo clung to its Fordist tradition of infrequent model shifts to achieve maximum economy of scale and did not perceive the radically new conditions brought about by the Japanese companies' accelerated rate of innovation. The car crisis at the start of the 1990s dramatically brought home the demands for greater efficiency and flexibility in product design, at Volvo as elsewhere.

Another area in which the Japanese industry sets the example is its collaboration with suppliers in long-term yet competitive relationships. Ford has developed a comprehensive so-called Q1 program as the basis for systematic assessment of the supplier firms' quality and delivery precision. (But reportedly Ford's package is nothing compared with the meticulous care with which Toyota is building its European supplier network.)

In their personnel management, Western auto firms, following the Japanese, are emphasizing the need for flexibility and more integrated approaches, for example, amalgamating production tasks with quality-control assignments. They are less active in pursuing other changes, such as enhancing job security and eliminating blue-collar and white-collar segregation, which in the Japanese case is closely linked to the potential for flexibility. As has been repeatedly emphasized in this book, a distinctive feature of Japanese manufacturing is the shop-floor focus, the meticulous attention to detail, and the striving for perfection. This has given birth to elaborate quality-control procedures, the continuous reduction of inventories to reveal imbalances and slack, and the never-ending *kaizen* activities.

These practices constitute a deeply ambiguous package, however. Some parts are irrefutable contributions, such as the dramatic reduction of set-up times (from several hours to a few minutes in the press shops), the integrated quality-control approach, and the widespread application of statistical analysis to discover and analyze deviations before they become errors. But other parts of the package, such as the drive for unconditional JIT control, are closely linked to the regressive working conditions in the Japanese system, including the widespread fragmentation and intense machine pacing of human tasks; the rigid demands to fulfill production quotas in all parts of the tightly coupled system, which require unconditional employee flexibility, including a willingness to work overtime on very short notice; the close surveillance of the individual and excessive regimentation of the workplace; and the failure to adapt the working environment, ergonomic conditions, and work pace to long-term human requirements.

In sum, the Japanese production system has made several important contributions, but it is simply not a global "best practice," as Womack, Jones, and Roos (1990) claim. The shortcomings are increasingly debated in Japan, where the acute labor shortage triggered higher demands at the end of the 1980s and in the early 1990s. Japanese companies actually had a much harder time recruiting workers in Japan than in the United States or Britain. Among Japanese youth, jobs in auto manufacturing got a bad reputation, as *"san kei* jobs," or 3 K— *kitsui, kitanai, kiken* ("hard, dirty, and dangerous").[3] One of the strategies employed by the companies to cope with this problem was to reduce their need for personnel by means of mechanization. In 1990, they declared that they planned to invest massively in modernizing production facilities and raising the rate of automation. Nissan planned a 20 percent automation of final assembly by the mid-1990s; Honda aimed even higher—at 30 percent.[4] This strategy was favored because of the access to cheap capital, the short lead times in product development, the close connection between production and design, and the high degree of standardization in manufacturing. The auto companies sought as well to increase their attractiveness in the labor market by making large investments in staff facilities, recreation centers, and so on.

The discontent with working conditions in the auto industry in Japan was not confined to new entrants to the labor market but seemed to encompass a majority of the regular employees. According to a large survey reported by JAW (the national federation of the unions within the auto industry) in 1989, very few employees would recommend to their children that they get jobs in the automobile industry; of all respondents, 43 percent answered they would not, 43 percent found the question difficult to answer, and only 4 percent gave a positive response. The pattern was basically the same for all employee categories, but sales and service staff were the most dissatisfied. (Reading the lyric description of the Japanese sales organizations in *The Machine That Changed the World,* this certainly comes as a surprise.)[5] The main reasons the production workers gave for their reluctance to recommend the auto industry were that the wages were too low for such hard work, there was too much overtime and holiday work and too much shift work and night work, and the work was too intensive (JAW 1989:29).

These results were supported by a workplace survey published in 1991. Two-thirds or more of the production workers in the auto industry reported too tight staffing, too much work, too much overtime, and too many difficulties to take paid holidays. Sixty-seven percent were not satisfied with their working environments, 62 percent regarded their work as excessively routine, and 72 percent did not think the company paid enough attention to human resource development.

As a result of these surveys, JAW started to campaign for goals such as shorter working hours; a prolongation of the model change time from four to six years; a reexamination of the JIT system (which in Japan is seen as a major source of traffic congestion); the adaptation of machines to people instead of people to machines, which is the case in the Toyota system; the integration of routine and segmented jobs; and the redesign of production lines to make them possible workplaces for elderly and female workers.

The motto of a Toyota plant opened in 1991 was "factory friendly to workers." Womack, Jones, and Roos emphasize the efficient space utilization of Japanese plants as one of their important advantages. In this new plant, however, space per worker was deliberately increased to create an improved work environment. The JIT principle of zero stocks was modified, and the plant distinguished between two types of waste (*muda*), unnecessary waste and waste that was considered necessary to provide human working conditions. Further, Toyota experimented with new work schedules to reduce overtime. At the same time, the organization was changed to create a more flexible and less hierarchical structure (Nomura 1992).

Many of the demands raised in the Japanese debate are strikingly similar to the goals of Sweden's work reforms and, more generally, to the European human-centered concept of work.[6] They emphasize the position put forward here that lean production should not be adopted lock, stock, and barrel.

Toward Postlean Production

Sweden's Accomplishments in Perspective

The dynamics of Japanese car production have been fueled by the fierce domestic competition in Japan's home market and by its strong and rising currency. In contrast, Swedish firms have encountered a uniquely demanding labor market. They have also been influenced by Sweden's less hierarchical culture and more deeply embedded democratic and egalitarian values. Thus, Sweden's contribution to the renewal of work organization and job design have occurred in areas in which Japanese management has never focused. Four contributions are especially noteworthy.

1. The integration of subdivided and monotonous mass-production work to more dignified and holistic tasks. The Swedish assembly trajectory has demonstrated that alternatives to repetitive and confined work structures are indeed possible. They are technically feasible, compatible with varied market demands, and socially highly desirable, in that they result in qualitative improvements in the working conditions, reducing physical work loads as well as mental stress.

2. The broad development of the physical work environment, especially the ergonomic aspects of manual workplaces, with the purpose of combatting repetitive strain injuries. At Uddevalla, this effort was explicitly related to the high proportion of female workers (40 percent) and the need for a comprehensive adaptation of tools and methods to human differences, recognizing that workers are not standard packages of the same size and with the same strength.

3. The efforts to make work systems less rigidly coupled and more adaptable to meeting diverse human needs. This too can be interpreted as a response to Sweden's advanced labor market, in which there was virtually no unemployment, high labor force participation, and a high share of women workers. The auto firms were not able to target an elite male work force, and they had to acknowledge that employees have important obligations outside work. Consequently, a demand

for total commitment Japanese style was neither possible nor desirable. Forms of production control that permanently rely on overtime for smooth functioning were out of reach for all large firms.

4. The high degree of involvement of unions in decision making and planning processes as independent partners with legitimate interests of their own. In contrast to the case in Japan, unions in Sweden had a strong workplace presence yet were integrated into national industrywide unions. The involvement of unions as independent partners sometimes caused controversies and complications, but it also enabled them to articulate complex social demands that Japanese enterprise unions found very difficult to do. When JAW adopted a more assertive and reformative stance, it had no means of getting the enterprise unions to pursue this policy since they were locked into the system of company competition.

Sweden's contributions have been marked by a distinctive shop-floor focus. Unfortunately, this did not include a consistent devotion to an increase in productivity. An important reason for this failure was the government policy of currency depreciations, which relaxed the profit squeeze on companies—quite the opposite of the situation in Japan, where the rising yen forced firms to upgrade even faster than before.

Creating a Synthesis

Many elements of the Japanese and Swedish trajectories could be combined. The introduction of "Japanese" forms of product development, with close collaboration between design and manufacturing (but without the excessive overtime so characteristic of the Japanese automakers) would strengthen and support the Swedish assembly concept, push integration further, and add to its intellectual qualities. The same is true of the Japanese firms' long-term and closely collaborative relations with their suppliers. But what about the Japanese preoccupation with standardization and procedures? This seems to be squarely incompatible with the emphasis on autonomy, freedom, and worker discretion heralded in human-centered production. In fact, the Swedish long-cycle assembly systems would benefit from much more attention to details, order, and discipline (concerning tools and quality-control procedures, for example) and from more systematic efforts to develop reliable standards for critical operations. Such efforts would help lagging teams, facilitate the training of new employees, and make it possible for qualified teams to concentrate on solving more complex problems and developing their methods. (Of course, complete standardization and proceduralization of the Toyota type, with "programmed worksheets" prescribing body postures and movements would not be compatible with the holistic work concept.) An analogy with sailing is apt here. Good crews maintain meticulous standards and discipline concerning their sails, sheets, and halyards, their ropes and tools, and their nautical instruments and safety equipment so that they may concentrate on the creative parts of the adventure, respond to unpredictable events, and deal with emergencies promptly. In the same vein, skilled work requires good procedures and standards. This has too often been overlooked in Sweden.

Recognizing the Options

Other features of the two approaches are difficult or impossible to reconcile. Firms have a choice between measuring their efficiency strictly in worker hours and considering the societal and human consequences of different manufacturing strategies in developing their goals for efficiency; between flexibility as a "one-way street," unilaterally demanding that employees conform to company needs, and the flexible design of manufacturing, to respond to employee needs; and between continuing the tradition of fragmentation and centralized control and reorienting one's view of work as capable of enhancing autonomy.

The options are there. Firms have choices concerning their work organization and their production design. Further, their decisions have important implications for the future quality of working and social life. To make these choices, however, it is essential to know the alternatives and not to simplify the problem. No one practice is suitable for all firms or all workers.

It is mandatory that unions become much more active, critical, and competent in choosing production strategies. This does not apply only to the United States, where the UAW at the national level neither took on lean production as a concept nor supported union locals facing it as a practice. This applies also in Europe, especially in Germany, where unions have been lulled into a false sense of security because of the successes of the auto industry in the 1980s. Lean production is now approaching on the fringes—in the United States, firms used the "southern strategy" to weaken unions; on the European continent, they play the "eastern card." In 1991 in Eisenach, in eastern Germany, where the Wartburg car was once produced, GM planned a "transplant" explicitly modeled on its Japanese joint ventures in North America, CAMI and NUMMI. Similarly, VW has tried to implement full-fledged lean production in its East German plant in Mosel where the well-known Trabis used to be manufactured (Jürgens et al.). Unions have the option of simply acquiescing to this managerial push or conducting analyses of their own and devising strategies for the selective synthesis of both lean and human-centered practices.

High unemployment, large income inequalities, deficient social protection, and low labor standards facilitate the adoption of the regressive features of lean production that are causing so much dissatisfaction in Japan. Advanced labor market policies, solid social security, and regulation of the work environment raise costs in the short term. In the long run, however, if firms, financiers, and management are committed to their industry, such selective disadvantages will stimulate innovation, upgrading, and sustainable competitive positions. To maintain the advanced social demands that are the basis for human-centered production, governments must play an important role. This is particularly true in Europe, where the much-delayed development of the "social dimension" of the integrated market could be a very important element in the movement toward postlean production.

Notes

Chapter 1

1. Volvo's acquisition of British Leyland was greeted by high expectations among the work force. Unfortunately, Volvo chose a very low-key approach—in striking contrast to the Japanese—which gave the local management abundant opportunities to obstruct the introduction of new work practices.

2. This has, for example, been reported by Tom Clarke (personal communication, September 1991). The combination of the considerable degree of freedom in a small-scale, greenfield plant and the commitment of a management fostered in the Volvo company culture seems to have resulted in this innovative approach. In Belgium, which is a very efficient production site for many European auto firms, the industrial culture seems to be much more entrenched and dominated by mass-production paradigms.

3. This combination of resentment and resignation is poignantly depicted in Kamata 1973 and mirrored in a number of surveys that show a consistently low level of job satisfaction in Japan. This theme will be dealt with in more detail in chapter 13.

4. The extent to which this managerial style is applied outside Sweden is a complicated issue. Forslin and Ågren (1987) found clear evidence of such a process in the case of White, a truck company bought by Volvo in 1981. Other Swedish corporations have a pronounced policy of "adopting local standards." This is the case of Electrolux, for example, which in the United States has a decidedly antiunion policy.

5. On the continual importance of national institutions in the development of manufacturing practice and industrial relations, see, for example, Lane 1989.

6. Jürgens, Dohse, and Malsch 1989 is the principal report on this project.

Chapter 2

1. Europe's technologically most eminent auto company, Daimler-Benz, came well after Honda. The greatest innovative activity among European companies, measured in this manner, was shown by the German manufacturer Bosch—"the technological powerhouse of the European motor industry" (Jones 1988:5).

2. This is according to Clark et al., *Product Development in the World Auto Industry*, referred to in Jones 1990:12. See also Clark and Fujimoto 1990.

3. This account of workers' prewar program and postwar struggles in Japan is based largely on Gordon 1990, which in compressed form presents the main argument of Gordon 1985.

4. A painstaking account of this conflict is in Cusumano 1985. He documents the strategic significance of the conflict and the coordinated strategy of the employers. The other auto companies—Toyota, for instance (where management had already asserted its standing in 1950 with the dismissal of two thousand workers)—supported Nissan wholeheartedly.

5. A national autoworkers' union was eventually organized, as a kind of umbrella organization. The national body did not wield any effective policy-making capacity, however, and could not change the competitive relations between the enterprise unions that were working in close cooperation with their respective managements.

6. Ohno began at Toyota in 1943 and made his career in the production division before becoming the CEO in 1970.

7. A central role in Toyota's reduction of its set-up times was played by Shigeo Shingo, author of *The Toyota Production System* and originator of the SMED concept (single minute exchange of die).

8. The changes in the machine shops were one of the major causes of the unsuccessful Toyota strike of 1950, after which two thousand men were dismissed.

9. Carl le Grand has emphasized the great importance of small companies in Japanese industry (the transport industry especially) and the great wage differentials between companies. See Le Grand 1985, especially page 34, for statistics on wage differentials at workplaces of varying sizes in Toyota City.

10. Toyota's production pyramid in the late 1970s, with its ten thousand companies, is described in Le Grand 1985:22.

11. As in Germany, components suppliers accounted for the majority of the Japanese industry's technological innovations during the 1980s, as measured by the number of patents registered in the United States. See Jones 1988.

12. In Toshiko Tsukaguchi's and my investigation of Japanese production pyramids in 1984, the wire harness and instrument maker Yazaki provided an example of such a structure. Accordingly, fourteen hundred of twenty-one hundred employees at one of the company's plants were women employed part time (so-called *paato*). Moreover, the company employed four thousand women who worked at home assembling wire harnesses for a very low wage per unit. They enjoyed no employment benefits.

13. "The protagonist of industrialization in successive historic epochs has shifted from the owner-entrepreneur, to the corporate manager, to the production engineer, because the latter is the only person with the technical knowledge to make imported technology work" (Amsden 1990:26).

14. The description of the *shokunoshikaku* and *satei* systems is based largely on Endo 1991 and Nomura 1990.

15. A detailed description of how this "individual guidance" worked at Toyota Auto Body may be found in Cole 1979. Cole summarizes on page 171: "It is apparent from this detailed apparatus of data-collection and record-keeping that a cornerstone of company personnel policy is a very individualized treatment of workers which involves the constant monitoring of individual plans and the actions designed to shape and produce the desired outcomes. . . . It should be noted that the only page the individual is allowed to see in this document is the fifth page [which lists the educational plans for the year and the records of education received]. . . . Otherwise the document is open only to management; union officials have no significant input or right of access."

16. In addition to the (largely male) permanent full-time employees, there are other groups of employees: part-time workers (*paato*), seasonal workers (*kikanko*), employees of subcontractors leased out to larger firms (*ukeoiko*), and family members and self-employed at the smallest suppliers. In the mid-1980s, the so-called part-time employees made up a good half of Japan's 12 million female wage earners. Their workday was often only slightly shorter than the normal day. The major difference between permanent full-time workers and the *paato* workers was that the latter were not embraced by the maximal employment relationship. The company accepted that these workers had other important duties (in the home), and so overtime and other "voluntary" efforts were not

required of them to the same extent. In exchange, their economic and social compensation were far below that enjoyed by permanent, full-time (male) employees: lower wages, inferior job security, small or nonexistent career possibilities, a fraction of the regular bonus, and so on.

17. The term *lifetime employment* is a misnomer because Japanese employees usually quit, more or less voluntarily, before sixty years of age; they often must then take much lower-paying jobs—at supplier firms, for example—since the severance pay does not suffice for a secure retirement.

18. The corresponding figure for the Federal Republic of Germany was at least 17 percent in the mid-1980s, according to Deutschmann and Weber 1987:42; the rate in Swedish assembly plants ranged from 25 to 30 percent in the late 1980s.

19. The Japanese wage systems are complicated and vary between companies. Toyota's system contained a group-based performance element and an individual evaluation as well (done by the foreman and his superior). Attitude and commitment weighed very heavily. Tokunaga (1984) analyzes Toyota's wage and rank-order systems; Nomura (1985) treats both Nissan and Toyota.

20. See, for example, Burawoy (1979), who discusses "output restrictions" as a theme in American industrial sociology.

21. Compare Schonberger 1982:61: "In Japanese plants, the production pace itself [the pace per hour] is not the most important thing. We have seen that it can be broken at any time by a stoppage of the line. While the pace is not important, the daily production quota is, and if there is much stopping and reworking, the operators may have to work longer in order to ensure that the daily quota is met."

22. Worker times for the selected operations were about nineteen hours for the Japanese factories in Japan, twenty hours in the Japanese transplants, twenty-seven hours in the American-owned plants, and thirty-six hours in the European-owned factories. The comparison between Japanese plants in Japan and in North America was methodologically simple since they manufacture the same products. The matter is more complicated when different companies and thereby products with different designs are compared (i.e., where productivity is affected by how well the products are prepared for efficient production). Even when the Japanese companies' robust, manufacturable designs are accounted for, considerable differences in productivity at the plant level remain.

23. For example; "Nummi's application form requires workers to specify the number of days missed each year for the previous five years and give reasons for absence in excess of ten days per year" (Parker and Slaughter 1988:18).

24. One worker's situation was described in the following way: "Brian Johnson scarcely dares to stay home from work when he is sick. . . . He is absent so seldom that he does not even know what compensation rules apply in the event of illness" (*Dagens Nyheter,* July 29, 1989).

25. See, for example, the article by regional director Bruce Lee, "Worker Harmony makes NUMMI Work," *New York Times,* Dec. 25, 1988.

26. One must also distinguish, as in Sweden, between the time formally allocated to training (e.g., because it is partly financed by public authorities) and the way this time is actually used. That these can be very different is testified to by Mazda workers in the article "Injury, Training Woes Hit New Mazda Plant," *Automotive News,* Feb. 13, 1989. A subforeman says: "It was protocol to record more training hours than actual training. . . . The important thing was to get the line time going." Another injured worker tells how it was made clear in the job interview that "no job here takes more than a half-hour to learn."

27. In MacDuffie's Ph.D. thesis (1991), problem solving on the shop floor plays a central theoretical role. There is a lengthy discussion of the integration of conception and execution, of production and innovation, and of the alleged holistic division of labor, which is supposed to characterize the transplants. Unfortunately, MacDuffie's field study of problem-solving activities at a Honda plant does not provide very substantive proof of comprehensive participation and training. The report from Honda is selective and anecdotal and stands out very unfavorably in comparison to MacDuffie's rigorous, systematic, and highly critical studies of two Ford and GM plants.

28. This applies as well to transplants with heavy investments in modern technology. At CAMI, which claimed in 1990 to have North America's most modern body shop (with over four hundred robots), there were just eighty-five skilled tradespeople out of a total of seventeen hundred employees.

At Diamond Star, the most automated transplant (with over one hundred robots in assembly alone), skilled tradespeople comprised a mere two hundred of the plant's twenty-three hundred workers.

29. According to Cusumano (1985:309), Toyota insisted in its application of this system that production quotas be met even when the line had been halted; the result was a strong social pressure even on highly pressed workers not to signal red.

30. Cole continues: "The increased responsibility given to workers occurs in a context in which management controls the training, the amount of job rotation, and the content of career patterns. This gives management enormous leverage in preventing the hardening of worker privilege."

31. See, for example, "What Happened to the American Dream?" *Business Week,* Aug. 19, 1991. This article describes Troy and Linda, who both worked in the service sector. Together they earned 44 percent less, adjusted for inflation, than Troy's father earned as a blue-collar worker at the same age.

32. This has been demonstrated in recent studies by Hiramoto (1991) and Sei (1991).

33. As yet, there are no solid studies comparing working conditions in the transplants with American-owned auto plants, collating working hours (extent of overtime and how it is ordered), work-related injuries, and so on. One hopes that American social researchers will not be satisfied with the MIT's authors' sweeping assertions but will confront this challenging issue.

ILR Press has fulfilled this request, at least in one important area, by publishing Richard Wokutch's important study (1992). Among Wokutch's rich empirical material is a comparison between Mazda's Michigan plant and corresponding American-owned operations. After a painstaking analysis of the facts and figures, Wokutch finds that repetitive traumas are considerably more frequent at the Mazda plant (disguised as "Jidosha USA"). He summarizes (195): "The obvious conclusion is that the stresses of the production system do indeed make soft-tissue disorders more of a problem at Jidosha USA. The problems seem to go to the very core of the production system, which elicits maximum efficiency from both workers and machinery. Although accidents must be avoided at all costs in this production system, slow-developing conditions such as CTDs are evidently viewed as less of a threat. Perhaps it is reasoned that workers with conditions such as CTDs can be replaced with only minimal disruption to production."

34. This tendency was reported by several Japanese specialists, such as Masami Nomura and Masayoshi Ikeda, at the symposium "Production Strategies and Industrial Relations in the Process of Internationalization," Sendai, Japan, Oct. 14–16, 1991.

Chapter 3

1. The companies' foreign assembly plants are included in these figures. The Swedish figures therefore include Volvo's operations in Belgium and Saab's in Finland but not the production of the Volvo 300 and 400 series in the Netherlands, since they were produced by a separate company, 70 percent of which was owned by the Dutch state (Volvo Car Bv).

2. In contrast to table 3-1, Volvo's Dutch production is included. The justification is that the products are developed as part of Volvo's product program, even though Volvo Cars in the Netherlands is independent from an ownership standpoint. In a rank ordering based on the *total sales* of cars and trucks in 1989 (published in *Business Week* on April 9, 1990), Volvo came in twentieth and Saab twenty-fifth.

3. These disappointments, together with the practical difficulties of attaining the hoped-for advantages of coordination and the structure's unclear forms for decision making, provoked grave doubts as to whether the deal was industrially justifiable and would last. See, for example, "Kompromisser och oklar styrning, Volvo och Renault—ett multinationellt missfoster" (Compromises and Muddled Control: A Multinational Monstrosity), *Affärsvärlden,* no. 9, 1990.

4. Volvo entertained ambitions of introducing its own drive train, but the idea met with little success since Americans are accustomed to choosing engines and the like from independent manufacturers such as Cummins and Detroit Diesel, which have their own extensive service networks.

5. Scania's CEO Leif Östling in the article "Nu väntar svåra år, sedan kan det lossna," in *Affärsvärlden,* no. 43, 1989.

Chapter 4

1. The concept of cluster is used here in the same way as Michael Porter uses it, to include not only prime manufacturers but also supporting and related industries, suppliers of specialized inputs and equipment, and so on. Thus, the forest-related cluster encompasses timber, pulp, and paper producers as well as makers of machinery and chemicals plus downstream industries such as manufacturers of prefabricated houses and furniture. See Porter 1990:333–41 and Sölvell, Zander, and Porter 1991:59–119.

2. This fundamental oversight in the established research on trade unions has been emphasized by Roger Molin in a comprehensive but still unpublished study. The data on Metall's organization come from Molin's study.

3. A summary in English of the 1985 report is presented in *Rewarding Work* (1987).

4. Kjellberg 1990 is an excellent analysis of the changing industrial relations system and employer strategies from the beginning of the century to 1990.

5. As a response, the government commissioned the National Commission on Productivity to investigate the causes of the stagnation and to make recommendations for policy changes. The committee initiated a number of studies and published its major report in 1991 (SOU 1991).

6. The birth of a child entitles the parents to eighteen months of leave from work, which they can divide between them as they see fit. The national insurance office replaces the income shortfall for twelve of these months; for the next three months, a minimum compensation of 60 crowns per day is paid (1991); for the last three months, no compensation is paid.

7. On March 1, 1991, new rules on sickness insurance came into effect, which meant a deterioration in benefits. According to these rules, an employee absent from work on account of illness receives 75 percent income replacement during the first three days of illness and 90 percent replacement for the following days of absence. (The rules had earlier prescribed 100 percent income replacement from the first day.) In the first months following this change, the rate of absenteeism on account of illness fell by 20 percent.

8. The two lines in question are the two-year mechanical line (which includes vocational training for the engineering industry) and the experimental three-year industrial technical line. See Skolöverstyrelsen 1990: 47. A considerably greater number of students—more than four thousand—applied to enter the automotive technical line, in the hope of finding work in auto repair shops and such.

9. These figures were provided by the admissions boards for the Södertälje, Uddevalla, and Gothenburg regions. The data for 1990 are preliminary.

10. The field work was commenced in 1983 with a questionnaire answered by 6,500 youth between sixteen and twenty-four years of age. Of these, 1,060 had had personal experience with industrial work; 880 could be interviewed; 490 of these had stayed and 380 had left.

11. IVA symposium, "Successful Automated Assembly Systems," Stockholm, Sept. 27, 1988.

12. The robotization of Swedish industry proceeded much more slowly during the 1980s than had been foreseen at the start of the decade. The robotics industry at that time had counted on a growth rate of 30 percent per year. That would have meant 10,000 robots installed by 1990. The actual figure at the start of 1989 was 3,000. Just 292 robots were installed in 1988 (*Ny teknik* 1989:12).

13. See Skantze 1988 and the article "Flexibel automatiserad montering," *Verkstäderna*, no. 11, 1988.

14. For example, at Saab's assembly plant in Trollhättan, the variant spread measured in time doubled from five to ten hours from 1982 to 1987, while production rose by 50 percent. At Volvo Bus at Borås, the knowledge requirements for assembly workers increased during the 1980s by 10 percent per year (measured in time). At Volvo LB, the production volume rose from 1985 to 1988 by about 15 percent, while the number of employees increased by 50 percent, on account of the increasing complexity.

Chapter 5

1. The statistical distribution of the time spread differed between experienced and inexperienced workers. For experienced workers the actual cycle time was Weibull distributed; for the inexperienced it was normally distributed.

2. Handling losses are understated because they are calculated according to the normal method, without accounting for working ahead. The differences between Volvo and Saab depend on the fact that Volvo has larger volumes, more facilities, and thereby a greater number of assembly flows on which to distribute variants.

3. I refer here exclusively to assembly. The same types of production designs are relevant for manual work in other production sections as well—in the body shops' final polishing and welding processes, for instance.

4. There are other technologically feasible possibilities—manual moving of the objects on air cushions, for instance. In that case, the handling losses are large in high-volume flows.

5. In his later book *Arbeidervilkår* (1975), Gulowsen emphasizes, on a more general level, the importance of trade unions for the development of worker influence and self-management.

6. The model was discussed in a series of seminars in the Swedish auto industry and proved to have considerable heuristic value.

Chapter 6

1. Note that this rate is not comparable to that at Borås, since Katrineholm's operations are considerably more extensive (in body work, among other areas).

2. Since 1988, Leyland Bus has been a part of Volvo Buses. The studies of the Borås plant were done in 1982 and 1987, before Leyland was acquired.

3. When a new vehicle came into production at Katrineholm, the designers had six months in which to propose improvements. The suggestion system (for the assemblers) was not open during this period; that is, workers were not entitled to any rewards if they submitted suggestions. After the six months, however, assemblers would get paid for changes that facilitated assembly. This system did not further cooperation in product preparation; naturally, the assemblers waited to make suggestions until they were paid for them. I was told about this system in discussions with assemblers and industrial engineers in 1988, in connection with the presentation of the results of the assembly survey (see chap. 11).

Chapter 7

1. This section is based mainly on a study done in April–May 1985, when planning for the Uddevalla plant had just begun (and the focus was on copying the Kalmar concept). The highly positive official evaluation, *Volvo/Kalmar Revisited* (Agurén et al. 1985), had come out in Swedish the year before. Our analysis of the factory, of its working conditions in particular, was especially critical at this stage.

2. SIFO had misinterpreted the replies. Fifty-seven percent were seeking work, not 94 percent as SIFO reported.

3. In the Volvo car division, comparisons are made regularly of the assembly plants in Sweden, in Belgium (at Ghent), and in Canada (at Halifax). Unfortunately, it was not possible to analyze the truck-assembly plant in Ghent in the same way because of the large differences in product mix between the Swedish and Belgian operations.

4. The industrial engineers emphasized in interviews the great difficulty in achieving changes on an already designed vehicle. The designing section's first reaction was that there must be defects in the materials. If this proved not to be the case, the next problem was that, by the time assembly problems were revealed in the plant, the vehicle was old (from the point of view of the designers).

Why waste effort on changes when a new model would come in one to two years? It was also difficult to ascertain who among the designers was responsible. To achieve a design change, the industrial engineers had to show how much the design problems cost in production. The designers then replied with a calculation of the costs of redesign. The decision was then made by the design section itself.

5. The Uddevalla project's heavy investment in the development of a wholly new type of technical information system should be seen against the background of these experiences at LB.

Chapter 8

1. Lennart Nilsson from the University of Gothenburg had worked for many years in the area of research and development within vocational training. He introduced the concept of "natural work" as a model to the project. According to Nilsson, such work is distinguished by the following: the worker has control over daily events; the work has a holistic character; the work has meaning for the individual; and the time allotted for a task is determined by the character of that task, instead of the other way around. Finally, the transfer of knowledge to a great extent takes place from one occupational generation to another. See Ellegård, Engström, and Nilsson 1991.

2. "Once lean production principles are fully instituted, companies will be able to move rapidly in the 1990s to automate most of the remaining repetitive tasks in auto assembly—and more. Thus by the end of the century we expect that lean-assembly plants will be populated almost entirely by highly skilled problem solvers. . . . The great flaw of neocraftsmanship is that it will never reach this goal, since it aspires to go in the other direction, back toward an era of handcrafting as an end in itself' (Womack, Jones, and Roos 1990:102).

3. This was confirmed in interviews I did in 1987 with assemblers at TC in Gothenburg: "At the start I took exactly as many screws as I needed, or put back those I didn't use. Then I noticed no one else did so. After a few days I had fallen into the usual pattern: you take a handful without a closer look, and you throw out those left over, into the cabin or onto the line."

4. An example was the problem of inspecting the bags by means of weighing. If a bag contained both heavy and light articles, the tolerance variation in the heavy articles would "drown" the light ones, so that one could not be certain if the bags contained the light articles or not. The tolerance spread was especially marked for rubber articles.

5. One may compare variant-rich, long-cycle assembly with the making of music. Learning a piano concert (a couple hours' cycle time) is a matter of remembering a great number of operations and carrying them out in the proper sequence, according to the right tempo, pitch, and so on. It is in this sense an exercise in manual dexterity. But who can learn and remember such a "manual task" without possessing at the same time an intellectual understanding of the composition's "functional grouping," harmony, and chord progression?

6. In Sweden it was not Volvo but the giant Swiss-Swedish electrotechnical corporation ABB that took the lead in attacking the traditional segregation of blue- and white-collar workers. In 1990, an aggressive companywide rationalization program was launched, with the objective to cut through-put times for all major products, from order to delivery, including engineering, manufacturing, and administration, by 50 percent. This tough corporate goal started a process of elimination of functional boundaries. In pioneering divisions, various professional specialties were integrated in mixed teams. The next step was to formulate identical employment contracts for hourly and salaried workers.

7. I was able to experience this personally, in a nearly unforgettable way, at two Volvo Forum conferences in 1986; on May 15–16 in Gothenburg and November 17–18 in Kungälv.

8. Volvo's vice-president for production, K.E. Nilsson, interviewed in "Låt oss vara smarta tillsammans," *Stockholmstidningen,* May 13, 1983.

9. I experienced such distrust between assemblers and the company very powerfully when I took part in a union course for Metall's delegates at TC; "TC 90—en ny monteringsfabrik," on October 29–30, 1986.

Chapter 9

1. Such items dominate the work environment section of the standard of living surveys conducted by the Institute for Social Research (Stockholm University) in 1968, 1974, and 1981.

2. Wikman had shown earlier that reliability (i.e., the probability that respondents would give the same answer on repeated occasions) was also clearly lacking in questions of the first and second type. See Wikman 1980.

3. Den Hertog (1978), among others, has reported such cases from the Dutch Philips Company.

4. These studies are an excellent illustration of the observation of the French philosopher Louis Althusser (following Marx) that "ideology has no history" (1976:132).

5. The only clear difference was that the physical environment was considered better at LB.

6. Similar questions were used in 1985 in a survey by Lars-Erik Karlsson (Luleå Institute of Technology) at AB Sunlight in Nyköping.

7. Some examples of such questions are the following: "Do you work under such time pressure that there are risks for mistakes and defects (for example, that something important is forgotten, must be done over again, is damaged, and so on.)?" "Does the job require total concentration and attention?" "Does the job require mainly that you repeat the same work operation many times an hour, hour after hour?" The answers are designed to get the respondent to report the incidence of a certain factor in terms of the proportion of the workday involved, from "nearly all the time" to "not at all." See Wikman 1989.

8. R can vary, as can gamma, between -1 and 1. The value 0 means no relation exists. A precise interpretation of, for example, gamma $= 0.3$ is difficult; the values are useful mainly for comparing the strength of different relations.

Chapter 10

1. In January 1986, line 1 had 880 employees, including those on long-term leave. The proportion of women was about 20 percent.

2. These figures include everyone in the sample, $N = 260$, after the internal nonresponses were taken into account.

3. Interviewed for the article "Ett liv på linan? Sällan!" (A Life on the Line? No Way!), *Metallarbetaren*, June 1987. Compare this with the words of the production manager at Electrolux in Spennymoor interviewed for the article "Electroluxkulturen nyckeln till framgång," *Dagens Nyheter*, July 29, 1989: "We try to simplify the job and divide it up into shorter operations as much as possible. . . . Many people in fact want to have the same monotonous job year in and year out. It's a kind of security for some people."

4. Krafcik accordingly writes (1988:12): "The most significant predictor of plant level quality is plant scale, which is a proxy for cycle time. This indicates that *reduced* cycle times are at least partial contributors to improved quality performance" (emphasis in original).

Chapter 11

1. Borås and Katrineholm had the same basic technical design. The difference between them was in the arrangement of work: at Katrineholm, the assemblers followed the chassis, so that each pair of assemblers built the entire chassis. At Borås, the work was strictly divided between stations.

2. TUN was closed down in 1989 in connection with a reduction of capacity within Volvo Cars in Gothenburg. Production was concentrated in the main factory, TC.

3. The survey at LB confirmed this analysis. A large majority of LB's workers (75 percent) had done the same type of work earlier at other plants within Volvo. They were asked in the survey to assess their current jobs in comparison to their previous ones. Their evaluation of LB varied closely depending on the reference point (i.e., which factory LB was compared with): the X plant—a traditional truck plant; TC/TA—a traditional car plant (TA—body welding, TC—trim and final

assembly); TLA—a shop for adjustment and custom outfitting of truck chassis; or Arendal—a smaller plant that, between 1974 and 1980, built trucks in a dock assembly system with very long work cycles. The former TC workers were clearly positive. Eighty-six percent claimed their LB job was better, while just 6 percent said it was worse than their earlier job. More than half thought LB was *much* better. The evaluations were positive for nearly all factors, including the work tempo and physical strains. Opposite results were found in the evaluations of the former Arendal workers. Nearly all were negatively disposed to LB on all points. The remaining groups fell between these two extremes.

4. A survey of different studies of the connection between mental stress/muscular tension and muscular-skeletal strains was compiled by Eklund et al. 1989.

5. The question was asked as follows: "Do you work part of the day under heavy time pressure, so that you are forced to hurry as much as you can to keep up?" The answers were: "No/A few hours or a day a week/Yes, about an hour every day/Yes, about half the day/Yes, the larger part of the day."

6. For the variable "headaches on the job," the differences are significant on the .005 level; for "stomach aches on the job," the significance level is .0002; for "distaste at the prospect of work," it is .0001; for "satisfied with the day's work," finally, it is .001.

7. Unfortunately, this question was not included in the questionnaires at TUN and LB.

Chapter 12

1. The internal nonresponse rate was very low, a sign that it was easy for the respondents to state who made the decisions in question. The question concerning the selection of group representatives was not included in the TC questionnaire, since such a position did not exist there. For the same reason, "group representative" was not included in the answers at TC.

2. This occurred partly through so-called wild rotation (i.e., alternation outside the control of first-line management). The TC management strove to bring this practice to a halt.

3. This is not the same, naturally, as a list of union priorities drawn up by the workers. Union work includes a great many issues not discussed here, above all wages and work times.

Chapter 13

1. Honda has an engineering division that is responsible for planning and building new plants and turning them over to the parent company in turn-key condition. Local adaptation is done through personnel selection, training, and the wage system.

2. It is remarkable that one cannot find support for this view in Trist et al.'s work, which contains a very careful empirical study of work forms in coal mining and is cautious in drawing conclusions of a general nature.

3. In April 1991, a group of researchers and company physicians from Volvo and Saab visited various automakers in Japan for the purpose of learning how work injury problems were handled and solved in that country. The group made field trips to a large number of plants belonging to Isuzu, Fuji, Aisin Warner, Toyota, and Mazda, among others. Their general impression of the working environment was discouraging: high noise levels, frequent exposure to oil haze, ergonomically unsuitable work positions, and everywhere an utterly intense work pace. The official view of the Japanese companies, however, was that they had no problems with work injuries. The strains that occurred arose, they claimed, because of deficient training of new workers or, in the case of older workers, because of age. The only company that acknowledged problems with work injuries and strains (such as CTDs) was Mazda at Hiroshima, which also appeared to have an ambitious program for combatting these problems.

4. See the interview with Yutaka Kume, Nissan's CEO, in *Automotive News,* December 11, 1989, and "Japan Makers on Spending Spree," *Automotive News,* October 8, 1990.

5. The main reason for the dissatisfaction among the sales staff seemed to be the excessive amount of overtime and holiday work.

6. At a labor-management seminar in May 1991 on the Swedish car industry at which the pros and cons of lean production were debated, a Japanese participant suggested that Volvo should build a plant of the Uddevalla type in Japan. Such a plant would get a long queue of job applicants, he asserted, and would be a great PR case for Volvo in Japan. Unfortunately, Volvo, like other Western producers, lacked the guts to undertake such a bold policy idea.

References

Adler, Paul. 1990. "Materials on New United Motor Manufacturing, Inc." Department of Industrial Engineering and Engineering Management, Stanford University.

———. 1991. "The 'Learning Bureaucracy': New United Motor Manufacturing, Inc." School of Business Administration, University of Southern California.

Ager, Harald and Ingemar Ander. 1945. "Flytande tillverkning." In *Handbok i industriell driftsekonomi och organisation* ("Flow Production," *in Handbook in Industrial Economy and Organization*), ed. Tarras Sällfors. Vol. 1:706–46. Stockholm: Natur och Kultur.

Agurén, Stefan, Reine Hansson, and K. G. Karlsson. 1976. *Volvo Kalmarverken* (The Volvo Kalmar Plant), trans. David Jenkins. Stockholm: Development Council, SAF-LO.

Agurén, Stefan, Christer Bredbacka, Reine Hansson, Kurt Inregren, and K. G. Karlsson. 1985. *Volvo/Kalmar Revisited.* Stockholm: Development Council, SAF-LO-PTK.

Althusser, Louis. 1976. Filosofi från proletär klasståndpunkt. (Philosophy from a Proletarian Perspective). Lund: Bo Cavefors Bokförlag.

Altmann, Norbert, Peter Binkelmann, Klaus Düll, and Heiner Stück. 1982. *Grenzen neuer Arbeitsformen.* Frankfurt: Campus Verlag.

Altshuler, Alan, Martin Anderson, Daniel Jones, Daniel Roos, and James Womack. 1984. *The Future of the Automobile.* Cambridge: MIT Press.

Amsden, Alice. 1990. "Third World Industrialization: 'Global Fordism' or a New Model?" *New Left Review* 182:5–31.

Arnström, Anders, and Peter Gröndahl. 1984. *Flexibel automatiserad montering—introduktion och sammandrag* (Flexible Automated Assembly: Introduction and Overview). Ivf-result 84614. Stockholm: Sveriges Mekanförbund.

Bengtsson, Lars, Christian Berggren, Paavo Bergman, et al. 1991. *90-talets industriarbete i Sverige* (Swedish Manufacturing Work in the 1990s). Stockholm: Carlsson Bokförlag.

Bergdahl, Anna, and Katarina Johansson. 1987. "Socioteknisk analys av personbilsmontering" (Sociotechnical Analysis of Car Assembly). Department of Industrial Organization, Chalmer's Institute of Technology, Gothenburg.

Berggren, Christian. 1986. *Uppbrott från bandet? Arbete och organisation i Volvos lastvagnsfabrik i Tuve* (An Alternative to the Assembly Line? Work Organization at the Volvo LB Truck Plant). Final report. Stockholm: Department of Work Science, Royal Institute of Technology.

Berggren, Christian, Torsten Björkman, and Ernst Hollander. 1991. *Are They Unbeatable?* Stockholm: Department of Work Science, Royal Institute of Technology.

Beynon, Huw. 1973. *Working for Ford.* Harmondsworth: Penguin Books.

Björklund, Lars, Roger Molin, and Thomas Sandberg. 1979. *Företagsdemokrati i sex verkstadsföretag* (Industrial Democracy in Six Engineering Plants). Lund: Studentlitteratur.

Björkman, Torsten, and Karin Lundqvist. 1981. *Från MAX till PIA. Reformstrategier inom arbetsmiljöområdet* (From MAX to PIA: Strategies for Reforming the Work Environment). Lund: Arkiv.

Blauner, Robert. 1964. *Alienation and Freedom: The Factory Worker and His Industry.* Chicago: University of Chicago Press.

Bluestone, Barry, and Bennett Harrison. 1988. *The Great U-Turn: Corporate Restructuring and the Polarizing of America.* New York: Basic Books.

Bolinder, Erik, Egon Magnusson, Carina Nilsson, and Magnus Rehn. 1981. *Vad händer med arbetsmiljön?* (What Is Happening with the Work Environment?). Stockholm: Tidens Förlag.

Borgström, Henric, and Martin Haag. 1988. *Gyllenhammar.* Stockholm: Bonniers.

Bratt, Christian. 1990. *Arbetsmarknaden i 18 länder* (The Labor Market in Eighteen Countries). Stockholm: Svenska Arbetsgivareföreningen.

Braverman, Harry. 1974. *Labor and Monopoly Capital.* New York: Monthly Review Press.

Burawoy, Michael. 1979. *Manufacturing Consent.* Chicago: University of Chicago Press.

Chinoy, E. 1955. *Automobile Workers and the American Dream.* New York: Doubleday.

Clark, Kim, and Takahiro Fujimoto. 1990. "The Power of Product Integrity." *Harvard Business Review,* November–December, 107–18.

Cole, Robert. 1979. *Work, Mobility and Participation: A Comparative Study of American and Japanese Industry.* Berkeley: University of California Press.

Crona, Göran, and Anders Leion. 1986. *Ungdomars erfarenhet av industriarbete* (Young Workers' Experiences of Industrial Work). Stockholm: Sifo Förlag.

Crowther, Stuart, and Philip Garrahan. 1988. "Invitation to Sunderland: Corporate Power and the Local Economy." *Industrial Relations Journal* 19 (1):51–59.

Cusumano, Michael. 1985. *The Japanese Automobile Industry.* Cambridge: Harvard University Press.

Cutler, Tony, Colin Haslam, John Williams, and Karel Williams. 1987. "The End of Mass Production?" *Economy and Society* 16 (3):405–38.

Dankbaar, Ben, Ulrich Jürgens, and Thomas Malsch, eds. 1988. *Die Zukunft der Arbeit in der Automobilindustrie.* Berlin: Edition Sigma.

den Hertog, Friso. 1978. *Arbeitsstrukturierung.* Bern: Verlag Hans Huber.

Dertouzos, Michael L., Richard K. Lester, Robert M. Solow, and the MIT Commission on Industrial Productivity. 1989. *Made in America: Regaining the Productive Edge.* New York: HarperPerennial.

Deutschmann, Christoph, and Claudia Weber. 1987. "Das Japanische 'Arbeitsbienen'-Syndrom." *PROKLA* 66:31–53.

Dohse, Knuth, Ulrich Jürgens, and Thomas Malsch. 1984. *From "Fordism" to "Toyotism:" The Social Organization of the Labour Process in the Japanese Automobile Industry.* Preprint 84–218. Berlin: Wissenschaftszentrum.

Eckerström, Gunnar, and Lars Södahl. 1980. *Ekonomisk analys av annorlunda fabriker* (Economic Analysis of New Production Principles). Working paper. Stockholm: Management Media.

Eklund, Jörgen, et al. 1989. "Psykisk belastning, armavlastning och muskelelektrisk signalstyrka vid datainmatning" (Mental Strain, Stress-Relieving of Arms, and Musculoelectrical Signal Intensity in Data Registering Work). Department of Occupational Medicine and Industrial Ergonomy, Linköping Institute of Technology.

Ellegård, Kajsa. 1989. *Akrobatik i tidens väv. En dokumentation av projekteringen av Volvos bilfabrik i Uddevalla* (A Documentation of the Planning for Volvo's Car Plant in Uddevalla). Gothenburg: Department of Cultural Geography, Gothenburg University.

Ellegård, Kajsa, Tomas Engström, Bertil Johansson, Mats I. Johansson, Dan Jonsson, and Lars Medbo. 1991. *The Possibilities of "Lean" Production: A Comparison between Different Production Flow Concepts in the Automotive Industry.* Gothenburg: Chalmers Institute of Technology.

Ellegård, Kajsa, Tomas Engström, and Lennart Nilsson. 1991. *Reforming Industrial Work: Principles and Realities in the Planning of Volvo's Car Assembly Plant in Uddevalla.* Stockholm: Swedish Work Environment Fund.

Endo, Koshi. 1991. "Satei (Personal Assessment) and Interworker Competition in Japanese Firms." Paper presented at the symposium "Production Strategies and Industrial Relations in the Process of Internationalization," Sendai, Japan, October.

Erixon, Lennart. 1990. "Produktivitetsproblemet" (The Productivity Dilemma). Produktivitetsdelegationen; Stockholm.

Feldman, Richard, and Michael Betzold. 1988. *End of the Line: Autoworkers and the American Dream.* New York: Weidenfeld & Nicolson.

Ford, Henry. 1924. *My Life and Work.* London: Heinemann.

Forslin, Jan, and Lars Ågren. 1987. *Volvo White Truck Corporation: The Best of Two Cultures?* Stockholm: Institute of International Business, Stockholm School of Economics.

Fucini, Joseph, and Suzy Fucini. 1990. *Working for the Japanese.* New York: Free Press.

Fujita, Eishi. 1988. "Labor Process and Labor Management: The Case of Toyota." *Review of Social Sciences* 28.

Garrahan, Philip, and Paul Stewart. 1989. "Working for Nissan," draft article for *Science as Culture* (October:13).

Gelsanliter, David. 1990. *Jump Start.* New York: Farrar, Straus, Giroux.

Gindin, Sam. 1989. "Breaking Away: The Formation of the Canadian Auto Workers." *Studies in Political Economy,* Summer:63–89.

Gordon, Andrew. 1985. *The Evolution of Labor Relations in Japan.* Cambridge, Mass.: Council on East Asian Studies.

———. 1990. "Japanese Labor Relations during the Twentieth Century." *Journal of Labor Research* 11 (3):239–52.

Grehn, Stig, and Margareta Pettersson. 1989. *Kan vi lära av Japan?* (Learning from Japan?) Stockholm: Swedish Metal Workers' Union.

Gulowsen, Jon. 1971. *Selvstyrte arbeidsgrupper, på vei mot industrielt demokrati?* (Autonomous Production Groups on the Road to Industrial Democracy). Oslo: Tanum.

———. 1975. *Arbeidervilkår. Et tilbakeblick på samarbeidsprosjektet LO-NAF* (Workers' Conditions: The Norwegian Labor-Management Cooperation Project Revisited). Oslo: Tanum/Norli.

Gunnarsson, Lars. 1980. *Att förändra arbetsprocessen: Volvo i Olofström och svensk industrisociologi.* (Changing the Work Process: Volvo at Olofström and Swedish Industrial Sociology). Lund: Studentlitteratur.

Gyllenhammar, Pehr G. 1973. *Jag tror på Sverige* (I Believe in Sweden). Örebro: Askild & Kärnekull.

Hack, Lothar. 1988. "Wie man die Wirklichkeit auf/um den Begriff bringt." In *Die Neuen Produktionskonzepte auf den Prüfstand,* ed. Thomas Malsch and Rüdiger Selz, 155–94. Berlin: Edition Sigma.

Hadenius, Stig. 1976. *Facklig organisationsutveckling: En studie av Landsorganisationen i Sverige* (The Organizational Structure of Unions in Change: A Study of the Swedish Trade Union Confederation). Stockholm: Rabén & Sjögren.

Hedberg, Magnus. 1967. *The Process of Labour Turnover.* Stockholm: Personnel Administration Council.

Helling, Jan. 1987. "Hondas väg mot mästerskap som biltillverkare" (Honda's Road to Manufacturing Excellence). Saab-Scania, Trollhättan.

Hill, Richard, Michael Indergaard Child, and Kuniko Fujita. 1988. *Flat Rock: Home of Mazda.* East Lansing: Department of Sociology, Michigan State University.

Hiramoto, Atsushi. 1991. "Subcontracting Strategies of Japanese Companies in Europe and Asia: A Case Study on the Electronics Industry." Paper presented at the symposium "Production Strategies and Industrial Relations in the Process of Internationalization," Sendai, Japan, October.

Holloway, John. 1987. "The Red Rose of Nissan." *Capital and Class* 32:142–64.

Hounshell, David. 1984. *From the American System to Mass Production, 1800–1932.* Baltimore: Johns Hopkins University Press.

Huxley, Wareham, et al. 1991. "Team Concept: A Case Study of Japanese Production Management in a Unionized Canadian Auto Plant." Paper presented at the Université Laval, Quebec, August.

Jain, Hen C., ed. 1980. *Worker Participation: Success and Problems.* New York, Praeger.

JAW (Confederation of Japan Automobile Workers' Unions). 1989. "Report on the Consciousness of Union Members" (in Japanese). Tokyo. November.

————. 1991. "Report on the Seventh Survey of Consciousness of Union Members" (in Japanese). *Rodo Chosa* (Labor Research), June: 32–71.

Jenkins, David. 1981. *QWL: Current Trends and Directions.* Issues in the Quality of Working Life no. 3. Toronto: Ontario Quality of Working Life Centre.

Jones, Daniel. 1985. *A Revolution in Automobile Manufacturing? Technological Change in a Mature Industry.* Papers in Science, Technology and Public Policy no. 9. Sussex: University of Sussex, Science Policy Research Unit.

————. 1988. "Measuring Technological Advantage in the Motor Vehicle Industry." IMVP International Policy Forum, MIT, May.

————. 1989. "The Competitive Outlook for the European Auto Industry." *International Journal of Vehicle Design,* May.

Jürgens, Ulrich. 1986. *Entwicklungstendenzen in der Weltautomobilindustrie bis in der 90er Jahre.* Preprint 86–218. Berlin: Wissenschaftszentrum.

————. 1991. "Internationalization Strategies of Japanese and German Automobile Companies." Paper presented at the symposium "Production Strategies and Industrial Relations in the Process of Internationalization," Sendai, Japan, October.

Jürgens, Ulrich, Knuth Dohse, and Thomas Malsch. 1989. *Moderne Zeiten in der Automobilfabrik.* Berlin: Springer-Verlag.

Kamata, Satoshi. 1973. *Japan in the Passing Lane.* New York: Random House.

Karlsson, K. G. 1969. *Vad är MTM?* (What Is MTM?). Stockholm: Brevskolan.

Karlsson, Lars-Erik. 1985. "Enkätundersökning vid AB Sunlight i Nyköping" (Survey Study at the Sunlight Plant in Nyköping). Luleå Institute of Technology.

Karlsson, Ulf. 1979. *Alternativa produktionssystem till lineproduktion.* Gothenburg: Department of Sociology, Gothenburg University.

Kern, Horst, and Michael Schumann. 1977. *Industriearbeit und Arbeiterbewusstsein.* Frankfurt: Suhrkamp Verlag.

———. 1984: *Das Ende der Arbeitsteilung?* Munich: Verlag C. H. Beck.

———. 1987. "Limits of the Division of Labour. New Production and Employment Concepts in West German Industry." *Economic and Industrial Democracy* 8(2).

Kjellberg, Anders. 1983. *Facklig organisering i tolv länder* (Trade Union Organizations in Twelve Countries). Lund: Arkiv Förlag.

———. 1990. "The Swedish Trade Union System: Centralization and Decentralization." Paper presented at the World Congress of Sociology, Madrid, July.

Klein, Janice. 1989. "The Human Costs of Manufacturing Reform." *Harvard Business Review,* March–April, 60–66.

Kodama, Fumio, Taizo Yakushiji, and Mieko Hanaeda. 1983. *Structural Characteristics of the Japanese Automotive Supplier Industry.* Working Paper Series no. 13. Ann Arbor: University of Michigan.

Krafcik, John. 1986. "Learning from NUMMI." IMVP Internal Working Paper.

———. 1988. *European Manufacturing Practice in a World Perspective.* IMVP International Policy Forum, MIT, May.

———. 1989. "Assembly Plant Performance and Changing Market Structure in the Luxury Car Segment." IMVP International Policy Forum, MIT, May.

Landqvist, Lars, and Marcus Papinski. 1984. *Systemlösningar för flexibel automatiserad montering* (Flexible Automated Assembly: System Solutions). Ivf-result 83616. Stockholm: Sveriges Mekanförbund.

Lane, Christel. 1989. *Management and Labour in Europe.* Aldershot: Edward Elgar.

Le Grand, Carl. 1985. *Underleverantörssystem och arbetsmarknadssegmentering—några särdrag i den japanska industrins organisering* (Subcontracting Structures and Labor Market Segmentation: Some Particularities in Japanese Industry). Stockholm: Institute for Social Research, Stockholm University.

Lindh, Björn-Eric. 1984. *Volvo: personvagnarna från 20-tal till 60-tal* (Volvo: The Passenger Cars from the 1920s to the 1960s). Malmö: Förlagshuset Norden.

———. 1987. *Saab: Bilarna de första fyrtio åren* (Saab: The Cars during the First Forty Years). Malmö: Förlagshuset Norden.

Linhart, Robert. 1978. *Året på bilfabriken* (The Year at the Auto Plant). Stockholm: Norstedts.

Littler, Craig. 1978. "Understanding Taylorism." *British Journal of Sociology* 2.

Luria, Dan. 1990. "Automation, Markets and Scale: Can Flexible Niching Modernize U.S. Manufacturing?" *International Review of Applied Economics* 4(2):127–65.

Lysgaard, Sverre. 1976. *Arbejderkollektivet* (The Worker Collective). Oslo: Universitetsforlaget.

MacDuffie, John Paul. 1991. "Beyond Mass Production: Flexible Production Systems and Manufacturing Performance in the World Auto Industry." Ph.D. diss., Sloan School of Management, MIT.

MacDuffie, John Paul, and Haruo Shimada. 1987. "Industrial Relations and 'Humanware.' " IMVP Policy Forum, MIT, May.

Meyer, Stephen, III. 1981. *The Five Dollar Day*. Albany: State University of New York Press.

Ministry of Industry. 1990. *Swedish Industry and Industrial Policy*. Stockholm: Svenska Dagbladets Förlags AB.

Molin, Roger. 1988. "Utglesning eller utbredning? Arbetsplatsförankringen inom svensk fackföreningsrörelse" (Diffusion or Dissolution? Workplace Strength in Swedish Trade Unions). Department of Business Economics, Uppsala University.

Nilsson, Lennart, and Bengt Pettersson. 1985. *Monteringsarbete ur lärandeperspektiv* (Assembly Work from a Learning Perspective). Gothenburg: Gothenburg University.

Nomura, Masami. 1985. *"Model Japan?" Characteristics of Industrial Relations in the Japanese Automobile Industry*. Berlin: Wissenschaftszentrum.

———. 1990. "Social Conditions for CIM in Japan: A Case Study of a Machine Tool Company." Paper presented at the conference "Company Social Constitution under Pressure to Change." Berlin, June.

———. 1992. "Farewell to 'Toyotism'? Recent Trends of a Japanese Automobile Company." Department of Economics, Okaya University.

Olsson, Christer. 1987. *Volvo Lastbilarna under sextio år* (Volvo Trucks during Sixty Years). Malmö: Förlagshuset Norden.

Parker, Mike. 1988. "New Industrial Relations, Myth and Shop Floor Reality: The 'Team Concept' in the U.S. Auto Industry." Paper presented at the conference "Work Relations in 20th Century America," Woodrow Wilson International Center for Scholars, March 28–30.

Parker, Mike, and Jane Slaughter. 1988: *Choosing Sides: Unions and the "Team Concept."* Boston: South End Press.

Philips, Åke. 1986. *Spridning av arbetsorganisatoriska idéer* (Diffusion of Work Organizational Innovations). Stockholm: Handelshögskolan/EFI.

Piore, Michael, and Charles Sabel. 1984: *The Second Industrial Divide: Possibilities for Prosperity*. New York: Basic Books.

Pontusson, Jonas. 1990. "The Politics of New Technology and Job Redesign: A Comparison of Volvo and British Leyland." *Economic and Industrial Democracy* 11:311–36.

Porter, Michael. 1990. *The Competitive Advantage of Nations*. London: Macmillan.

Rehder, Robert. 1990. "Japanese Transplants: After the Honeymoon." *Business Horizons*, January–February, 1–12.

References

Riksförsäkringsverket (National Board for Social Insurances). 1989. *Varför ökar sjuktalet?* (Why Are the Figures of Reported Sickness Increasing?). Report 1989: 1. Stockholm.

SAF. 1986. Wage and Total Labour Costs for Workers: International Survey. Stockholm.

————. 1988. "Var finns arbetskraften?" (Where Are the Workers?). Stockholm.

Sällfors, Tarras. 1939. *Arbetsstudier inom industrien* (Industrial Time and Motion Studies). Stockholm: Sveriges Industriförbund.

Sandberg, Thomas. 1982. *Work Organization and Autonomous Groups.* Lund: Liber-Förlag.

Schonberger, Richard. 1982. *Japanese Manufacturing Techniques.* New York: Free Press.

Sei, Shoichiro. 1991. "Is Technical Innovation All? A Hidden Meaning of Social Relationships behind the Product Development Stage in Japanese Automotive Industry." Paper presented at the symposium "Production Strategies and Industrial Relations in the Process of Internationalization," Sendai, Japan, October.

Shimada, Haruo. 1988. "Japanese Trade Unionism: Postwar Evolution and Future Prospects." *Labour and Society* 13 (2): 203–23.

Shingo, Shigeo. 1981. *The Toyota Production System.* Tokyo: Japan Management Association.

Skantze, Jesper. 1988. *Att projektera och bygga flexibla automatiska monteringssystem* (Implementing Flexible Automated Assembly). Ivf-result 88607. Stockholm: Mekan-förbundets förlag.

Skolöverstyrelsen (National Board of Education). 1990. *Gymnasieskolan hösten 1989* (Admissions to Senior High School, Fall 1989). Report 89:47. Stockholm.

Smith, Adam. 1979. *The Wealth of Nations.* Harmondsworth: Penguin Books.

Sölvell, Örjan, Iva Zander, and Michael Porter. 1991. *Advantage Sweden?* Stockholm: Norstedts.

SOU. 1991. *Drivkrafter för produktivitet och välstånd* (Contributors to Wealth and Productivity). Stockholm: Produktivitetsdelegationen.

Statistiska Centralbyrån. 1985. *Arbetsmiljön i siffror. Miljöstatistisk Årsbok* (Statistical Yearbook for the Work Environment). Stockholm: SOS.

————. 1989. *Arbetsmarknaden i siffror, 1970–88* (Labor Market Statistics, 1970–88). Stockholm.

Sundgren, Per. 1978. "Införandet av MTM-metoden i svensk verkstadsindustri, 1950–56." (The Implementation of the MTM Method in the Swedish Engineering Industry, 1950–56). *Arkiv för studier i arbetarrörelsens historia* 13–14:3–33.

Svenska Metallindustriarbetareförbundet (Swedish Metal Workers' Union). 1985. *Det goda arbetet.* (Summarized in English in *Rewarding Work* [1987].) Stockholm.

————. 1989. *Solidarisk arbetspolitik för det goda arbetet.* (Solidaristic Work Policy to Achieve Rewarding Work). Stockholm.

Sveriges Arbetsledareförbund (SALF). 1989. *Ledning, organisation och medbestäm-mande i den goda bilfabriken* (Management, Organization, and Participation in the Ideal Car Factory). Stockholm.

Sveriges Tekniska Attachéer (Swedish Technical Attachées). 1990. "Arbetsmiljö i japanska fabriker i Storbritannien" (Working Conditions at Japanese Plants in Great Britain). Stockholm.

Taylor, Frederick Winslow. 1911. *The Principles of Scientific Management.* New York: Harper.

Tidds, Joseph. 1989. "Next Steps in Assembly Automation." IMVP International Policy Forum, MIT, May.

Tokunaga, Shigeyoshi. 1984. *Some Recent Developments in the Japanese Industrial Rela-tions with Special Reference to Large Private Enterprises.* Berlin: Wissenschaftszentrum.

Törnqvist, Anders, and Peter Ullmark, eds. 1989. *When People Matter.* Stockholm: Swedish Council for Building Research.

Trist, E., et al. 1963. *Organizational Choice.* London: Tavistock Publications.

Turner, Lowell. 1988. *NUMMI in Context.* Berkeley: Department of Political Science, University of California.

Volvo Trucks. 1981. "Hälso- och miljöundersökning Bana 2, X-hallen," (Survey of Occupational Health and Job Satisfaction on the Assembly Line at the X Plant). Gothenburg.

———. 1986. "Resultat av arbetsmiljökartläggningen vid VLAB. Avd 29200, resp 29300" (Results of the Work Environment Study at Volvo Trucks, Department 29200 and 29300). Gothenburg.

Walker, Charles, and Robert Guest. 1952. *The Man on the Assembly Line.* Cambridge: Harvard University Press.

Ward's Automotive Yearbook. 1988. Detroit: Ward's Communication.

Westlander, Gunnela. 1978. *Vad är psykosociala frågor?* (What Are Psychosocial Prob-lems?) Stockholm: Arbetarskyddsnämnden.

Wickens, Peter. 1987: *The Road to Nissan.* London: Macmillan.

Wikman, Anders. 1980. *Svarsprecisionen i surveyundersökningar om levnadsförhållan-den* (Response Precision in Survey Studies of Standards of Living). Methodological Problems in Individual and Household Statistics no. 14. Stockholm: Statistiska Centralbyrån.

———. 1982. "Kan man mäta den faktiska arbetsmiljön och andra levnadsförhållanden med hjälp av surveyfrågor?" (Is It Possible to Measure the Real Work Environment with Survey Methods?). Preliminary version. Statistiska Centralbyrån, Stockholm.

———. 1989. "Att beskriva arbetsmiljön hjälp av surveyfrågor: Slåtrapport från arbets-miljprojektet" (Using Survey Methods to Describe the Work Environment: Final Report from the Work Environment Study). Preliminary version. Statistiska Central-byrån, Stockholm. May 15.

Wild, Ray. 1975a. "On the Selection of Mass Production Systems." *International Journal of Production Research* 5.

————. 1975b. *Work Organization: A Study of Manual Work and Mass Production.* Bristol: Wiley.

Willman, Paul. 1988. "The Future of the Assembly Line in the U.K. Car Industry." In *Die Zukunft der Arbeit in der Automobilindustrie,* ed. Ben Dankbaar, Ulrich Jürgens, and Thomas Malsch, 211–25. Berlin: Edition Sigma.

Womack, James P., Daniel T. Jones, and Daniel Roos. 1990. *The Machine That Changed the World.* New York: Rawson Associates.

Wokutch, Richard E. 1992. *Worker Protection, Japanese Style: Occupational Safety and Health in the Auto Industry.* Ithaca, N.Y.: ILR Press.

Wood, Stephen. 1989. "What's This Fuss about Post-Fordism?" Background paper for session at the Center for Working Life, Stockholm, April.

World Motor Vehicle Data Book. 1990. Detroit: Motor Vehicle Manufacturers Association of the United States.

Index

ABS. *See* antilock brakes
Adler, Paul, 31, 32, 44, 45, 46
Affärsvärlden, 60
Agurén, Stefan, 122, 124, 125, 126
AGVs. *See* centrally controlled carriers
Ahlqvist, Björn, 64
Altmann, Norbert, 20, 99, 185, 186, 214
Altshuler, Alan, 36
Amsden, Alice, 28
andon device, 46–47
Angiers, France (Scania Trucks), 67
"anthropocentric production systems," 11, 13, 20; in Uddevalla, 13. *See also* postlean production, human-centered synthesis
antilock brakes, 102, 124
Arendal (Volvo Cars), 109, 130, 131, 144, 146, 244
ASEA/ABB, 72, 187, 189
assembly-line regime, xi, 3, 4, 6, 8, 10–12, 14, 90, 151, 194–206, 241–43; balancing losses, 91, 92, 195; birth of, 20, 90; and handling losses, 91, 92; vs. neocraftism, 241–42; physical demands of, 5, 12, 90, 194–98, 200–201, 204; system analysis of, 90–97, 206–20; system losses in, 91, 92; and variant losses, 91, 92, 195. *See also* five-plant comparative questionnaire
"attitudes 85," 190
Audi, 61
Auto-liv, 58
automotive industry, American, 3, 23, 34, 36, 41, 44, 50, 85; and adversarial labor relations, 6; and differences from Japanese automotive industry, 23, 34, 36; and differences from Swedish automotive industry, 85; "drill sergeant style" management in, 6; egalitarianism, lack of, 50; job insecurity in, 3, 5, 34; low import share of, 57; and skilled trades workers, 44; and union concessions, 41

automotive industry, German, 57, 58, 61, 64, 250, 255; components industry and patents in, 58; import share of, 57; and Japanese competition, 250, 255
automotive industry, Japanese, xii, 4–8, 10, 14, 16, 18–23, 25–29, 31–34, 36, 43, 45, 46–48, 54, 55, 58, 153, 204, 232, 233, 245, 250, 252; absence of reciprocity in, 6; acquiescent unions in, 16, 25; and advanced components manufacturers, xii, 16, 250; "BMW line," 63; and career system, 33; and collective worker action, elimination of, 8, 36; dependent work force in, 16, 25, 34; disciplinary measures in, 8; and flexible volume production, 18; foremen, position of, 32; and intense domestic rivalry in, 16; and "inventoryless" manufacturing, 26, 36, 251; and just-in-time delivery, 5, 6, 16, 23, 26, 29, 43, 45, 251; and *kaizen* activities, 31, 42, 51, 55, 243, 251; and long hours regime, criticism of, 54, 251, 252; and personnel evaluation, 33, 34, 36; and personnel selection, 8, 10; rhythm and intensity of assembly line, 5, 26, 32; *san kei* jobs in, 251; shop-floor focus within, 16, 25, 28, 251; team organization, supporting management in, 7, 8, 10, 32; and total productive maintenance, 89; vertical hierarchy in, 31, 34; and wages, 32, 34; working conditions in, 5–8, 10, 16, 21, 31, 46, 54, 55, 233, 251, 252; and zero defects, 6, 26. *See also* lean production regime, Japanese; transplants, Japanese
automotive industry, Swedish, 6–8, 10, 15–20, 21, 56, 58–59, 61–73, 81, 84–93, 98–101, 103, 119–45, 184, 232, 237, 243, 248, 253, 254; assembly design, evolution of, 92, 93, 100, 121, 243, 253; and assembly line, questioning of, 7, 9, 10, 17, 20, 71, 86, 92, 94, 120, 184, 233, 243, 253; bus business within, 20, 56, 58, 59, 66–68,

automotive industry, Swedish (*cont.*)
70, 86, 103; and climate for change, 11, 71, 81, 84–87, 120, 233; contributions of, 232, 255; and differences from Japanese, 7, 10, 14, 16, 20, 56, 248, 253–54; ergonomic advances within, 17, 84, 253; and first-line management, role of, 7; internationalization of, 57, 58, 66–71, 87; and lifetime service contracts, 16; and low unemployment, 11, 71, 253; and postlean production, 253, 254–56; and postlean synthesis, creation of, 255, 256; production design in, 6, 7, 9, 10, 11, 15, 20, 21, 184, 233, 253; robotization in, 85, 86; trade union participation and influence in, 8, 11, 17, 71, 81, 84, 88, 254; truck business within, 20, 56, 58, 59, 64, 65–70, 86; upscale niche strategy, 59, 232, 237; work load injury debate, impact of, 84; work organization and worker autonomy, relationship between, 98

balancing losses, 91, 92, 110
Beek, Van, 90
Bendix, Richard, 54
Bengtsson, Lars, 247
Bergdahl, Anna, 92
Berggren, Christian, 5, 39, 42, 53
Betriebsräte, 73. *See also Facharbeiter*
Betzold, Michael, 5
Björklund, Lars, 191, 222
Björkman, Torsten, xii, 5, 39, 42, 53, 187, 188, 189
Blauner, Robert, 4, 5, 6, 8
"blue-collar blues," 10
Bluestone, Barry, 3
BMW, 57, 61, 250
body welding, 20
Bolinder, Erik, 187
Borås, 15, 68, 69, 92, 99, 108–15, 118, 130–33, 146, 152, 163, 165, 191, 206, 208, 211, 213–17, 219, 239, 242, 244, 248, 249; and autonomy and time pressure, ambiguities of, 213, 215; five-plant questionnaire of, 191, 206, 208, 209, 211–15, 219, 242; and Leyland Bus, acquisition of, 99; MTM piece rates, dissatisfaction with, 115, 117, 206; parallel dock assembly in, 109–11, 114, 116, 130, 244; and physical strains, complaints of, 215; technical design, development of, 110–13; and workers' job assessments, 209–11, 214–17, 242; working conditions in, 115, 116, 215, 242; working conditions and assembly design, relation between, 208, 212, 213, 215, 219, 242
Braverman, Harry, 18
Brazil, 14, 18, 28, 37, 63, 69, 73, 80, 82; Japanese transplants in, 37; and labor-management debate, 18; 1990 recession in, 14; Swedish transplants in, 69; wage differentials in, 73
British Leyland Company, 15; and Volvo Buses, acquisition by, 15

B10M, 108
Buick City (Flint, Michigan), 52
Business Week, 147, 237

CAMI/GM-Suzuki (Ontario, Canada), 5, 42, 49, 255
Canada, 36, 42
Canadian Auto Workers' (CAW) union, 42, 43, 54; and Japanese production methods, rejection of, 42, 54
Canadian Auto Workers Research Group on CAMI, 49
carpal tunnel syndrome, 52
CAW. *See* Canadian Auto Workers' union
Central Bureau of Statistics, 187, 189, 191, 202
centrally controlled carriers, 92, 237
Chalmers Institute of Technology, 151
Child, Michael Indergaard, 51
Chinoy, E., 4
Clark Michigan, 60
codetermination, 78. *See also* labor unions, Swedish
Codetermination Law (MBL), 78–79
Cole, Robert, 8, 48
Competitive Advantage of Nations, The, 18
"compliance bureaucracy," 31
computer-controlled transmission, 102
craft production, 3, 4, 153. *See also* "neocraft" systems
Crona, Göran, 85
Crowther, Stuart, 37
cumulative trauma disorders (CTDs), 12, 52, 160; and lean production systems, 52; and whole-car design, reduction of, 160
Curitiba (Brazil), and participative workers' culture, encouragement of, 15; Volvo greenfield site in, 15
Cusamano, Michael, 22, 26, 27, 31
customization: and Japanese firms, 19
Cutler, Tony, 18

Dagens Nyheter, 89
Daimler-Benz, 61, 64, 250
Das Ende der Arbeitsteilung?, 18, 19
den Hertog, Friso, 90
Dertouzos, Michael L., 3
Deutschmann, Christoph, 34, 54; and "social heteronomy," 54
Diamond Star (Mitsubishi-Chrysler), 5, 6, 38, 41; and assembly robots, 38; and UAW local, 41
division of labor, 7, 18, 32, 43, 75, 95, 98, 151, 205; economic limits of, 18; horizontal, 7; vertical, 95
dock assembly: introduction of, 14; vs. complete assembly, 93
Dohse, Knuth, 20, 30

Eckerström, Gunnar, 110
economies of scale, 18
Electrolux (Mariestad), 40, 41, 58, 86; and Auto-liv,

58; and intensive personnel data, 40; robotization, plans for, 41, 86; work organization, forms for, 41

Electrolux (Spennymoor, England), 40, 41; and job insecurity, 41

electronically controlled brakes, 102

End of the Line: Auto Workers and the American Dream, 5

Endo, Koshi, 33

Engineering Employers' Federation, 77

Engineering Industry Employers, 107

Engström, Tomas, 159

enterprise unionism, 24

ergonomic research, 210

Ericsson, 72

Erixon, Lennart, 80

European GM, 250

"Evaluation of Work Organizational Development in the Volvo Group," xi

Facharbeiter, 72, 73

FAM. *See* flexible automated assembly

Feldman, Richard, 5

Five-plant comparative questionnaire, 191–94, 196–205, 208–20, 221–31, 241, 242; and actual vs. desired influences, 224–28, 230; assembly tools, design of, 195, 198; autonomy and time pressure, ambiguities of, 212, 214; and correlation coefficient, 192; and desire for holistic work, 220; and important union issues, 230, 231; improvement, assemblers' desire for, 216, 220, 241; influence and well-being, connection between, 227; and mental strains, measurement of, 198, 227; monotony, assessment of, 195, 199, 200, 204; new organizational form and shop-floor influence, 221, 233; physical strains, measurement of, 194–96, 210–11, 220, 227, 242; psychosomatic symptoms, reporting of, 200, 204, 214, 227; repetitiveness, assessment of, 197; severe negative feelings, reporting of, 200, 201, 203, 214, 215, 216; union influence, desire for, 227–30; weariness, reports of, 210, 220; worker composition of, 209; working conditions and assembly design, relationship between, 206, 210, 211, 220, 227, 242

"flexibility debate," 3

flexible automated assembly (FAM), 85

flexible line assembly, 92

flexible specialization, 18, 19; contridictory effects of, 119

flexible volume production, 18, 19, 28; and small-batch manufacturing, 28

Ford, Henry, 10, 13, 40, 44, 49, 93, 203; and "assembly hall of 1903," 13; technical control, principle of, 93; and worker preference for monotony, 10

Fordism, 4, 5, 14, 20, 32, 34, 43, 44, 50, 56, 97, 137, 205, 234–35, 250; and birth of mechanical assembly line, 20, 205; company-employee

relationship with, 34; and lean production, 6, 50; and post-Fordist debate, 18, 87

Ford Michigan Truck Plant, 5

Ford Motor Company, 4, 14, 22, 25, 26, 27, 40, 52, 165; and adoption of lean procedures, 4, 52; and labor's share of the value added, 27; and production process, development of, 22; standardization, development of, 14; and work simplification, 26

foremen, Japanese, 32; as union representative, 32

"fragile product design," 62. *See also* Saab 9000

Fucini, Joseph, 5, 42; and Mazda union mobilization, 42

Fucini, Suzy, 5, 42

Fujita, Eishi, 30, 32, 35

Fujita, Kuniko, 51

"The Future of the Automobile," xi, xii

Future of Work in the Automobile Industry, The, 20

Garrahan, Philip, 37, 49

Gelsanliter, David, 42

General Motors, 13, 36, 40, 51, 62, 85, 86, 153, 165, 171, 172, 182, 235, 255; and comparison with Japanese transplants, 51, 255; flexible automated assembly in, 85, 86; and management of Saab Automobile, Inc., 62

Germany, 18, 57, 72, 73, 74, 75, 80, 82; and labor debates, 18; labor segmentation and divided representation, 74, 75; and unions, strength of, 72, 75; wage differentials in, 73

Ghent, Belgium, 14, 15, 16. *See also* Volvo (Ghent)

Gilbreth, Frank, 31

Gindin, Sam, 42

GM. *See* General Motors

Gordon, Andrew, 24, 27

Gothenburg (Sweden), 12, 13, 15, 69, 70, 84, 87, 100, 108, 109, 122, 124, 128, 129, 130, 132, 134, 135, 147, 153, 158, 170, 223, 237; and TC assembly plant, 87, 99, 123, 136, 147, 153, 158; TLA shop and custom outfitting, 129, 136; and X plant, 129, 130, 131, 135, 136, 190, 223. *See also* Volvo Trucks; LB plant

Grehn, Stig, 31

Grenzen neuer Arbeitsformen, 185

Guest, Robert, 4

Gulowsen, Jon, 95, 96, 186

Gyllenhammar, Pehr G., 14, 88, 121, 127, 146; and Kalmar innovations, 121, 122, 127; and long-term trade union collaboration, 88

Hadenius, Stig, 76

Halifax, Canada (Volvo), 154, 166

Halle 54 (VW), 86

Hamtramck-Poletown (Detroit), 36

hancho, 32

handling losses, 91, 92

Hansson, Reine, 122

Harrison, Bennett, 3

Highland Park, Michigan, 32, 90, 205

Hill, Richard, 51
Hino, 65
holistic assembly, 243, 254
Hollander, Ernst, 5, 39, 43, 53
Holtback, Roger, 64, 237
Honda (Japan), 36, 37, 63, 165, 252; and
  Aeordeck, 63; in Britain, plans for, 37
Honda (Ohio), 5, 22, 48, 53; and pace-of-work
  issues, 53
human-centered production. See "anthropocentric
  production systems"
Huxley, Wareham, 49

IKEA, 158
"Industrial Democracy in Europe," 191
industrial democracy tradition, 222
industrial districts, Italian, 18
industrial sociology, 17, 18, 20, 43, 115, 184–91;
  American, 19, 35; and degradation of labor, 17;
  and flexible specialization, 18; German, 20, 43,
  115, 184, 185, 186; mental effort, questions
  about, 188; mental strains, questions about, 188,
  189, 190; and "output restrictions," 35; and
  requalification, 18; research in, 17; and survey
  method problems, 186–91
industrial work, 18, 23–25, 31–33, 36, 72, 73; and
  American national contracts, 25; in Britain, 28;
  and European social welfare policy, 25; in
  Germany, 28, 72, 73; in Italy, 18; in Japan, 23–
  25, 28, 31–33, 36
Industriearbeit und Arbeiterbewusstsein, 18, 19, 184
Infiniti (Nissan), 250
Institute for Social Research (Munich), 20
Institute for Social Research (Stockholm), 188
integrated assembly, 93
International Motor Vehicle Program (MIT), 36
"inventoryless" manufacturing, 26, 36, 251

Japan, 7, 8, 16–20, 23–25, 28, 30, 31, 35, 36, 43,
  46, 56, 57, 254; and independent labor unions,
  rise and fall of, 23–25; industrial dualism in, 25;
  and promotion system in, 31; technology,
  borrowing of, 28; total work time in, 34–35; and
  yen, rising of, 254
Japanese Auto Workers' Union (JAW), 17, 252,
  254; "new industrial policy," demands for, 17,
  254
Japan National Railways Union, 27
Jenkins, David, 11
JIT. See just-in-time delivery
Johansson, Bertil, 152
Johansson, Katarina, 92
Jones, Daniel T., 3, 6, 13, 17, 18, 19, 29, 40, 49,
  51, 53, 165, 184, 195, 233, 238, 239, 240, 242,
  251, 252; and The Machine That Changed the
  World, 3, 19, 29, 49, 165, 242
Jürgens, Ulrich, 20, 30, 72
just-in-time delivery, 5, 6, 16, 23, 43, 45, 46, 195,

235, 252; and incompatibility with worker
  autonomy, 45, 46, 252; reexamination of, 252

kaizen activities, 31, 42, 51, 55, 243; rejection of,
  by CAW, 42; speed-up and work intensification
  with, 42, 51
Kalmar (Volvo), 12, 13, 15, 21, 48, 56, 63, 69, 70,
  88, 99, 119–29, 132, 133, 146, 148, 149, 151,
  155, 157, 160, 167, 169, 171, 178, 182, 236–38,
  240, 243–46; AGVs in, 121, 123, 125, 127, 128,
  132; and assembly ergonomics, improvement of,
  121; buffers and worker autonomy, effects on,
  121, 127, 128; dock assembly in, 121, 125, 126,
  128, 243; functional assembly in, 121; and
  intensive rationalization, 123, 125–28, 236; job
  rotation within, 121; MOST system within, 123,
  124; and physical strains, 126, 160; planning for,
  12, 120–23; 236; and productivity levels, 15,
  123, 124; results-based wage system within, 123,
  127; sociotechnical design, innovations in, 119–
  21, 124, 126, 236, 245; synchronization
  problems in, 125; and tilting contrivance, 121;
  vs. Uddevalla, 120, 128, 129, 151, 236, 238; and
  Volvo 760, 236; and Volvo 960, 236
kanban system, 26
Karlsson, K. G., 122
Karlsson, Lars-Erik, 186
Karlsson, Ulf, 97
Katrineholm (Scania bus), 68, 69, 98, 101–3, 105–
  8, 114, 117, 118, 155, 191, 208–10, 214, 217–
  20, 244, 248; assembly design of, 68, 105, 106,
  108, 109, 117, 155; autonomy and time pressure,
  ambiguities of, 214; vs. Borås, 117–18; and
  competitive "craft work," 101, 102; and five-
  plant questionnaire, worker verification of, 191,
  208, 214, 220; improvement, assemblers' desire
  for, 217–20; and K chassis, 101; and length of
  service, significance of, 219–20; and N chassis,
  101; organizational change, ambiguities of, 106;
  stability within, high level of, 118; and
  Taylorism, retreat from, 108; variety and
  responsibility within, 217, 220; wage system in,
  107; worker composition of, 209; and workers'
  job assessments, 209, 210, 214, 217, 220; and
  working conditions and assembly design,
  relations between, 210, 214, 220
Kawasaki (United States), 47
K chassis, 101
Kern, Horst, 18, 19, 184, 185, 186, 189
kitsui, kitanai, kiken (san kei) 54, 251
Kjellberg, Anders, 77, 79
Klein, Janice, 45
kōchō, 32
Korea, 28
Krafcik, John, 37, 62, 147
kumichō. See foremen, Japanese

Labor and Monopoly Capital, 18
labor process school, 18, 19

labor unions, Swedish, 73–85; blue-collar workers in, 74–76; and codetermination, 78–79; and coordinated national wage bargaining, 74, 77; features of, 74; and job security legislation, 78; repetitive strain injuries, 81; and solidaristic wage policy, 73, 80, 85; white-collar workers in, 74–76; and women's participation in workforce, 74, 83; and work load injury debate of 1987–88, 83, 84; and workplace clubs, 76, 77; and workplace organization, 76, 81

Labour government (Sweden), 80

large-batch manufacturing, 29

LB (Volvo Gothenburg), 12, 13, 15, 21, 69, 190–92, 206, 213, 214, 217–19, 221–31, 237, 239, 240, 242, 246, 249; AGVs, use of, 237; autonomy and time pressure, ambiguities of, 214; and five-plant questionnaire, worker verification of, 191, 192, 206, 209, 213, 218, 219, 221–23, 228–31; length of service, significance of, 219; and MTM, 206; and new organizational form and shop-floor influence, 221, 223; worker composition of, 209; and workers' job assessments, 209, 213, 214, 218, 242; working conditions and assembly design, relation between, 213, 214, 231, 242

LB (Volvo Trucks), 92, 96, 98, 99, 129–32, 135–38, 140–46, 149, 152; AGVs, use of, 132; vs. Arendal, 132; vs. Borås, 132; dock assembly, renaissance for, 143, 145; flexible specialization, contradictory effects of, 119, 136–38, 140, 141, 144, 145; new work organization in, 119, 131, 134–36, 138–42; production design in, 132, 133, 137–39, 152; relations between assembly and industrial engineers, 139, 140, 144; and Tuve site, 15, 129, 130, 144; working conditions, effects of production design on, 119, 130, 135–39; vs. X plant, performance of, 136, 137, 139, 143

lean production regime, Japanese, 3–6, 8, 9, 13, 17, 19, 23, 43, 50, 53, 55, 153, 232, 233, 243; advent of, 5; and carpal tunnel syndrome, 52; and conduct code, 53; expansion of, 5, 43; factory regime of, 6, 51–53, 55; "management by stress" in, 49–50, 51; and mandatory company uniforms, 6, 48; and need for synthesis with human-centered manufacturing, 17; and perfect attendance, 6, 53; and personal articles, prohibition of, 6, 48; positive features of, 50, 153; and strict conduct of rules, 6, 51, 53; and systemized sanctions, 6, 53; working conditions under, 43, 50–53, and work injuries, intolerance for, 52

Leion, Anders, 85

Lester, Richard K., 3

Lexus (Toyota), 250

lifetime service contracts, 16

Littler, Craig, 29, 30

LO, 75, 76, 77, 79, 80, 122, 187, 188; and Metall, 78, 80; and Municipal Workers' union, 77; and Rationalization Council, 122; and SAF negotiations, 77, 79, 122; working conditions, investigations of, 187–88

Lohn und Leistung, 115

Lordstown, 11

low-cost rationalization, 23

Lundqvist, Karin, 187, 188, 189

Luria, Dan, 18

luxury car makers, British, 153

Lysgaard, Sverre, 35, 36

Machine That Changed the World, The, 3, 13, 19, 29, 49, 153, 165, 218, 242, 250, 252; and Japan's competitive strategies, analysis of, 250

Made in America, 3

Malmö. *See* Saab (Malmö)

Malsch, Thomas, 20, 30

"management by stress," 46, 50. *See also* lean production regime, Japanese

Masami, Nomura, 253

mass consumption, 50

mass production, 3, 4, 28, 29, 50, 90, 96, 232; degrading work in, 232; "end of," 18; and mass consumption, 50

Massenarbeiter, 72, 73

MATCH program (Volvo), 170

Mazda (Flat Rock, Michigan), 5, 38, 40–43, 50–54; cumulative trauma injuries within, 52, 53; and ergonomics training program in, 43; and *kaizen* techniques, 51; and paid absence allowance days, 53; symptoms surveys, union access to, 43; teamwork in, 51; and tight attendance, 43

MBL. *See* Codetermination Law

Mercedes, 61

Metall, 7, 12, 30, 75, 77, 78, 80, 81, 107, 133, 134, 146, 147, 149, 182, 231, 248; and development of collective competence, 7; and new work organization development, 7, 78, 81, 231, 248; and "Rewarding Work," 81; self-management, issues of, 248; and team decision-making, 7, 248; and Uddevalla, 79, 146, 149; work environment agenda for, 78; work reform agenda for, 78, 80, 81

Metallarbetaren, 88

Metal Workers' Union (Sweden). *See* Metall

Michigan Injured Workers, 52

Ministry of Industry (Sweden), 72

Mitsubishi, 38

Molin, Roger, 191, 222

Mosel (VW), 255

MOST system, 123, 124

MTM piece rate, 111, 115, 117

muda, 6, 253

multiskilling, 43–44

multitasking, 23, 43, 44, 98

Municipal Workers' Union, 77

N chassis, 101, 103, 107

nenko systems, 24, 33, 34

"neocraft" systems: vs. assembly lines, 241, 243
New York Times, 40, 164, 165, 238
Netherlands, 60, 66; Scania Trucks in, 66
Nilsson, Lennart, 140, 150
Nippondenso, 250
Nissan (Japan), 24, 25, 27, 31, 36, 252; and
    absenteeism, 31; and differences with Toyota, 27;
    and labor's share of value added, 27; training and
    promotion, 31
Nissan (Sunderland, England), 7, 37, 40, 44, 48–
    49, 146, 161, 238, 250; assembly line, revival of,
    238; and company enculturation, 44; foremen,
    role, 48–49; and industrial relations, 37;
    personnel selection for, 44; pricing policies in, 37;
    product development for, 37; and supplier
    relations, 37; and teamworking, 48–49
Nissan (Tennessee), 5, 22, 38, 42, 50, 52–53, 85;
    job security within, 50; and incidence of work
    injury, 53
"no-dismissal" pledges, 24
North America, 7, 37, 85; and unionized Japanese
    transplants, 7, 37
Norway, 95; sociotechnical tradition within, 95
NUMMI (Toyota-GM), 31, 32, 36, 38, 40, 43, 44,
    46, 48, 52, 245, 255; maintenance
    standardization within, 44; People's Caucus in,
    43; and "technical Taylorism," 31–32; and UAW
    local, isolation, of, 42

Office for the Study of Automotive Transportation,
    37
Ohno, Taichi, 26, 27; and cycle-times
    rationalization, introduction of, 26
Olofström (Volvo), 87, 166
"optimal batch sizes," 26
orthodox line assembly, 92. *See also* assembly-line
    regime
Oskarshamn (Scania cab plant), 156
Östling, Leif, 67
Otto cycle engine, 245
"output restrictions," 35

paid absence allowance days (PAA), 53, 54
Parker, Mike, 46
Pelletier, Rob, 54
People's Caucus, 43
Pettersson, Bengt, 140
Pettersson, Margareta, 31
Philips Group, 90
piece rates, 77, 103, 108, 113; and MTM, 113;
    negotiations over, 77; Scania bus and, 103, 108
Piore, Michael, 18, 19
Plaza agreement, 22
poka-yoke principle, 26
polyurethane adhesing (PUR), 151
Pontusson, Jonas, 120
Porter, Michael, 18, 19, 233
"post-Fordist Age," 4
postlean production, 21, 232, 253, 254, 255, 256;

human-centered synthesis with, 232, 255, 256;
    and manufacturing synthesis, strategy for, 21,
    253; and Swedish accomplishments in, 253, 254,
    255
process industries, 248
"Production Project 90," 169
"Production Strategy P 90—Final Assembly," 171–
    72, 174
PRV engine, 64
PUR. *See* polyurethane adhesing

Q1 program, 251
qualification policy, 98
quality circles, 5, 35
quality-control system (QC), 16, 49, 103

rationalization activities. *See kaizen*
Rationalization Council, 122
rationalized line assembly, 15, 170; in Belgium, 15;
    and Kalmar (Volvo), use of, 123, 125, 126–28
Renault Corporation, 14, 64, 66, 70, 88; and
    alliance with Volvo, 14, 64, 66, 70, 88; and value
    differences from Volvo, 14, 64
repetitive strain injuries, 81. *See also* carpal tunnel
    syndrome; cumulative trauma disorders
requalification, 18
reskilling, 23, 43, 98
"Rewarding Work," 81
right from the beginning (RFB), 169
robotization, 38, 41, 85, 86
Roos, Daniel, 3, 6, 13, 18, 19, 29, 40, 49, 51, 53,
    165, 184, 195, 233, 238, 239, 240, 242, 251,
    252; and *The Machine That Changed the World,*
    3, 19, 29, 49, 165
Rover, 57
Royal Institute of Technology (Stockholm), 136,
    247
Rubenowitz, Sigvard, 190

Saab Automobile, Inc., 62; and GM management
    of, 62
Saab (Malmö), xii, 11, 13, 61, 69, 88
Saab 9000, 61, 62, 92
Saab-Scania Group, 11, 13, 56–58, 60–62, 67, 85,
    87, 88, 89, 99, 101, 103, 155, 165, 237, 234;
    bus division within, 11, 14, 58, 59, 64, 65, 67,
    68, 72, 97, 101, 103, 105–8, 114–18, 155, 234,
    243; car division within, 59, 68, 165; and civil
    and military aircraft, 59; dock assembly,
    introduction of, 14, 243; and foreign suppliers,
    dependence on, 57; and German luxury market,
    challenge to, 61; independence, end of, 62; and
    industrial engines, 59; merger between, 60;
    ownership structure of, 59, 60; product range of,
    59; and Saab 9000, 61; truck division within, 11,
    14, 58, 59, 64, 67, 68
Sabel, Charles, 18, 19
SAF. *See* Swedish employers' national confederation
SALF. *See* Union of Foremen and Supervisors

Sällfors, Tarras, 203
Sandberg, Thomas, 186, 191
sanka, 48
san kei jobs (3K), 54, 251
satei. See wage-setting practice, Japanese
Saturn project (GM), 166
Scania Buses, 11, 14, 58, 64, 65, 67, 68, 72, 97,
    101, 103, 105–8; 114–18, 155, 234, 243;
    efficiency problems in, 234; and integrated
    parallel assembly, 234
Scania Trucks, 11, 14, 58, 59, 64, 66, 67, 84;
    Angiers, France, facility of, 67; design and
    production centralization within, 66;
    internationalization of, 67; youth recruitment
    problems for, 84
SCB. *See* Central Bureau of Statistics
Schonberger, Richard, 36, 47
Schumann, Michael, 18, 19, 184, 186, 189
scientific management, 18, 29, 31, 203; and flexible
    mass production at Toyota, 29; Swedish
    advocates of, 203
self-management, partial, 95, 96
"semiautonomous groups." *See* self-management,
    partial
semiconductors, 19, 250
seniority systems, Japanese, 24, 33, 34
Shimada, Haruo, 24
Shingo, Shigeo, 26, 28, 30
shokunoshikaku, 33
sh'tauke, 27
SIF. *See* Union of Clerical and Technical Employees
    in Industry
SIFO, 84, 85, 90; and study of youth in industrial
    work, 84; and "Volvo Monitor," 190
sixteen-valve engine, 61. *See also* Saab-Scania group
SKF, 58
Skövde gasoline engine factory (Volvo), 69, 243
small-batch manufacturing, 26, 28, 29
Social Democratic party, 74, 78; and industrial
    reformism, 78
Södahl, Lars, 110
Södertälje, 66, 84, 102. *See also* Scania Trucks
solidaristic wage policy, Swedish, 73, 85. *See also*
    labor unions, Swedish
Solow, Robert M., 3; and *Made in America,* 3
Statistiska Centralbyrån, 188
Stewart, Paul, 49
Stockholm, 84
Stockholmstidningen, 170
Sweden, 7–12, 14, 15, 17, 18, 20, 60, 63, 66, 69,
    70, 73, 74–76, 78, 81, 82, 84, 90, 145, 232, 240,
    246, 253–55; alternative forms of production in,
    15, 17, 253; "BMW" line, 63; "democratize the
    workplace," 17; economic concentration, high
    degree of, 72; and ergonomics, 17, 253; high
    employment levels in, 19, 74, 81, 82, 232, 253;
    high job security in, 17, 74, 78; labor
    segmentation in, 73; 1990 recession in, 14, 80;
    product and labor market, changes in, 13, 17, 69,

71, 72, 81; and the reform of working life, 9, 12,
    17, 78, 79, 84, 232, 253; and Social Democratic
    party, 74, 78, 80; and sociotechnical engineering,
    232; universal welfare system in, 85; and work
    leaves, legislation for, 82, 83
Swedish Academy of Engineering Science, 85
Swedish employers' national confederation (SAF),
    76, 77, 122; and centralized bargaining,
    introduction of, 79; and LO, negotiations with,
    77, 79, 122; and Rationalization Council, 122
"Swedish management style," 17
Swedish Metal Workers' Union. *See* Metall
Swedish trade union federation. *See* LO

takt time, 121
Taylor, Frederick, 31, 35, 40
Taylorism, 10, 11, 13, 23, 29, 30, 31, 32, 41, 94,
    232, 245, 247, 248; in British management, 41;
    chain of command with, 94; "one-best-way"
    principle, 245; revolt against, 10, 232;
    specialization feature of, 94; strict hierarchy with,
    94; and Toyotism, 23, 31; "verticalized
    relations," 94; and work intensification and line
    speed, 32
TC (Volvo-Gothenburg), 9, 10, 15, 16, 21, 87,
    132, 136, 142, 147, 153, 167, 170, 171, 173,
    174–83, 191, 192–204, 206, 211, 213, 214,
    216–31, 234, 235, 240–47; assembly line,
    redesign of, 173–81, 182, 244; autonomy and
    time pressure, ambiguities of, 211, 213, 214; as
    brownfield site, 173–81, 182, 244; and direct
    influence of workers, 222, 223, 227, 230; and
    five-plant questionnaire, 191, 192, 205, 208–31;
    "General TC Plan 90," 170, 175, 179–81;
    internationalization, 87; job rotation and CTD
    reduction, 171, 197, 241; job rotations and
    worker distaste for, 10, 197, 200, 204; and MAX
    experiences of, 175–99, 244; and mechanization,
    obstacles to, 172; new organizational form and
    shop-floor influence, 221, 223; and MTM, 167,
    206, 208; production design of, 10, 15, 87, 174–
    82, 194–97, 199, 200–204; and Project Chassis,
    175, 179, 180, 181; and Project Door, 178, 179;
    and Project TC 90, 174, 191; PUR window
    adhering within, 172; robotization, failure
    within, 182; turnover in, 173, 178, 179, 182,
    197, 202; and union influence, desire for, 227–
    29; and Volvo 200, 166, 167, 175; and Volvo
    700, 166, 167, 175; workers' job assessments.
    209–11, 214, 216, 217, 218, 241; work
    satisfaction, lack of, 214, 216, 241, 242; working
    conditions and assembly design, relation between,
    206–20, 241–42
teamwork, Japanese, 47, 48
3K. *See san kei* jobs
Tornqvist, Anders, 121
Torslanda (Volvo TC), 92, 98, 123, 130, 163, 166,
    167, 171, 173, 174, 182, 190, 236; line

Torslanda (Volvo TC) (*cont.*)
dissatisfaction within, 173, 174; and "Production Project 90," 169, 174; productivity level of, 167
Toshiba, 24
total productive maintenance (TPM), 89
Toyoda, Shoichiro, 55
Toyota (Japan), 26–36, 39, 47, 55, 65, 252–54; and bonuses, 31; and Corolla, 28; dense management within, 32, 36; flexible labor deployment within, 32; foremen, position within, 32; and Hino, 65; and job training for, 30; labor process in, 30; and labor's share of the value added, 27; large-batch manufacturing synthesis in, 29; and "learning bureaucracy," 32; and machine-paced assembly line, 30; and *muda,* 253; and overtime, 35; and personnel policy within, 27, 34, 36; and production system, 27–30, 36, 252; quality circles in, 31; and rigorous shop-floor focus, 28; and *satei* system, 33–34; teamwork, elusiveness of, 47; total work time within, 35; and vacation days, 35; and vertical integration, retreat from, 27; work intensity, increase of, 30, 32; work process, in, 30
Toyota (Kentucky), 5, 7, 14, 38, 39, 48; and production systems in, Swedish contrast, 20
Toyota Production System, The, 26
Toyota Revolution, 23, 25, 26
Toyota System, 8, 20, 22, 23, 25, 56; and Toyota Revolution, 23, 25
Toyotism, 14, 22, 23, 28, 31, 35, 36, 43, 46; and employment relations, 23; evolution and transplantation of, 22, 23; labor deployment with, 23, 43; and managerial structure, 23; and maximal employment relations, 35, 36; and short total production runs, 28; small-batch manufacturing with, 28; and Taylorism, extension of, 29, 31; work process with, 23
Trabis, 255
trailing axle bogies, 102
"transcendent production," 13, 16, 238
transplants, Japanese, xii, xiii, 8, 14, 16, 20, 36–39, 43, 44, 47, 48, 50, 51, 52–54, 153, 194, 204, 233; and *andon,* 39; bonus systems of, 39; in Britain, 37, 44, 233, 250; and carpal tunnel syndrome, incidences of, 152; cumulative trauma injuries within, 52; and declining American unionism, 41; disciplinary measures within, 38, 40; and dismissals, 38; dress code, 48, 53; and egalitarianism, 50; factory layouts of, 38, 57; health problems, reports of, 45; and high work intensity in, 3, 9, 40, 45, 47, 51, 52, 53, 153; and JIT system, 43, 45, 46; and *kaizen* method, 39, 42, 51; lean staffing with, 38; and manufacturer-supplier relations, 51; and multitasking, 44; and "no-fault attendance," 38, 42, 48; in North America, xii, 5, 8, 14, 37, 38, 42, 45, 47, 48, 50–52, 153, 233; and outsourcing, 204; overtime within, 39, 51–52; and personnel evaluation, 39, 40, 47, 53, 233;

and personnel selection, 39, 40, 47, 53, 233; and pride in workmanship, 16, 50; and robotization, 38; shop-floor focus in, 50, 53; and social conditions, significance of, 39–40; statistical process control of, 45; and trade unions, weakening of, 54, 233; and wage-setting, 233; and worker autonomy, loss of, 45
transplants, Swedish, 63, 66, 67, 88, 89, 154, 234; in Asia, 154; in Belgium, 88, 89; in Britain, 234; in Canada, 154; in France, 67; in Latin America, 68; in Scotland, 66; in United States, 63
Trist, E., 246
Trollhättan (Saab), 69, 86, 91, 160, 203, 234, 247; industrial engineering, losses within, 91; and modernization projects, 69, 86
TUN (Volvo), 98, 167, 169, 171, 191, 192, 206, 210, 213, 217, 221–27, 229, 230, 242; autonomy and time pressure, ambiguities of, 213–14; and five-plant questionnaire, 191, 192, 206, 208, 209, 213, 214, 217, 221–30, 242; and important union issues, 230; improvement, assemblers' desire for, 217; and MTM, 206, 208; new organizational forms and shop-floor influence, 221, 223; production design within, 169, 171; right from the beginning result, 169; union influence, desire for, 227, 229; worker composition of, 209; and workers' direct influence 222; workers' job assessments for, 209; working conditions and assembly design, relation between, 208, 213, 214, 242
Turner, Lowell, 40
Tuve. *See* LB (Volvo Trucks)

U & R. *See* utility and repair personnel
UAW. *See* United Auto Workers
Uddevalla (Volvo) 12, 13, 15, 16, 21, 44, 56, 63, 69, 70, 79, 84, 88, 100, 119, 120, 124, 127, 129, 136, 146–66, 175, 183, 193, 197, 206, 211, 236–41, 246, 249, 253; absenteeism rate within, 44, 163, 241; AGVs in 157; and automated materials handling process, 13, 163; and complete car-building teams, 12, 152, 155, 164; and comprehensive ergonomic effort, 154, 159, 160, 162–64; and computer-integrated information system, 13; and development of work, qualitative, 154, 162; vs. Ghent plant, 164; and GM leadership, criticism of, 166; individualized materials provision, 146, 150, 154–58, 164, 238; media criticism of, 164, 238, 240; new assembly tools, comprehensive development of, 13, 160; opening of, 63, 99, 146, 148, 154; and parallel final assembly, evolution, 146, 151–55; parallelization vs. pure line assembly, 151–53; production design, changes in, 150–54, 162, 164, 166; productivity levels within, 13, 15, 16, 44, 152, 163, 164, 240, 241; and PUR, 151, 158; and repetitive strains, reduction of, 253; and strong trade union participation in, 12, 79, 146, 149, 152, 162;

technical information flow and language within, 158–59; 162–63; and transcendent production, 238; and "Uddevalla Ultra," 150; and unique building design, 155; vocational training in, 13, 150–53, 162; and Volvo 900 series, 16, 163; wage system in, 161, 164; wholly tilted assembly in, 153–55, 158, 160–61; and working conditions within, 162, 164, 253; and work cycles, long, 12, 44, 128, 146, 151, 155, 159, 163; and youth recruiting difficulties, 84

Ullmark, Peter, 121

Umeå (Volvo Trucks), 240, 244, 249

Union of Civil Engineers, 76

Union of Clerical and Technical Employees in Industry, 75, 134

Union of Foremen and Supervisors, 76, 134, 161

United Auto Workers (UAW), 41, 42, 43, 255; and concessions to Japanese companies, 42, 43

United States, 14, 17, 18, 22, 25, 28, 36, 37, 57, 63, 73; and automotive unionization, 25; Japanese transplants in, 36, 37; 1990 recession in, 14; and Volkswagen transplant, 37; Volvo market in, 14, 63; wage differentials in, 73

University of Gothenburg, 190

University of Michigan, 37

utility and repair personnel (U & R), 161, 194, 195, 221

Veckans Affärer, 164

vertical integration, 27

VME, 60

Volkswagen, 85, 86, 172, 182, 255; flexible automated assembly within, 85; robotization in, 182; "VW liner," 22

"Volvism," 14, 87; lack of, 87

Volvo Buses, 15, 67, 68, 70, 89, 99, 109, 110–15, 118, 234, 239; and Brazilian greenfield site, 15; in Britain, 89; and British Leyland Company, acquisition of, 15, 68, 69, 234; efficiency problems within, 234; and integrated parallel assembly, 234; long cycle assembly, 99

Volvo Car BV (Netherlands), 60

Volvo (Chesapeake, Virginia), 63, 245

Volvo Components, 100

Volvo 480, 63

Volvo (Ghent), 14–16, 63, 69, 88, 89, 136, 145, 164–66, 173, 175, 181, 182, 236, 240, 245, 246; and AGVs, 175; automotive factories in, 14, 88, 166, 173; benefits, curtailment of, 14; and elevated productivity levels, 15, 16, 63, 145, 164; job security, weakness of, 14, 89; and TPM, 246; trade union movement in, 89; truck factories in, 14, 88, 136; and unemployment, 14; Volvo 700, introduction of, 63, 175; Volvo 800, break in, 181

Volvo Group trajectory, 3, 10, 11, 13, 21, 55–56, 70–72, 77, 79, 84–88, 101, 119–46, 153, 154, 165, 169–73, 182, 232, 236, 237, 243, 245, 246, 250; and alternative production, search for, 11,

14, 86, 153, 232, 243, 245; Asian plants of, 154; bus divisions of, 58–60, 67–70, 99, 101, 109–15, 118, 234, 239; and car assembly costs, 100; and commercial vehicles, international position in, 14, 58, 59, 65; "culture of," 13, 14, 71, 88; and customized requests, 14; and flexible automated assembly, 85, 86; foreign suppliers, dependence on, 57, 165; French Renault, co-ownership of, 64; and German luxury market, challenge to, 61; holistic assembly in, 232; and "Japan Wave," 170; and marine and industrial engines, 59, 60; MATCH campaign of, 170; and North American operation, 14, 154; outsourcing, dependency on, 59; ownership structure within, 59, 60; passenger car market of, 15, 57, 58, 60, 62, 66, 68, 70, 100; personnel, selection of, 88; piece rates, negotiations of, 77; "Production Project 90," 169, 245; truck divisions of, 14, 58, 64–70, 87, 99, 119; and upscale niche strategy, 59, 63; and Volvo 140, 66; Volvo 700, 63, 173; and work organization, transformation of, 87, 89, 153, 232. *See also* Gyllenhammar, Pehr G.

"Volvo Monitor," 190, 191

Volvo 960, 120, 128, 236

Volvo Now, 144

Volvo 140 series, 66

Volvo-Renault complex, 88

Volvo 700, 63

Volvo 740, 92, 237

Volvo 760, 120, 236

Volvo Trucks (Gothenburg), 12, 13, 15, 66, 67, 69, 70, 87, 89, 92, 109, 119, 129, 130, 135–44, 190, 237, 239, 246; and Brazilian greenfield site, 15, 66, 89; dock assembly, renaissance for, 143–44; and Ghent site, 136, 145; and Gothenburg site, 69, 70, 84, 87, 109, 129, 130, 132, 134; internationalization of design and production, 66, 67, 87; LB factory, 119, 129; Taylorist backlash in, 131; United States, operations of, 89; and White acquisition, 66; and workers' survey, description of, 190; and youth recruitment difficulties, 84. *See also* LB (Volvo Trucks)

Volvo (Uddevalla). *See* Uddevalla (Volvo)

VTV-nytt, 190

wage-setting practice, Japanese, 8, 33, 34, 233

Walker, Charles, 4

Wallenberg family, 60, 61; and sixteen-valve engine, launching of, 61

Warren, Jim, 52

Wartburg car, 255

Washington Monthly, 53

Weber, Claudia, 34, 54; and "social heteronomy," 54

Weber, Max, 31

Westlander, Gunnela, 219; and "Berit case," 219

White Truck Corporation, 66; and acquisition of, by Volvo, 66

whole-car design, 160, 181–83; and cumulative

whole-car design (*cont.*)
  trauma disorders, reduction of, 160; in TC, 181–
  83
Wickens, Peter, 44, 48
Wikman, Anders, 188, 191
Wild, Ray, 90
wildcat strikes, 10
Wolfsburg (VW), 86, 182
Womack, James P., 3, 6, 13, 17, 18, 19, 29, 40, 49,
  51, 53, 165, 184, 195, 233, 238, 239, 240, 242,
  251, 252; and *The Machine That Changed the
  World,* 3, 19, 29, 165
Working for the Japanese, 5, 51

Workington (Leyland plant), 15
work load injury debate, 83, 84
work organization forms: ambiguous effects of,
  184–91, 193; and deficiencies, 185; and direct
  worker influence, 186, 190; and discrepancies,
  185; and disparities, 185
workplace clubs, 77. *See also* labor unions,
  Swedish
World War II, 74

yen: rule of, 22, 254

zero defect, 6

About the Author

Christian Berggren is an associate professor in the Department of Work Science at the Royal Institute of Technology in Stockholm. He is the author of major works in Swedish and German about new production strategies and work organization in the automotive industry.